T0181477

Bridging the Gap between Requirements Engineering and Software Architecture

Azadeh Alebrahim

Bridging the Gap between Requirements Engineering and Software Architecture

A Problem-Oriented and Quality-Driven Method

With a foreword by Maritta Heisel

 Springer Vieweg

Azadeh Alebrahim
Duisburg, Germany

Dissertation Universität Duisburg-Essen, 2016

ISBN 978-3-658-17693-8   ISBN 978-3-658-17694-5   (eBook)
DOI 10.1007/978-3-658-17694-5

Library of Congress Control Number: 2017935953

Springer Vieweg

Printed on acid-free paper

This Springer Vieweg imprint is published by Springer Nature
The registered company is Springer Fachmedien Wiesbaden GmbH
The registered company address is: Abraham-Lincoln-Str. 46, 65189 Wiesbaden, Germany

To my dear parents and dear brother Babak

Foreword

Developing software that perfectly fits its purpose is a truly non-trivial task. For many years, the CHAOS research of the Standish Group shows that the majority of software projects still cannot be considered to be successful, but are challenged or even fail. The reasons for this undesirable situation are manifold, but an insufficient understanding of the problem is one of them. Different studies indicate that in average software development projects, more effort is devoted to testing than to requirements analysis and design. This distribution of effort has the disadvantage that software quality is taken into account mostly at the end of the software development process, when the product already exists. It appears to be promising to spend more effort in analyzing the problem to be solved and developing an adequate design. In this way, software quality can be addressed right from the beginning, and there is hope that the necessary testing effort will decrease at least as much as the effort for the early phases increases. It is a universal truth that quality cannot be tested into a product, but has to be built into it.

The advantages of thoroughly conducting requirements engineering and design become even more apparent when the software development follows a model-based approach. This means that the results of the different phases of the software development lifecycle are expressed by means of models. Software development then consists in developing a series of models, representing the software to be built from different angles and on different levels of abstraction. It is not completely unrealistic to assume that in the not-too-far future it will be possible to generate working code from models, such that the coding phase of the software development lifecycle will disappear. Generating code from models would be a similarly important step towards using higher-level constructs in software development as was the introduction of higher-level programming languages and compilers that made writing machine code unnecessary. When code can be generated from models, then also testing would have to be conducted in a different manner than it is done today. The coherence between models would play an important role in quality assurance for software.

Besides models, patterns are one more mechanism that helps to make software development more systematic and less error-prone. First identified in architecture, patterns now are an established tool that can support all activities of the software development lifecycle. Patterns are templates for the intermediate artifacts of software development. They abstract from incidental properties of such artifacts and only represent the essence that is important for using the artifact. Patterns are used by instantiation, i.e., the essence represented by the pattern is concretized for the problem situation at hand. Pattern- and model-based software development fit together very well and have the potential to lead to software of high quality.

Of course, the most important software quality is correctness. Even though developing correct software is still not mastered sufficiently – as all of us experience with more or less frustration in our regular software use – most of the existing software engineering approaches focus on the functional behavior of the software to be built (or maintained). However, the importance of quality requirements (also called non-functional requirements) is not to be under-estimated. Nobody wants to use a software that is perceived as unacceptably slow, comes with an incomprehensible user interface, or exposes its users to security threats. As a consequence, quality requirements deserve a thorough and systematic treatment, in much the same way as functional ones.

This book presents a comprehensive method to address quality requirements in software development in a systematic way. It particularly addresses two very important software qualities, namely performance and security. Performance is crucial for the practical acceptance of software systems. At the same time, it is in conflict with almost all other desirable software properties. For example, building up pleasant user interfaces or employing cryptographic mechanisms use processor power and hence slow down the software. Hence, an appropriate balance between performance and other software qualities has to be found. Security, on the other hand, is a problem of growing importance to our society. In regular intervals, reports on security breaches appear in the media. Almost every enterprise has been subject to attacks. At the same time, legislation demands an appropriate protection of data. This means that security also becomes a matter of compliance and thus its consideration will become mandatory in many areas.

The QuaDRA method proposed in this book is model- and pattern-based, and it addresses a wide variety of of important issues to be taken into account when considering quality requirements. An important fact is that software qualities cannot be assessed without taking into account the environment in which the software operates. For example, a software system may be secure against attacks of laymen, but not against professional attackers. It can be fast enough when human users are in the loop, but not for automatic control processes. The models that are set up using the QuaDRA method not only represent quality requirements in an explicit way, but also relate such requirements those parts of the environment that are relevant for satisfying them.

Another problem for which quality-aware solutions are lacking concerns requirements interactions. Before attempting to construct a software system, it should be made sure that all requirements that have been elucidated and selected for realization can indeed be satisfied at the same time. This cannot be taken for granted, especially when performance plays an important role. The QuaDRA method offers a systematic way of identifying and eliminating undesired interactions between quality requirements.

After having identified and modeled a set of requirements to be implemented, i.e., having understood the problem in detail, it is necessary to move to a solution of the problem. A first and crucial step toward an implementation is the development of an appropriate software architecture that not only reflects the functional requirements but also the quality requirements. The QuaDRA method allows software developers to select architectural solutions for quality requirements in the form of patterns. Selecting such patterns leads to a refinement of the requirements, which in turn leads to a refinement of the software architecture. Thus, it follows the twin-peak paradigm which postulates that requirements and software architecture have to be developed together, moving not only from the problem space to the solution space but also vice versa.

It has to be noted that using the QuaDRA method is not a question of all-or-nothing. Parts of the method can be integrated into existing software processes in a non-obtrusive way. Moreover, readers who want to know more about the state of the art can find a wealth of useful references. All in all, the reader of this book finds concrete and comprehensive guidance for quality-aware software development.

Duisburg Germany,   *Maritta Heisel*
November 2016

Preface

Scope

Two essential activities in the software development process are requirements engineering (RE) and software architecting. The focus of RE is on eliciting, analyzing, and managing requirements. Software architecting is concerned with providing an abstraction of the system as a blueprint to manage the complexity of software systems. The development of software architectures is a challenging task, even when the requirements for a software system are clear. Requirements in general and quality requirements in particular drive the architecture of a software system, whereas decisions made in the architectural phase can affect the achievement of initial requirements and thus change them. The common way of traditional software development processes such as the waterfall model is to build a software architecture from requirement descriptions. This process considers the forward development process from requirements to the software architecture, it however does not consider the impact of design decisions on initial requirements. The problem of the linear software development processes is twofold. On the one hand requirements are elicited, analyzed, and specified in isolation without considering the impact of architecture artifacts. On the other hand, design decisions are made without managing the conflicts and making necessary changes in the requirements. Hence, requirements and software architecture evolve together. According to the intertwining nature of requirements and architectures at each level of refinement, requirement descriptions cannot be considered in isolation and should be co-developed with architectural descriptions iteratively and concurrently. There is, however, no structured solution on how to perform the co-development of requirements and software architecture. With this book, we aim at providing a comprehensive and structured approach that supports the intertwining relationship of requirements and software architecture. We propose a framework for the *Problem-oriented and Quality-based Co-Development of Requirements and Architecture (QuaDRA)*. QuaDRA guides the software engineer in co-developing the requirements and early software architecture in an iterative and concurrent manner, taking into account quality requirements.

Content

This book first systematically identifies the lack of methodological support for development of requirements and software architecture in the state-of-the-art. We systematically derive the meta-requirements for such a method. Later we use the extracted meta-requirements as evaluation criteria for building a comparative evaluation framework aiming at analyzing the state-of-the-art methods. To gather the state-of-the-art, we conducted a systematic literature review. Applying the evaluation framework to the state-of-the-art showed that none of the compared methods fulfills all the meta-requirements. To close this gap, this book proposes the *QuaDRA* framework as a problem-oriented approach comprising eight phases. It provides an instantiation of the twin peaks model, in which we move back and forth between two peaks for co-developing requirements and software architecture. QuaDRA includes several structured methods. These methods guide software engineers in quality- and pattern-based co-development of requirements and early software architecture design alternatives in an iterative and concurrent manner. The QuaDRA framework provides support for developing a single system. We further show how to enhance it for supporting a software product line development. Finally, we validate the QuaDRA framework by applying the systematic evaluation framework. The evaluation framework provides a basis for comparing QuaDRA with the state-of-the-art based on the previously defined evaluation criteria. The comparative evaluation demonstrates that QuaDRA exhibits a substantial progress over the state-of-the-art.

Audience

This book is aimed at practitioners such as software engineers working in the areas of requirements engineering and software architecture design. Particularly, novices and less experienced software engineers benefit from this book as it provides detailed guidance on how to develop software architectures from quality requirements in a systematic way. It is also intended for researchers who aim at investigating the relationship between requirements engineering and software architecture and how the activities in each phase restrict the scope of consideration in the other phase. As this book provides a novel software development method compared to the traditional software development approaches, it can be served as a supplementary reading for the undergraduate courses in the software engineering discipline. This book pays a particular attention to the quality requirements security and performance. Therefore, it can be used to teach the graduate courses in the requirements engineering and software architecture with focus on quality requirements and their systematic integration into the software architecture.

Cologne Germany,   *Azadeh Alebrahim*
November 2016

Acknowledgements

I would like to express my deepest thanks to my supervisor Prof. Maritta Heisel for her patient guidance, encouragement, and advice she has provided throughout my PhD. She has always supported me with valuable feedback on various research papers as well as on this thesis. I am truly thankful for her selfless dedication to both my personal and academic development. She has not only been a teacher, but also a friend and advisor for me.

I would also like to express my sincere gratitude to Prof. Christine Choppy for previous joint work and for her support and valuable feedback on my thesis.

My cordial thanks go to my colleagues at the working group Software Engineering at the paluno institute and the external doctoral candidates for their support and helpful comments during research sessions. In particular, I would like to thank Stephan Faßbender, Nazila Gol Mohammadi, Denis Hatebur, and Rene Meis for the joint work on some of the research topics.

I would also like to thank our project partner Prof. Michael Goedicke for collaboration on the GenEDA project, various research papers, and being a supportive co-organizer of our VAQUITA workshop. My special thanks go to Martin Filipczyk for enjoyable working sessions.

I am grateful to Prof. Bashar Nuseibeh, Dr. Yijun Yu, and Dr. Thein Than Tun for their hospitality, support, and inspiring discussions during my visit at the Open University.

My thanks also go to Joachim Zumbrägel and Katja Krause for supporting me in technical as well as organizational issues at the University of Duisburg-Essen.

I would also like to thank Christina Menges to proof read countless pages of barren technical material.

Finally, I want to express my appreciation to my dear parents and my supportive brother Babak for their patience, endless support, and never failing faith in me.

They experienced all of the ups and downs of my studies throughout the years. Last but not least, I would like to express my deep gratitude to my beloved partner Martin for his continuous support, understanding, and encouragement.

This research was partially supported by the German Research Foundation (DFG) under grant numbers HE3322/4-1 and HE3322/4-2.

Contents

Acronyms

A1	Architecture Alternative 1
A2	Architecture Alternative 2
A3	Architecture Alternative 3
AD	Architecture Description
ADD	Attribute Driven Design
ADL	Architecture Description Language
AHP	Analytic Hierarchy Process
ALMA	Architecture Level Modifiability Analysis
ALPSM	Architecture Level Prediction for Software Maintenance
ALRRA	Architecture Level Reliability Risk Analysis
AMI	Advanced Multi-metering Infrastructure
ANP	Analytic Network Process
AO	Aspect-Oriented
AO-CAM	Aspect-Oriented Component and Aspect Model
AORE	Aspect-Oriented Requirements Engineering
AOSD	Aspect-Oriented Software Development
ARID	Active Reviews for Intermediate Design
ARQ	Additional Research Question
ASAAM	Aspectual SAAM
ATAM	Architecture Trade-off Analysis Method
AtE	Authenticate then Encrypt
ATL	Atlas Transformation Language
ATRIUM	Architecture generaTed from RequIrements applying a Unified Methodology
AUML	Agent UML
CBSD	Component-Based Software Development

CSM	Core Scenario Model
DK	Domain Knowledge
E&A	Encrypt and Authenticate
EC	Exclusion Criteria
ERA	Excellence in Research for Australia
ESAAMI	Extending SAAM by Integration in the Domain
EtA	Encrypt then Authenticate
FT	Flex Time
FTF	First Things First
GCM	Generic Component Model
GO	Goal-Oriented
GQAM	Generic Quantitative Analysis Modeling
GRM	Generic Resource Modeling
H	High
HAN	Home Area Network
HLAM	High-Level Application Modeling
HRM	Hardware Resource Modeling
IC	Inclusion Criteria
ICT	Information and Communication Technology
IEC	International Electrotechnical Commission
ISO	International Organisation for Standardization
KM	Knowledge Management
L	Low
LAN	Local Area Network
LB	Load Balancer
LC	Life-Cycle
LMN	Local Metrological Network
M	Medium
M2M	Model-to-Model
MAC	Message Authentication Code
MARTE	Modeling and Analysis of Real-Time and Embedded systems
MDD	Model-Driven Development
MRQ	Main Research Question
MVC	Model-View-Controller
MW	Master-Worker
NFP	Non-Functional Properties
NFR	Non-Functional Requirements
NIMSAD	Normative Information Model-based Systems Analysis and Design
OOAD	Object-Oriented Analysis and Design
OVM	Orthogonal Variability Modeling

PAC	Presentation-Abstraction-Control
PAM	Performance Analysis Modeling
PASA	Performance Assessment of Software Architecture
PL	Project Leader
PLC	Power Line Communication
PM	Product Manager
PoPeRA	Problem-oriented Performance Requirements Analysis
PREVISE	PRoblEm-oriented VarIability RequirementS Engineering
QA	Quality Attribute
QADA	Quality-driven Architecture Design and quality Analysis
QAW	Quality Attribute Workshop
QuaDRA	Quality-based Co-Development of Requirements and Architecture
QVT	Query, View, Transformations
RBAC	Role-Based Access Control
RE	Requirements Engineering
RIT	Requirements Interaction Table
RQ	Research Questions
SA	Software Architecture
SAAF	Software Architecture Analysis of Flexibility
SAAM	Scenario-based Architecture Analysis Method
SAAMCS	SAAM founded on Complex Scenarios
SAAMER	SAAM for Evolution and Reusability
SACAM	Software Architecture Comparison Analysis Method
SAEM	Software Architecture Evaluation Model
SAM	Schedulability Analysis Modeling
SAR	Software Review Architecture
SBAR	Scenario-based Architecture Reengineering
SEI	Software Engineering Institute
SIG	Softgoals Interdependencies Graph
SLR	Systematic Literature Review
SPE	Software Performance Engineering
SPL	Software Product Lines
SPLE	Software Product Line Engineering
SPT	Schedulability, Performance, and Time specification
SRM	Software Resource Modeling
SSL	Secure Sockets Layer
ToE	Target of Evaluation
UCM	Use Case Maps
UML	Unified Modeling Language
VAQUITA	VAriability for QUalIties in SofTware Architecture

VD	Variability Dependency
VP	Variation Point
WAN	Wide Area Network

Chapter 1
Introduction

Abstract There exist two challenges in developing requirements and software architecture in current research for which satisfactory solutions are still sought. The first one refers to methods for building software architectures based on requirements. This task is even more challenging when software qualities have to be addressed in the software development. The other challenge refers to the process for bridging the gap between requirements and software architecture. This process is currently based on experience, communication, and intuition of software engineers. Such processes can hardly be used by novices and less experienced software engineers. This chapter outlines how this book aims to address the identified challenges by presenting the QuaDRA framework, which is a comprehensive approach for the iterative and concurrent co-development of requirements and software architecture with regard to quality requirements, in particular security and performance.

1.1 Problem Statement

Managers, software engineers, and users call for *cheaper, faster*, and *securer* software [71]. The analysis and design of quality requirements have not received as much attention as functional requirements in recent years [172]. One reason is that quality requirements (also known as non-functional requirements) are less well understood than functional requirements [71]. They are often integrated into the implementation phase of the software development process as an after-thought [172].

Many software systems fail to achieve their quality objectives due to neglecting quality requirements. Errors of neglecting or not properly considering quality

requirements are acknowledged to be among the most expensive errors being difficult to correct [93]. Problems such as loss of productivity, loss of revenues, loss of
customers, cost overruns, etc. arise when software systems are constructed without
having quality requirements such as performance in mind [221]. Software products
which are developed without considering quality requirements face a failure rate
of 60% or higher [40].

Fixing such problems afterwards is costly or even hardly possible [219]. Therefore, not or not properly dealing with quality requirements might lead to software
that is more expensive than initially planned. The earlier the errors and miscon-
ceptions are identified, the easier and cheaper is their elimination. Hence, there
is room for improving this situation with fully incorporating quality requirements
into all phases of the software development life cycle.

Two essential activities in the software development process are requirements
engineering and software architecting. Requirements engineering (RE) is concerned with activities in the problem space. It aims at achieving a proper understanding of the problem to be solved. Requirements elicitation as one part of RE
aims at discovering the problem that needs to be solved and identifying the system
boundaries. The focus of the requirements engineer when eliciting requirements is
on the problem domain rather than on solutions to those problems. In a roadmap
for RE, Nuseibeh & Easterbrook [183] identified defining richer models for capturing and analyzing quality requirements as one major challenge for RE in the
years ahead.

In RE, properties of the entities of the environment and assumptions about them
are called *domain knowledge*. Domain knowledge is often undocumented and tacit
in the minds of the people involved in the process of software development [197].
The common ad-hoc nature of gaining domain knowledge is error-prone. Hooks
and Farry [127] report on a project where 49% of requirements errors were due
to incorrect domain knowledge. Capturing inadequate assumptions about the environment of the flight guidance software led to the crash of a Boeing 757 in Colombia in December 1995 [178].

The reason for such errors is likely the lack of awareness and attention on the
importance of capturing and using domain knowledge when constructing software.
Fabian et al. [94] conclude in their survey about security RE methods that it is not
yet state of the art to consider domain knowledge. The software development process involves knowledge-intensive activities [202]. It is an open research question
how to elicit domain knowledge as part of the software development process correctly for effective requirement engineering [181].

van Lamsweerde [161] and Jackson [133] underline the importance of eliciting
domain knowledge in addition to the elicitation of requirements to obtain correct

specifications. However, there is sparse support in capturing and modeling domain knowledge.

For almost every software system various stakeholders with diverse interests and expectations exist [107]. These interests give rise to different sets of requirements. The combination of these sets causes unwanted *interactions* or *conflicts* among the requirements. The achievement of one quality requirement might affect the achievement of other quality requirements negatively. Hence, on top of incorporating quality requirements into the software development process, the interactions among functional and quality requirements have to be identified and resolved during the software development process.

Unlike RE, software architecting is concerned with the solution space. The software architecture plays a vital role to the success of a software project [213]. The development of software architectures is a challenging task, even when the requirements for a software system are clear. Requirements in general and quality requirements in particular drive the architecture of a software system.

It is commonly agreed that for building upon common knowledge and best practices, the use of architectural patterns [62, 215] is valuable [45, 62]. Besides their functional properties, each architectural pattern has benefits and drawbacks regarding the achievement of quality requirements. Therefore, choosing the appropriate architectural pattern is not trivial. The existing approaches are imprecise or do not provide any aid for finding appropriate patterns [52] to address quality requirements. The selection of appropriate architectural patterns is therefore critical for a successful software development.

Beside architectural patterns that contribute to the achievement of quality requirements positively as well as negatively, there exist mechanisms and patterns that improve a certain quality attribute of the system, such as performance and security [211, 96]. Different mechanisms and patterns can satisfy a certain quality requirement to a certain degree [72, 44]. In some cases, the mechanism that fits best to a certain quality requirement cannot be selected. The reason is that tradeoffs have to be made due to conflicting quality requirements. Therefore, solution alternatives for achieving quality requirements have to be identified, captured, and modeled appropriately.

Constructing a software architecture that achieves not only its functional requirements, but also the desired quality requirements is a challenging task [73]. The current techniques for incorporating quality requirements into software architectures are even less developed than the ones that concentrate on functional requirements only. Therefore, the transition from requirements to software architectures is still a field of ongoing research [32]. Architectural design must be derived from requirement models in such a way that the knowledge gained in the requirements engineering phase is used in a systematic way in the software architecture.

RE and software architecture have been performed separately for many years [53]. The common way of the traditional software development processes such as the waterfall development process is to build a software architecture from requirement descriptions. This process considers the forward development process from requirements to the software architecture, it however does not consider the other way round, namely the impact of design decisions on initial requirements. The problem in the linear software development approaches is that on the one hand requirements are elicited, analyzed, and specified in isolation without considering the impact of architecture artifacts. On the other hand, design decisions are made without managing the conflicts and making necessary changes in the requirements.

Beside the common and traditional approaches utilizing requirements for creating the software architecture, there have been increasing efforts regarding the relationship between requirements and architecture in recent years [32, 102]. De Boer and van Vliet [53] review different opinions regarding this relationship between requirements as problem description and software architecture as solution description. They propose a closer collaboration between the two communities to profit from the research results that each community provides.

Requirements are supposed to be the architectural drivers [45, 38], whereas decisions made in the architectural phase can affect the achievement of initial requirements and thus change them. Hence, requirements and software architecture evolve together [239]. Little research and guidance is available that acknowledges the intertwining relationship of the two fields, thus proposing the iterative and incremental co-development of requirements and software architecture [182, 195, 177]. According to the intertwining nature of requirements and architectures at each level of refinement, requirement descriptions cannot be considered in isolation and should be co-developed with architectural descriptions iteratively, known as *Twin Peaks* model as proposed by Nuseibeh [182].

The international workshop on the Twin Peaks of requirements and architecture (TwinPeaks) [1, 2, 3, 77, 4] provides a platform for researchers and practitioners from the fields of RE and software architecture since 2012 to discuss their experiences, identify open issues, and directions towards addressing open issues. Regarding the intertwining relation of requirements and architecture, the effects of design decisions on requirements has been explored in [152, 90]. There exist some attempts regarding the selection of architectural patterns based on quality requirements [217, 176].

There is, however, no comprehensive approach for co-development of requirements and architecture artifacts. Hence, supporting the interplay between requirements and software architecture remains a challenging task and an open problem in software engineering research [124]. Although the twin peaks model emphasizes the co-development of requirements and software architecture in an iterative and concurrent manner, it, however, does not propose any structured solution on how to perform the co-development of requirements and software architecture [195]. This task is even more challenging when software qualities such as security and performance have to be addressed in the software development.

1.2 Research Questions & Contribution

In this section, we first describe in Section 1.2.1 the research questions we aim at addressing in this book. Then, we provide an overview of our contributions and relate them to the research questions in Section 1.2.2.

1.2.1 Research Questions

In the previous section, we mentioned existing challenges in developing requirements and software architecture for which satisfactory solutions are still sought. We highlight these challenges once again in summary in order to derive the research questions:

- there exists a gap in research regarding methods for building software architectures based on requirements. This task is even more challenging when software qualities have to be addressed in the software development.
- the process for bridging the gap between requirements and software architecture is currently based on experience, communication, and intuition of software engineers. Such methods can hardly be used by novices and less experienced software engineers.

Considering these open research problems, we derive four research questions (RQ). These research questions address the challenges in dealing with quality requirements in requirements engineering and software architecture:

RQ 1 What are the meta-requirements that a systematic method for quality-aware development of requirements and software architecture should fulfill?

RQ 2 Is there a lack of methodological support in existing research for fulfilling these meta-requirements?

RQ 3   If yes, how can a new process provide guidance in developing requirements and software architecture with respect to quality requirements considering the identified meta-requirements?

RQ 4   Does the new process fulfill the identified meta-requirements? How can
this process be validated in a structured way with respect to the identified meta-
requirements?

Furthermore, we define an additional research question that deals with an essential requirements engineering concept:

RQ 5   How can the new process of developing requirements be extended for
supporting important concepts of requirements engineering such as Software
Product Lines (SPL)?

1.2.2 Contribution

With this book, we aim at providing a comprehensive and structured approach that
contributes to the open research problems discussed earlier. To this end, we first
identify the meta-requirements for quality-aware development of requirements and
software architecture in a structured way. In order to provide evidence for the
identified meta-requirements, we reviewed empirical studies including literature
reviews, interviews, surveys, and group discussions. Based on the identified meta-
requirements, we develop a framework for comparative evaluation of state-of-the-
art in this area. To gather the state-of-the-art methods, we conducted a systematic
literature review. Applying the comparative evaluation framework to the selected
methods, we identify the lack of systematic and methodological guidelines. Consequently, we contribute to the research questions RQ 1 and RQ 2. Figure 1.1 illustrates the contributions of this work and the related research questions addressed
by the contributions.

Overview of the QuaDRA Framework

As an attempt to respond to the identified need for a method in software engineering which supports the development of requirements and software architecture with respect to quality requirements, we propose the framework[1] *Problem-
oriented and **Qua**lity-based Co-**D**evelopment of **R**equirements and **A**rchitecture*

---

[1] "A framework helps to structure one's thinking similar to a method / methodology. It also
provides a structure to help connect a set of models or concepts. A framework can be perceived as

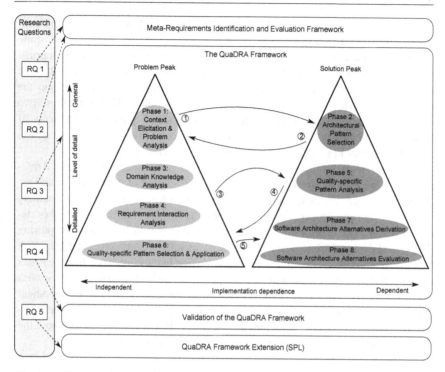

Fig. 1.1: Contributions of this work and related research questions

(QuaDRA) that guides the software engineer in co-developing the requirements and early software architecture design in an iterative and concurrent manner, taking into account quality requirements. The goal of the QuaDRA framework is to meet the identified meta-requirements. With this comprehensive framework, we aim at addressing the research question RQ 3.

In the following, we take a closer look at the constituent parts of the framework's title. The proposed framework is a *problem-oriented* approach. The reason is that we make use of problem frames [133] as a basis for our framework. We introduce problem frames and their benefits in Chapter 2 (see Section 2.1.2 on page 22).

---

an integrating meta-model through which concepts, models, and methodologies can be structured and their interconnections or differences displayed to assist understanding or decision making. A methodology differs from a framework in that a methodology always implies a time-dependent order of thinking and/or action stages [136]."

Quality requirements are the key element of the QuaDRA framework. We consider security and performance as quality requirements, because they are quite different in nature. Security requirements can often be transformed into functional ones. For example, the confidential transmission of data can be achieved through encryption, which is an added functionality. Performance requirements, on the other hand, can hardly be transformed into functional ones. Therefore, these two kinds of requirements are appropriate representatives of quality requirements. If these two can be treated in a similar way, we may hope that our results are generalizable for other kinds of quality requirements as well.

The framework's title contains the constituent parts *Requirements* and *Architecture*, as we emphasize the concurrent *co-development* of requirements and architecture design. Software design consists of two levels of refinement, namely the high-level (or coarse-grained) design and the low-level (or fine-grained or detailed) design. The main result of the high-level design is the architecture capturing the general design decisions, including the main software structure. The QuaDRA framework aims at constructing a high-level design in the context of the *twin peaks* model [182] providing a suitable starting point for the low-level design to be built upon. The *twin peaks* model proposes the concurrent and iterative co-development of requirement descriptions and architectural descriptions. It is based on the intertwining nature of requirements and architectures. In the following, we show the phases of the QuaDRA framework and the related inputs and outputs.

Closer Look into the QuaDRA Framework

Figure 1.2 shows the QuaDRA framework in the order in which the phases have to be executed. The phases of the process are visualized using ellipses. The control flow is given by directed solid arrows. The artifacts used within the process, i.e. the inputs for and outputs of the phases, are shown as notes. These artifacts can be either externally given as visualized by the lane "external input" in the top of Fig. 1.2, or generated within the framework as visualized by the lane "input/output" in the bottom of the figure. The input and output relations are shown as dashed arrows. In the following, we describe how and in which order each phase has to be performed.

Phase 1 (*Context Elicitation & Problem Analysis*) is concerned with modeling the context as well as modeling the functional and quality requirements. *Existing documents including functional and quality requirements* are required as input for this phase. The functional requirement models are extended with representations for modeling quality requirements. As output we obtain a *context diagram* representing the problem description involving all domains related to the problem to be

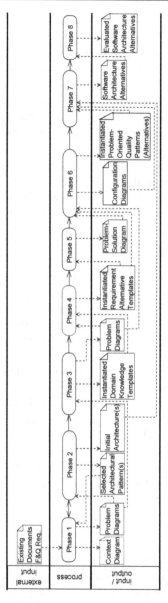

Fig. 1.2: Phases of the QuaDRA Framework and the related inputs and outputs

solved, their relations to each other and to the software to be constructed. *Problem diagrams* representing subproblems to model functional requirements provide another output of this phase. The problem diagrams contain annotations that represent quality requirements. Quality requirements complement functional requirements.

The requirement models provide a basis for selecting appropriate architectural patterns in Phase 2 (*Architectural Pattern Selection & Application*) (see arrow 1 in Fig. 1.1). Hence, as input for Phase 2, we demand the *problem diagrams* from the previous phase. The selected architectural patterns contribute to the satisfaction of the modeled quality requirements. The selected patterns might lead to the refinement of requirement models set up in Phase 1 by further decomposition of subproblems. For example, when selecting a distributed architectural pattern the subproblems have to be tailored to the selected pattern. Hence, a feedback from the solution space to the problem space is required (see arrow 2 in Fig. 1.1). As output for Phase 2, we obtain *initial architecture(s)* instantiating the *selected architectural pattern(s)* using the refined problem diagrams. Selecting different architectural patterns provides one way to produce architecture alternatives that satisfy quality requirements in different ways.

We propose a method in Phase 3 (*Domain Knowledge Analysis*) for eliciting, modeling, and using quality-related domain knowledge. In RE, properties of the entities of the environment and assumptions about them are called *domain knowledge*. Domain knowledge is required in addition to the elicitation of quality requirements for detecting and resolving requirement interactions in the next phase. This method augments the requirement models with required domain knowledge for performance and security requirements by providing domain knowledge templates. Hence, *problem diagrams* are needed as input. This phase has to be performed after selecting the architectural pattern(s) in Phase 2. The reason is that the refined problem diagrams due to the pattern selection are required for this phase. We obtain *instantiated domain knowledge templates* for each refined quality requirement and each project. *Problem diagrams* enriched with the required domain knowledge represent another output of this phase. The outputs of this phase are used in the next phase for detecting requirement conflicts.

Detecting potential interactions among functional requirements as well as among quality requirements (performance and security requirements) and resolving such interactions is achieved in Phase 4 (*Requirement Interaction Analysis*). To this end, we propose two methods for detecting interactions between functional requirements as well as quality requirements which both make use of the *problem diagrams*. To restrict the set of potential conflicting requirements between quality requirements, we provide the performance analysis method PoPeRA with respect to available resources and usage profiles. Finally, we propose a method that creates alternatives for remaining conflicting requirements as a resolution strategy. To this end, we take *instantiated domain knowledge templates* as input and extend them with alternatives for quality requirements. In doing so, we obtain *instantiated requirement alternative templates*. All proposed methods for this phase require the elicited domain knowledge (*instantiated domain knowledge templates*) in addition to the *problem diagrams* as input in order to detect and resolve the potential conflicts. Hence, this phase has to be performed after Phase 3. As output, we obtain the *instantiated requirement alternative templates* that are used in Phase 6 as input.

We selected appropriate architectural patterns in Phase 2 to support the achievement of quality requirements. In addition, we need mechanisms and patterns such as *load balancer* for performance and *encryption* for security that aim at achieving a particular quality requirement. We call these mechanisms and patterns *quality-specific patterns*. Such quality-specific solutions are, however, not directly suitable for requirements analysis based on problem frames. They have to be adapted in such a way that they can be applied to the requirement models in the next phase. The adapted quality solutions which are represented as problem diagrams are called *problem-oriented quality (security / performance) patterns*. Phase 5 (*Quality-specific Pattern Analysis*) provides a catalog of such patterns (see arrow 3 in Fig. 1.1) that can be selected and applied in Phase 6 (*Quality Solution Identification & Analysis*) in order to satisfy quality requirements (see arrow 4 in Fig. 1.1). Having quality requirement alternatives from the previous phase and *problem-oriented quality patterns*, we are able to provide a link from quality requirement alternatives to quality-specific solution alternatives. This mapping serves as an intermediate model to bridge the requirements and software architecture. The intermediate model is called *problem-solution diagram* which is used in Phase 6 as input.

After generating requirement alternatives in Phase 4 and setting up the *problem-solution diagram* in Phase 5, we are able to select and apply *problem-oriented quality patterns* for incorporating the quality-specific solutions in the requirement models. The selection and application of these patterns is achieved in Phase 6 (*Quality-specific Pattern Selection & Application*) of the framework (see arrow 4 in Fig. 1.1) by proposing a structured method. It provides the basis for deriving quality-based software architecture alternatives in Phase 7. By doing this, we obtain subproblems that contain solution approaches with regard to security and performance. They are called *instantiated problem-oriented quality patterns*. We can create alternatives for achieving security and performance requirements by producing different instances of the problem-oriented quality patterns. In order to know which architecture alternative is responsible for achieving which requirement alternatives we set up a *configuration diagram* for each architecture alternative. It contains the requirements to be achieved by the corresponding architecture alternative and the solutions involved in the architecture alternative for addressing those requirements.

In Phase 7 (*Software Architecture Alternatives Derivation*), the *instantiated problem-oriented quality patterns* from the previous phase have to be transformed into software architecture alternatives for achieving quality requirements in different ways (see arrow 5 in Fig. 1.1). As input in addition to *instantiated problem-oriented quality patterns* we require the *initial architecture(s)*, and the *configuration diagrams* to derive *software architecture alternatives*.

To examine to what extent the derived architecture alternatives fulfill the elicited and modeled quality requirements, the resulting architecture alternatives from the previous phase have to be evaluated in Phase 8 (*Software Architecture Alternatives Derivation & Evaluation*). We present an evaluation of software architecture alternatives based on an established architecture evaluation method. As input we require the derived *software architecture alternatives*.

Validation of the QuaDRA Framework

In the aforementioned phases, we described how the QuaDRA framework can guide the software engineer in co-developing requirements and software architecture with taking into account quality requirements in an iterative and concurrent manner. Now, we need to validate whether this new process fulfills the identified meta-requirements. To this end, we make use of the comparative evaluation framework which we developed before. We apply this framework to the QuaDRA method in order to investigate whether and to what extent the identified meta-requirements are fulfilled. This contributes to the research question RQ 4.

QuaDRA Framework Extension (SPL)

We provide an extension of the QuaDRA framework which augments the capabilities of the problem frames approach in the area of requirements engineering in dealing with the established requirements engineering paradigm Software Product Lines (SPL) [194]. Hence, the QuaDRA extension contributes to the research question RQ 5. We extend Phase 1 of the QuaDRA framework (*Context Elicitation & Problem Analysis*) in a way that it can be used for SPL. The so enhanced requirement models contain annotations to deal with variability for SPL.

Summary of the Contributions

The contributions of this work can be summarized as follows:

- **Systematic identification of the lack of methodological support** for quality-aware development of requirements and software architecture (see Chapter 3).

  – Systematic derivation of meta-requirements that a method for quality-aware development of requirements and software architecture should fulfill, and their classification.
  – A structured evaluation framework for comparative evaluation of such methods.
  – A systematic literature review for obtaining the state-of-the-art methods.
  – A comparative evaluation of the state-of-the-art methods.

- **A comprehensive and structured development framework** that guides software engineers in co-developing the requirements and early software architecture design alternatives in an iterative and concurrent manner taking into account quality requirements.

  – A method and a UML profile for modeling quality requirements (see Chapter 4).
  – A method for systematic selection of architectural patterns (see Chapter 5).
  – A method for eliciting, modeling, and using quality-related domain knowledge (see Chapter 6).
  – A method for detecting potential interactions among functional requirements (see Chapter 7).
  – A method for detecting potential interactions among quality requirements (see Chapter 7).
  – A method for performance requirements analysis and restricting the set of potential interactions (see Chapter 7).
  – A method for resolving requirement conflicts by generating requirement alternatives (see Chapter 7).
  – Identifying, structuring, and analyzing quality-specific solutions (see Chapter 8).
  – An intermediate model and a UML profile for providing a mapping of quality requirement alternatives to the quality-specific patterns. The intermediate model contains rationales for choosing among alternatives (see Chapter 8).
  – A method for selecting and applying quality-specific solutions (see Chapter 9).
  – A method for deriving software architecture alternatives (see Chapter 10)
  – Evaluating software architecture alternatives (see Chapter 11).

- **Validating the fulfillment of meta-requirements through the development framework** by applying the comparative evaluation framework (see Chapter 12).
- **An extension of the development framework.** A method and a UML profile for augmenting the problem frames approach with Software Product Lines (see Chapter 13).
- **Demonstrating the application of the framework** by a case study illustrating the quality-aware co-development of requirements and software architecture alternatives (throughout the whole book).

1.3 Outline

This dissertation presents the QuaDRA framework, which is a comprehensive approach for the iterative and concurrent co-development of requirements and software architecture with regard to quality requirements, in particular security and performance. We provide an instantiation of the twin peaks model, in which we move forth and back between two peaks for co-developing requirements and software architecture. Furthermore, we provide an extension for the QuaDRA framework, in which we integrate the notion of SPL. The QuaDRA framework and its extension provide answers to the research questions given in the previous section. In Fig. 1.3, we show which chapter is going to provide answers to which research question.

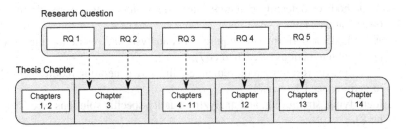

Fig. 1.3: Mapping between the research questions and chapters of the dissertation contributing to them

The remainder of this book is structured as follows. Chapter 2 outlines basic concepts, notations, and terminologies in the RE and software architecture fields that our approach relies on. In addition, we describe the concepts of variability modeling, which provide the foundation for the framework extension. Furthermore, we provide an overview of a software architecture evaluation method that is used for evaluating software architectures. A description of the case study that we have chosen to show the applicability of our approach provides the final part of this background chapter.

The main contribution of this dissertation, which is the co-development of requirements and software architecture with regard to quality requirements (QuaDRA framework), is described in Chapters 3 - 12. First, we systematically identify the lack of methodological support for quality-aware development of requirements and software architecture in Chapter 3. To this end, we systematically derive the meta-requirements for such a method and provide a classification of them. Identified meta-requirements are then structured in an evaluation framework which is used for comparing state-of-the-art methods that have been selected by performing a systematic literature review. As the comparative evaluation shows that none of these methods fulfills the identified meta-requirements, we propose our QuaDRA framework in Chapters 4 - 11 considering these meta-requirements.

In Chapter 4, we present a method for modeling quality requirements and decomposing the problem diagrams with regard to design decisions. This comprises Phase 1 of our comprehensive approach, which is accommodated in the problem peak. In order to be able to model quality requirements using the UML profile for problem frames, we extend this profile with new stereotypes for annotating quality requirements.

Chapter 5 describes Phase 2 of the QuaDRA framework, in which we move to the solution peak. We present a method that provides support for selecting appropriate architectural patterns with respect to quality requirements. In this method, we relate problem diagrams to relevant architectural patterns by means of a question catalog. An initial architecture is then derived by instantiating the selected architectural pattern.

Chapter 6 presents Phase 3 of our framework accommodated in the problem peak. In this chapter, we show which domain knowledge should be collected in addition to requirements. Then, we present a method for eliciting, modeling, and using quality-related domain knowledge.

Chapter 7 is devoted to Phase 4 of our framework and is located in the problem peak. This phase is concerned with the management of requirement interactions. In the first part of this chapter, we provide a method for detecting negative interactions among functional requirements. The second part shows how we detect interactions between quality requirements. In the third part of this chapter, we have a deeper look at the workload of the system and the available resources processing that workload. The reason is that the lack of resources is the essence of most performance problems. We present a method for **P**roblem-oriented **P**erformance **R**equirements **A**nalysis (PoPeRA) that guides the software engineer and performance analyst in identifying potential performance problems early in the requirements analysis phase. This third part aims at restricting the scope of potential conflicts among quality requirements identified in the second part by analyzing the required resources and the usage profiles. In the fourth part of this chapter, we describe the resolution of negative interactions by proposing a method that systematically generates alternatives for remaining conflicting requirements.

In Chapter 8 describing Phase 5 of the QuaDRA framework, we re-use the knowledge which is located in the solution space such as mechanisms and patterns (also known as *tactics*) that target the achievement of security and performance requirements (quality-specific solutions). We adapt the existing security and performance patterns for requirement analysis. As a result, we derive problem-oriented quality (security / performance) patterns that can be applied to subproblems in order to satisfy security and performance requirements. In the second part of this chapter, we provide a mapping between the quality requirement alternatives (obtained from the previous phase) in the problem peak and the quality-specific solution alternatives in the solution peak as an intermediate model.

Chapter 9 describes Phase 6 of our framework. We propose a method for systematically selecting quality-specific patterns and applying them to the problem diagrams by instantiation. Thus, we integrate solution approaches for security and performance requirements already in the problem space.

The so enhanced requirement models facilitate deriving high-level architecture alternatives from the requirement models, which is the aim of Chapter 10 describing Phase 7. To this end, we make use of requirement models that already contain quality-specific solution approaches and derive architecture alternatives from these models.

The derived software architectures are then evaluated with respect to security and performance in Phase 8 described in Chapter 11. To this end, we apply the architecture evaluation method Architecture Trade-off Analysis Method (ATAM), which is selected from the set of existing architecture evaluation methods. The selection is achieved by our developed comparative evaluation framework in a systematic way.

For comparing the state-of-the-art methods, we developed an evaluation framework in Chapter 3. In Chapter 12, we apply this evaluation framework to our developed QuaDRA framework in order to validate whether the identified gaps in Chapter 3 are addressed by QuaDRA .

In Chapter 13, we describe how the problem-oriented requirements engineering may be enhanced with the concepts of SPL. In the QuaDRA framework, we have provided support for developing a single system. In Chapter 13, we show

how to enhance the problem-oriented requirements engineering for supporting a product-line development. We extend the problem frames approach with a notation for modeling variability by providing a UML profile. Furthermore, we propose the **PR**obl**E**m-oriented **Va**r**I**ability Requirement**S** **E**ngineering (PREVISE) method, which conducts requirements engineering in software product lines considering quality requirements. Our method covers domain engineering as well as application engineering.

In the very last chapter, namely Chapter 14, we conclude this work by providing a summary of the results. Furthermore, we discuss the research questions and provide a critical review of how we addressed the research questions in this book. Finally, we provide suggestions for future research directions.

Chapter 2
Background

Abstract This chapter introduces fundamental basic concepts, notations, and terminologies for requirements engineering as well as software architecture that the proposed QuaDRA framework and its extension rely on. In addition, the UML profiles used throughout this book, life-cycle expressions used for describing the relation between the requirements in different methods of the QuaDRA framework as well as variability modeling used in the extension of QuaDRA are introduced. Finally, the description of the real-life case study smart grid used to illustrate the application of QuaDRA is presented.

2.1 Requirements Engineering

Understanding and describing the problem that the software has to solve in a precise way is the first thing to do when developing a software [68]. Requirements engineering (RE) as a sub-discipline of software engineering consists of requirements development and requirements management [240]. It covers a structured set of activities in discovering, documenting, and maintaining a set of requirements for a computer-based system [223]. The requirements of a software system consist of functional requirements and quality requirements (also known as non-functional requirements or NFRs).

We introduce definitions and descriptions of the quality requirements security and performance in Section 2.1.1. Problem frames as the basis for our problem-oriented requirements engineering is described in Section 2.1.2.

2.1.1 Quality Requirements

For the success of software projects, quality requirements are as critical as functional requirements as the software without considering the necessary quality properties may be too slow, unusable, or insecure [73, 40]. However, they are often neglected in practice or poorly described in requirement documents [251].

There is no consensus in the software engineering community regarding the definition of quality requirements (also known as non-functional requirements [184]). Often, they are referred to as "-ilities" such as reliability or "-ities" such as security. Nevertheless, there are quality requirements that end neither with "-ility" or "-ity" such as performance [73]. Chung & Sampaio do Prado Leite [73] introduce the notion of *satisficing* when talking about achieving quality requirements[1]. It refers to the nature of quality requirements that cannot be addressed absolutely but in a "good enough sense". The notion of satisficing reflects the sense of good enough.

Eliciting, modeling, and managing quality requirements is one of the important challenges in requirements engineering. Quality requirements are considered as the most expensive and complex ones to deal with [72, 93]. They tend to interfere, conflict, or contradict with each other. Achieving a particular type of quality requirements might hurt the achievement of other types of quality requirements [91, 72]. This negative impact reveals the need for making trade-offs between conflicting quality requirements to fulfill the overall software goal/purpose. Performance and security requirements represent such conflicting requirements. In the following, we describe these requirements and give definitions for them.

Security Requirements

Security is often an afterthought in designing software. Security requirements are not considered explicitly and therefore not integrated in the software architecture [211]. Hence, there is a need for explicitly and systematically addressing security as early as possible in the software development life cycle.

In the international standard ISO/IEC 25010 (SQuaRE) [130] which is the successor of ISO/IEC 9126-1, security is defined as one of the characteristics for product quality properties. It is divided into the five subcharacteristics *confidentiality*, *integrity*, *non-repudiation*, *accountability*, and *authenticity*. In this book, we fo-

---

[1] Quality requirements or non-functional requirements are treated as *softgoals* in the NFR Framework introduced by Chung & Sampaio do Prado [73].

cus on confidentiality, integrity, and authenticity which are defined in the standard ISO/IEC 25010 as follows:

Confidentiality is defined as the *"degree to which a product or system ensures that data are accessible only to those authorized to have access."*

Integrity is defined as the *"degree to which a system, product or component prevents unauthorized access to, or modification of, computer programs or data."*

Authenticity is defined as the *"degree to which the identity of a subject or resource can be proved to be the one claimed."*

Performance Requirements

According to Bass et al. [45], quality requirements are not completely dependent on design or on implementation. Performance has partially architectural dependencies and partially non-architectural dependencies. For example, it depends on the amount of communication between components, on the allocation of the functionalities to each component, on the usage of shared resources, which are all architectural dependencies. On the other hand, performance depends also on the choice of algorithms to implement the functionalities and on how efficient the implementation of such algorithms is, which are both non-architectural dependencies.

Performance depends upon the load to the system and the resources available to process the load [47]. Therefore, for performance assessment, performance requirements and domain knowledge are used. Performance requirements describe the response time characteristics of the system-to-be. Domain knowledge represents assumptions on the system-to-be such as the workload and the constraints on resource usage.

In the international standard ISO/IEC 25010 (SQuaRE) [130] performance efficiency (performance hereafter) is defined as one of the characteristics for product quality properties. It is composed of the subcharacteristics *time behavior*, *resource utilization*, and *capacity*. Time behavior including *response time* and *throughput* is defined as *"the degree to which the response and processing times and throughput rates of a product or system, when performing its functions, meet requirements."* In this book, we focus on response time.

2.1.2 Problem Frames

Problem frames are a means to describe software development problems. They were proposed by Michael Jackson [133], who describes them as follows:

"A problem frame is a kind of pattern. It defines an intuitively identifiable problem class in terms of its context and the characteristics of its domains, interfaces and requirement."

A problem frame is described by a *frame diagram*, which basically consists of *domains*, *interfaces* between them, and a *requirement*. Domains describe entities in the environment. Jackson distinguishes the domain types *biddable domains* that are usually people, *causal domains* that comply with some physical laws, and *lexical domains* that are data representations.

In *problem diagrams*, *interfaces* connect domains, and they contain *shared phenomena*. Shared phenomena may be events, operation calls, messages, and the like. They are observable by at least two domains, but controlled by only one domain, as indicated by the name of that domain and "!". In Fig. 2.1 the notation $MD!\{data\}$ (between *MeterData* and *SubmitMD*) means that the phenomenon *data* is controlled by the domain *MeterData* and observed by the machine *SubmitMD*.

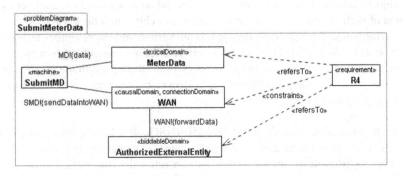

Fig. 2.1: Problem Diagram for submitting meter data to external entities

When we state a requirement, we want to change something in the world with the software to be developed. Therefore, each requirement constrains at least one domain. Such a constrained domain is the core of any problem description, because it has to be controlled according to the requirements. A requirement may refer to several other domains. The requirement *R4* in Fig. 2.1 constrains the domain *WAN*.

It refers to the domains *MeterData* and *AuthorizedExternalEntity*[2]. The task is to construct a *machine* (i.e., software) that improves the behavior of the environment (in which it is integrated) in accordance with the requirements.

Requirements analysis with problem frames proceeds as follows: first the environment in which the machine will operate is represented by a *context diagram*. A context diagram consists of machines, domains and interfaces. Then, the problem is decomposed into subproblems, which are represented by *problem diagrams*. A problem diagram consists of a submachine of the machine given in the context diagram, the relevant domains, the interfaces between these domains, and a requirement. Figures 2.1 shows a problem diagram in UML notation.

We use problem frames in this book as a basis for requirements engineering. The use of problem frames has the following benefits:

- It takes the surrounding environment of the software into consideration [133].
- It allows decomposing the overall software problem into simpler subproblems, thus reducing the complexity of the problem. The reason is that the complexity of each single problem diagram is independent of the size of the system. Moreover, the number of problem diagrams increase linearly even for large systems [133].
- It enables us to check for inconsistencies in different parts of the model due to its semi-formal structure [115].
- It makes it possible to annotate problem diagrams with quality requirements and additional information such as domain knowledge, particularly when considering quality requirements [17].
- It allows us to obtain detailed information from the structure of problem diagrams. Such information enables us to perform interaction analysis and optimization, whereas other requirements engineering approaches such as scenario-based approaches and use cases do not contain detailed information for such analyses [6].
- It not only helps to understand the software problem, but also supports in solving that problem. The structure of the problem diagrams and the properties of the involved domains facilitate the development of corresponding architecture components that reflect the problem characteristics. Hence, software architectures can be derived from requirement models expressed as problem diagrams [69].

---

[2] This example is taken from the case study smart grid which we introduce later on in this chapter.

2.2 Software Architecture Concepts

In this section, we provide an overview of the main concepts and definitions of software architecture and architecture terminology (Section 2.2.1 and Section 2.2.2), architectural patterns and quality-specific patterns (Section 2.2.3 and Section 2.2.4), Viewpoint models (Section 2.2.5), architecture description languages (Section 2.2.6), and architecture evaluation (Section 2.2.7).

2.2.1 Definition of Software Architecture

The need for having a software architecture (SA) discipline has been recognized in the sixties, seventies, and eighties with growing complexity of software systems [192, 80]. But the formal work in the area of software architecture began in the 1990s [187, 80].

Hofmeister et al. [126] describes software architecture as a blueprint of a system bridging the system requirements and implementation. It does not provide a comprehensive refinement of the system, but an abstraction of the system to manage complexity.

It is generally acknowledged that there is no common agreement on the definition of software architecture [104, 222, 35]. More than 150 definitions of the software architecture from the literature and from practitioners are collected by the Software Engineering Institute (SEI) at Carnegie-Mellon University[3] [78]. One of the most used definitions for software architecture is provided by Bass et al. [44]:

"The software architecture of a program or computing system is the structure or structures of the system, which comprise software elements, the externally visible properties of those elements, and the relationship among them."

Rozanski and Woods [204] describe two key parts of this definition, namely *system structures* and *externally visible properties* more detailed. Two types of system structure exist for software architecture:

- The *static structure* forms the design-time organization of the software. It includes the elements of the software and their relationships.
- The *dynamic structure* describes the run-time elements of the software and their interactions.

Externally visible properties of the system are manifested in two different ways, namely *externally visible behavior* and *quality properties*:

---

[3] http://www.sei.cmu.edu/architecture/

- *Externally visible behavior* specifies what the system does. It defines the functional interactions between the system and its environment.
- *Quality properties* specify how the system does it. They are non-functional properties of the system that are externally visible such as performance and security.

To a software problem, there might be more than one possible solution, known as *candidate architectures*. According to Rozanski and Woods [204]:

"A candidate architecture for a system is a particular arrangement of static and dynamic structures that has the potential to exhibit the system's required externally visible and quality properties."

In this book, we explore the solution space to identify candidate architectures with respect to quality requirements. The candidate architectures or alternative architectures stem from various architectural patterns having different impact on quality requirements or quality strategies help satisficing quality requirements.

Rozanski and Woods [204] define an *Architecture Description (AD)* as

"a set of products that documents an architecture in a way its stakeholders can understand and demonstrates that the architecture has met their concerns."

Products in this context is referred to *architectural models*, *scope definition*, *constraints*, and *principles*.

2.2.2 Difference between Architecture and Design

In the previous section, we gave an overview of existing definitions of software architecture. In this section, we discuss how architecture is different from design. This difference matters for this book as we have been developing a method including requirements analysis and software architecture. Therefore, we need to know for our method

- where are the boundaries to design
- which decisions are "architectural" and which are "non-architectural"

Perry & Wolf [192] clearly distinguish in their definitions between architecture and design. They define *architecture* as follows:

"Architecture is concerned with the selection of architectural elements, their interactions, and the constraints on those elements and their interactions necessary to provide a framework to satisfy the requirements and serve as a basis for the design."

Design is defined by Perry & Wolf [192] as:

"Design is concerned with the modularization and detailed interfaces of the design elements, their algorithms and procedures, and the data types needed to support the architecture and to satisfy the requirements."

Hence, the design phase consists of two levels: high-level structure and low-level structure of the software[4]. Software architecture (or architectural design) is concerned with the design and implementation of the high-level structure of the software [156, 174], whereas detailed design (or non-architectural design) is concerned with the design and implementation of the low-level structure of the software. From the perspective of the architecture, detailed design is part of the realisation [194, pp 116,117].

According to Hofmeister et al. [126], software architecture is placed after requirements and domain analysis and before detailed design, coding, integration, and testing. This provides an approximate order of executing the tasks, it however does not mean that the analysis phase must be finished before the design phase begins. Overlaps and iterations between tasks exist. As described in Section 2.1, in the requirements engineering phase the requirements of the system are elicited, analyzed, and managed. It results in requirements that provide the key input to the software architecture design. Requirements may need to be changed according to the software architecture tasks. The software architecture guides the implementation tasks, including detailed design, coding, integration, and testing.

According to Clements et al. [78], decisions that are concerned with satisfying functional and quality requirements can be seen as "architectural decisions". Decisions that result in element properties that are not visible are "design decisions" and not "architectural decisions". Typical examples for design decisions are the choice of data structures and algorithms.

Rozanski & Woods [204] state that "a concern, problem, or system element is *architecturally significant* if it has a wide impact on the structure of the system or on its important quality properties such as performance, scalability, security, reliability, or evolvability." Whether something is architecturally significant is a subjective decision which is driven by the judgement of the architect, its skill and expertise, and the circumstances of each individual system [204].

---

[4] Also called coarse-grained design and fine-grained design

2.2.3 Architectural Patterns

The software architecture is to a large extent influenced by its quality requirements [56, 44, 126]. It has to fulfill the defined functional requirements as well
as the desired quality requirements [56, 44, 126]. Developing such a software architecture that achieves its quality requirements is one of the most demanding
tasks [39]. Architectural patterns in general contribute to the satisfaction of desired quality requirements.

Architectural styles have been investigated for many years in different areas of
computer science [175]. According to Bass et al. [44], an architectural style is
*"a specialization of element and relation types, together with a set of constraints
on how they can be used."*

We use the term *architectural pattern* as a synonym for *architectural style* as
suggested by Bass et al. [44] and Hofmeister et al. [126]. The idea of software
patterns stems originally from Christopher Alexander, a professor of building architecture, who published a series of books about patterns, pattern language, and
catalog of patterns in building architecture [98].

Architectural patterns [62, 215, 33] describe the high-level structure and behavior of software systems. They represent well-proven generic solutions to problems that arise recurrently at the architectural design level. An architectural pattern
has three essential parts: a *problem* definition, a description of the problem's *context*, and a corresponding *solution* to the problem [109, 33]. Besides satisfying
functional requirements, architectural patterns aim at satisfying several quality requirements. Applying an architectural pattern results in *consequences* regarding
the fulfillment of quality requirements. Positive consequences are documented as
benefits whereas the negative consequences are labeled as *liabilities*. Patterns may
have different variants that extend their functionality and/or come with different
benefits and liabilities.

In the literature, there is no consensus on the classification of patterns, regarding their philosophy, the way of describing patterns, and the granularity of architectural patterns. For example, *interpreter* is a classical design pattern introduced
by Gamma et al. [103]. It, however, can be treated like an architectural pattern,
since it is a central and externally visible component [33]. Hence, there is no single catalog of architectural patterns to be used by software architects. We decided
to select the patterns from Buschmann et al. [62], which are among the best set of
the existing architectural pattern collections.

2.2.4 Quality-specific Mechanisms and Tactics

Architecture tactics or *Tactics* are established and proven strategies that can be used to help fulfill a particular quality requirement [44, 204]. From an architectural view a tactic may affect the overall architecture only slightly or, in some cases, an implemented tactic may not be visible in the architecture at all. For example, a client/server architecture could be augmented by a "Heartbeat" tactic to address availability [44]. It enables the server to know which clients are still alive; however, this modification is neither an architectural pattern nor is its implementation guaranteed to modify existing architectural views.

Introduce concurrency is an example for a performance tactic. It proposes to process the requests in parallel by processing different event streams on different threads for processing different sets of activities. This tactic describes a coarse-grained solution to help achieve response time requirements. Such a tactic can be mapped to more fine-grained mechanisms such as *master-worker*. The same holds for security tactics. For example, *maintain data confidentiality* can be achieved by the fine-grained mechanism *encryption*. To this end, we make use of such fine-grained mechanisms instead of tactics in the QuaDRA framework. These mechanisms are briefly described in the following.

2.2.4.1 Security patterns and mechanisms

Encryption   is an important means to achieve confidentiality. A plaintext is encrypted using a secret key and decrypted either using the same key (symmetric encryption) or a different key (asymmetric encryption). One advantage of symmetric encryption is that it is faster than asymmetric encryption. The disadvantage is that both communication parties must know the same key, which has to be distributed securely or negotiated. In asymmetric encryption, there is no key distribution problem, but a trusted third party is needed that issues the key pairs.

RBAC   Verifying permission is a frequently recurring problem in security relevant systems. Hence, it has been treated in several access control patterns for the design phase [248, 211]. Access control patterns define security constraints regarding access to resources. Role-Based Access Control (RBAC) provides access to resources based on functions of people in an environment, known as roles, and the kind of permission they have, known as rights.

Digital signature   is an important means for achieving integrity and authenticity of data. Using the digital signature, the Sender produces a signature using the private key and the data. The receiver ensures that the data is created by the known sender using the public key.

MAC is an important means for achieving integrity and authenticity of data. Message Authentication Code (MAC) uses a secret key and the data to generate a MAC. The verifier uses the same secret key to detect changes to the data.

2.2.4.2 Performance patterns and mechanisms

Load Balancer is a mechanism that is used to distribute computational load evenly over two or more hardware components. The load balancing pattern consists of a component called Load Balancer, and multiple hardware components that implement the same functionality. The load balancer can be realized as a hardware or a software component [96].

Master Worker makes it possible to serve requests in parallel, similarly to load balancing. In contrast to load balancing that uses hardware components, the master-worker pattern provides a software solution. It consists of a software component called Master and two or more other software components, called Worker. The task of the master is to divide the request into parallel tasks and to forward them to the workers, which manage the smaller tasks [96].

First Things First ensures that the most important tasks will be processed if not every task can be processed. The problem that this pattern aims at solving is that a temporary overload of inbound requests is expected. This situation may overwhelm the processing capacity of a specific resource. The First Things First pattern uses the strategy of prioritizing tasks and performing the important tasks with high priority first. In the case of a permanent overload, applying this pattern would cause the starving of low-priority tasks [220].

Flex Time reduces the load of the system by spreading it temporally. That is, it moves the load to a different period of time where the inbound requests do not exceed the processing capacity of the resource. The problem that this pattern solves is that an overload of the system is expected. The inbound requests exceed the processing capacity of a specific resource. Flex Time is only applicable when some tasks can be performed at a different period of time [220].

2.2.5 Viewpoint Models

As the architecture of a software system is a complex construct, it cannot be described in one single model. There are several representations of one or more structures and abstraction levels for software architecture, each of which describes a separate concern of the architecture [204]. However, ISO/IEC/IEEE 42010 [131], which replaced IEEE Recommended Practice for Architectural Description of Software Intensive Systems [129], provides no commitment what structures (commonly called *views* [204]) are required for software architecture. This ambiguity in defining a software architecture and its constituents makes the understanding and communication between the involved groups of stakeholders inefficient and error-prone [222].

Common architectural view models summarized from the literature [174] are *Kruchten's 4+1 view model* [156], *SEI viewpoint model* [80], *Siemens 4 view model* [126], and *Raozanski & Woods view model* [204, 245]. Table 2.1 shows the views of each view model classified into *requirement view*, *design view*, and *realization view*. These view models can be extended with further views if required, for example for representing quality requirements.

Table 2.1: Overview of common view models

View model	Requirement view	Design view	Realization view
4+1	use case view	logical view	development view
		process view	physical view
Siemens	-	conceptual view	code view
		module view	execution view
SEI	-	functional view	code view
		concurrency view	development view
			physical view
Raozanski & Woods	context view	functional view	development view
		information view	deployment view
		concurrency view	operational view

2.2.6 Architecture Description Languages vs UML

As the architecture description of a software system is essential for communication among stakeholders and for being a basis for later phases of software development, it should be unambiguous. Informal box and arrow diagrams are used by most of the architects, which are highly ambiguous [187]. Hence, there have been some attempts in the software engineering research community to specify design specific languages, called *Architecture Description Languages (ADLs)* [80]. ADLs are a means for representing the architecture of a software system in a formal way [187]. Some prominent ADLs are *Rapide* [170], *Darwin* [171], *UniCon* [214], etc. However, the ADLs did not become very popular among the practitioners except for a few in a specific domain [187].

In contrast, the *Unified Modeling Language (UML)* [235] is being widely adopted to describe architectural constructs. UML is originally not constructed to support architecture descriptions, since it does not support architectural concepts (for example layers) and the successive refinement of design from the architectural abstractions [80]. UML lacks formal semantics and is therefore a source of ambiguity and inconsistency [187]. However, UML has received much attention from practicing architects as its facilities can be tailored to describe architectures. The following reasons might contribute to the popularity of UML [187]:

- Providing a graphical representation of the software architecture. Most of the ADLs are textual and less appealing to the software architects.
- Supporting multiple views which are important to the software architecture.
- Many tools are available for UML. ADLs lack supporting tools.
- UML is a general-purpose modeling language in contrast to most of the ADLs that are constructed for domain-specific applications.

2.2.7 Architecture Evaluation

Finding errors during requirements analysis or early design and correcting them is less costly than finding the same errors during testing. An architecture represents the results of early design decisions. Architecture evaluation helps finding those errors early to avoid failure. An architecture evaluation determines how suitable the architecture is with respect to a set of goals and how problematic with respect to another set of goals. The results of an architecture evaluation are information and insights about the architecture [80]. Architecture Trade-off Analysis Method (ATAM) is one of the well-known methods for evaluating architectures [204]. ATAM consists of nine steps categorized in four groups *presentation* (Steps 1 - 3), *investigation and analysis* (Steps 4 - 6), *testing* (Steps 7 and 8), and *reporting* (Step 9). The steps are summarized as follows:

1. **Present the ATAM**: ATAM is described to the assembled participants by the evaluation leader.
2. **Present the business drivers**: The business goals motivating the development effort and the primary architectural drivers (for example high security) are described by the project manager.
3. **Present the architecture**: The architecture is described by the architect focusing on how business drivers are addressed.

4. **Identify the architectural approaches**: The architect identifies architectural approaches.
5. **Generate the quality attribute utility tree**: Quality attributes comprising system utility (performance, security, etc.) are elicited, specified down to the level of scenarios, and prioritized.
6. **Analyze the architectural approaches**: Architectural approaches addressing scenarios identified in the previous step are elicited and analyzed. In this step, architectural risks, nonrisks, sensitivity points, and trade-off points[5] are identified.
7. **Brainstorm and prioritize scenarios**: Scenarios are prioritized involving all the stakeholders.
8. **Analyze the architectural approaches**: This step re-applies Step 6 using the highly ranked scenarios from the previous step. In this step, additional architectural approaches, risks, nonrisks, sensitivity points, and trade-off points might be identified.
9. **Present the results**: The information collected during the ATAM steps is presented to the assembled stakeholders by the ATAM team.

2.3 UML Profiles

UML is a widely used notation to express analysis and design artifacts. Therefore, we use the *UML profile for problem frames* [115] and the *Architecture profile* [70] that extend the UML meta-model to support problem-oriented requirements analysis as well as the representation of quality-based software architecture with UML. These profiles can be used to create the diagrams for the problem frames approach. The description of UML4PF is given in Section 2.3.1 while the Architecture profile is described in Section 2.3.2. In addition, we introduce the dependability profile [114] in Section 2.3.3 that we use for annotating security requirements. The MARTE profile [233] used for annotating performance requirements is described in Section 2.3.4.

---

[5] The terms risk, nonrisk, sensitivity point, and trade-off point are defined in Chapter 11 (see Section 11.5 on page 367) when applying ATAM.

2.3.1 UML profile for Problem Frames

Hatebur and Heisel proposed a UML profile for problem frames [115] that extends
the UML meta-model. It allows one to express Jackson's original notation in UML.
Côté et al. [81] developed an Eclipse-Plugin, called UML4PF, that facilitates representing the different diagrams occurring in the problem frame approach in UML.
The developed plug-in contains a number of validation conditions in terms of OCL
expressions [236] to check the consistency of model elements within one single diagram as well as between different diagrams.

Diagram types

Five kinds of diagrams exist in the UML profile for problem frames, namely the
context diagram, problem frame, problem diagram, domain knowledge diagram,
and *technical context diagram*. To represent these diagrams the corresponding
stereotypes ≪ContextDiagram≫, ≪ProblemFrame≫, ≪ProblemDiagram≫,
≪DomainKnowledgeDiagram≫, and ≪TechnicalContextDiagram≫ have to
be applied. These stereotypes extend the meta-class *Package* in the UML meta-
model, as illustrated in Fig. 2.2. The context diagram and the technical context
diagram are special cases of a domain knowledge diagram.

Fig. 2.2: Diagram types

Domain types

Domains are represented by classes (extending the meta-class *Class*) with the
stereotypes ≪Domain≫ and ≪Machine≫. More specific stereotypes are defined for different types of domains such as ≪BiddableDomain≫, ≪Causal-

Domain≫, and ≪LexicalDomain≫. To describe the problem context, a *connection domain* (≪ConnectionDomain≫) between two other domains may be necessary. Connection domains establish a connection between other domains by means of technical devices. Examples are video cameras, sensors, or networks. This kind of modeling allows one to add further domain types, such as ≪Display-Domain≫ (introduced in [82]), being a special case of a causal domain. Domain types are shown in Fig. 2.3.

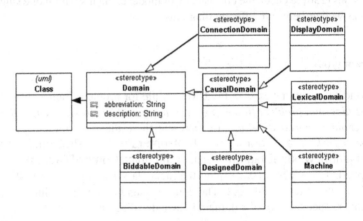

Fig. 2.3: Domain types

Statement types

As depicted in Fig. 2.4, domain knowledge (≪DomainKnowledge≫) and requirements (≪Requirement≫) are special kind of statements. Using the attribute *description* of the stereotype ≪Requirement≫, a requirement can be textually described. Assumptions (≪Assumption≫) and facts (≪Fact≫) represent special kinds of domain knowledge.

Interface types

In problem diagrams, *interfaces* connect domains. For representing interfaces, we use associations with the stereotype ≪connection≫ (extending the meta-class

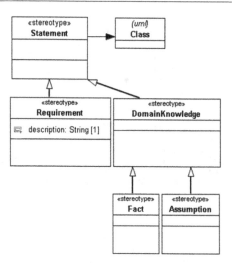

Fig. 2.4: Statement types

Association). Using the attribute *description* of the stereotype ≪connection≫, a textual description to an interface can be given. For annotating the interfaces in a more precise way, more specific connections such as ≪call_return≫ and ≪stream≫ are available as shown in Fig. 2.5.

Dependency types

Each requirement constrains at least one domain. This is expressed by a dependency from the requirement to a domain with the stereotype ≪constrains≫. A requirement may refer to several domains in the environment of the machine. This is expressed by a dependency from the requirement to a domain with the stereotype ≪refersTo≫. These dependencies extend the meta-class *Dependency* of the UML meta-model.

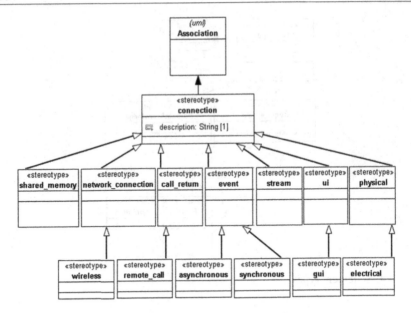

Fig. 2.5: Interface types

UML4PF Tool Support

For supporting requirements analysis with problem frames the tool UML4PF [81] is developed as an Eclipse plug-in[6]. It contains the UML profile for problem frames which allows creating problem diagrams as class diagrams in UML. For creating problem diagrams, we use Papyrus[7] as the graphical editor, which is available as an Eclipse plug-in, open-source, and EMF-based. Nevertheless, any other EMF-based editor can be used for creating the different diagram types.

UML4PF maintains a set of validation conditions expressed in OCL[8] which can be validated using another Eclipse plug-in for OCL. The components of UML4PF are shown in Fig. 2.6. Boxes highlighted in gray denote components that UML4PF re-uses and those in white represent those components particularly created for UML4PF. The features of UML4PF can be summarized as follows:

Requirements Editor   supports adding new requirements in a textual form.

---

[6] http://www.eclipse.org/

[7] https://eclipse.org/papyrus/

[8] http://www.omg.org/spec/OCL/2.0/

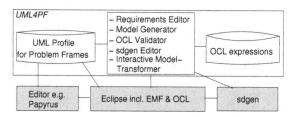

Fig. 2.6: Components of the UML4PF Tool (taken from [81])

Model Generator   automatically generates model elements.
OCL Validator   checks OCL expressions for validity and consistency of the requirement models.
sdgen Editor   supports editing sequence diagrams.
Interactive Model Transformer   supports creating software architectures using
interactive model transformations.

2.3.2 Architecture Profile

We describe the structural view of software architectures by composite structure
diagrams consisting of components and connectors.

Component types

For modeling components in the composite structure diagrams, the UML meta-
class *Class* is extended by the stereotype ≪Component≫. For each machine
in the context diagram, one or more architectures are developed. The stereotypes
≪Initial_architecture≫, ≪Implementable_architecture≫, and ≪Layered_ar-
chitecture≫ indicate different stages of the software architecture development
(see Fig. 2.7). Furthermore, the stereotypes ≪Hardware≫ and ≪Software≫
are introduced for representing hardware and software components.
   There are different stereotypes that can be used for the machine domain. If
the machine domain represents a distributed system, one uses the stereotype
≪distributed≫. By a local system such as a single computer, the stereotype
≪local≫ is used as shown in Fig. 2.8. It offers the attributes *Multiprocessor* for
stating whether the system is a multiprocessor system, *MemorySpeed* for giving

the memory speed, and *OS* for describing the operating system. The stereotype ≪process≫ expresses a process on a certain platform. A process can be described by the attributes *Multiprocessor* and *usedOS*. The stereotype ≪task≫ represents a single task within a process with the attribute *usedOS* for describing the used operating system.

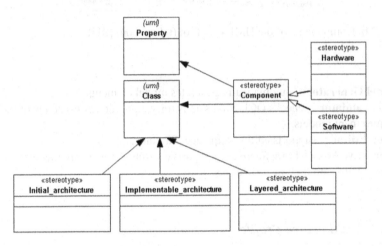

Fig. 2.7: Technical component types

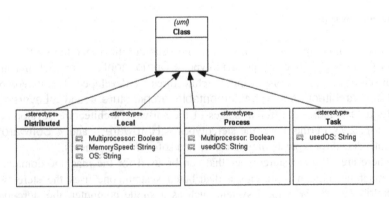

Fig. 2.8: Component types

Connector types

For modeling connectors in software architectures, we use the same stereotypes that we used for interfaces in the UML profile for problem frames. The stereotypes for connectors, however, extend the meta-class *Connector* instead of the meta-class *Association* for interfaces.

2.3.3 Dependability Profile

We use the UML profile for dependability proposed by Hatebur and Heisel [114] to annotate problem diagrams with security requirements.

Modeling confidentiality

For modeling a confidentiality requirement, the stereotype ≪Confidentiality≫ has to be applied. It is a specialization of the stereotype ≪Dependability≫, as shown in Fig. 2.9, which extends the meta-class *Class* in the UML meta-model. The stereotype ≪Confidentiality≫ states that the confidentiality of the domain which is constrained in the problem diagram should be preserved by the *stakeholder* and its disclosure should be prevented from the *attacker*. The constrained domain is a causal domain. The attackers should be described in detail. The objective, skills, equipment, knowledge, preparation time, and the attack time have to be described. For describing the attackers, the stereotype ≪Attacker≫ (not shown in Fig. 2.9) has to be used which is a special biddable domain.

Modeling integrity

For modeling an integrity requirement, the stereotype ≪Integrity≫ has to be applied which is similarly to the stereotype ≪Confidentiality≫, a specialization of the stereotype ≪Dependability≫, as shown in Fig. 2.9. The stereotype ≪Integrity≫ states that the data or service of the domain which is constrained in the problem diagram (*constrainedByFunctional*) must be either correct or the domain which is influenced by a violation (*influencedViolation*) must perform an action (*actionIfViolation*).

Modeling authenticity

An authenticity requirement can be modeled using the stereotype ≪Authenticity≫. It is a specialization of the stereotype ≪Dependability≫ (see Fig. 2.9). The stereotype ≪Authenticity≫ states that access to the influenced domain (*influenced*) must be permitted for known domains (*known*) and must be denied for unknown domains (*unknown*).

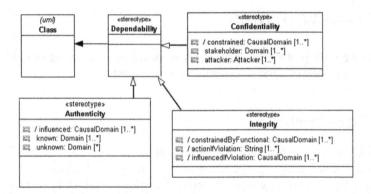

Fig. 2.9: Relevant stereotypes of dependability profile

2.3.4 MARTE Profile

The UML profile for Modeling and Analysis of Real-Time and Embedded systems (MARTE) [233] adopted by OMG consortium extends the UML modeling language to support modeling of performance and real-time concepts. MARTE replaced the UML profile for Schedulability, Performance, and Time specification (SPT) [232]. The MARTE profile consists of the three main packages *MARTE foundations*, *MARTE design model*, and *MARTE analysis model*, shown in Fig. 2.10.

The package *MARTE foundations* contains elements to be reused by two other packages. It consists of the sub-packages for defining core elements (*CoreElements* package), modeling non-functional properties (*NFP* package), time properties (*Time* package), generic resource modeling (*GRM* package), and resource allocation (*Alloc* package).

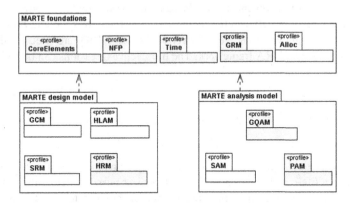

Fig. 2.10: Package structure of the MARTE profile

The packages *MARTE design model* and *MARTE analysis model* are structured for designing systems and annotating system properties for analysis purposes. The package *MARTE design model* contains the sub-packages *Generic Component Model package (GCM)* that supports the modeling of component-based systems, *High-Level Application Modeling package (HLAM)* for modeling of high-level features, *Software Resource Modeling (SRM)*, and *Hardware Resource Modeling (HRM)* for detailed modeling of software and hardware resources.

The package *MARTE analysis model* contains the sub-packages *Generic Quantitative Analysis Modeling (GQAM)*, *Schedulability Analysis Modeling (SAM)*, and *Performance Analysis Modeling package (PAM)*. The package *GQAM* provides generic concepts for analysis modeling that are further specialized by the packages *PAM* for analysis of performance properties and *SAM* for analysis of schedulability properties.

To model performance requirements and domain knowledge, we use the packages *CoreElements*, *NFP*, *Time*, *GRM*, *HRM*, *GQAM*, and *PAM*. There is an open-source implementation of the MARTE specification based on Eclipse[9] provided by Papyrus UML[10], which we use to annotate our requirements analysis models with performance analysis properties.

---

[9] http://www.eclipse.org/

[10] https://www.eclipse.org/papyrus/

2.4 Life-Cycle Expressions

The problem frames approach decomposes the overall problem into smaller sub-problems that fit to problem frames. We use lightweight *life-cycle expressions* to describe the relation between the requirements of the corresponding problem diagrams to be achieved to solve the overall problem. They are used in different methods of the QuaDRA framework. The life-cycle expressions can be built using the following syntax.

$$LC ::= R \mid (LC) \mid [LC] \mid LC^* \mid LC^+ \mid$$
$$LC; LC \mid LC \mid LC \mid LC \parallel LC$$

The syntactical elements have the following semantics. Each requirement R represents a life-cycle expression. Round braces are used to define the evaluation order of the expression for a clear precedence of the operators. Let L and M be life-cycle expressions, then

- $[L]$ is the life-cycle, where L is optionally executed.
- L^* is the life-cycle, where L is executed 0 or more times.
- L^+ is the life-cycle, where L is executed at least once.
- $L; M$ is the life-cycle, where at first L is executed and then M.
- $L \mid M$ is the life-cycle, where either L or M is executed.
- $L \parallel M$ is the life-cycle, where L and M are executed concurrently.

2.5 Variability Modeling

In software product line engineering (SPLE), orthogonal variability modeling (OVM) describes an approach to capture a product line's variability. In contrast to other approaches, which integrate variability into existing design artifacts, (e.g. using UML profiles, cf. [256]) OVM explicitly captures variability in distinct models. Using traceability links, elements from OVM models can be connected to arbitrary design or development artifacts or elements within these artifacts, e.g. requirements, a state within a UML state machine, or implemented classes [194].

OVM comprises a set of model elements that allow for modeling variability. The central model element is the abstract *variation point (VP)*. A VP defines a place where single products may differ. Since a VP is an abstract model element, an instance must either be an *internal* VP or an *external* VP. Internal VPs are visible only to the developers, whereas external VPs are visible to every stakeholder. This visibility concept allows for creating views that contain only elements that are relevant for non-developers.

Since an OVM model defines the variability of an entire SPL, it provides a concept to derive products. Several model elements (including VPs) support a selection concept. A single product is defined through all elements that have been selected. To indicate a choice for the developer, selectable VPs may be *optional*. In contrast, if a VP is considered essential, it is declared *mandatory*. A mandatory VP must be selected for every product.

While VPs define where products may differ, *variants* define how they differ. Variants and VPs are linked through *variability dependencies (VD)*, where a variant has to be associated with at least one VP (in turn, a VP must be associated with at least one variant). Similar to VPs, variability dependencies may be either *optional* or *mandatory*. If a VP is selected and is associated with a variant through an optional VD, this very variant may be selected. However, if the association is a mandatory one, the variant must be selected.

To ensure flexibility in the product derivation, OVM offers the possibility to define *alternate choices*. An alternate choice groups a set of variants that are associated with the same VP through optional dependencies and defines a minimum and a maximum value. In product derivation, a number of n with $minimum \leqslant n \leqslant maximum$ variants have to be selected if their corresponding VP has been selected.

Since in practice relationships and interactions between variants and VPs can be observed, OVM allows for defining these relationships through *variability constraints*. Variability constraints can be set up between two variants, two VPs, or a variant and a VP. OVM provides two types of variability constraints: *requires* and *excludes*. The *requires* constraint is directed from a source to a target element and requires the target to be selected if the source has been selected. The *excludes* constraint is undirected and prevents selecting one element if the other element has been selected.

2.6 Case Study Smart Grid

To illustrate the application of our framework, we use the real-life case study of smart grid. As sources for real functional and quality requirements, we consider diverse documents such as *"Application Case Study: Smart Grid"* and *"Smart Grid Concrete Scenario"* provided by the industrial partners of the EU project NES-

SoS[11], the *"Protection Profile for the Gateway of a Smart Metering System"* [155] provided by the German Federal Office for Information Security[12], *"Smart Metering Implementation Programme, Overview Document"* [106] and *"Smart Metering Implementation Programme, Design Requirements"* [105] provided by the UK Office of Gas and Electricity Markets[13], and *"D1.2 Report on Regulatory Requirements* [201]" and *"Requirements of AMI (Advanced Multi-metering Infrastructure")* [200] provided by the EU project OPEN meter[14].

The smart grid case study is suitable for illustrating the applicability of the methods proposed in the QuaDRA framework due to the following reasons:

Consideration of quality requirements: In the smart grid case study, different kinds of quality requirements have to be taken into account. We list them in the following:

> **Security:** For instance, a smart grid involves a wide range of data that should be treated in a secure way. Additionally, introducing new data interfaces to the grid (smart meters, collectors, and other smart devices) provides new entry points for attackers. Therefore, special attention should be paid to security concerns.

> **Performance:** The number of smart devices to be managed has a deep impact on the performance of the whole system. This makes performance of smart grids an important issue.

Considering these different kinds of quality requirements in the smart grid case study allows us to illustrate:

- the elicitation and modeling of quality requirements (*Phase 1: context elicitation & problem analysis*, Chapter 4)
- the selection of architectural patterns (*Phase 2: architectural pattern selection*, Chapter 5)
- the capturing of quality-related domain knowledge and its integration in the requirement models (*Phase 3: domain knowledge analysis*, Chapter 6),
- the exploration of quality-specific solution alternatives (*Phase 5: quality solution identification & analysis*, Chapter 8).

Consideration of stakeholders: Due to the fact that different stakeholders with diverse and partially contradicting interests are involved in the smart grid, the

---

[11] http://www.nessos-project.eu/

[12] www.bsi.bund.de

[13] http://www.ofgem.gov.uk

[14] http://www.openmeter.com/

requirements for the whole system contain conflicts or undesired mutual influences. Therefore, the smart grid is a very good candidate to illustrate

- the applicability of our method for detecting interactions among functional and quality requirements (*Phase 4: requirement interaction analysis*, Chapter 7),
- the resolution of interacting requirements by generating requirement alternatives, selecting, and applying quality-specific solution alternatives (*Phase 6: quality solution selection & application*, Chapter 9),
- the derivation of architecture alternatives (*Phase 7: quality-based software architecture alternative derivation & evaluation*).

We give a description of smart grids in Section 2.6.1. Section 2.6.2 presents the functional requirements of the smart grid case study that we use throughout this work. The relevant security and performance requirements are given in Sections 2.6.3 and 2.6.4.

2.6.1 Description of Smart Grids

To use energy in an optimal way, smart grids make it possible to couple the generation, distribution, storage, and consumption of energy. Smart grids use information and communication technology (ICT) which allows for financial, informational, and electrical transactions.

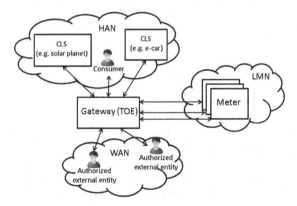

Fig. 2.11: The context of a smart grid system

Figure 2.11 shows the simplified context of a smart grid system based on the protection profile [155]. We first define the terms specific to the smart grid domain taken from the protection profile:

Gateway　represents the central communication unit in a *smart metering system*. It is responsible for collecting, processing, storing, and communicating *meter data*.

Meter data　refers to meter readings measured by the meter regarding consumption or production of a certain commodity.

Meter　represents the device that measures the consumption or production of a certain commodity and sends it to the gateway.

Authorized external entity　could be a human or IT unit that communicates with the gateway from outside the gateway boundaries through a *Wide Area Network (WAN)*. The roles defined as external entities that interact with the gateway and the meter are *consumer, grid operator, supplier, gateway operator, gateway administrator, ...* (for the complete list of possible external entities see the protection profile [155]).

WAN (Wide Area Network)　provides the communication network that interconnects the gateway with the outside world.

LMN (Local Metrological Network)　provides the communication network between the meter and the gateway.

HAN (Home Area Network)　provides the communication network between the consumer and the gateway.

LAN (Local Area Network)　provides the communication network that interconnects domestic equipment or metrological equipment[15].

Consumer　refers to the end user or producer of commodities (electricity, gas, water, or heat).

2.6.2 Functional Requirements

The functionality of the smart grid is described as use cases. The use cases given in the documents of the open meter project are divided into the three categories *minimum*, *advanced*, and *optional*. Minimum use cases are necessary to achieve the goals of the system, whereas advanced use cases are of high interest, but might not be absolutely required, and optional use cases provide add-on functions. As treating all 20 use cases would go beyond the scope of this work, we decided to

---

[15] In protection profile, LAN is referred to as hypernym for LMN (Local Metrological Network) and HAN (Home Area Network).

consider only the use case *Meter Reading for Billing*. This use case is concerned with gathering, processing, and storing meter readings from smart meters for the billing process. The considered use case belongs to the category *minimum*.

The protection profile [155, p.18] states that "*the Gateway is responsible for handling Meter Data. It receives the Meter Data from the Meter(s), processes it, stores it, and submits it to external parties.*" Therefore, we define the requirements *R1-R3* to receive, process, and store meter data from smart meters. The requirement *R4* is concerned with submitting meter data to authorized external entities. The gateway shall also provide meter data for consumers for the purpose of checking the billing consistency (*R5*). Requirements with their descriptions are listed in Table 2.2.

Table 2.2: Requirements for smart metering

Requirement	Description	Related functional requirement
R1	Smart meter gateway shall receive meter data from smart meters	-
R2	Smart meter gateway shall process meter data from smart meters	-
R3	Smart meter gateway shall store meter data from smart meters	-
R4	Smart meter gateway shall submit processed meter data to authorized external entities	-
R5	The gateway shall provide meter data for consumers for the purpose of checking the billing consistency	-
R6	The gateway shall provide the protection of integrity when receiving meter data from a meter via the LMN	R1
R7	The gateway shall provide the protection of confidentiality when receiving meter data from a meter via the LMN	R1
R8	The gateway shall provide the protection of authenticity when receiving meter data from a meter via the LMN	R1
R9	Data shall be protected from unauthorized disclosure while persistently stored in the gateway	R3
R10	Integrity of data transferred in the WAN shall be protected	R4
R11	Confidentiality of data transferred in the WAN shall be protected	R4
R12	Authenticity of data transferred in the WAN shall be protected	R4
R13	The gateway shall provide the protection of integrity when transmitting processed meter data locally within the LAN	R5
R14	The gateway shall provide the protection of confidentiality when transmitting processed meter data locally within the LAN	R5
R15	The gateway shall provide the protection of authenticity when transmitting processed meter data locally within the LAN	R5
R16	Data shall be protected from unauthorized disclosure while temporarily stored in the gateway	R1

R18	The time to retrieve meter data from the smart meter and publish it through the WAN shall be less than 5 seconds (together with R20, R22, R24)	R1
R19	The time to retrieve meter data from the smart meter and publish it through the HAN shall be less than 10 seconds (together with R21, R23, R25)	R1
R20	The time to retrieve meter data from the smart meter and publish it through the WAN shall be less than 5 seconds (together with R18, R22, R24)	R2
R21	The time to retrieve meter data from the smart meter and publish it through the HAN shall be less than 10 seconds (together with R19, R23, R25)	R2
R22	The time to retrieve meter data from the smart meter and publish it through the WAN shall be less than 5 seconds (together with R18, R20, R24)	R3
R23	The time to retrieve meter data from the smart meter and publish it through the HAN shall be less than 10 seconds (together with R19, R21, R25)	R3
R24	The time to retrieve meter data from the smart meter and publish it through WAN shall be less than 5 seconds (together with R18, R20, R22)	R4
R25	The time to retrieve meter data from the smart meter and publish it through the HAN shall be less than 10 seconds (together with R19, R21, R23)	R5

2.6.3 Security Requirements

To ensure security of meter data, the protection profile [155, pp. 18, 20] demands protection of data from unauthorized disclosure while received from a meter via the LMN (*R7*), temporarily or persistently stored in the gateway (*R9, R16*), transmitted to the corresponding external entity via the WAN (*R11*), and transmitted locally within the LAN (*R14*). The gateway shall provide the protection of authenticity and integrity when receiving meter data from a meter via the LMN, to verify that the meter data has been sent from an authentic meter and has not been altered during transmission (*R6, R8*). The gateway shall provide the protection of authenticity and integrity when sending processed meter data to an external entity, to enable the external entity to verify that the processed meter data has been sent from an authentic gateway and has not been changed during transmission (*R10, R12, R13, R15*).

2.6.4 Performance Requirements

The report *"Requirements of AMI"* [200, p. 199–201] demands that the time to retrieve meter data from the smart meter and publish it through the WAN shall be less than 5 seconds. Since we decompose the whole functionality, from retrieving meter data to publishing it, into requirements *R1-R4*, we also decompose this performance requirement into the requirements *R18* (related to *R1*), *R20* (related to *R2*), *R22* (related to *R3*), and *R24* (related to *R4*). The requirements *R18*, *R20*, *R22*, and *R24* shall be fulfilled in a way that in total they do not need more than 5 seconds.

Further, the report *"Requirements of AMI"* states that for the benefit of the consumer, actual meter readings are to be provided to the end consumer device through HAN. It demands that the time to retrieve meter data from the smart meter and publish it through HAN shall be less than 10 seconds. Similar to the previous requirement, we decompose this requirement into the requirements *R19* (related to *R1*), *R21* (related to *R2*), *R23* (related to *R3*), and *R25* (related to *R5*). These requirements together shall be fulfilled in less than 10 seconds.

Chapter 3
Framework for Identifying Meta-Requirements

Abstract As motivated in the very first chapter, this book is an attempt to address the need for a software engineering method to bridge the gap between requirements engineering and software architecture with respect to quality requirements. This chapter identifies what is needed for such a method by 1) identifying the meta-requirements that such a method should fulfill and developing an evaluation framework based on the identified meta-requirements, 2) capturing the state-of-the-art in this area by conducting a systematic literature review and producing an overview of existing work, 3) analyzing the existing work by applying the evaluation framework. Our evaluation underlines the lack of systematic guidelines and methods for quality-aware development of requirements and software architecture. It shows that none of the existing methods fulfills all meta-requirements we identified before. In further chapters of this book, we describe our QuaDRA framework which addresses the gap identified in this chapter by providing a method supporting the development of requirements and software architecture with respect to quality requirements.

3.1 Introduction

Substantial research in the fields of requirements engineering as well as software architecture has been done for many years, however, in isolation [53, 186]. The problem with existing software development approaches is that on the one hand requirements are elicited, analyzed, and specified in isolation without considering the impact of architectural decisions. On the other hand, design decisions are made without managing conflicts and making necessary changes in the requirements. As requirements engineering and software architectural design affect each other, it is neither feasible nor reasonable to separate them.

The software engineering community has been dealing with solving the problem of how to go from the problem space to the solution space using a methodological guidance [238]. Still, there exists a gap in research regarding methods for building software architectures based on requirements. Little research has been done to overcome this gap [102]. This task is even more challenging when software qualities have to be addressed in the software development.

The other challenge deals with the ad-hoc nature and experience-based development of software systems which provide difficulties for inexperienced software architects following the current software development methods in practice. According to Galster et al. [102], the process for bridging the gap between requirements and software architecture is currently based on experience, communication, and intuition of software engineers. Examples of such methods are the Attribute Driven Design (ADD) method [244, 48, 37] and the QASAR method [55] that rely heavily on the software architect to find suitable solutions for the satisfaction of quality requirements [39]. Such methods can hardly be used by novices and less experienced software architects.

The goal of this chapter is to discover whether the existing approaches fulfill the meta-requirements (characteristics) needed for such methods. To this end, we first need to find answers for the following two questions:

- What are the meta-requirements that a method for quality-aware development of requirements and software architecture should address?
- What are the existing methods for quality-aware development of requirements and software architecture?

Hence, in the first part of this chapter, we identify criteria for a method bridging the gap between both phases with regard to quality requirements. These criteria are used later on in this chapter to evaluate and analyze the existing methods. For identifying these criteria, we reviewed empirical studies related to quality requirements and software architecture such as interviews, group discussions, and experience reports. These works provide direct evidence from real case studies. Herewith, we find an answer for the first question.

Comparing and evaluating methodologies is not a trivial task. Depending on who does the evaluation (e.g., developer, user, etc.) and what the evaluation criteria are (e.g., implementation cost), the evaluation process and its conclusions might vary. Therefore, it is crucial to perform the evaluation by means of a systematic approach considering all relevant criteria. Hence, we develop a structured framework by means of the identified requirements. The framework is used later on in this chapter to analyze the state-of-the-art methods. Our framework draws upon various sources for accurate selection of the components, elements, and evaluation questions [136, 88, 35, 34, 173].

In order to find an answer for the second question, we first searched secondary studies such as surveys, reviews, and mapping studies[1] to figure out whether there exist relevant studies that describe methods for quality-aware development of requirements and software architecture. As the found studies did not directly address the topic in question as desired, we conducted a systematic analysis. Our analysis is a systematic study based on a Systematic Literature Review (SLR) [36, 145, 147, 149]. In the second part of this chapter, we report on the conducted SLR and selected methods.

Having answers for both questions, we are able to investigate whether the methods obtained from the SLR fulfill the identified meta-requirements. To this end, we perform a comparative evaluation of the selected methods by applying our framework. Our analysis acknowledges that substantial research has been done in the area of requirements engineering as well as software architecture separately. Nevertheless, there is not much effort on providing support for systematic development of both phases with respect to quality requirements in a unified process. The analysis shows that none of the existing methods fulfill all meta-requirements we identified before. The main finding of our review is the identification of a need for a unified and quality-aware method which supports the development of requirements and software architectures.

The rest of this chapter is organized as follows. In Section 3.2, we describe the derivation of meta-requirements for a method for quality-aware development of requirements and software architecture. We describe the NIMSAD framework [136] and its terminology in Section 3.3. It is used as a basis for our evaluation framework. Section 3.4 proposes our framework along with reasoning for selecting its components. Section 3.5 reports on a secondary study that is related to our topic, however does not cover all the issues. We describe our research methodology for conducting the SLR in detail in Section 3.6 and the results of our study in Section 3.7. Section 3.8 is devoted to the application of our framework for analyzing methods resulted from our systematic review. Threats to validity are reported in Section 3.9. We conclude this chapter in Section 3.10.

---

[1] A mapping study is intended to identify gaps in the set of primary studies, where new or better primary studies are required [61].

3.2 Meta-Requirement Derivation

In the following, we describe the meta-requirements that we identified for a method that supports the quality-aware development of requirements and software architecture.

In order to be able to reason about the need for such meta-requirements, we reviewed 11 empirical studies related to quality requirements and software architecture. The reviewed empirical studies include literature reviews, interviews, surveys, and group discussions. These works provide direct evidence for meta-requirements from real case studies.

We divide the meta-requirements into the three categories *"essential"*, *"recommended"*, and *"optional"*. *Essential meta-requirements* are required and must be fulfilled when developing such a method. That is, we cannot speak of a "method supporting the quality-aware development of requirements and software architecture" if the essential meta-requirements are not fulfilled.

Recommended meta-requirements are of high interest, but might not be absolutely required. That is, we can still speak of a "method supporting the quality-aware development of requirements and software architecture" if not all recommended meta-requirements are met. In such a case, we are concerned with a method which is not optimal for our purposes but still acceptable.

Optional meta-requirements represent those meta-requirements that must not be necessarily fulfilled for a "method supporting the quality-aware development of requirements and software architecture". Their fulfillment, however, provides additional characteristics that are useful.

We found strong evidence from empirical studies that underlines our classification into essential, recommended, and optional meta-requirements. In order to give reasoning for derived meta-requirements, we provide an overview of the empirical studies and their findings. Table 3.1 shows an overview of the empirical studies, the type of study analysis, and the population involved.

In the first empirical study Svensson et al. [228] have conducted a systematic literature review, in which 18 empirical research studies related to the management of quality requirements have been investigated. The aim of this SLR was to provide researchers with future research directions by collecting existing empirical evidence on quality requirements.

The second empirical study is an exploratory study carried out by Ameller et al. [30]. It investigates how software architects deal with quality requirements. The authors interviewed 13 architects from 12 organizations.

We reviewed another empirical study which has been performed by Svensson et al. [50] in industry to discover and describe how quality requirements are handled in practice. The study uses semi-structured interviews, which enable exploratory

Table 3.1: Overview of empirical studies

#	Title	Type of Analysis	Population	Reference
1	Managing Quality Requirements: A Systematic Review	SLR	1.560 candidate studies, 18 selected studies	[228]
2	How do Software Architects Consider Non-functional Requirements: An Exploratory Study	Interviews	13 software architects	[30]
3	Quality Requirements in Practice: An Interview Study in Requirements Engineering for Embedded Systems	Interviews	5 product managers, 5 project leaders	[50]
4	The Bad Conscience of Requirements Engineering: An Investigation in Real-world Treatment of Non-functional Requirements	Interviews	14 (different roles)	[54]
5	A survey of Architecture Design Rationale	Questionnaire	81 software architects	[230]
6	Requirements Engineering in the Development of Large-Scale Systems	Experience report	-	[151]
7	Software Architects' Experiences of Quality Requirements: What We Know and What We Do Not Know?	Interviews	20 software architects	[85]
8	Questionnaire Report on Matter Relating to Software Architecture Evaluation	Questionnaire	50 (different roles)	[29]
9	Mature Architecting - A Survey about the Reasoning Process of Professional Architects	Questionnaire	53 software architects	[121]
10	Naive Architecting - Understanding the Reasoning Process of Students	Questionnaire	22 students	[120]
11	Transition from Requirements to Architecture: A Review and Future Perspective	Review	Not specified	[102]

discussions between the researchers and the interviewees. Five companies have participated in the study with one product manager (PM) and project leader (PL) of each company.

The fourth empirical study is an interview study, in which professionals of two companies have been interviewed about the problems they face regarding quality requirements and their treatments [54]. A total of 14 professionals with different experiences, responsibilities, and roles have been interviewed. All of them were involved with product development in some way. The aim of this case study was to document the state-of-the-practice regarding management of quality requirements in industry and to corroborate the sparse literature of quality requirements. Borg et al. [54] report on findings regarding the problems related to quality requirements. The authors conclude that identified problems reflect the fact that problems related to quality requirements occur throughout the entire software development process.

Tang et al. [230] conducted a question-based survey consisting of 30 questions. 81 professionals with three or more years of experience in software development working in a designer or architect role have participated in this study. The aim of the survey was to investigate the perception of practitioners of the value of design rationale and how they use and document the rationale related to their design decisions.

The sixth empirical study is an experience report from a large-scale industrial project. Konrad and Gall [151] present requirements engineering challenges they faced and lessons learned in a large-scale system with more than 4.000 requirements. The challenges and lessons learned have been reviewed by requirements engineering experts. They agreed that similar challenges exist across projects at numerous companies.

The seventh empirical study is an interview study, in which 20 software architects working in large projects and having at least 10 years of experience have been interviewed [85]. The goal of this study was to investigate how software architects deal with quality requirements in large and contract-based software system development projects.

Almari & Boughton [29] conducted a survey in the form of a questionnaire to discover the factors influencing the relationship between quality requirements, software architecture, and its evaluation. 50 participants with different roles such as architect, designer, and developer responded to 23 questions. The majority of the participants had between 5 and 10 years of experience.

van Heesch & Avgeriou [121] conducted a survey with 53 industrial and experienced software architects. The aim of this questionnaire was to understand and describe reasoning practices during three general architecting activities *architectural analysis*, *architectural synthesis*, and *architectural evaluation*. The population under study has been working in industry for at least five years and has been responsible for software architecture design for at least two years.

A different survey from the same authors has been conducted with 22 undergraduate students as inexperienced software architects [120]. The aim of the study was to investigate the basic reasoning process of inexperienced designers and to identify potential areas for improvement. In a first phase the students have been asked to design an architecture. After that, the students filled in a questionnaire.

Galster et al. [102] conducted a review on existing approaches bridging the gap between requirements and software architecture. This work targets methods covering both early phases of software engineering. The authors evaluate the suitability of current approaches. At the end, they define criteria that a method covering requirements engineering and software architecture must meet.

In the following, for each identified meta-requirement we provide first our reasoning followed by corroboration through experience reports and studies from practice that we listed in Table 3.1. Subsequently, we conclude the reasoning by deciding on the category of each meta-requirement. Table 3.2 (see page 69) provides a mapping of identified meta-requirements and the empirical studies, in which the corresponding meta-requirement is addressed. A "*" in a cell of the Table 3.2 states that there exists a positive empirical evidence from the related empirical study for the corresponding meta-requirement. A "*-" means that the corresponding meta-requirement has been evidenced for not being important in the related empirical study. This is only the case for the meta-requirement *tool support* in two empirical studies.

3.2.1 Essential Meta-Requirements

Eliciting and documenting quality requirements in a systematic and structured way

Our reasoning: In Chapters 1 and 2, we reasoned about the critical role of quality requirements in software development. To determine whether a software architecture can achieve its quality requirements, the quality requirements must be elicited and documented in a structured and comprehensive way [39]. Reviewing empirical studies related to quality requirements underlines this statement as described below.

Corroboration: One of the findings of the first empirical study (see Table. 3.1) is that there is no clear view on how to elicit quality requirements [228]. There are some works that propose to relate quality requirements and design approaches for ensuring the basic understanding of the design problem [111, 84, 89].

The interviews from the second empirical study [30] show that in 10 out of 13 projects, the quality requirements have not been elicited until the architecture design phase. The customers either did not mention the desired quality requirements at all or provided only indications in the form of cost or efficiency. In those projects, in which the architects elicit the quality requirements (10 out of 13 projects), the quality requirements have only been elicited based on the experience of the architects. In addition, Ameller et al. [30] report that from 13 architects that have been interviewed, only 4 architects documented the quality requirements. Nine architects did not document quality requirements at all.

According to Svensson [50], every fourth quality requirement is dismissed at some stage. One explanation for dismissing quality requirements is that they are lower prioritized than functional requirements. The results of this empirical study reveal that all the companies face the challenge of getting QR into the projects.

The interviews run by Daneva et al. [85] reveal that the majority of interviewed software architects (14 out of 20) use checklists for eliciting requirements. Also the majority of the software architects (15 out of 20) specify quality requirements based on predefined templates in natural language.

One of the problems identified by Borg et al. [54] is related to elicitation and documentation of quality requirements. The interviewees state that *quality requirements are discovered too late* or *many of quality requirements are never discovered*. The most effective solution to the problem as suggested by the interviewees would be to make quality requirements a part of the agenda.

van Heesch & Avgeriou [121] found out that most industrial software architects consider a deep understanding of the problem space and the requirements- particularly quality requirements- as essential. Also less experienced architects have tried to understand quality requirements and considered them as important [120].

Conclusion: From these empirical studies we conclude that quality requirements are considered as essential for the architecting activities. However, they are often elicited late in the software development phase, namely in the software architecture design phase and not early in the requirements engineering phase as it is desired for avoiding costly errors in the downstream software development activities. In addition, these studies reveal the lack of proper documentation of quality requirements in most projects. It seems that eliciting and documenting quality requirements in a systematic and structured way is often not integrated in the process of software development in practice. Hence, "eliciting and documenting quality requirements in a systematic and structured way (abbreviated as *quality req.*)" is considered as an *"essential"* meta-requirement for such a method under investigation.

A structured method and extensive guidelines

Our reasoning: Most software architecture methods provide only a coarse-grained description of the proposed method. They are currently based on experience, communication, and intuition of software engineers [102]. Such methods can hardly be used by novices and less experienced software architects. The decision-making process as one of the challenging activities during architecting is often described as an ad-hoc and creative process relying to a large extent on the experience and expertise of the architects [120, 253].

Corroboration: According to the results of the study with experienced software architects, van Heesch & Avgeriou [121] recommend guiding inexperienced architects in almost all architecting activities. These activities include understanding the problem space and the requirements- particularly quality requirements-, negotiating and relaxing requirements, capturing design rationale and documenting them adequately, searching for architecture alternatives and identifying dependencies among them, validating solution candidates for quality requirements and finding optimal trade-offs among them, and evaluating the architecture as a whole.

Conclusion: To avoid that architecting and designing systems are being done in an ad-hoc and unsystematic manner and successfully only by experienced software engineers, the method has to involve a number of steps to be performed. In addition, it should explicitly be provided in which order certain steps have to be executed. In addition to the structuring of the method, explicit guidelines and heuristics must be provided in order to support inexperienced software architects in achieving the goal of the method. Hence, we define "a structured method and extensive guidelines (abbreviated as *guidance*)" as an *"essential"* meta-requirement, as according to van Heesch & Avgeriou [121] inexperienced software architects rely on extensive description and guidance that support them in developing the required artifacts.

Use of unified notations and languages as well as a combination of semi-formal and natural language

Our reasoning: A method which supports the systematic development of requirements and software architecture, has to create the artifacts for each of the phases [216]. One of the essential properties of each method is the language or the notation it uses [173]. Also for capturing software architecture, using an appropriate notation is important [35].

Corroboration: Regarding the language and notation to use for describing software architecture, in the study conducted by Almari & Boughton [29] the majority of the respondents found a combination of semi-formal language and natural language as the best. Also the authors underline this combination as a good one as non-developer stakeholders can understand these languages easier. This questionnaire study reveals that great effort is needed to increase the awareness, knowledge, and use of software architecture not only in practice, but also in academic institutions.

The same questionnaire survey [29] reveals that an alarming 50 percent of the respondents either used models infrequently or did not use models at all for the architecture description. One main factor discouraging the use of modeling technique for the architecture description is "the difficulty in integrating these models with other artifacts" [29]. This statement reveals that participants find standalone models less useful in the process of software development than those models that can be used throughout the software development.

Conclusion: Hence, we conclude that a software development process covering requirements engineering and software architecture must create artifacts for these two phases. As an *"essential"* meta-requirement, we define "the use of unified notations and languages as well as a combination of semi-formal and natural language for producing the artifacts as essential (abbreviated as *RE descr., design descr.*)".

Use of reusable knowledge

Our reasoning: Addressing quality requirements on the architecture level relates to identifying solutions for achieving quality requirements. The experienced architects make use of their existing design knowledge or external knowledge repositories such as patterns, styles, or tactics in order to find solutions for addressing quality requirements [159, 125]. Architectural patterns [62, 215] are solutions to problems that arise recurrently in software design. Architectural patterns have benefits and drawbacks regarding quality requirements, thus they can affect quality requirements positively or negatively. Strategies and mechanisms to improve a certain quality attribute in the system are called Tactics by Bass et al. [44][2]. In contrast to architectural patterns that affect quality requirements, such mechanisms specifically contribute to the fulfillment of a particular quality requirement.

Corroboration: Experienced architects participating in the survey conducted by van Heesch & Avgeriou [121] have frequently searched for different solutions for achieving quality requirements. They were also aware of dependencies between some of the solutions, and pros and cons of each solution. In contrast, the inexperienced architects in the other study do not seem to be aware of the limitations and constraints of the solutions for fulfilling quality requirements. For addressing quality requirements, Galster et al. [102] define supporting the reuse of existing architectural knowledge such as patterns and mechanisms as requirements for a method bridging the gap between requirements and software architecture.

Conclusion: Hence, we conclude that a quality-aware software development process covering requirements engineering and software architecture must include

---

[2] Tactics and quality-specific mechanisms or solutions are used as synonyms in this book

step-by-step and systematic ways for finding solutions such as patterns, styles, and tactics to achieve quality requirements. In addition, the limitations and constraints of those solutions must be considered. We define "the use of reusable knowledge, namely architectural patterns as well as tactics for achieving specific quality requirements (abbreviated as *knowledge reuse*)" as an *"essential"* meta-requirement.

3.2.2 Recommended Meta-Requirements

Traceability support between requirements and architecture artifacts

Our reasoning: The relations between requirements and software architecture artifacts as well as within each artifact should be captured to keep track of them, their origins, and their changes [102, 191].

Corroboration: One of the challenges reported by Konrad and Gall [151] is concerned with traceability. For all development artifacts including requirements, a full bi-directional traceability should be established. The authors report that creating and maintaining the trace links was a difficult task. The reason for that is that a high amount of time and effort is required to keep track of changes. Also Tang et al. [230] underline the lack of processes that guide the designers in tracing design decisions during the software development. Also Galster et al. [102] recommend supporting traceability for tracking design decisions and the rationale behind them.

Conclusion: Hence, we reason "traceability support between requirements and architecture artifacts (abbreviated as *traceability*)" as a *"recommended"* meta-requirement from the above-mentioned studies.

Capturing and documenting design rationale in a systematic way

Our reasoning: A software architecture can be seen as the result of complex decisions, which are usually called architectural design decisions [134, 57, 237]. Architectural decisions are essential for the success or failure of a project [120]. When building a software architecture based on requirements, a huge amount of information should be managed for taking the right design decisions. To this end, rationales behind design decisions, particularly design decisions due to the satisfaction of quality requirements, should be captured in order to support subsequent implementation and maintenance of the software system. The need for documenting and using architecture design rationale has been recognized by researchers and practitioners [44, 57]. However, there is little empirical evidence on the importance of design rationale [230].

Corroboration: The importance of design reasoning and design rationale in the area of software architecture has been emphasized in the survey conducted by Tang et al. [230]. The findings of this survey reveal that the majority of designers captures reasoning and considers it as important for justifying the architectural decisions. The authors of this survey hypothesize that designers unknowingly pay more attention to the positive rationales to support the design decisions than to the negative rationales. They paid special attention to the documentation of discarded design choices. They found that 36% of the respondents do not document discarded decisions. One reason for this might be that there is no software development methodology or guideline that mandates the documentation of discarded decisions. Documenting such decisions, however, may help newbies in a project to understand the reasons for discarded design alternatives.

Although the frequency of documenting design rationales is relatively high, the findings of the survey provide no insight whether the rationales are sufficiently documented so that other designers can understand them without additional assistance [230]. One of the main reasons for not documenting design rationale given by the participants is the lack of processes as well as proper tools that guide the designers in capturing, maintaining, and tracing design rationale during the software development.

The results of the survey with inexperienced software architects show that documenting design rationale is one of the areas that needs to be improved [120]. Documenting design rationale includes documenting why an option was selected over another option and what the possible limitations and constraints were. In contrast, the survey with experienced software architects [121] reveals that these architects are aware of the importance of documenting rationales behind design decisions. They, however, do not use any systematic process for documenting the reasoning part of decision making.

Conclusion: We conclude from the reviewed studies that software architects, particularly inexperienced architects, rely on methods that guide them in capturing design rationale and ensure that design rationale is sufficiently and systematically documented. Hence, we define "capturing and documenting design rationale in a systematic way (abbreviated as *design rationale*)" as a *"recommended"* meta-requirement.

Detecting conflicts and interactions among (quality) requirements as well as resolving such interdependencies

Our reasoning: Some quality requirements such as security and performance are conflicting due to their nature. For such quality requirements identifying the conflicts and making trade-offs are often necessary. Hence, any approach that deals with quality requirements has to take trade-off analysis into account. This involves the systematic treatment of conflicts among requirements [172, 102]. Trade-off analysis can be done on the requirements as well as on the architecture level.

Corroboration: Svensson et al. [228] report that there is no unified view in the current practice with respect to handling dependencies between artifacts. The results of another empirical study conducted by Svensson et al. [50] show that interdependencies among (quality) requirements are a major problem in market-driven software development. In 3 out of 5 companies, no elicitation, analysis, or documentation of interdependencies involving quality requirements was conducted at all. The problem includes detection of interdependencies as well as dealing with them. According to Svensson et al. [50], one explanation for this is that the companies have more focus on functional requirements than quality requirements since functional requirements are easier to handle than quality requirements.

In a different survey, Borg et al. [54] report that one of the primary problems related to the management of quality requirements is the difficulty to manage conflicting quality requirements. The solution for minimizing conflict-related problems suggested by the respondents is to focus on the most important types of quality requirements and to improve the competence regarding knowledge about quality requirements. From our point of view, this suggestion contributes only to a limited extent to solving the problem.

The findings of the survey conducted by Daneva et al. [85] reveal that the software architects use no systematic and structured method for validating quality requirements in terms of consistency checking or detecting negative interactions among quality requirements. Most software architects use common sense practices such as documentation reviews.

van Heesch & Avgeriou [120] found out that inexperienced software architects are not aware of risks, e.g. due to conflicting requirements and consequently do nothing to mitigate them. The same authors conducted another study with experienced software architects [121]. The results show that experienced architects are continuously involved in the negotiating process and relaxing the requirements if conflicting or hard to implement. Some architects mentioned these activities as the most important activities. In a different study, Farenhorst et al. [95] found out that more experienced architects (in terms of working years) consider auditing activities and quality assurance as more important.

Also in the review conducted by Galster et al. [102] supporting trade-off analysis is considered as important. It is defined as a requirement for a method that covers both early phases of software development.

Conclusion: From the above-mentioned strong empirical evidences, we conclude that trade-off analysis must be considered as a "*recommended*" meta-requirement. This meta-requirement includes "detecting conflicts and interactions among (quality) requirements as well as resolving such interdependencies (abbreviated as *trade-off analysis*)".

Supporting architecture alternatives

Our reasoning: There might exist various solutions for achieving quality requirements, as they can be satisficed to different levels. Also conflicts and trade-off analysis lead to discovering the potential alternatives for conflicting quality requirements. Hence, a method that deals with quality requirements should allow the development of various architecture alternatives [159, 102].

Corroboration: The study with experienced architects performed by van Heesch & Avgeriou [121] reveals that is advisable to search for alternative design options in order to fulfill quality requirements. This requires knowing the solution space well when making design decisions in order to be able to choose suitable solution candidates. van Heesch & Avgeriou [120] found out in a different study conducted with inexperienced software architects that they often do not consider multiple design options at the same time. Supporting the development of various architecture candidates is also considered as important by Galster et al. [102]. They define it as a requirement that must be fulfilled.

Conclusion: According to these studies, we define "supporting architecture alternatives (abbreviated as *arch. alternatives*)" as a "*recommended*" meta-requirement. This includes different solution candidates such as patterns and tactics for achieving quality requirements, as well as alternatives for the overall software architecture.

Supporting feedback loops between requirements and software architecture

Our reasoning: The common way of the traditional software development processes such as the waterfall development process is to build a software architecture from requirements. This process considers the forward development process from requirements to the software architecture, it however does not consider the other way around, namely the impact of design decisions on initial requirements. The problem in the linear software development approaches is that on the one hand requirements are elicited, analyzed, and specified in isolation without considering the impact of architecture artifacts. On the other hand, design decisions are made without managing the conflicts and making necessary changes in the requirements [32]. According to Jansen et al. [135] the architecting process consists of a cycle of activities to be followed iteratively until the architecture is complete. Hence, it is necessary to provide feedback loops in the architecting process to enable the software system to respond to changes in the problem space as well as in the solution space.

Corroboration: In the survey study with experienced architecture [121], many architects have stated that the architecture is refined and developed iteratively. According to the survey performed by Ameller et al. [30], the architects state that quality requirements are elicited following an iterative process. Also, Galster et al. [102] define providing a recursive and iterative method for bridging the gap between requirements and software architecture as an important requirement to be satisfied.

Conclusion: Developing requirements and software architecture in an iterative manner is recommended in the empirical studies as described above. "Supporting feedback loops between requirements and software architecture (abbreviated as *iterative dev.*)" should be a part of the quality-aware approaches developing requirements and software architecture. Hence, we define this meta-requirement as a *"recommended"* one.

Support for the evaluation of the software architecture

Our reasoning: Evaluation of software architecture is essential to ensure whether and to which extent quality requirements have been addressed in the software architecture. Some software architecture methods ensure the consideration of quality requirements with non-architectural evaluation methods such as model checking, inspection, and testing [173]. However, most software architecture methods do not provide an explicit way of evaluating the resulted software architecture with respect to quality requirements.

Corroboration: The empirical study reported in [30] emphasizes the lack of evaluation based on the satisfaction of quality requirements. It reports that 11 out of 13 interviewed architects claimed the satisfaction of all quality requirements by the end of the project. They, however, answered vaguely when asked how they have validated them. They further commented that the evaluation is only discussed with the customer as it is not easy to test. Based on the report by Ameller et al. [30], eight interviewees performed some validation regarding usability, efficiency, accuracy, and reliability. However, all of them presuppose an implemented system. None of them performed any evaluation of the software architecture. In one extreme case regarding the validation of quality requirements, the respondent stated that they wait until the customer complains as the customer will notice when something does not work properly.

Also the findings of the interview study conducted by Svensson et al. [50] underline the problem of evaluating quality requirements in software projects in practice. The companies face the challenge of "how to know when the quality level is good enough?".

A comparison of results between two studies with experienced architects [121] and less experienced architects [120] shows that experienced architects usually think of pros and cons of the design options. They are aware of dependencies among different design options. We can conclude that the more experienced architects consider the evaluation of design decisions and the evaluation of the architecture as a whole belonging to the architecting activities, though it does not seem to be performed in a systematic manner. The results of the second study with inexperienced architects reveal that they do not critically evaluate their decisions. Also validating design decisions against each other has been neglected by novices.

Conclusion: These studies, in particular the study performed by van Heesch & Avgeriou [120] with inexperienced software architects, show strong evidence for a method which provides "support for the evaluation of the software architecture (abbreviated as *arch. evaluation*)". Hence, we include it as a "*recommended*" meta-requirement.

3.2.3 Optional Meta-Requirements

Co-development of requirements and software architecture in an iterative and concurrent manner

Our reasoning: Though the iterative and incremental co-development of requirements and software architecture has been acknowledged in the literature [182, 195, 177], supporting the interplay between requirements and software architecture remains a challenging task in software engineering research [124].

Corroboration: Tang et al. [229] suggest in their empirical study to refine and formulate the problem and solution space at the same time, which is in line with the Twin Peaks model [182]. This statement can be corroborated in the work by Doerr et al. [89]. They argue that elicitation of functional requirements, quality requirements, and architecture must be performed in an intertwining manner.

Conclusion: Co-development of requirements and software architecture in an iterative and concurrent manner is recommended in the research. We also found few empirical studies that underline this. The Twin Peaks model itself proposing this paradigm comes from the experiences of its author in industrial environments [182]. Hence, we define "co-development of requirements and software architecture in an iterative and concurrent manner (abbreviated as *concurrent codev.*)" as an *"optional"* meta-requirement.

Defining architectural views

Our reasoning: Architectural views are considered as the crucial constituents of the architecture description [102, 191, 159]. Different architectural views [204] can be defined for a software architecture, each of which represents a specific perspective of the software architecture design. Table 2.1 in Chapter 2 (see page 30) provides an overview of the common architectural view models. However, there is no consensus about the number and nature of the architectural views between the researchers and practitioners [44, 156, 126]. According to [41], the architects have to choose those views that they think as appropriate based on the needed engineering leverage of each view and the interests of the stakeholders.
Corroboration: In the review and future perspectives conducted by Galster et al. [102], the support of different architectural views is considered as a requirement for a method bridging the gap between requirements and software architecture.

Conclusion: We consider "defining architectural views (abbreviated as *arch. views*)" as an *"optional"* meta-requirement, as we did not find strong evidence for it in the empirical studies we reviewed. Since there is no consensus on the number and nature of the architectural views, it can be hardly defined which kinds of architectural views are required. It is interesting to examine whether there will be a consensus in the state-of-the-art methods regarding this meta-requirement. We discuss this later on in Section 3.8 when reporting on the results of the comparative evaluation of existing methods.

Tool support

Our reasoning: According to Kazman [142], one of the obstacles to the widespread application of software development methods in the industry is the overhead produced by tedious and time-consuming tasks of such approaches. A tool can provide support for some time-consuming and error-prone tasks of a method. In the following, we can see whether this claim can be corroborated by the empirical studies we reviewed.

Corroboration: According to the survey performed by Ameller et al. [30], none of the architects use any specific tools for managing quality requirements. They are even not willing to use a decision support tool for the process of architectural decision-making. The majority of the interviewed architects "do not trust", or "do not believe in automatic things" or "cannot imagine that this can be done". Also Daneva et al. [85] report on not using tools for validating quality requirements. The results of this study reveal that common sense practices such as documentation reviews and building up communication processes are simple and powerful ways of performing such activities. Galster et al. [102] do not support this opinion regarding tools for supporting software engineers by applying methods as well as architecting activities. They propose having a formal approach enabling tool support for checking consistency of the architectural artifacts. This statement, however, does not unambiguously underline providing tool support, but providing a certain level of formalism that enables consistency checks.

Conclusion: According to these studies, tools are not used in practice. Among the studies we reviewed, we could not find any evidence for considering a tool as necessary for using a method. However, this is no evidence that a tool might not be supportive by some tasks. For example, a tool might be useful for tedious tasks such as consistency checking. Hence, we define "tool support" as an *"optional"* meta-requirement.

Table 3.2: Identified requirements and related evidence from empirical studies

Emp. Study	QR	Guidance	QR Ful- fill.	Descr.	Trace.	Design Rat.	Trade-off Anal.	Arch Alt.	Iterative Dev.	Arch Eval.	Concurrent Co-dev.	View Types	Tool Sup- port
1	*						*						
2	*								*	*			*_
3	*						*			*			
4	*						*						
5				*	*						*		
6				*									
7	*						*						*_
8			*										
9	*	*	*			*	*	*	*	*			
10	*		*			*	*	*		*			
11			*	*	*	*	*	*	*			*	*

3.2.4 Method Characteristics

In addition to the three categories *"essential"*, *"recommended"*, and *"optional"* for meta-requirements for a method under investigation, we define a new category, namely *"method characteristics"*. This category is concerned with those characteristics that every software engineering method exhibits. Examples for such characteristics are *development phase* and *application domain*. Such kinds of characteristics might also be used for comparison of the methods:

Development phase

refers to the software development phases. It includes requirements engineering, architecture (or early design), and detailed design (or late design) phases. In addition, sub-phases in each development phase can be considered if available, for example, *elicitation* within the requirements engineering phase. Although we compare requirements engineering and software architecture methods, nevertheless some methods might include other development phases such as the implementation phase as well.

Method input/ method output

It is important to know which artifacts are required as input and which ones are produced as output of a method. It is also essential to specify on which abstraction level the required input and produced output artifacts are provided.

Application domain

It might also be of importance to know whether a method can be used in general or is developed only for a specific application domain.

User Skill

As mentioned before, we place value on inexperienced software engineers as users of the method under investigation. Hence, user skill refers to the skills that an inexperienced software engineer needs additionally for applying the method at hand. Certainly, it is of advantage if less specific knowledge is required for applying a method.

3.3 The Evaluation Framework NIMSAD

We use the NIMSAD (Normative Information Model-based Systems Analysis and Design) evaluation framework [136] as a basis for developing our framework along with other sources (see Section 3.4). NIMSAD introduced by Jayaratna is a generic and methodology-independent framework for understanding and evaluating any methodology. The aims of the NIMSAD framework are to support: 1) understanding of problem-solving processes in general and of any nature, 2) evaluating methodologies, their structure, steps, form, nature, etc., and 3) drawing conclusions.

NIMSAD has arisen from problem solving in industry and consultancy practice. Forsell [97] describes the advantages of applying the NIMSAD framework as follows: 1) it has a wide scope, 2) it is not restricted to the evaluation of any particular category of methodologies, 3) it is practical and has already been used in several real-life case studies, and 4) it considers different use situations. The NIMSAD framework considers the evaluation of a methodology as a dynamic activity. The evaluation can be conducted before, during, and after the application of a methodology. However, the framework does not attempt to rank the evaluated methodologies.

According to the NIMSAD framework, an effective application of a methodology depends upon the person who applies the methodology, the context in which the methodology is practiced, and the methodology itself. The NIMSAD framework proposes therefore to consider four essential components during the comparison of methodologies. Figure 3.1 illustrates these four components. These components are:

The problem situation (the methodology context): This refers to the situation in which the methodology is intended to be used.

The intended problem solver (the methodology user): This includes the users and stakeholders of the methodology.

The problem-solving process (the methodology): This describes the methodology to be evaluated.

The evaluation of the above three: This helps to measure the effectiveness of the *problem-solving process* and the *problem solver* in the *problem situation*.

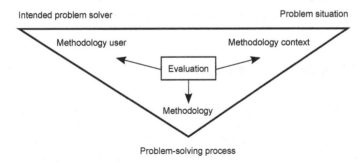

Fig. 3.1: The components of the NIMSAD framework

In the following, we describe each of these components as they are important to gain an understanding of the framework.

3.3.1 Methodology Context

The first component of the NIMSAD framework is concerned with the problem situation in which the methodology is intended to be used, i.e., the method context.

The problem situation is an essential component as the effectiveness of a method can only be measured within its context. Methodology context has a current situation and a desired situation. It is the current situation that a methodology user tries to change with the help of a methodology to gain the desired situation in which the problem is solved. For the methodology context we need to know what information a method uses, what problem the method tries to solve with this information, how the method is going to solve the problem, etc.

3.3.2 Methodology User

The second component is concerned with the role of the intended problem solver, i.e., the user of the method. The success of effective design and development of a method depends among other things on the personal characteristics of the methodology user. The intended problem solvers tend to select some elements of the situation as being relevant and dismiss some others as being irrelevant. The motivation and skills of the methodology user might affect this selection. Thus, this is addressed in the methodology user component of the NIMSAD framework.

3.3.3 Methodology Contents

The third component is the problem solving process, which is represented by the methodology itself. A methodology guides and assists a problem solver to understand the problem situation and to overcome it. The NIMSAD framework proposes three phases for the problem solving process, namely problem formulation, solution design, and solution implementation. The problem formulation phase is concerned with understanding the situation of concern and the problems to be solved by the use of the methodology. The solution design phase aims at producing an agreed and acceptable design specification of the methodology. The implementation phase is considered as the outcome of the problem solving process. The realization of the methodology is achieved in the implementation phase.

3.3.4 Evaluation

The fourth component of the framework and the most important one brings the three above mentioned elements together by evaluating the methodology. The evaluation helps measuring the effectiveness of the problem solving process and the problem solver in the problem situation. This component is concerned with the assessment of the methodology and the degree of assistance it provides by means of models, concepts, structure, techniques, etc. The evaluation of a methodology should reveal to what situation the methodology would be suitable for, how it is to be used, and how the benefits can be measured.

3.4 Our Proposed Evaluation Framework

In this section, we introduce our evaluation framework as an analysis tool. We use this framework for comparative evaluation of methods bridging the gap between requirements and software architecture with respect to quality requirements. The framework can easily be modified and extended to desirable features.

The evaluation framework shown in Table 3.3 consists of *Components, Elements, Evaluation Questions*, and *Category* (Columns of the table). The column "category" specifies whether the meta-requirement is an *"essential"*, a *"recommended"*, an *"optional"* meta-requirement, or a *"method characteristic"*.

For developing the evaluation framework, we make use of various sources for accurate selection of its constituents:

1. The first source is the NIMSAD framework. The overall structure of our framework is based on the NIMSAD framework. It involves four essential components for method evaluation, namely method context, method users, method content, and evaluation. These four components are depicted in the first column of Table 3.3.

2. The second source for our evaluation framework is the application of the NIMSAD framework to different software engineering methods [34, 173]. In addition, we made use of the works defining the technical and non-technical issues that a method should address [88, 35]. These works have influenced the second column of the framework, mainly the elements of the components *context, user*, and *validation*.

3. The third source are the meta-requirements that we derived in the previous section from various empirical studies. These requirements have influenced the elements of the component *contents*.

Table 3.3: The components and elements of the framework and the evaluation questions

Component	Elements	Evaluation Questions	Classification
Context	Development phase	Which phases are covered by the method?	Method characteristic
	Method input	What are the required inputs for the method?	Method characteristic
	Method output	What are the produced outputs of the method?	Method characteristic
	Application domain	For which application domain is the method developed?	Method characteristic
User	User skill	What specific skills does an inexperienced software engineer require to accomplish tasks required by the method?	Method characteristic
Content	Quality req.	How are quality requirements elicited and documented?	Essential
	Guidance	How much support for applying the method by the user is provided by the reported method?	Essential
	Knowledge reuse	To what extent is making use of reusable knowledge supported?	Essential
	RE descr.	Which RE artifacts are created by the method? Which notation/language is used by the method to represent RE models, diagrams, and other artifacts it creates? Which RE approach is used for creating the artifacts?	Essential
	Design descr.	Which design artifacts are created by the method? Which notation/language is used by the method to represent design models, diagrams, and other artifacts it creates? Which design approach is used for creating the artifacts?	Essential
	Traceability	To what extent is traceability between requirements and design artifacts supported?	Recommended
	Design rationale	To what extent is capturing the rationales behind design decisions supported?	Recommended
	Trade-off analysis	Whether and to what extent is trade-off analysis supported?	Recommended
	Arch. alternatives	To what extent are alternative architectures supported?	Recommended
	Iterative dev.	To what extent is the iterative development of requirements and software architectures supported?	Recommended
	Concurrent co-dev.	To what extent is the intertwining and concurrent co-development of requirements and software architecture supported?	Optional
	Arch. views	Whether and which views are used for representing the RE and design artifacts?	Optional
	Tool support	Are there tools to support the method and its artifacts? Which activities of the methods are supported by the tools?	Optional
Validation	Arch. evaluation	Whether and how does the method evaluate the satisfaction of quality requirements in the produced software architecture?	Recommended

3.5 Related Review

We only found one secondary study related to our study. Galster et al. [102] present a review and future perspective regarding the transition between the two important phases of requirements engineering and software architecture within the software development life cycle. This review emphasizes the lack of systematic guidelines and methods providing support for building architecture based on requirements. Moreover, it defines requirements and suitability criteria such as providing traceability and capturing architectural rationale for a transition process. We captured these requirements in our evaluation framework described in Section 3.4. However, this review lacks some issues that are essential for our study: 1) It does not focus on quality requirements and their fulfillment. 2) It is performed in 2006. Hence, it does not consider the whole time span we are interested in. 3) It is not performed in a systematic way. 4) It does not capture all characteristics that are essential and recommended for such methods such as capturing and eliciting quality requirements in a proper way, evaluation of the software architecture, and providing guidance (see Section 3.2).

3.6 Research Method

The aim of the SLR was to identify existing methods for developing requirements and software architecture with respect to quality requirements. Hence, we developed a process shown in Fig. 3.2 on the basis of the systematic literature review literature [146, 149, 148, 59]. In the following, we describe our process comprising the three phases *planning*, *conducting*, and *reporting* in detail.

3.6.1 Planning Phase

Our process starts with the **planning phase** comprising three steps *Step 1 - research questions specification*, *Step 2 - need identification*, and *Step 3 - review protocol development*.

In the first step, we defined research questions according to the problem we identified before (see Section 3.1). We aim at finding existing methods for quality-aware development of requirements and software architecture.

In the second step, we searched secondary studies such as surveys, reviews, and mapping studies to find out whether there exists already such a systematic

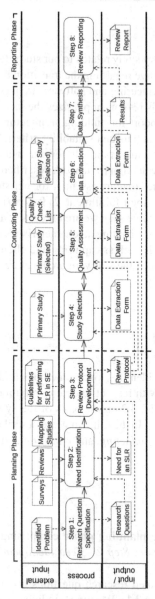

Fig. 3.2: Overview of our process

review that provides an extensive overview of existing methods regarding bridging the gap between requirements and software architectures with respect to quality requirements. As we found no studies that directly address the topic in question as desired, we decided to perform a systematic literature review. Hence, we defined in the third step a protocol that describes the review process. In the following, we describe each step in detail.

Step 1 - Research Questions Specification

We aim at reviewing the existing literature for identifying methods to develop requirements and software architecture with regard to quality requirements. To this end, we define one *main research question (MRQ)* and several *additional research questions (ARQ)* as illustrated in Table 3.4. The MRQ aims at identifying the existing methods in our research field. The ARQs aim at extracting the characteristics of the reported methods. In the third column of Table 3.4, we give a type for the RQs which is either *content* or *quality*. The former refers to the characteristics of the methods we want to extract and the latter relates to the quality of the methods. We answer to the ARQs related to quality (*ARQ 24* and *ARQ 25*) in the *quality assessment* step, in which we assess whether the selected papers exhibit a certain quality to be qualified for the *data extraction* step.

The ARQs serve as specific criteria for comparative evaluation of the reported methods, which is described later on in this chapter. The ARQs can mainly be mapped to the meta-requirements for such methods that we captured in the evaluation framework (see Section 3.4). Table 3.5 shows how the ARQs are mapped to the identified meta-requirements.

Step 2 - Need Identification

The aim of this step is to find related secondary literature such as surveys and reviews, which might be relevant. In case we would find such systematic surveys that can answer our research questions, there is no need for conducting a systematic review any more. As mentioned in Section 3.5, we only found one secondary study related to our study. In Section 3.5, we gave four reasons why this review does not cover all the desired aspects regarding a method for quality-aware development of requirements and software architecture. Hence, we confirm the need for conducting an SLR.

Table 3.4: Research questions

RQ	Question	Type
MRQ	Which methods are reported for developing requirements and software architecture with respect to quality requirements?	Content
ARQ 1	Which SE phases are involved in the reported methods?	Content
ARQ 2	What is the input of the reported method?	Content
ARQ 3	What is the output of the reported method?	Content
ARQ 4	Which application domains are the reported methods developed for?	Content
ARQ 5	Which specific user skills are required for applying the reported methods?	Content
ARQ 6	Which quality attributes are considered in the reported methods?	Content
ARQ 7	How is the process support by the reported methods?	Content
ARQ 8	How are quality requirements addressed in the software architecture in the reported methods?	Content
ARQ 9	Which existing approach is used for the requirements engineering phase?	Content
ARQ 10	Which notation or languages are used for requirements in the reported methods?	Content
ARQ 11	Do the reported methods create requirements artifacts?	Content
ARQ 12	Which existing approach is used for the architecture design phase?	Content
ARQ 13	Which notation or languages are used for architectures in the reported methods?	Content
ARQ 14	Do the reported methods create design artifacts?	Content
ARQ 15	Do the reported methods support traceability concepts?	Content
ARQ 16	Do the reported methods support capturing of design rationale?	Content
ARQ 17	Do the reported methods deal with conflicts and trade-off analysis?	Content
ARQ 18	Do the reported methods support the creation of architecture alternatives?	Content
ARQ 19	Do the reported methods support the iterative development of requirements and architecture?	Content
ARQ 20	Do the reported methods support the intertwining and concurrent co-development of requirements and architecture?	Content
ARQ 21	Which views are used in the reported methods?	Content
ARQ 22	Do the reported methods provide tool-support for creating its artifacts?	Content
ARQ 23	Do the reported methods support architecture evaluation?	Content
ARQ 24	How detailed are the steps and structure of the reported methods defined?	Quality, Content
ARQ 25	How rigorously are the reported methods evaluated?	Quality

Step 3 - Review Protocol Development

The aim of this step is to define a protocol that describes the review process which will be carried out in the *conducting phase*. A literature review protocol includes two perspectives. On the one hand, the main parts of the protocol are written before conducting the review itself. On the other hand, results following the protocol are also stored in the protocol. In this chapter, we describe both perspectives while describing the Steps 1 to 8 of Fig. 3.2.

The review protocol includes a *data extraction form* that we prepared to be filled in in the *conducting phase*. We prepared an excel sheet that has been used as the *data extraction form*. As this literature review has been performed by only one

Table 3.5: Mapping between ARQs and derived meta-requirements

ARQ	Derived meta-requirement	Category
ARQ 1	Involved phase	Method characteristic
ARQ 2	Method input	Method characteristic
ARQ 3	Method output	Method characteristic
ARQ 4	Application domain	Method characteristic
ARQ 5	User Skill	Method characteristic
ARQ 6	Quality req.	Essential
ARQ 7, ARQ 24	Guidance and method struc-ture	Essential
ARQ 8	Knowledge reuse	Essential
ARQ 9, ARQ 10, ARQ 11, ARQ 12, ARQ 13, ARQ 14	RE and design descr.	Essential
ARQ 15	Traceability	Recommended
ARQ 16	Design rationale	Recommended
ARQ 17	Trade-off analysis	Recommended
ARQ 18	Arch. alternatives	Recommended
ARQ 19	Iterative dev.	Recommended
ARQ 20	Concurrent co-dev.	Optional
ARQ 21	Arch views	Optional
ARQ 22	Tool support	Optional
ARQ 23	Arch. evaluation	Recommended

researcher, it was more convenient to use an Excel sheet for this purpose instead of preparing a data extraction form which is usually used by literature reviews conducted by several researchers. Preparing such forms requires more effort. Hence, we decided to store the data in an Excel file.

3.6.2 Conducting Phase

The **conducting phase** consists of four steps: *Step 4 - study selection, Step 5 - quality assessment, Step 6 - data extraction*, and *Step 7 - data synthesis*. In this phase, we conducted the SLR according to the review protocol by selecting the relevant studies in a stepwise manner (Step 4). The selected studies have been checked for its quality according to a quality check list (Step 5). In Step 6, we extracted the relevant data according to the queries in the data extraction form. The extracted data has been analyzed in Step 7 in order to answer the research questions. In the following, we describe each step in detail.

Steps 4 and 5 - Study Selection and Quality Assessment

In this section, we describe our strategy for searching and selecting relevant studies including the search sources and search terms. For finding relevant studies, we performed manual, automated, and "snowball" search. Fig. 3.3 illustrates the mechanism underpinning the selection process and the quality assessment. It refines the Steps 4 and 5 of Fig. 3.2 by describing their sub-steps.

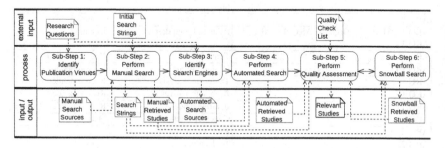

Fig. 3.3: Mechanism underpinning the selection process

Sub-Step 1 - Identify Publication Venues
Search sources comprise search engines and publication venues. Publication venues are used for performing manual search. Researchers use relevant conference proceedings or journals for retrieving relevant studies. According to our defined research questions, we identified relevant publication venues as search sources for manual search.

We considered specific journal papers and conference proceedings with the ranking A and B. We selected the publication venues according to the Australian ERA (Excellence in Research for Australia) Outlet Ranking[3]. As conference proceedings, we conducted the manual search within 5 publication venues (ECSA[4], QoSA[5], RE[6], REFSQ[7], and WICSA[8]). In addition, we selected two journals JSS[9]

---

[3] http://lamp.infosys.deakin.edu.au/era/

[4] European Conference of Software Architecture

[5] International ACM Sigsoft Conference on the Quality of Software Architectures

[6] IEEE International Requirements Engineering Conference

[7] International Working Conference on Requirements Engineering: Foundation for Software Quality

[8] Working IEEE/IFIP Conference on Software Architecture

[9] Journal of Systems and Software

and INFSOF[10].

Sub-Step 2 - Perform Manual Search
We first conducted a manual search between 2005 and 2010 within particular publication venues. As a basis for constructing the search strings for the manual search, we used the MRQ. During the manual search, we revised the search strings and added synonyms and alternative spellings to cover the maximum possible set of primary studies treating the topic.

The main search terms were linked with the Boolean operator "AND" and the synonyms and alternative spellings with the Boolean operator "OR" as shown in Table 3.6. Doing this, we obtained the search string "*SS1 AND SS2*" which is composed of search strings from Table 3.6.

Table 3.6: Search strings

Search string	
SS1	"quality concerns" **OR** "quality requirements" **OR** "quality attributes" **OR** "non-functional requirements" **OR** "non-functional properties" **OR** "NFR" **OR** "NFRs"
SS2	"architecture" **OR** "software architecture" **OR** "design" **OR** "architectural design" **OR** "software design"

We defined exclusion and inclusion criteria (EC, IC) as given in Table 3.7. We excluded studies according to the exclusion criteria EC1–EC3 linked with the boolean operator "OR". We included studies according to the inclusion criteria IC1–IC9 linked with the boolean operator "AND". We considered IC2 and IC3 as inclusion criteria, since our focus is on methods addressing quality requirements. Additionally, we considered IC4 and IC5 as inclusion criteria as well, as we believe that a method which should support the systematic development of requirements and software architecture, has to create the artifacts for each of the phases. These criteria guided the researcher in the decision whether to include or exclude studies.

We performed the selection process for manual search as well as for automated search in three rounds as follows:

- First round: In this round, we scanned the studies by "title and abstract" to remove the irrelevant papers according to the selection criteria. In case a paper was considered completely irrelevant, the researcher did not protocol it at all. The studies, in which the researcher was not sure about their relevance have been included in the set of candidate studies for the second round.

---

[10] Information and Software Technology

Table 3.7: Exclusion and Inclusion Criteria

Exclusion Criteria	
EC1	Published as book
EC2	Published as keynote, road map
EC3	Published as research review, and survey summarizing other research
Inclusion Criteria	
IC1	Focus on developing requirements and software architecture with regard to quality requirements
IC2	Consideration of quality requirements
IC3	Fulfillment of quality requirements on the architecture level
IC4	Creation of requirements description
IC5	Creation of architecture description
IC6	Publishing time between 1.2005 and 12.2010
IC7	In the form of conference, journal papers
IC8	Subject area: computer science
IC9	Language: English

- Second round: The candidate studies from the first round have been further investigated in the second round according to the selection criteria. For this round, we included additional sections of the papers, namely "introduction, discussion, and conclusion". Again, the studies, in which the researcher still was not sure about their relevance have been included in the set of candidate studies for the next round.

- Third round: The candidate studies from the second round have been scanned by their full text according to the selection criteria. The resulting set of studies has gone through a quality assessment before extracting data from the final set of selected studies.

Sub-Step 3 - Identify Search Engines

Search engines are used for conducting automated search. Researchers use such search engines to scan the online data bases for retrieving relevant studies according to some defined search strings. For the automated search, we used the established literature search engines Scopus[11], and Science Direct[12]. We did not include ACM Digital Library and IEEE Xplore since publications listed in their catalog could also be found through the meta search engine Scopus.

Sub-Step 4 - Perform Automated Search

We conducted the automated search between the same time span as for manual search. We used the search terms which have been revised and evaluated during the manual search. For retrieving relevant studies from the automated search, we

---

[11] http://www.scopus.com/

[12] http://www.sciencedirect.com/

used the same exclusion and inclusion criteria that we used for the manual search. The results obtained from automated search complemented the results retrieved from the manual search.

Sub-Step 5 - Perform Quality Assessment
Within quality assessment (Step 5 in Fig. 3.2), the papers selected in the manual search as well as in the automated search were investigated further regarding their quality. To this end, we used a *quality check list* given in Table 3.8. We used it to record the quality of a paper consisting of four questions based on Table 6 in [149].

Each question had to be answered with a value from the set of possible values defined in the check list. The paper that had been assigned at least one value defined as "stop quality" was rejected from further analysis. This is only the case for the question about the credibility of the papers. Along with the set of possible values for each question, the table provides numeric values that were used to calculate a quality score by summing up the respective numeric value for each answer. We chose a threshold of 0 for the quality scores to select the final set of studies. In the end, the studies which reached the threshold were included in the final selection of papers that went into data extraction. The threshold of 0 quality points was chosen to include as many papers as possible for our investigation.

Question 1 in Table 3.8 is concerned with the credibility of the method and findings reported in the paper at hand. Here the main question is if we can trust the statements claimed in the paper. As one factor for credibility of the paper we considered the type of the paper. We divided the types of the papers into the three categories *poster paper or idea paper (value: -1)*, *Short paper or position paper (value: 0)*, and *full paper (value: 1)*. Only for a poster or short paper, we excluded the paper immediately. The reason for the exclusion was less about the length of the paper, but more about the lack of detailed content of the paper. This was the case only for 2 studies.

Question 2 deals with the evaluation reported in the paper. We considered the three cases *real-life case study or big experiment (value: 1)*, *desktop example or small experiment (value: 0)*, and *no evaluation (value: -1)*. None of these values led to exclusion of the study.

Question 3 is concerned with the results of the evaluation and the quality of the result reporting. Here, the questions are whether the results are conclusive and connected to the initial research questions, whether all evidence is given in a way the reader can comprehend them, whether important statements are given on the base of evidence found in the results, and whether the reporting is clean? As possible values, we considered the three options *everything clear and coherent (value: 1)*, *some flaws (value: 0)*, and *major flaws (value: -1)*. None of these values led to exclusion from the study.

Question 4 deals with the method itself and its details. We are interested in the structure of the method. The main question here is how detailed the method is described. As possible values, the three following options are given: *step by step and very detailed (value: 1), relatively detailed (value: 0),* and *vaguely conveyed (value: -1).* None of these values led to exclusion from the study.

Table 3.8: Quality Check List

Question	Possible Values	Stop Quality
1: How credible are the findings?	credible(1), partially credible(0), not credible(-1)	Yes (if -1)
2: How rigorously is the method evaluated?	real-life case study / big experiment(1), desktop example / small experiment(0), no evaluation(-1)	No
3: How clear and coherent is the reporting?	everything clear and coherent(1), some flaws(0), major flaws(-1)	No
4: How detailed is the method conveyed?	step by step and very detailed (1), relatively detailed (0), vaguely conveyed (-1)	No

Sub-Step 6 - Perform Snowball Search

In addition to the manual and automated search, we performed a snowball search. For the "snowball" search, we did not take the time span into account to be able to find relevant studies published before 2005 as well. In the snowball search, we scanned the references in the selected papers obtained from manual as well as automated search. These studies are those which have passed the quality assessment step. For selecting relevant studies from the snowball search, we performed the same three rounds as for the manual and automated search. The studies retrieved from the snowball search have to go through the *quality assessment*. The final set of relevant studies is composed of search results from manual search, automated search, and snowball search that have been qualified in the *quality assessment*.

During the selection process, we identified duplicate papers, which we retrieved from more than one search engine as well as by the manual search. We kept only one of the duplicate studies in the final set of relevant studies. For the papers which describe the same method, we aggregated the results.

Step 6 - Data Extraction

To extract and store data, we developed an excel sheet as an *extraction form* filled out for the selected studies obtained from the *quality assessment* step. The extraction form contains meta information such as title, abstract, author names, publication venue, and publication year related to each paper obtained from the *study selection* step. In addition, it contains answers to the quality check list shown in Table 3.8 from the *quality assessment* step.

We extracted and elicited data in order to answer the MRQ and ARQs represented in Table 3.4. According to Table 3.5, the ARQs are mapped to meta-requirements that we derived from empirical studies in Section 3.2. Having collected this data, we are able to perform a comparative evaluation of selected methods using the evaluation framework described in Section 3.4.

In Section 3.7, we report on the results on the systematic literature review and draw conclusions from the results. This corresponds to *Step 7* and *Step 8* in Fig. 3.2.

3.7 Results and Discussion

In this section, we present the results (*conducting phase*, Step 7 in Fig. 3.2) we derived from extracting data and draw conclusions from the results (*reporting phase*, Step 8 in Fig. 3.2).

For the manual search, we searched 5 conference proceedings and 2 journals from 2005 to 2010. We scanned 2304 papers within 7 publication venues. For the automated search, we scanned 806 papers obtained from the general search engine Scopus and 74 obtained from Science Direct. From the manual and automated search, we selected 44 papers and for the snowball search, we selected 11 papers for the *study selection* step. One paper out of 7 selected papers describes the same method or report on a method we already selected. For such papers, we aggregated the results of data extraction to avoid bias in the results. As the final result, we extracted data for 6 papers (see Table 3.9).

Table 3.9: Study selection according to the selection process

	Manual and automated search		Snowball search	
Round	Selected	Excluded	Selected	Excluded
First round	44	-	11	-
Second round	13	31	7	4
Third round	7	6	3	4
Quality assessment	4	3	3	0

Table 3.10 shows the final list of 6 papers we selected for data extraction. The aggregated paper is marked in *italic font* in the column *Reference*.

Table 3.10: Selected methods (answer to the MRQ)

#	Title	Name	Reference
1	ATRIUM: Software architecture driven by requirements	ATRIUM	[179], *[180]*
2	Tactics based approach for integrating non-functional requirements in object-oriented analysis and design	Marew et al.	[172]
3	Integrating a software architecture-centric method into object-oriented analysis and design	Sangwan et al.	[208]
4	Knowledge based quality-driven architecture design and evaluation	Ovaska et al.	[185]
5	Towards MDD transformation from AO requirements to AO architecture	Sánchez et al.	[207]
6	Towards requirements-driven software development methodology: The Tropos project	Tropos	[65]

In the following, we first give a brief overview of the selected methods in Section 3.7.1. Then, we discuss the results of the SLR by answering the research questions for each method in Section 3.7.2.

3.7.1 Description of Selected Methods

In this section, we provide a brief description of the selected methods.

3.7.1.1 ATRIUM

Architecture generaTed from RequIrements applying a Unified Methodology (ATRIUM)[179, 180] is an aspect-oriented methodology that supports the development of architectures from requirements. The intertwining of requirements and software architectures is supported by ATRIUM. It pays special attention to traceability support between requirements and software architecture. ATRIUM consists of three main activities. In the first activity, goals of the system are defined taking informal requirements into account. The ISO/IEC 25010 [130] is used for defining quality requirements. Catalogues of patterns form the other input for this activity. The output is a goal model which is based on KAOS [159] and the NFR framework [72]. Quality requirements are then refined into *operationalizations* which describe design decisions and design rationale made to satisfy requirements. Requirements and operationalizations are related by means of *contribution* relationships illustrating the effect of solutions on the requirements. In addition, architectural patterns are applied by the architect to address quality requirements. They are classified according to their positive and negative contributions to quality requirements. ATRIUM provides no systematic and methodical selection of architectural patterns.

The second activity is concerned with defining architectural scenarios using sequence diagrams. Architectural scenarios describe the system behavior under certain operationalization decisions. Each scenario describes the interaction of architectural and environmental elements to satisfy specific requirements.

In the third activity, a proto-architecture is generated from the scenario model using Model-to-Model (M2M) transformations. The proto-architecture is a first draft of the final architecture description that can be refined in a later stage of the software development process. The target architecture description language (ADL) is PRISMA [190] which combines component-based software development (CBSD) and aspect-oriented software development (AOSD).

ATRIUM is supported by a tool called MORPHEUS. It includes a requirements tool to describe requirement meta-models, a scenario editor for describing the scenarios, and a graphical environment for describing the proto-architecture obtained from the scenario model. Although the authors claim that ATRIUM is designed for the concurrent definition of requirements and software architecture, we cannot comprehend this kind of development according to the available documents. Nevertheless, in our comparative evaluation, we consider this meta-requirement as fulfilled as this is claimed by the authors of this method.

3.7.1.2 Marew et al.

This method aims at incorporating quality requirements into the analysis and design phases of the existing object-oriented analysis and design (OOAD) [172]. For modeling quality requirements, the NFR framework [72] is used. For realizing quality requirements, tactics [44] are used as operationalization in the NFR framework. The method considers trade-off analysis after the tactics are applied. During trade-off analysis, the relationship among quality requirements is analyzed. According to the results of this activity, it is possible to go back to other phases and redo the application of tactics.

This method uses the idea of aspect-oriented development to implement some tactics by defining classpects (the use of the aspect idea in a class). In the design phase, the tactics are integrated in the existing functional design. Some tactics require restructuring and redesigning the existing design. The method does not make use of architectural patterns and styles. Hence, architecture alternatives that might result from the application of different architectural patterns are not considered by Marew et al. Traceability between different artifacts is only partially provided. For example, in the SIG graph (Softgoals Interdependencies Graph) based on the NFR framework, NFRs and tactics are related. However, we did not find trace links between NFRs and class diagrams. The proposed method provides no support for evaluating the resulting architecture.

3.7.1.3 Sangwan et al.

Sangwan et al. [208] combine the object-oriented analysis and design (OOAD) methodology which heavily focuses on functional requirements with the methods Quality Attribute Workshop (QAW) [42] and Attribute Driven Design (ADD) [244, 48, 37] in order to incorporate quality requirements into the software development process. First the goals of the system are elicited using the QAW approach. The next step is to link the goals to quality requirements. Scenarios are used for specifying quality requirements.

The starting point is the system considered as a monolithic component which has to be iteratively elaborated to a coarse-grained architecture by applying ADD. This component is then recursively decomposed to sub-components. Tactics are applied to satisfy quality requirements. It is mentioned that trade-offs among quality requirements and potential conflicts among tactics should be tackled. However, no systematic approach to deal with these conflicts and making trade-offs is described. It seems that trade-off analysis strongly relies on the experience of the people performing it. Architectural patterns can also be applied in this approach. However, it is unclear whether there is a systematic method for selecting among the set of architectural patterns. For elaborating the high level architecture produced by ADD and specifying the fine-grained architectural detail, the standard OOAD techniques are applied.

3.7.1.4 Ovaska et al.

A quality-aware, model-driven, ontology-orientated, and domain-specific software architecture method is proposed by Ovaska et al. [185]. The specific domain this method is tailored to is the embedded system domain. This method consists of three main phases: modeling quality attributes (QA), representing quality properties in architectural models, and evaluating quality fulfilment from models and code. In the first phase, two models are created; the QA ontology model which captures the knowledge related to a specific quality requirement and the QA requirements model which uses the QA ontology to define and update the quality requirements. In the second phase, architectural patterns, generic and domain-specific design patterns, and tactics are used for addressing quality requirements in the software architecture. In this approach, tactics are called *means* such as security means. The third phase is concerned with prioritizing quality requirements, performing a trade-off analysis between them, and achieving quality requirements according to their priority. Low priority quality requirements are considered as *nice to have* requirements. Although the use of architectural styles, patterns, and tactics might lead to different architectures depending on the priorities of the requirements, the creation of architecture alternatives is not addressed in this method. Similar to the three methods described before, also the Ovaska et al. method does not consider the evaluation of the resulted architecture with respect to quality requirements.

This method uses UML for both requirements engineering and software architecture. This allowed for developing a semi-automated tool based on the open source platform Eclipse. The tool provides support for the whole design flow from requirements to design.

3.7.1.5 Sánchez et al.

An aspect-oriented and a model-driven approach to derive software architecture descriptions from requirements is proposed by Sánchez et al. [207]. The first step is concerned with aspect-oriented requirements engineering (AORE). The goal of this step is to collect requirements and capturing and analyzing concerns (functional and quality concerns) which results in textual requirements. The second step is concerned with AO requirements modeling. A UML model is constructed for modeling textual requirements as a set of scenarios. In the third step, the scenario model from the previous step is transformed into an AO architectural model using predefined model-driven development (MDD) transformations. The architectural model is expressed in UML containing a structural view and a behavioral view. The structural view contains components, ports, interfaces, and connections. The behavioral view involves the exchange of messages between components. Quality requirements are addressed in the architectural model by means of aspects.

In this method, it is possible to generate several candidate architectures corresponding to different design decisions by defining several transformations. Nevertheless, it is the responsibility of the software architect to select the best one, as there is no support for evaluating the software architectures and selecting the most suitable software architecture provided. Trade-offs between quality requirements can be reflected in the architectural model, if they are already considered in the AORE step. However, there is no approach provided that describes how to deal with interacting quality requirements and scenarios in the AORE step. Trace links between scenarios and the architecture model might implicitly exist using the transformation rules that are used for transformation from scenarios to the architectural model. However, there is neither explicit support for traceability in this method given, nor exists support for capturing design rationals.

For this method, the authors did not develop any specific tool. They made use of standard tools and languages, whenever possible. For example, for the AORE step, the tool to be used depends on the AORE process chosen. For the scenario model and the architectural model, any UML tool can be used as these models are based on UML. For transformation, QVT (Query, View, Transformations) [234] as an OMG standard is used.

3.7.1.6 Tropos

Castro et al. [65] propose a development framework, named Tropos which adopts the i* organizational modeling framework and uses it for modeling early and late requirements, architectural, and detailed design. The early requirements analysis is concerned with the intentions of stakeholders to be modeled as goals. In the i* framework, stakeholders are represented as actors. *Strategic dependency models* and *strategic rational models* are used for modeling the relationships among actors and capturing rationales. Late requirement analysis is concerned with modeling requirements containing functional and quality requirements. In this step, functional requirements are operationalized. Quality requirements are either operationalized or metricized.

The task in the architectural design step is to select among (organizational) architectural styles. For evaluating and analyzing architectural styles against quality requirements, the NFR framework is used. Softgoals are refined to sub-goals that are more specific and precise for evaluating architectural styles against them. Design rationale is represented as dashed clouds in the goal model. After selecting the appropriate architectural style, the responsibilities are assigned to the actors. The detailed design step focuses on introducing additional detail for each architectural component. A set of stereotypes and tagged values are defined for accommodating the Tropos concepts within UML. Class diagrams and sequence diagrams are used for representing the detailed design.

Tropos provides partial support for traceability. For example, relations between softgoals and architectural styles are established, whereas from goals to sequence diagrams and class diagrams no trace links are provided. Regarding trade-off analysis, there is no methodical support for detecting and resolving conflicts among quality goals. There is only the possibility for representing such dependencies among goals in the goal model. Tropos considers different architectural styles and selects among them. Nevertheless, it derives only one software architecture at the end of the design phase which is implemented. Regarding the evaluation, only architectural styles are compared with respect to their impact on softgoals. There is no support given for the evaluation of the resulting architecture regarding the achievement of softgoals.

3.7.2 Results of the SLR

In the following, we present the results of our synthesis by answering the research questions shown in Table 3.4. Tables 3.11, 3.12, 3.13, 3.14, and 3.15 represent the answers to *ARQ 1–ARQ 25*. The first column (*Method*) lists the selected papers as the answer to the MRQ.

Table 3.11 illustrates the answers to *ARQ 1–ARQ 5*. As an answer to the *ARQ 1* (*SE phase*), we classified the SE phases to requirements engineering (*RE*), architecture (*Arch*), and design (*Design*). As we can see, all methods cover the phases requirements engineering and architecture design. *Input* and *Output* of each method are addressed in *ARQ 2* and *ARQ 3*. The majority of the methods takes as input an *informal description of the requirements* (*informal requirements* in Table 3.11). The output of the methods varies depending on the requirements engineering and architecture approach they use. *Application domain* is addressed in *ARQ 4*. The majority of the methods can be applied in general. Only the method *Ovaska et al.* is domain specific. It is specified for embedded systems.

ARQ 5 is concerned with the skills that an inexperienced software engineer needs to know or learn in addition to conventional software engineering knowledge. We assume that UML and some types of UML diagrams such as class diagrams, activity diagrams, use case diagrams, and sequence diagrams are known to novices software engineers, as this material is supposed to be the standard material being taught in undergraduate courses. In contrast, goal-oriented modeling (*GO* in Table 3.11) needed for the methods *ATRIUM*, *Marew et al.*, and *Tropos*, aspect-oriented paradigm (*AO*) needed for the methods *ATRIUM Marew et al.*, and *Sánchez et al.*, model-driven development (*MDD*) needed for the methods *ATRIUM*, *Ovaska et al.*, and *Sánchez et al.* might not belong to the standard material of the undergraduate courses.

Table 3.11: Answers to ARQ 1–ARQ 5

MRQ	ARQ 1	ARQ 2	ARQ 3	ARQ 4	ARQ 5
Method	SE Phase	Input	Output	App Dom.	User Skill
ATRIUM	RE[13], Arch.[14]	Informal requirements	Proto arch.	General	GO[15], AO[16], MDD[17], AO-ADL[18]
Marew et al.	RE, Design	Informal requirements	Goal model, class diagram, sequence diagram, deployment diagram	General	GO, AO
Sangwan et al.	RE, Arch, Design	Business concept model, business process model, business goals	Interfaces specification, detailed component design, component architecture	General	QAW[19], ADD[20], OOAD[21]
Ovaska et al.	RE, Arch, Design	Informal requirements	Requirements quality attribute ontology models, architecture models	Embedded system	MDD, QADA[22]
Sánchez et al.	RE, Arch	Informal requirements	Component, sequence diagrams	General	AO, MDD, AO-CAM[23]
Tropos	RE, Arch, Design	Stakeholder intentions	SD[24] model, SR[25] model, formal Tropos specification, NFR[26] diagram, Agent class diagram, sequence diagram, collaboration diagrams, plan diagram	General	GO

Table 3.12 shows the answers to *ARQ 6–ARQ 8* and *ARQ 24*. *ARQ 6* is concerned with eliciting and documenting quality requirements. As we can see, in con-

---

[13] Requirements Engineering

[14] Architecture

[15] Goal-Oriented Concept

[16] Aspect-Oriented Concept

[17] Model-Driven Development

[18] Aspect-Oriented Architecture Description Language

[19] Quality Attribute Workshop

[20] Attribute Driven Design

[21] Object-Oriented Analysis and Design

[22] Quality-driven Architecture Design and quality Analysis

[23] Aspect-Oriented Component and Aspect Model

[24] Strategic Dependency

[25] Strategic Rationale

[26] Non-Functional Requirement

trast to the results we obtained from empirical studies and experience reports from practice (see Section 3.2), requirements elicitation and documentation in academia is largely performed in a systematic way using well established methods and notations such as goal modeling and UML.

To investigate whether architecting and designing systems is being done in an ad-hoc and unsystematic manner and only by experienced software engineers, *ARQ 7* and *ARQ 24* aim at finding out how well the process is supported by the selected methods and how detailed these methods are structured and described. These questions are related to the essential meta-requirement *Guidance* (see Table 3.5). The aim of these questions is to discover how suitable the selected methods are for less experienced software engineers. As we can see, only *ATRIUM* provides guidelines and case studies that help the user in applying the method (*ARQ 7*). As an answer to *ARQ 24*, we observe that *ATRIUM* provides a very detailed and step by step description of the method as well.

ARQ 8 investigates how quality requirements are addressed in the software architecture. This ARQ is related to the essential meta-requirement *knowledge reuse*. As we can see in Table 3.12, only two methods *Sangwan et al.* and *Ovaska et al.* use architectural patterns as well as tactics (also called quality means) for achieving quality requirements. The other methods use either architectural patterns or tactics (also called mechanisms or quality means). In a suitable software architecture both patterns and tactics have to be used as they contribute to the satisfaction of quality requirements in different ways.

Table 3.12: Answers to ARQ 6–ARQ 8, and ARQ 24

MRQ	ARQ 6	ARQ 7	ARQ 24	ARQ 8
Method	Q Req.	Guidance	Method Structure	Knowledge Reuse
ATRIUM	Elicitation, documentation	Yes	Step by step	Architectural patterns, design patterns
Marew et al.	Elicitation, documentation	No	Step by Step	Tactics
Sangwan et al.	Elicitation, documentation	No	Step by step	Architectural patterns, tactics
Ovaska et al.	Elicitation, documentation	No	Relatively detailed	Architectural patterns, design patterns, quality means
Sánchez et al.	Elicitation, documentation	No	Relatively detailed	Mechanisms
Tropos	Elicitation, documentation	No	Step by step	Organizational architectural styles, social patterns

Table 3.13 shows the answers to *ARQ 9–ARQ 14*. *ARQ 9* and *ARQ 12* are concerned with the known RE as well as architecture approaches that are used in the selected methods. For example, *Marew et al.* uses the *NFR framework* and *Tropos* uses *i** as their requirements engineering approaches. The methods *Marew et al.*

and *Tropos* do not use any known approach for the architecture phase. *Ovaska et al.* uses QADA (Quality-driven Architecture Design and quality Analysis) as the architecture approach.

ARQ 10 and *ARQ 13* deal with the notations and languages used for creating the requirements artifacts as well as architecture artifacts. Some methods use *UML* or notations similar to UML and some methods use *goal notations* for creating the requirements artifacts. These might be different kinds of goal notations. For example, *ATRIUM* uses *KAOS* and the *NFR framework*, which is distinguished from the goal notation *i** in *Tropos*. For creating the architecture artifacts, the majority of methods uses *UML* or its variants such as *Agent UML (AUML)* used in *Tropos*.

ARQ 11 and *ARQ 14* are concerned with the artifacts created in the requirements engineering phase as well as in the architecture phases. *Atrium* creates a *goal model* and a *scenario model* for describing the requirements, whereas *Sánchez et al.* uses *sequence diagrams* as requirement descriptions. The artifacts that are created in the architecture phase are different. However, most of the methods create a structure diagram such as a *class diagram*. The second frequent diagram for representing the software architecture is the *sequence diagram* for describing the behavior.

Table 3.13: Answers to ARQ 9–ARQ 14

MRQ	ARQ 9	ARQ 10	ARQ 11	ARQ 12	ARQ 13	ARQ 14
Method	RE Descr.			Design Descr.		
ATRIUM	KAOS, NFR framework, scenario	Goal notation	Goal model, scenario model	UML[27], AO-ADL	UML	AO-ADL, structure diagram
Marew et al.	NFR framework	Goal notation	Goal model	-	UML	class, sequence, deployment diagrams
Sangwan et al.	QAW, use cases	UML	Quality attribute scenarios, use case model, business type model	ADD, OOAD	UML	Class, component diagram
Ovaska et al.	-	UML	Requirements quality attribute ontology models	QADA	UML	Collaboration, structure, sequence, state, deployment diagram
Sánchez et al.	Scenarios	UML	Sequence diagram	AO-CAM	UML	Component, sequence diagram
Tropos	i*	Goal notation	SD model, SR model, formal tropos specification	-	Goal notation, AUML[28]	NFR requirements, class, sequence, plan diagrams

Table 3.14 shows the answers to *ARQ 15–ARQ 19* and *ARQ 23. ARQ 15* is concerned with providing support for traceability. It is only fully supported by *ATRIUM* and *Sangwan et al.*. The rest of the selected methods support traceability either partially or not at all. For example, *Marew et al.* provide traceability between NFRs and tactics in the SIG graph, but not between NFRs and the class diagrams. Also *Tropos* provides partial traceability support, namely only between softgoals and architectural styles.

As discussed in Section 3.2, particularly inexperienced architects rely on methods that guide them in capturing design rationale and ensure that design rationale is sufficiently and systematically documented. With *ARQ 16*, we aim at finding answers on how well the selected methods support capturing design rationale behind design decisions. Only *ATRIUM* and *Tropos* support the documenting of design rationale when making design decisions. For the rest of the methods, we did not find any hint regarding design rationale in the documentation of the methods.

We found strong empirical evidence in Section 3.2 for taking trade-off analysis as a meta-requirement into account. This meta-requirement corresponds to *ARQ 17*. Only three methods *Marew et al.*, *Sangwan et al.*, and *Ovaska et al.* support trade-off analysis. *ATRIUM* and *Tropos* provide the possibility to represent such trade-offs. They, however, do not provide any systematic method for detecting as well as resolving conflicts.

Creation of architecture alternatives (*ARQ 18*) is not supported by the most of the methods. Only *ATRIUM* and *Sánchez et al.* provide the possibility to generate several candidate architectures corresponding to different design decisions by defining several transformations. They, however, do not include the creation of architecture alternatives in their method steps. In *Tropos*, one can choose among different architectural styles for creating the resulting software architecture. However, the method is designed for creating only one resulting software architecture and not candidate architectures.

Regarding the iterative software development (*ARQ 19*), some of the methods such as *ATRIUM, Marew et al.*, and *Ovaska et al.* support the iterative development as recommended in the empirical studies described in Section 3.2.

As discussed in Section 3.2, evaluation of software architecture is essential to ensure whether and to which extent quality requirements have been addressed in the software architecture. Evaluating software architecture is addressed in *ARQ 23*. As we can see in Table 3.14, none of the methods consider the evaluation of software architectures. For example, in *Sánchez et al.* it is possible to create candidate architectures based on different transformations. Nevertheless, it is the responsi-

---

[27] Unified Modeling Language
[28] Agent UML

bility of the software architect to select the best one, as there is no support for evaluating the software architectures and selecting the most suitable software architecture provided. Only *Tropos* provides partial support for evaluation by evaluating the architecture styles to be chosen for the final architecture. However, there is no support in *Tropos* for evaluating the final software architecture with respect to quality requirements.

Table 3.14: Answers to ARQ 15–ARQ 19 and ARQ 23

MRQ	ARQ 15	ARQ 16	ARQ 17	ARQ 18	ARQ 19	ARQ 23
Method	Traceability	Design Rationale	Trade-off Analysis	Arch. Alt.	Iterative Dev.	Arch. Eval.
ATRIUM	Yes	Yes	No	Partially	Yes	No
Marew et al.	Partially	No	Yes	No	Yes	No
Sangwan et al.	Yes	No	Yes	No	No	No
Ovaska et al.	No	No	Yes	No	Yes	No
Sánchez et al.	No	No	No	Partially	No	No
Tropos	partially	Yes	No	Partially	No	Partially

Table 3.15 shows the answers to *ARQ 20–ARQ 22* and *ARQ 25*. Co-development of requirements and software architecture in an iterative and concurrent manner is recommended in the literature. We also found few empirical studies that underline this as discussed in Section 3.2. *ARQ 20* is concerned with concurrent development of requirements and software architecture. This is only answered with *yes* by the *ATRIUM* approach. All other approaches do not support the intertwining development of the two phases.

There is no consensus on the number and nature of the architectural views. Hence, it can be hardly defined which kinds of architectural views are required. All the selected studies provide at least a structural view for representing the software architecture (*ARQ 21*). The behavioral view is considered in the majority of the methods as well.

ARQ 22 addresses tool support by the selected methods. According to the studies we discussed before (see Section 3.2), tools are usually not used in practice. Nevertheless, there is no evidence that a tool might not be supportive by some tasks. As we can see in Table 3.15, tool support is only provided by the methods using the MDD technique as it is hardly possible to transform one model into another model without tool support. These methods are *ATRIUM*, *Ovaska et al.*, and *Sánchez et al.* to some extent.

Method evaluation addressed by *ARQ 25* is one of the questions asked by the quality assessment. It is classified into *big experiment* representing real-life case studies, *small experiment* representing small case studies or desktop examples, and *no evaluation.* All the selected methods used at least a small experiment for their evaluation.

Table 3.15: Answers to ARQ 20–ARQ 22, ARQ 25

MRQ	ARQ 20	ARQ 21	ARQ 22	ARQ 25
Method	Concurrent Dev.	Arch. Views	Tool Support	Method Eval.
ATRIUM	Yes	Not explicitly (structural)	Yes	Big experiment
Marew et al.	No	Structural, behavioral, deployment	No	Small experiment
Sangwan et al.	No	Structural	No	Big experiment
Ovaska et al.	No	Structural, behavioral, deployment, development	Yes	Big experiment
Sánchez et al.	No	Structural, behavioral	Partially	Small experiment
Tropos	No	Structural, behavioral	No	Small experiment

3.8 Comparative Evaluation

This section deals with evaluating the selected methods based on the meta-requirements derived in Section 3.2 and the comparative evaluation framework developed in Section 3.4. First, we describe how we perform the value assignment to the criteria (meta-requirements) to make the selected methods comparable in Section 3.8.1. Then, we show the application of the evaluation framework to the methods we have selected from our systematic review.

3.8.1 Value Assignment Schema

It is not a trivial task to quantify the results we obtained from the previous section. However, we need to some extent a quantification to make the methods comparable. We decided to use a 3-score scale consisting of +, o, and - for assigning values to the meta-requirements, as it might be easier to handle than other scoring systems. In the following, we describe for each meta-requirement a mapping between the answer of the related ARQ (obtained from the previous section) and the assigned values. To show such a mapping, we provide one table for each meta-requirement, in which the first column of the table represents the *"meta-*

requirement", the second column shows the *"related ARQ"*, the third column gives the possible answers to the ARQ (*"answer to ARQ"*), and the fourth column represents the values we assigned (+, o, -) for making the meta-requirement comparable with other methods (*"assigned value"*).

User skill

As described before (see Section 3.2), user skill refers to the skills that an inexperienced software engineer needs additionally for applying the method at hand. Certainly, it is of advantage if less specific knowledge is required for applying a method. Therefore, we assigned values to the meta-requirement *user skill* according to the number of skills an inexperienced software architect requires to learn additionally to be able to apply a method. This is shown in Table 3.16.

Table 3.16: Mapping between meta-requirements and their assigned values

Meta-requirements	Related ARQ	Answer to ARQ	Assigned value
User Skill	ARQ 5	4 needed skills	-
		3 needed skills	o
		1-2 needed skill	+

Eliciting and documenting quality requirements in a systematic and structured way

We defined eliciting and documenting quality requirements in a systematic and structured way as an *"essential"* meta-requirement that must be integrated in the process of software development. Hence, we assigned the values to this meta-requirement as illustrated in Table 3.17.

Table 3.17: Mapping between meta-requirements and their assigned values

Meta-requirements	Related ARQ	Answer to ARQ	Assigned value
Quality requirements	ARQ 6	Structured and systematic elicitation and documentation	+
		Vaguely elicitation and documentation	o
		No elicitation and documentation	-

Guidance and method structure

As discussed before, the methods have to involve a number of steps to be performed. It should explicitly be provided in which order the certain steps have to be executed. In addition to the structuring of the method, explicit guidelines and heuristics must be provided in order to support inexperienced software architects in achieving the goal of the method. Hence, we define the following values for the criteria *guidance and method structure* shown in Table 3.18.

Table 3.18: Mapping between meta-requirements and their assigned values

Meta-requirements	Related ARQ	Answer to ARQ	Assigned value
Guidance and method structure	ARQ 7, ARQ 24	"Yes" and "step by step"	+
		"Yes" and "relatively detailed"	o
		"No" and "step by step"	o
		"No" and "relatively detailed"	-

Knowledge reuse

A quality-aware software development process covering requirements engineering and software architecture must include step-by-step and systematic ways for finding solutions using architectural patterns and tactics[29] to achieve quality requirements. The assigned values for this "essential" meta-requirement are illustrated in Table 3.19.

Note that the use of patterns and tactics is manifested in the state-of-the-art as a common and an established principle for fulfilling quality requirements. Since all the considered methods in our study make use of patterns and/or tactics for achieving quality requirements, the value assignment shown in Table 3.19 is sufficient for comparing the selected methods. However, there might exist approaches (i.e., in the future) that use other principles for achieving quality requirements. For such a case, Table 3.19 has to be extended or modified in order to consider other principles for achieving quality requirements.

---

[29] Also known as mechanisms or quality means

Table 3.19: Mapping between meta-requirements and their assigned values

Meta-requirements	Related ARQ	Answer to ARQ	Assigned value
Knowledge reuse	ARQ 8	"Architectural patterns" and "tactics[30]"	+
		"Only architectural patterns"	o
		"Only tactics"	o
		"No architectural patterns" and "no tactics"	-

RE and design descriptions

From the empirical studies we concluded that the use of models, the use of unified notations and languages as well as a combination of semi-formal and natural language for producing the artifacts are important. The assigned values to this "essential meta-requirement" are shown in Table 3.20.

Table 3.20: Mapping between meta-requirements and their assigned values

Meta-requirements	Related ARQ	Answer to ARQ	Assigned value
RE and design descriptions	ARQ 9, ARQ 10, ARQ 11, ARQ 12, ARQ 13, ARQ 14	"unified language for RE and architecture" and "semi-formal"	+
		"unified language for RE and architecture" and "only natural language"	o
		"different languages for RE and architecture" and "semi-formal"	o
		"different languages for RE and architecture" and "only natural language"	-

Traceability support between requirements and architecture artifacts

We defined traceability as a "recommended" meta-requirement which can be supported fully, partially, or not at all by the selected methods. Table 3.21 shows the mapping of the fulfillment of this meta-requirement to values we assigned.

Capturing and documenting design rationale in a systematic way

As described in Section 3.2, software architects, particularly inexperienced architects, rely on methods that guide them in capturing design rationale and ensure that design rationale is sufficiently and systematically documented. A method can

Table 3.21: Mapping between meta-requirements and their assigned values

Meta-requirements	Related ARQ	Answer to ARQ	Assigned value
Traceability	ARQ 15	Yes	+
		Partially	o
		No	-

fully, partially, or not at all support the capturing and documenting design rationale in a systematic way. The value assignment is shown in Table 3.22.

Table 3.22: Mapping between meta-requirements and their assigned values

Meta-requirements	Related ARQ	Answer to ARQ	Assigned value
Design rationale	ARQ 16	Yes	+
		Partially	o
		No	-

Detecting conflicts and interactions among (quality) requirements as well as resolving such interdependencies

Trade-off analysis as a *"recommended"* meta-requirement should be integrated in the process of software development. This includes detecting conflicts and inter-actions among (quality) requirements as well as resolving such interdependencies. The values assigned to this meta-requirement are displayed in Table 3.23.

Table 3.23: Mapping between meta-requirements and their assigned values

Meta-requirements	Related ARQ	Answer to ARQ	Assigned value
Trade-off analysis	ARQ 17	"Detection" and "resolution"	+
		"Only detection"	o
		"Only resolution"	o
		"No detection" and "no resolution"	-

Supporting architecture alternatives

We defined supporting architecture alternatives as a *"recommended"* meta-requirement. It refers to architecture alternatives to be created for the overall software architecture that achieve quality requirements to different satisfaction levels. Some
methods do not consider the creation of such candidates for the final software
architecture. They, however, consider solution candidates such as patterns and tactics for achieving quality requirements. We call this as a "partial" fulfillment of
this meta-requirement. Table 3.24 shows the related assigned values.

Table 3.24: Mapping between meta-requirements and their assigned values

Meta-requirements	Related ARQ	Answer to ARQ	Assigned value
Architecture alterna-tives	ARQ 18	Yes	+
		Partially	o
		No	-

Supporting feedback loops between requirements and software architecture

To ensure that the software system responds adequately to changes, there should
exist at least feedback loops between the phases requirements engineering and
software architecture. Hence, developing requirements and software architecture
in an iterative manner is "recommended" in the empirical studies. See Table 3.25
for the defined mapping.

Table 3.25: Mapping between meta-requirements and their assigned values

Meta-requirements	Related ARQ	Answer to ARQ	Assigned value
Iterative develop-ment	ARQ 19	Yes	+
		No	-

Co-development of requirements and software architecture in an iterative and concurrent manner

Co-development of requirements and software architecture in an iterative and concurrent manner is recommended in the research. As we did not find much empirical evidences, we defined it as an "optional" meta-requirement which can be supported by the methods or not. Table 3.26 shows the related assigned values.

Table 3.26: Mapping between meta-requirements and their assigned values

Meta-requirements	Related ARQ	Answer to ARQ	Assigned value
Concurrent co-development	ARQ 20	Yes	+
		No	-

Defining architectural views

Table 2.1 in Chapter 2 (see page 30) provides an overview of the common However, there is no consensus on the number and nature of the architectural views. Hence, it can be hardly defined which kinds of architectural views are required. According to Smolander et al. [222], the most appropriate set of architectural view cannot be objectively specified in general. Based on the prevalent situation and characteristics of the organizations and software projects, the architectural views have to be selected. This dissension regarding the appropriate set of architectural views makes it hard to assign values for this meta-requirement. Therefore, for this "optional" meta-requirement we assign values according to the view types used in the selected methods shown in Table 3.27.

Table 3.27: Mapping between meta-requirements and their assigned values

Meta-requirements	Related ARQ	Answer to ARQ	Assigned value
Arch. views	ARQ 21	"structural" and "behavioral" and "deployment" or "development"	+
		"structural" and "behavioral"	o
		"structural"	-

Tool support

We could not find any evidence for considering a tool as necessary for using a method. Hence, we defined this meta-requirement as "optional". Some methods provide full tool support for their methods, some only partially, and some do not provide a tool at all. This is reflected in Table 3.28.

Table 3.28: Mapping between meta-requirements and their assigned values

Meta-requirements	Related ARQ	Answer to ARQ	Assigned value
Tool support	ARQ 22	Yes	+
		Partially	o
		No	-

Support for the evaluation of the software architecture

Studies with inexperienced software architects show strong preferences for a method which supports the evaluation of the software architecture. Some methods include the evaluation of the resulting software architecture and some do not consider this at all. There exist methods which only partially support the evaluation by for example evaluating the architectural pattern candidates with respect to quality requirements. The value assignment is illustrated in Table 3.29.

Table 3.29: Mapping between meta-requirements and their assigned values

Meta-requirements	Related ARQ	Answer to ARQ	Assigned value
Architecture evaluation	ARQ 23	Yes	+
		Partially	o
		No	-

3.8.2 Framework Application

Table 3.30 shows the application of the evaluation framework to the methods we have selected from our systematic review. The dark gray rows show the *essential* meta-requirements, which are *quality requirements, guidance, knowledge reuse,* and *RE and design descriptions*. The light gray rows indicate the *recommended* meta-requirements, which include *traceability, design rationale, trade-off analysis, architecture alternatives*, and *iterative development*. The non-colored rows are the *optional* meta-requirements, which are *concurrent co-development, architecture views*, and *tool support*. In addition, we take into account the *method characteristic user skill* for the comparative evaluation of the selected methods, as the number of new skills to learn by a novice software architect might have an impact on the application of the method. In the previous section (see Section 3.8.1), we described the value assignment schema that we use for comparative evaluation (see Table 3.30).

Table 3.30: Comparative evaluation of selected methods

Component	Elements	ATRIUM	Marew et al.	Sangwan et al.	Ovaska et al.	Sánchez et al.	Tropos
User	User skill	-	+	o	+	o	+
Contents	Quality requirements	+	+	+	+	+	+
	Guid. and method struc.	+	o	o	-	-	o
	Knowledge reuse	o	o	+	+	o	o
	RE and design description	o	-	+	+	+	o
	Traceability	+	o	+	-	-	o
	Design rationale	+	-	-	-	-	+
	Trade-off analysis	-	+	+	+	-	-
	Architecture alternatives	o	-	-	-	o	o
	Iterative development	+	+	-	+	-	-
	Concurrent co-development	+	-	-	-	-	-
	Architecture views	-	+	-	+	o	o
	Tool support	+	-	-	+	o	-
	Architecture evaluation	-	-	-	-	-	o

As we can see in Table 3.30, we cannot find any method among the set of selected methods that fulfills all the meta-requirements or nearly all of them. We discuss the fulfillment of the meta-requirements by the selected methods by category. We first consider the category *essential* meta-requirements that can be considered as *must have* meta-requirements as argued in Section 3.2. Two methods

Sangwan et al. and *Ovaska et al.* fulfill three of the four meta-requirements. The meta-requirement *guidance and method structure* cannot be fully fulfilled by these methods. One reason for this can be that these methods are not designed for inexperienced software architects and novices. Hence, they do not place importance on guiding the user providing a step by step method and detailed guidance.

The *recommended* meta-requirements do not need to be fulfilled necessarily by the selected methods. Nevertheless, they have been recommended repeatedly in research and empirical studies from practice as described in Section 3.2. Hence, we expect the methods to fulfill the most of these meta-requirements, if not all of them can be fulfilled by one single method. From six *recommended* meta-requirements, the three meta-requirements *traceability*, *design rationale*, and *iterative development* are fulfilled by the *ATRIUM* method. The other methods fulfill even less meta-requirements. In *ATRIUM*, the meta-requirement *trade-off analysis* is not considered at all. *Trade-off analysis* includes detection and resolution of conflicts and interdependencies among quality requirements. Regarding *architecture alternatives*, only alternatives for architectural patterns are taken into account which lead to selecting only one architectural pattern for the final architecture. Hence, the resulting final architecture does not include any alternatives. Moreover, *ATRIUM* does not evaluate to what extent the resulting final software architecture satisfices the elicited and modeled quality requirements (meta-requirement *architecture evaluation*).

Two of three *optional* meta-requirements that can be considered as *nice to have* meta-requirements are fulfilled by *ATRIUM* and *Ovaska et al.*. *ATRIUM* not only develops the requirements and software architecture in an iterative manner, it also takes the concurrent co-development of these artifacts into account. In addition, a tool is developed to support the user in applying the method.

Regarding the category *method characteristic*, we only considered *user skill* in Table 3.30. Only three out of 6 selected methods cover this characteristic. Another characteristic that might be interesting for comparison is the *application domain* (not shown in Table 3.30). The majority of the methods can be applied in general. Only the method *Ovaska et al.* is domain specific. It is specified for embedded systems which causes a restriction in applying this method as it is not universally applicable (see Table 3.11 on page 92).

Our evaluation underlines the lack of methodological support for a systematic development of both phases with respect to quality requirements in a unified process. The main finding of our review was the identification of a need for a unified method which supports the development of requirements and software architectures. In further chapters of this book, we describe our QuaDRA framework which addresses the gaps identified in this chapter by providing a method supporting the development of requirements and software architecture with respect to quality requirements. We will apply later on in this book the evaluation framework to the QuaDRA method in order to validate whether the identified gaps are addressed.

3.9 Threats to Validity

For quantitative research (such as experiments) in software engineering, four main types of validity threats, namely *conclusion, internal, construct,* and *external* are discussed by Wohlin et al. [242]. Among these four main types of validity threats, the internal validity is classified as the one with the highest priority [243]. We identified three types of validity threats that apply to our empirical study. We report on these threats and the mitigation strategies we applied to control the identified threats.

Internal validity threat refers to bias in designing the study and performing the review that affect the outcome of the review. We identified three internal threats regarding the conduction of the SLR. The first internal threat is associated with ambiguity, incompleteness, and inconsistency of the *data extraction form*. To mitigate this threat, we constructed the extraction form according to the research questions represented in Table 3.4 which are derived based on the identified requirements and the evaluation framework.

The second internal threat to validity concerns the design of the study in general. To mitigate this internal threat, we developed our protocol in advance, which has been reviewed by external reviewers within our working group.

Another important threat when performing systematic literature reviews refers to the completeness of search terms. In order to cover the possible maximum number of relevant studies, we took into account the synonyms and alternative spellings in the search strings. We first conducted the manual search using the defined initial search terms. Then, we revised and validated search terms during the manual search. The validated search terms have been used for the automated search. All studies found by the manual search have also been found by the automated search. This indicates a very high *quasi-sensitivity*. It is an important criterion that is used to evaluate the quality and performance of search strategies [254].

There exists an additional internal threat regarding the application of our comparative evaluation framework and the value assignment schema. Using the value assignment schema (see Section 3.8.1), we described how we defined the possible values for the defined meta-requirements and how we assigned values to the methods. It might be a bias regarding the value assignment, as it has been done by a single researcher. We tried to mitigate this bias by describing the value assignment process and the comparison process thoroughly and transparently in Sections 3.8.1

and 3.8.2 so that it can be easily understood. In addition, the single researcher has been carrying out research and collecting experiences in the fields of requirements and architecture and related methods for 6 years. This might mitigate the risk of bias regarding this internal threat as well. Nevertheless, we cannot fully eliminate this internal threat.

External validity threat deals with the generalization of the results. Due to a huge number of papers in the literature, there exists the possibility of not covering all relevant papers. To reduce this kind of validity threat, we conducted the snowball search in addition to the manual and automated search. We did not constrain the snowball search by publication year as we did for the manual and automated search. Hence, we reduced the external validity threat, which occurs due to a biased time span selection.

Construct validity threat is concerned with the relation between the measures used in the review and the outcomes of the review. We identified one construct validity, which might occur when the metrics and measures represented in the extraction form do not reflect the results of the study appropriately. To reduce this threat, we constructed the extraction form according to the research questions. In addition, we used metrics described in the literature to convey the results in a suitable way. Furthermore, the researcher involved in the study is experienced in this area which reduces the likelihood of using inappropriate metrics in the extraction form.

3.10 Contributions

In this chapter, we identified the lack of systematic and methodological guidelines for quality-aware development of requirements and software architecture. Our contributions can be captured as follows:

- **Systematic identification of meta-requirements** that a method for quality-aware development of requirements and software architecture should fulfill. We derived 19 meta-requirements.
- **Classification of identified meta-requirements** in *essential* which must be fulfilled, *recommended* which might not be absolutely required, *optional* which do not necessarily need to be fulfilled, and *method characteristics*.
- **Corroborating the identified meta-requirements** through direct evidence from empirical studies. We reviewed 11 empirical studies related to quality requirements and software architecture including literature reviews, interviews, surveys, and group discussions.

- **Developing a structured framework** for analyzing and comparing the state-of-the-art methods. It is structured in *Components*, *Elements*, *Evaluation Questions*, and *Classification*. The evaluation framework can easily be modified and extended to desirable features.
- **Systematic selection of the state-of-the-art methods** by conducting a systematic literature review. We scanned 2304 papers within 7 publication venues by conducting manual, automated, and snowball search. As the final result, we extracted data for 6 papers.
- **Defining a value assignment schema** for making the selected methods comparable. We selected a 3-score scale consisting of +, o, and - for assigning values to the meta-requirements
- **Comparative evaluation of the selected methods** by applying the developed framework. The evaluation showed that none of the compared methods fulfills all the meta-requirements or nearly all of them. Our evaluation underlines the lack of methodological support for systematic development of both phases with respect to quality requirements in a unified process.

Chapter 4
Phase 1: Context Elicitation & Problem Analysis

Abstract This chapter shows the modeling of the environment, functional as well as quality requirements in a problem-oriented requirements engineering method. We build upon functional models based on the problem frames approach in order to extend them with annotations for modeling quality requirements.

4.1 Introduction

Quality requirements are harder to deal with than functional requirements in different respects. It is often not clear how to express quality requirements in such a way that they can be analyzed appropriately. Properly modeling quality requirements should allow the analyst to unambiguously state what the requirement is, to set it into relation with other (functional or non-functional) requirements, and to determine if it is satisfiable at all.

Although the treatment of quality requirements in software development is not yet as well mastered as the treatment of functional requirements [45], it has recently caught more attention. Quality requirements such as security and performance requirements must be elicited, analyzed, and documented as thoroughly as functional ones.

As described in Chapter 2, we use the problem frames approach [133] as the basis for requirements analysis. The problem frames approach provides many advantages as mentioned in Chapter 1. It, however, does not provide support for dealing with quality requirements [51]. Hence, we extended the previous requirements analysis approach based on problem frames [114] by explicitly taking into account quality requirements in such a way that they can be analyzed appropriately. To this end, we enriched the analysis models with annotations for quality requirements. The so enhanced problem descriptions form the starting point for later phases of the software development process such as architectural design. For this purpose, we have extended the UML profile for problem frames [115].

This chapter, which represents Phase 1 of the QuaDRA framework is based on our work presented in [17]. The author of this book is the main author of this publication. We had useful and valuable discussions with Denis Hatebur and Maritta Heisel regarding modeling quality requirements.

The rest of this chapter is organized as follows. In Section 4.2, we describe our proposed extension to the UML profile for problem frames. The method for modeling quality requirements and its application is described in Section 4.3. Related work is discussed in Section 4.4. Section 4.5 summarizes the contribution of this chapter.

4.2 UML4PF Extension for Quality Requirements

UML [235] provides extension mechanisms such as stereotypes and tagged values that can be used to extend the UML meta-model. In order to provide support for modeling quality requirements we make use of such extensions. We add three new stereotypes to the UML profile for problem frames which currently contains only the stereotype ≪Requirement≫ to indicate a functional requirement. We introduce the stereotypes ≪QualityRequirement≫ and ≪FunctionalRequirement≫ to distinguish between a quality requirement and a functional requirement. Both stereotypes have to be applied to UML classes. The stereotype ≪complements≫ has to be applied to a UML dependency. It shows the relationship between a functional requirement and a quality requirement. It has a class with the stereotype ≪QualityRequirement≫ as the source and a class with the stereotype ≪FunctionalRequirement≫ as the target. Table 4.1 lists the new stereotypes, their description and the UML element they extend, and Fig. 4.1 shows the structure of the UML profile extension.

We extend the existing list of OCL expressions in the UML profile for problem frames by identifying a new consistency condition for quality requirements:

A quality requirement is connected to at least one functional requirement by a dependency with the stereotype ≪complements≫.

Furthermore, some existing consistency conditions expressed with OCL have to be modified in order to provide support for modeling quality requirements. Some examples of such modifications are given in Appendix A.

Table 4.1: Stereotypes defined for the UML profile extension

Stereotype	Applies to	Description
≪QualityRequirement≫	Class	Represents a quality requirement
≪FunctionalRequirement≫	Class	Represents a functional requirement
≪complements≫	Dependency	Represents a dependency from a quality requirement (class with stereotype ≪QualityRequirement≫) to a functional requirement (class with stereotype ≪FunctionalRequirement≫)

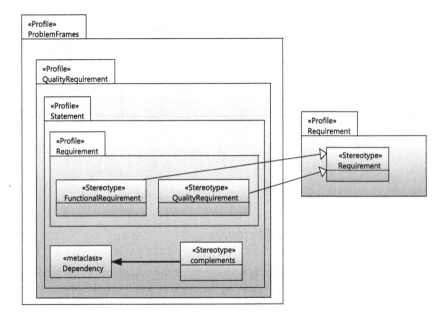

Fig. 4.1: Structure of the UML profile extension for modeling quality requirements

4.3 Method for Problem-oriented Requirement Analysis

Our method for problem-oriented requirement analysis is shown in Fig. 4.2. The artifacts in the top of Fig. 4.2 represent the external inputs for the steps of the method. Those in the bottom of the figure represent the output of the steps providing input for further steps. *Step 1 - Problem Context Elicitation* and *Step 2*

- *Functional Requirements Modeling* provide support for eliciting the context and modeling functional requirements, which are proposed by Hatebur & Heisel [114]. We extended this method by providing support for modeling quality requirements such as performance and security (*Step 3 - Quality Requirements Modeling*). In addition, we describe the impact of architectural decisions which are made on the architecture level and make them visible on the requirement level. This is highlighted in gray in Fig. 4.2.

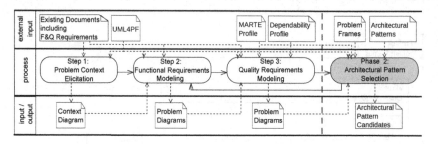

Fig. 4.2: Overview of Phase 1

Step 1 - Problem Context Elicitation

This step (*Step 1* in Fig. 4.2) aims at understanding the system-to-be, the problem it shall solve, and therefore understanding the environment it should influence according to the requirements. Existing documents including functional and quality requirements (F&Q Requirements in Fig. 4.2) are used as input for this step. We obtain a problem description by eliciting all domains related to the problem to be solved, their relations to each other and the software to be constructed. To elicit the problem context, we set up a *context diagram* consisting of the *machine* (software-to-be), related *domains* in the environment, and interfaces between these domains. Creating a context diagram is the first step in the software development process based on problem frames.

Application of Step 1 - Problem Context Elicitation

To elicit the problem context for the smart grid example (see Section 2.6 on page 43), we set up a context diagram consisting of the machine *Smart Meter Gateway*, the domains *LMN, HAN, WAN, MeterData, AuthorizedExternalEntities, Consumer Data, ...* and interfaces between these domains. The context diagram for the smart grid example is shown in Fig. 4.3. The machine *Smart Meter Gateway* collects and processes the recordings from the causal domain *SmartMeter*, and stores them into the lexical domain *MeterData*. The machine is also responsible for distributing the *MeterData* to external entities.

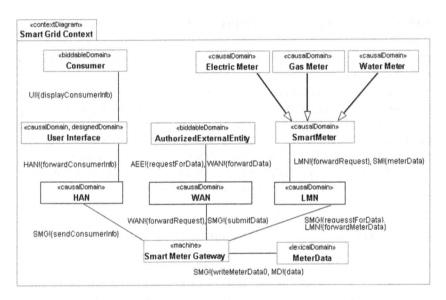

Fig. 4.3: Context diagram of smart grid

According to [155], a *SmartMeter* could be an *Electric Meter*, a *Gas Meter*, or a *Water Meter* that are causal domains. The *SmartMeter* communicates with the machine *Smart Meter Gateway* through the network *Local Metrological Network (LMN)*. The machine *Smart Meter Gateway* requests meter data from the *SmartMeter* via the *LMN* (*SMG!{requestForData}, LMN!{forwardRequest}*). The *SmartMeter* sends the requested meter data through the *LMN* to the machine *Smart Meter Gateway* (*SM!{meterData}, LMN!{forwardMeterData}*).

The machine *Smart Meter Gateway* communicates with the outside world such as the biddable domain *AuthorizedExternalEntity* through the network *Wide Area Network (WAN)*. The *AuthorizedExternalEntity* requests meter data through the *WAN* (*AEE!{requestForData}*, *WAN!{forwardRequest}*). The machine *Smart Meter Gateway* sends the requested meter data to the *AuthorizedExternalEntity* through the *WAN* (*SMG!{submitData}*, *WAN!{forwardData}*).

The biddable domain *Consumer* can access the Gateway via the *User Interface* (*UI!{displayConsumerInfo}*) through the network *Home Area Network (HAN)* (*SMG!{sendConsumerInfo}*).

Step 2 - Functional Requirements Modeling

This step (*Step 2* in Fig. 4.2) is concerned with decomposing the overall problem into subproblems, which describe a certain functionality, as expressed by a set of related functional requirements. The functionality of the software is the core, and all quality requirements are related in some way to this core. In addition to existing documents, we make use of the context diagram to provide input for this step. We set up *problem diagrams* representing subproblems to model functional requirements. A problem diagram consists of one submachine of the machine given in the context diagram, the relevant domains, the interfaces between these domains, and a requirement referring to and constraining problem domains.

Application of Step 2 - Functional Requirements Modeling

As mentioned in the description of the smart grid case study in Section 2.6 (see page 43), we consider the use case *Meter Reading for Billing* of the smart grid example. This use case is concerned with gathering, processing, and storing meter readings from smart meters for the billing process, and submitting the meter readings to the authorized external entities. We set up a problem diagram for this use case, which is shown in Fig. 4.4. The *AuthorizedExternalEntity* sends a request to the machine *HandlingSmartMeterData* through the network *WAN* (*AEE!{requestForData}*, *WAN!{forwardRequest}*). The machine *HandlingSmartMeterData* sends a request to the *SmartMeter* (*HSMD!{requestForData}*) via the network *LMN* (*LMN!{forwardRequest}*). As an answer to the request, the *SmartMeter* sends the meter readings (*SM!{meterData}*) to the machine *HandlingSmartMeterData* through the network *LMN* (*LMN!{forwardMeterData}*). The machine *HandlingSmartMeterData* stores meter readings into the lexical domain *MeterData* (*HSMD!*{*writeMeterData*}). The *MeterData* is sent to the *AuthorizedExternalEntity* through the *WAN* (*HSMD!*{*submitData*}, *WAN!*{*forwardData*}). The requirement *HandlingMeterData* constrains the domains *WAN* and *MeterData*. It refers to the domain *SmartMeter*.

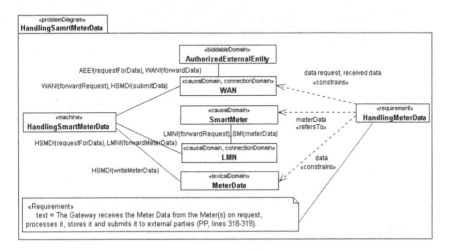

Fig. 4.4: Problem diagram related to the use case *Meter Reading for Billing*

Figure 4.4 contains several functional requirements. Hence, we split it into more simple problem diagrams, each of which describes one functional requirement. We define 5 functional requirements. To provide billing information to external parties and also to the consumer, the gateway receives the meter data from the meter(s) (*R1*), processes it (*R2*), and stores it (*R3*). The gateway submits the stored data to external entities (*R4*). The stored data can also be provided to the consumer to allow her to verify an invoice (*R5*). Table 4.2 illustrates the functional requirements *R1-R5* and their description.

We set up problem diagrams to model the functional requirements *R1-R5*. In this step, we only describe the problem diagram for the functional requirement *R4* shown in Fig. 4.5. In the next step of the method, we show all the problem diagrams for the requirements *R1-R5* including the quality requirements. The problem diagram *SubmitMeterData* in Fig. 4.5 describes that the machine *SubmitMD* should receive the data from the domain *MeterData* (*MD!*{*data*}) and sends it through the *WAN* (*SMD!*{*sendsDataIntoWAN*}) to the *AuthorizedExternalEntity* (*WAN!*{*forwardData*}). The functional requirement *R4* constrains the

Table 4.2: Functional Requirements *R1-R5*

Requirement	Description
R1	Smart meter gateway shall receive meter data from smart meters
R2	Smart meter gateway shall process meter data from smart meters
R3	Smart meter gateway shall store meter data from smart meters
R4	Smart meter gateway shall submit processed meter data to authorized external Entities
R5	The gateway shall provide meter data for consumers for the purpose of checking the billing consistency

domain *WAN* as the data has to be sent into the *WAN*. It refers to the domains *MeterData* and *AuthorizedExternalEntity*.

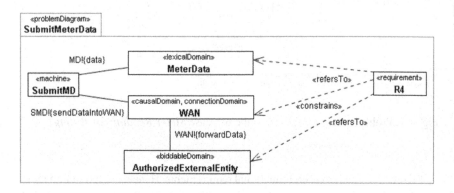

Fig. 4.5: Problem diagram related to the functional requirement *R4*

Step 3 - Quality Requirements Modeling

To analyze and integrate software quality in the software development process, quality requirements (obtained from existing documents) have to be modeled and integrated as early as possible in the requirement models. Modeling quality requirements is achieved in this step (*Step 3* in Fig. 4.2).

In the problem frames approach the focus is only on functional requirements [51]. We extended the UML-based problem frames approach by providing a way to attach quality requirements to problem diagrams [17]. We represent quality requirements as annotations in problem diagrams. Since UML lacks notations to specify and model quality requirements and quality-specific domain knowledge, we use different UML profiles to add annotations to the UML models. We use a UML profile for dependability proposed by Hatebur & Heisel [114] to annotate problem diagrams with security requirements (see Section 2.3.3 on page 39). For example, we apply the stereotypes ≪integrity≫, ≪confidentiality≫, and ≪authenticity≫ to represent integrity, confidentiality, and authenticity requirements.

To provide support for annotating problem descriptions with performance requirements, we use the UML profile MARTE (Modeling and Analysis of Real-time and Embedded Systems) [233] adopted by OMG consortium for modeling performance-specific annotations (see Section 2.3.4 on page 40).

Application of Step 3 - Quality Requirements Modeling

In the smart grid example, besides the functionalities that the gateway has to provide, it is also responsible for the protection of authenticity, integrity, and confidentiality of data temporarily or persistently stored in the gateway, transferred locally within the *LMN*, transferred in the *WAN* and *HAN*. The number of smart devices to be managed has a deep impact on the performance of the whole system. This makes performance of smart grids an important issue beside security.

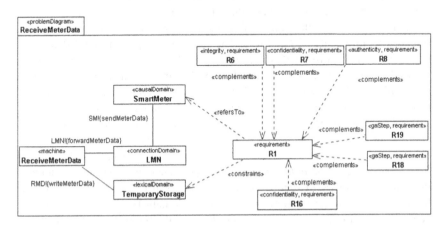

Fig. 4.6: Problem diagram related to functional requirement *R1* and its corresponding quality requirements

In this step, we enrich the problem diagrams set up in the previous step with annotations for quality requirements. To this end, we make use of the UML profile extension introduced in Section 4.2. We apply the dependency «complements» from the quality requirement to its related functional requirement. It represents that each quality requirement complements its related functional requirement. The problem diagram *ReceiveMeterData* shown in Fig. 7.1 describes the functional requirement *R1*, the related security requirements *R6*, *R7*, *R8*, and *R16* and the corresponding performance requirements *R18* and *R19*. It describes that the *Smart-Meter* sends meter data (*SM!{sendMeterData}*) through LMN to the machine *ReceiveMeterData* (*LMN!{forwardMeterData}*). The machine stores the received meter data temporarily in the *TemporaryStorage* (*RMD!{writeMeterData}*). The requirement *R1* constrains the domain *TemporaryStorage* and refers to the domain *SmartMeter*.

The problem diagram for receiving meter readings (see Fig. 7.1) is annotated with security requirements *R6* (integrity), *R7* (confidentiality), *R8* (authenticity), and *R16* (confidentiality) which complement the functional requirement *R1*. The confidentiality requirement *R7* is concerned with protecting confidentiality during transmission of meter data, whereas the confidentiality requirement *R16* shall protect the confidentiality of meter data during storage. Security requirements are represented using the stereotypes «confidentiality», «integrity», and «authenticity». The performance requirements *R18* and *R19* also complement the functional requirement *R4*. Performance requirements are indicated by the stereotype «gaStep». Table 4.3 illustrates the quality requirements related to the functional requirement *R1* and their description.

Figure 7.2 describes the functional requirement *R2* and its corresponding performance requirements *R20* and *R21*. The functional requirement *R2* states that the *smart meter gateway shall process meter data from smart meters*. The machine *ProcessMeterData* processes the stored meter data in the domain *TemporaryStorage* (*PMD!{readData,writeData}*). Table 4.4 illustrates the performance requirements related to the functional requirement *R2* and their description.

Problem diagram *StoreMeterData* shown in Fig. 7.3 describes the functional requirement *R3* stating that the *smart meter gateway shall store meter data from smart meters*. The machine *StoreMeterData* receives meter data from the domain *TemporaryStorage* (*TS!{data}*) and stores it permanently in the lexical domain *MeterData* (*StMD!{writeMeterData}*). The functional requirement *R3* refers to the domain *TemporaryStorage* and constrains the domain *MeterData*. It is complemented by the confidentiality requirement *R9*[1] and the performance requirements

---

[1] For temporary storing meter data, there is no integrity requirement defined by [155].

Table 4.3: Security and performance requirements related to functional requirement *R1*

Quality Requirement	Description
R6	The gateway shall provide the protection of integrity when receiving meter data from a meter via the LMN
R7	The gateway shall provide the protection of confidentiality when receiving meter data from a meter via the LMN
R8	The gateway shall provide the protection of authenticity when receiving meter data from a meter via the LMN
R16	Data shall be protected from unauthorized disclosure while temporarily stored in the gateway
R18	The time to retrieve meter data from the smart meter and publish it through WAN shall be less than 5 seconds (together with R20, R22, R24)
R19	The time to retrieve meter data from the smart meter and publish it through HAN shall be less than 10 seconds (together with R21, R23, R25)

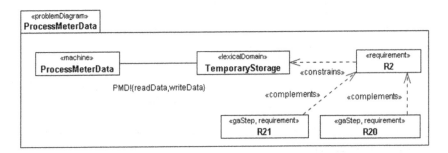

Fig. 4.7: Problem diagram related to functional requirement *R2* and its corresponding quality requirements

R22 and *R23*. Table 4.5 illustrates the performance and security requirements related to the functional requirement *R3* and their description.

The functional requirement *R4* is described by the problem diagram *Submit-MeterData* shown in Fig. 7.4. We described this problem diagram in detail in the previous step. In this step, we annotate it with the security requirements *R10* (integrity), *R11* (confidentiality), and *R12* (authenticity) as well as the performance requirement *R24* which complement the functional requirement *R4*. Table 4.6 illustrates the performance and security requirements related to the functional re-

Table 4.4: Security and performance requirements related to functional requirement *R2*

Quality Requirement	Description
R20	The time to retrieve meter data from the smart meter and publish it through WAN shall be less than 5 seconds (together with R18, R22, R24)
R21	The time to retrieve meter data from the smart meter and publish it through HAN shall be less than 10 seconds (together with R19, R23, R25)

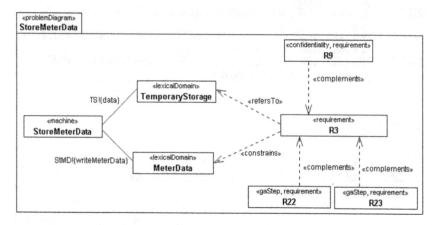

Fig. 4.8: Problem diagram related to functional requirement *R3* and its corresponding quality requirements

quirement *R4* and their description. The notes in Fig. 7.4 represent descriptions of quality requirements.

Figure 7.5 illustrates the problem diagram *PublishConsumerInfo* describing the functional requirement *R5* stating that *the gateway shall provide meter data for consumers for the purpose of checking the billing consistency*. The machine *PublishConsumerInfo* receives meter data from the domain *MeterData* (*MD!*{*data*}) and sends it through the network *HAN* (*PCI!*{*sendsConsumerInfo*}) to the *User Interface* (*HAN!*{*frowardConsumerInfo*}). The *User Interface* provides meter data to the *Consumer* (*UI!*{*displayConsumerInfo*}). The functional requirement *R5* refers to the domains *MeterData* and *Consumer*. It constrains the domain *User Interface*. The security requirements *R13* (integrity), *R14* (confidentiality), and *R15* (authenticity) complement the functional requirement *R5* as well as the performance re-

Table 4.5: Security and performance requirements related to functional requirement *R3*

Quality Requirement	Description
R9	Data shall be protected from unauthorized disclosure while persistently stored in the gateway
R22	The time to retrieve meter data from the smart meter and publish it through WAN shall be less than 5 seconds (together with R18, R20, R24)
R23	The time to retrieve meter data from the smart meter and publish it through HAN shall be less than 10 seconds (together with R19, R21, R25)

Table 4.6: Security and performance requirements related to functional requirement *R4*

Quality Requirement	Description
R10	Integrity of data transferred in the WAN shall be protected
R11	Confidentiality of data transferred in the WAN shall be protected
R12	Authenticity of data transferred in the WAN shall be protected
R24	The time to retrieve meter data from the smart meter and publish it through WAN shall be less than 5 seconds (together with R18, R20, R22)

Table 4.7: Security and performance requirements related to functional requirement *R5*

Quality Requirement	Description
R13	The gateway shall provide the protection of integrity when transmitting processed meter data locally within the LAN
R14	The gateway shall provide the protection of confidentiality when transmitting processed meter data locally within the LAN
R15	The gateway shall provide the protection of authenticity when transmitting processed meter data locally within the LAN
R25	The time to retrieve meter data from the smart meter and publish it through HAN shall be less than 10 seconds (together with R19, R21, R23)

quirement *R25*. Table 4.7 illustrates the performance and security requirements related to the functional requirement *R5* and their description.

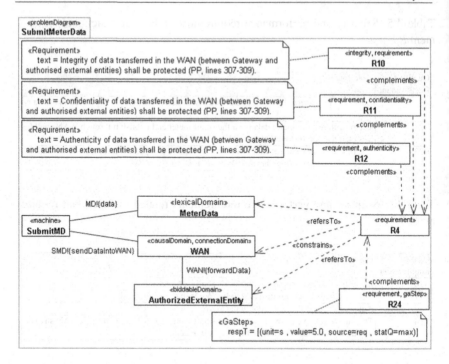

Fig. 4.9: Problem diagram related to functional requirement *R4* and its corresponding quality requirements

Further Iterations due to Architectural Pattern Selection

Design decisions on the architecture level might affect the initial requirements and the problem diagrams describing those requirements accordingly. For instance, a decision about the kind of distribution of the software, e.g., client-server, peer-to-peer, or standalone might lead to further decomposition of the subproblems. For distributed applications, the subproblems often have to be split in such a way that each subproblem is allocated to only one of the distributed components. We might need to introduce connection domains, e.g., networks.

Analogously to splitting the problem diagrams, we also have to split the functional requirements and the corresponding quality requirements. Hence, there is a need for further iterations regarding the decomposition of problem diagrams when

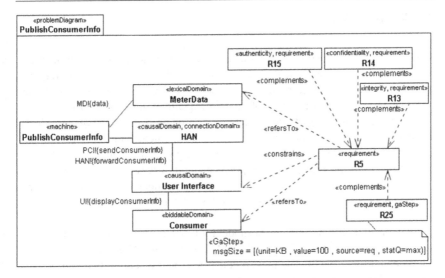

Fig. 4.10: Problem diagram related to functional requirement *R5* and its corresponding quality requirements

taking design decisions. To this end, by taking design decisions, we have to go back to this phase and check whether a further decomposition is required.

The next chapter (see Chapter 5) is concerned with making architectural decisions regarding the selection of architectural patterns. Depending on the selected architectural pattern(s), this design decision might affect the decomposition of the problem diagrams as well as the quality requirements. Hence, we might need to go back to *Step 2 - Functional Requirements Modeling* to decompose or merge subproblems as appropriate according to the selected architectural pattern. Decomposition or merging of functional subproblems might have an impact on quality requirements. Therefore, we need to go back to *Step 3 - Quality Requirements Modeling* as well and check for appropriateness of modeled quality requirements.

In Chapter 5, we describe the second iteration according to the design decision we make.

4.4 Related Work

Modeling and representing requirements have been a subject of research in the past. Although the requirements engineering community categorizes the requirements into functional requirements and quality requirements (or non-functional requirements), there is still a lack of modeling quality requirements [73].

Lencastre et al. [165] define a meta-model for problem frames using UML. Their meta-model considers Jackson's entire requirements engineering approach based on context diagrams, problem frames, and problem decomposition. In contrast to our UML profile and our proposed method, it only addresses the analysis of functional requirements and does not support the modeling of quality requirements. There is also no consideration of the OCL integrity conditions in their meta-model.

Seater et al. [212] present a meta-model for problem frame instances. They provide a formalization for requirements and specifications. Consequently, their integrity conditions ("wellformedness predicates") focus on correctly deriving specifications from requirements. In contrast, our UML profile concentrates on the structure of problem frames and the different domain and phenomena types. Additionally, we extend the problem frames approach and the UML profile for problem frames with stereotypes for modeling and analyzing quality requirements.

Hall et al. [108] provide a formal semantics for the problem frame approach. Their model focuses on a formal specification language to describe problem frames and problem diagrams. As compared to our UML profile and proposed method, their approach neither considers integrity conditions nor the modeling and analyzing of quality requirements.

Lin et al. [168, 167] introduce the notion of anti-requirement as the requirement of a malicious user. Such anti-requirements are described by so-called abuse frames imposed by malicious users in a specific problem context. Abuse frames take the viewpoint of a malicious user in contrast to traditional problem frames. Such abuse frames facilitate the identification and analysis of threats. Modeling anti-requirements as abuse frames can be seen as complementary to our work. It supports the identification of threats driving the elicitation and modeling of security requirements which can be performed using our problem-oriented requirements analysis method proposed in this chapter.

In the area of goal-oriented requirements engineering, approaches such as i* [249], KAOS [158], and the NFR framework [72] have treated the modeling of soft-goals. In these approaches, goal models are mostly represented in tree-like structures that define the intentions of different stakeholders at different levels of abstraction [193]. Goals can be classified into two different categories: hard-goals and soft-goals. Hard-goals may refer to the functional properties of the system behavior, whereas soft-goals represent quality preferences of the stakeholders. Goal models are defined for providing an interface to the stakeholders. Hence, they are represented in a higher abstraction level than requirements. They need to be refined into requirements. Thus, goal models can be seen as complementary to our proposed UML profile and method.

Use cases are widely accepted as a means for eliciting functional requirements. However, there is controversy about their suitability for eliciting and representing quality requirements [25]. Some approaches propose to combine quality requirements with use cases and misuse cases (negative form of uses cases [25]). Cysneiros & do Prado Leite [83] show how to reflect quality requirements in the UML models. They make use of some UML artifacts such as use cases, class diagrams, and sequence diagrams to deal with quality requirements and to integrate quality requirements into class diagrams. Alexander [25] suggests to combine use cases and misuse cases to improve the efficiency of eliciting functional and quality requirements. In particular, safety and security requirements can be elicited using such combinations of use cases and misuse cases. One approach for eliciting security threats and requirements based on use cases is proposed by Sindre & Opdahl [218]. It extends traditional use cases to cover misuses by proposing guidelines for how to describe misuse cases and method guidelines for eliciting security requirements with misuse cases.

4.5 Contributions

In this chapter, we investigated how to provide support for modeling quality requirements in addition to functional requirements. Our contributions can be summarized as follows:

- A UML profile that extends the UML profile for problem frames by specific stereotypes. Using this extension quality requirements can be annotated in the requirement models. Our extension includes new OCL expressions as well as the modification of some existing OCL expressions for checking the consistency of new introduced elements with the existing ones.
- A method for requirements analysis based on the problem frames approach with regard to quality requirements. Our method provides support for modeling quality requirements such as performance and security using the extension of the UML profile for problem frames. The method takes into account design decisions made in the architecture level. Such design decisions might affect the initial requirements and the corresponding problem diagrams. Our method proposes how to reflect the design decisions in the requirement level to decompose

the problem diagrams accordingly. In order to keep the requirement models and the architectural models consistent, it is required to re-apply the method after making every design decision. The method has to be re-applied until the architecture is stable and no more design decisions have to be made.

- The created requirement models in this chapter (Phase 1) provide the basis for the remaining phases of the QuaDRA framework such as domain knowledge analysis, requirement interaction detection and resolution, performance requirements analysis, quality-specific solution analysis, and architecture alternatives derivation.

Chapter 5
Phase 2: Architectural Pattern Selection & Application

Abstract Existing solutions for deriving architectures from requirements mostly rely on experienced architects. Besides the required experience, it is often a problem that the decision is not properly reasoned and documented. In this chapter, we propose a method to select appropriate architectural patterns with regard to given quality requirements. This process is based on the characteristics of the software to be built as well as on the properties of the architectural patterns. Our proposed process connects requirements and architecture, guides even less experienced software engineers through the pattern selection process, provides support for decision making, and makes the decision rationale transparent. In the second part of this chapter, we use the result of the pattern selection process in order to derive an initial architecture based on that result.

5.1 Introduction

In addition to functional requirements, to a large extent quality requirements govern the software architecture [44, 126, 56]. Creating software architectures that meet the desired quality requirements is not a trivial task [226, 186]. Often, more than one quality requirement has to be considered for constructing a software system. The reason is that different stakeholders might have different views on various quality requirements and their importance [137].

It is commonly agreed that for building upon common knowledge and best practices the use of patterns as architecture solutions is valuable [44, 62]. Patterns describe solutions for commonly recurring problems in software development, including the context in which a pattern is applicable. Patterns are found in various software development phases, such as Fowler's analysis patterns [98] for business engineering, Jackson's problem frames [133] for the requirements level, architectural patterns [62, 215] for the architecture level, and design patterns [103] for the design level.

Taking into account different quality requirements requires knowledge about benefits and liabilities of architectural patterns with respect to different quality requirements [226]. Deciding on an appropriate architectural pattern among a set of architectural pattern candidates with regard to different quality requirements is often performed in an intuitive and ad-hoc manner. Such decisions rely on the experience of senior software developers [225].

Pattern catalogs [62, 103] are used in architectural design methods that aim to give guidance for deriving architectures from requirements (e.g. [44, 126]). In these methods, pattern catalogs are used as a reference to find solutions for an architectural problem by choosing appropriate patterns from the catalog.

Especially for novice software architects, pattern catalogs are an appropriate source for finding suitable patterns for a particular design problem since making design decisions is a complex and challenging task for junior designers [122]. Choosing the appropriate architectural pattern in a catalog is, however, not trivial. Although several approaches exist for deriving architectures from requirements (e.g. [69, 253]), most solutions rely on experienced architects for proposing and choosing feasible architectural solutions. The existing approaches are imprecise or do not provide any aid for finding appropriate patterns from catalogs [52]. It is therefore critical to develop architecture systematically and without strong dependencies on experienced architects. The experienced architect on the other hand has an interest in finding multiple design alternatives before making a decision while favoring well-known solutions [121]. Both aspects could be satisfied by a method to systematically choose suitable patterns from a pattern catalog.

In the first part of this chapter which represents Phase 2 of the QuaDRA framework, we propose a process which provides support for selecting appropriate architectural patterns. Our process is based on the problem frames approach [133]. It takes problem diagrams as input which are used to identify problem frames. Based on a problem frame, the architect is asked a specific set of questions regarding the problem at hand. Based on the answers given to the questions in the question catalog, the *architectural pattern candidates* which might be relevant are shown to the software architect. Each of the patterns in our catalog is annotated with information about benefits and liabilities regarding software qualities. As not every quality or consequence has the same importance for the final decision, the qualities and consequences are ranked using a decision method. Based on this ranking, the *architectural pattern candidates* are ranked as well.

The method is of interest for both, the experienced and the inexperienced architect. Both can benefit from the process as it grounds decisions by making them explicit and providing some reasoning for decisions as it captures relevant problems and qualities. It also shows alternatives which should only be discarded for good reasons. Additionally, all this reasoning and decision making is documented to allow others to comprehend the reasons for an architecture at hand. This can be useful when evolving the architecture after some time, but also when the architecture is assessed by reviewers before the architecture is actually implemented. Additionally, the inexperienced architect gets some guidance for selecting architectural patterns, which an experienced architect probably does not need.

From our experiences regarding the proposed method, we see the following benefits. First, it supports both the experienced and the less experienced software architect in selecting an appropriate architectural pattern for a given problem. It makes the decisions and according reasons explicitly visible. Second, it is problem-oriented which follows the basic idea of most pattern forms and mitigates the risk of being too solution-oriented. A solution-oriented process would lead to the problem that it is hard to make good decisions if the architect cannot imagine if and which offered solution could work. Besides, being solution-driven always bears the risk of neglecting parts of the original problem. Third, the effort for selecting a pattern is minimized as the process relies on questions which are convenient to answer even when coming to complex decisions. If the system's requirements are available as problem diagrams, no extra input is needed for our process. Additionally, the solution space is iteratively reduced, which enables one to stop right at the point where solution selection is feasible. Hence, in many cases the effort for the software architect is reduced since it is not necessary to conduct the full process. Fourth, the process contains structured and transparent decision making steps, which clarify the decision rationale. In the second part of this chapter, we use the result of our pattern selection process in order to derive an initial architecture based on that result. The initial architecture provides a basis to solve the software development problem described by the problem descriptions. It uses the already selected architectural pattern(s) to implement the functional requirements with regard to quality requirements.

This chapter is based on our joint work with our colleague Stephan Faßbender and our project partner Martin Filipczyk. The concept of using problem frames for selecting among architectural patterns has been developed jointly. Stephan Faßbender elaborated this concept into the pattern selection process. External inputs and artifacts required for the selection process have been developed jointly. The application of the method to the smart grid case study has been done by the author of this book. This work has been actively discussed with the architecture

community at the MiniPLoP [110] and with the pattern community at the Euro-
PLoP [9].

The remainder of this chapter is organized as follows. We describe the relation between problem frames, architectural patterns, and question catalog in Section 5.2. The external inputs for our process are described in Section 5.3. Our
pattern selection process is given in Section 5.4. Section 5.5 illustrates the application of our process to the case study smart grid. We describe how to derive an
initial architecture by applying the selected architectural pattern(s) in Section 5.6.
Section 5.7 presents related work, while Section 5.8 concludes this chapter and
summarizes the contribution.

5.2 Artifacts and their Relations

To understand how the pattern selection works one has to understand how the
artifacts used for the pattern selection process are related. Therefore, Fig. 5.1 gives
an overview of the entities we use in our process as well as their relationships. The
entities are visualized by rectangles and the relationships are depicted by solid
arrows.

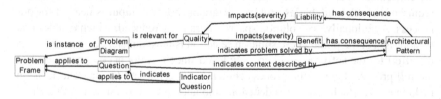

Fig. 5.1: Relations between artifacts needed for pattern selection

The requirements we need to execute our process have to be captured within
problem diagrams. A problem diagram is an instance of a *problem frame*. We assembled a set of *architectural patterns* from which the solution will finally be
selected. Each pattern has a description of its context and the problem it might be
applied for. From these descriptions we derived questions which, when answered
positively, indicate that the *context* or *problem* might apply for the system (relation between question and architectural pattern annotated with "indicates problem
solved by" or "indicates context described by"). For example, considering the architectural pattern *Pipes and Filters*, the context is described as "*Processing data*

streams". From this context we derive the question "*Q6: is the system-to-be related to processing of data streams?*. It is possible that patterns share parts of the same context or problem.

Some of the questions directly *apply to* problem frames (relation between question and problem frame annotated with "applies to"). This means that whenever a specific problem frame is identified, the related question is being asked. For example, the question "*Q6: is the system-to-be related to processing of data streams?* has to be asked, when the problem frame *transformation* is identified. This question indicates the context described by the architectural pattern *Pipes and Filters*.

For many questions such relations cannot be established directly. But the relation can be established if the problem diagram for which the problem frame was identified embodies certain characteristics. For example, a question might only apply for a problem frame in case one domain has a specific behavior. Taken the model building frame consisting of the lexical domain *Model* and the causal domain *Sensor* as an example (see Fig. B.5 for the model building frame in Appendix B.1) the causal domain *Sensor* provides the information from which the model is built. The lexical domain *Model* shall then reflect the result of the model building. Therefore, the lexical domain *Model* is constrained and the domain *Sensor* is referred to by the corresponding requirement. One question might only apply for this frame in case the *Sensor* domain is only accessible via low level hardware functions. *Indicator questions* aim at identifying such a characteristic (relation between indicator question and problem frame annotated with "applies to"). For developing the indicator questions, we generalize the questions derived from the patterns by using placeholders for the generic parts of the question. Within our process, these placeholders are being replaced with one or more elements from the problem frames that reference an indicator question.

For example, by asking the indicator question "*IQ2: is the functionality provided by Element1 a low level hardware functionality?*", **Element1** is the placeholder that has to be replaced with the *Sensor* domain from the model building frame. If an indicator question is answered positively, it indicates the corresponding question (relation between indicator question and question annotated with "indicates"), meaning that the corresponding question is relevant. The corresponding question in this case is "*Q3B: is there low level (hardware) functionality to be provided by the system?* which indicates the *problem* solved by the architectural pattern *Layers*. The concept of *indicator questions* becomes clearer in the next section when we describe the external input for our process.

Up to this point, the relations are sufficient to connect problem diagrams and architectural patterns. Note that the problem frames as defined by Jackson can only be used to represent functionality. They do not support the modeling of qualities directly. Hence, by now the architectural patterns and problem frames are only connected based on the functionality. For decision support for choosing an architectural pattern considering qualities, we need further artifacts and relations. When applying an architectural pattern, various *consequences* in terms of *benefits* (relation between architectural pattern and benefit annotated with "has consequence") and *liabilities* (relation between architectural pattern and liability annotated with "has consequence") for certain software *qualities* can be observed[1]. While benefits have a positive effect on certain qualities, liabilities have a negative influence on certain qualities (relations between benefit and quality, and liability and quality annotated with "impacts (severity)"). The influence of a benefit or liability on a quality can differ regarding their *severity*. Since our extension to the problem frames notation allows for augmenting problem diagrams with qualities which are relevant for the functionality at hand (see Chapter 4), qualities related to consequences might be relevant for fulfilling certain requirements as demanded by the problem diagrams (relation between quality and problem diagram annotated with "is relevant for"). The quality extension is limited to the problem diagrams and is therefore not usable for extending problem frames. This is due to the fact that qualities can differ for every problem under consideration, which is represented by a problem diagram, while the functionality as represented by the corresponding frame remains the same.

5.3 External Input for the Process

For our process, we need to create a set of external inputs that are needed for the various steps. To this end, we use architectural patterns from [62], which provide the starting point for creating external inputs. An overview of the architectural patterns that we use is given in Table 5.1. The type of the architectural patterns is taken from [62].

5.3.1 Question Catalog (Questions)

From the architectural patterns, we derive questions that constitute the question catalog. The question catalog contains the *questions* and *indicator questions*. The question catalog is required as external input for the Step 2 of our process (see the overview of the process in Fig. 5.3). Note that it is not required to know the steps of

---

[1] By the terms *consequences*, *benefits*, and *liabilities*, we use the wording from architectural pattern descriptions.

Table 5.1: Architectural Patterns

Type	Name	Identifier
From Mud to Structure	Layers	AP1
From Mud to Structure	Pipes and Filters	AP2
From Mud to Structure	Blackboard	AP3
Distributed Systems	Broker	AP4
Interactive Systems	Model-View-Controller (MVC)	AP5
Interactive Systems	Presentation-Abstraction-Control (PAC)	AP6
Adaptable Systems	Microkernel	AP7
Adaptable Systems	Reflection	AP8

the process in this section. In this section, we only intend to describe the creation of the external input which should be comprehensible without any knowledge of the process.

The questions target the *context* and the *problem* of the architectural patterns (see relation between question and architectural pattern annotated with "indicates problem solved by" or "indicates context described by" in Fig. 5.1 in Section 5.2). From these descriptions we derive questions which, when answered positively, indicate that the *context* or *problem* might apply for the system. We describe the derivation of the questions using the two architectural patterns *Pipes and Filters* and *Blackboard*. The context of the architectural pattern *Pipes and Filters* is given as follows:

"**Context**: Processing data streams ([62] (p. 54))."

From this *context*, we derive the question *Q6: Is the system-to-be related to processing of data streams?*

The context of the architectural pattern *Blackboard* is given as follows:

"**Context**: An immature domain in which no closed approach to a solution is known or feasible ([62] (p. 72))."

From this *context*, we derive the question *Q8: Is the domain of the system-to-be immature and no solution for the problem the system shall solve is known?*

We follow this procedure also for the *problem* part of the architectural patterns *Pipes and Filters* and *Blackboard*. Doing this, we obtain Table 5.2. *Q6* and *Q7*

Table 5.2: An Excerpt of the Question Catalog (questions)

Identifier	Question
Q6	Is the system-to-be related to processing of data streams?
Q7	Is one key functionality to transform input data to output data?
Q7A	Is it possible to handle the data as a stream?
Q7B	Are there several transformation steps?
Q7C	Is the transformation to be changed frequently?
Q7D	Are steps of the transformation to be carried out by different parties or parts of the system?
Q8	Is the domain of the system-to-be immature and no solution for the problem the system shall solve is known?
Q9	Is there a transformation of data for which the transformation is (partly) unknown?

(and the related sub-questions) are derived from the *context* as well as the *problem* of the architectural pattern *Pipes and Filters*. *Q8* is derived from the *context* of the architectural pattern *Blackboard*, while questions *Q7* and *Q9* are derived from the description of its *problem*. As we can observe, the question *Q7* is common in the *problem* part of both architectural patterns. The complete list of the questions is given in Appendix B.2.

5.3.2 Question Catalog (Indicator Questions)

Indicator questions constitute one part of the question catalog. They are required as external input for the Step 2 of our process (see the overview of the process in Fig. 5.3). For developing the indicator questions, we generalize the questions derived from the patterns by inserting placeholders for the generic parts of the questions. Within our process, these placeholders are replaced with one or more elements from the problem frames.

To make the process of developing indicator questions more comprehensible, we provide some examples. Considering the questions *Q7A*, *Q7B*, and *Q7C* from the previous example, we develop indicator questions *IQ11-IQ15* by generalizing the questions (see Table 5.3). The placeholder **Element1** of the indicator questions has to be replaced by elements of the problem frames. We describe this in more detail in Section 5.4. The complete list of indicator questions is shown in Appendix B.2.

Table 5.3: Examples of developing indicator questions

Question	Indicator Question
Q7A: Is it possible to handle the data as a stream?	IQ11: Is it possible to handle **Element1** as a stream?
Q7B: Are there several transformation steps?	IQ12: Has **Element1** been transformed before or will **Element1** be used in another transformation afterward?
Q7B: Are there several transformation steps?	IQ13: Has **Element1** been transformed before?
Q7B: Are there several transformation steps?	IQ14: Will **Element1** be used in another transformation afterward?
Q7C: Is the transformation to be changed frequently?	IQ15: Is it expected that the transformation described by **Element1** will change frequently?

5.3.3 Relations between Problem Frames and Questions

Another external input for Step 2 of our process is the relation between the problem frames and the (indicator) questions (see relation between indicator question and problem frame annotated with "applies to" in Fig. 5.1 in Section 5.2). As an example we show the relation between indicator questions and the problem frame *transformation* in Table 5.4. A complete set of the relations between the indicator questions and problem frames is given in Appendix B.3.

Such a table also contains the information how in the template the **elements** of the indicator questions have to be replaced with the elements of the problem frames. As an example, consider *IQ11* from the previous example: *IQ11: Is it possible to handle Element1 as a stream?* According to Table 5.4, **Element1** has to be replaced once with the lexical domain *Inputs* and once with the lexical domain *Outputs*. Having replaced these elements with the domains of the *transformation* frame, we obtain two indicator questions *IQ11: Is it possible to handle Inputs as a stream?* and *IQ11: Is it possible to handle Outputs as a stream?*

Another example is *IQ15: Is it expected that the transformation described by Element1 will change frequently?* In this case, **Element1** has to be replaced once with the requirement domain *Transformation*.

Table 5.4 also relates the questions directly to the problem frame (see relation between question and problem frames annotated with "applies to" in Fig. 5.1 in Section 5.2). For the case of *transformation* frame, questions *Q6* and *Q9* are directly related to this frame and can be asked without having any indicator questions in between (see the right part of Table 5.4).

As described before, questions and indicator questions are related (see relation between indicator question and question annotated with "indicates" in Fig. 5.1 in Section 5.2). In Table 5.5, we show an excerpt of the relations between the indica-

Table 5.4: Problem Frame *Transformation* and related Indicator Questions

Transformation			
<<connection>> TM!C2	<<lexicalDomain>> Outputs	<<constrains>> Y3	
<<machine>> TransformMachine			<<requirement>> Transformation
!!Y1 <<connection>>	<<lexicalDomain>> Inputs	Y4 <<refersTo>>	

Indicator Questions			Question
Identifier	ELEMENTS		*Identifier*
	ELEMENT	*Replacement*	
IQ4	ELEMENT1	Inputs	
	ELEMENT1	Outputs	
IQ6	ELEMENT1	Inputs	Q6, Q9
	ELEMENT1	Outputs	
IQ8	ELEMENT1	Inputs	
	ELEMENT1	Outputs	
IQ11	ELEMENT1	Inputs	
	ELEMENT1	Outputs	
IQ13	ELEMENT1	Inputs	
IQ14	ELEMENT1	Outputs	
IQ15	ELEMENT1	Transformation	
IQ21	ELEMENT1	Transformation	
IQ22	ELEMENT1	Inputs	
	ELEMENT1	Outputs	

tor questions with the questions. It shows how the indicator questions *IQ11-IQ15* from the previous example are related to the questions. Beside this relation, Table 5.5 also contains the information if an indicator question is domain or problem frame specific. In the first case which applies to *IQ11*, the indicator question has only to be asked once regardless in how many problem diagrams it is contained. In the second case such as in *IQ12-IQ15* it depends on the problem frame and therefore on the problem diagram. In this case, the indicator question has to be asked for each problem diagram matching the problem frame. The complete list of these relations is illustrated in Appendix B.3.

5.3.4 Benefits and Liabilities of Architectural Patterns

We distill benefits and liabilities of the architectural patterns to a short form and map them to the software qualities defined in the ISO/IEC 25010 standard [130] (see relations between architectural pattern and benefit, and architectural pattern and liability annotated with "has consequence" and relations between benefit and quality, and liability and quality annotated with "impacts(severity)" in Fig. 5.1 in Section 5.2). Benefits and liabilities of architectural patterns and their relation to

Table 5.5: An Excerpt of Indicator Question Properties (external input; used in Step 2)

Identifier	Indicated Question	Problem Frame Specific	Domain Specific
IQ11	Q7A	No	Yes
IQ12	Q7B	Yes	No
IQ13	Q7B	Yes	No
IQ14	Q7B	Yes	No
IQ15	Q7C	Yes	No

software qualities are required as external input for Step 6 of our process. Table 5.6 shows the benefits of the architectural pattern *Pipes and Filters* and their mapping to the qualities. Liabilities of the architectural pattern *Pipes and Filters* with their relation to the software qualities are illustrated in Table 5.7. The complete list of benefits and liabilities is given in Appendix B.4.

Table 5.6: Benefits and their relation to qualities

Identifier	Benefit	Quality
B1	Reuse is improved	Reusability
B1a	Reusable knowledge source	Reusability
B4	(Ex)changeability is improved	Maintainability (Modularity, Modifiability), Portability (Replaceability)
B6	Flexibility is improved	Maintainability (Modifiability, Testability), Portability (Replaceability, Adaptability), Compatibility (Interoperability)
B6a	Enables experimentation	Maintainability (Modifiability, Testability)
B6b	Portability is improved	Portability (Replaceability, Adaptability)
B6c	Interoperability is improved	Compatibility (Interoperability)
B7	Rapid prototyping is possible	Maintainability (Analyzability, Modifiability, Testability)
B8a	Enables parallel processing	Efficiency[2] (Resource utilization)

---

[2] *Performance*, is referred to as *efficiency* in ISO/IEC 25010 standard [130].

Table 5.7: Liabilities and their relation to qualities

Identifier	Benefit	Quality
L2a	Sharing state might be expensive	Efficiency (Resource utilization, Capacity)
L2b	Might introduce additional transformation overhead	Efficiency (Resource utilization, Capacity)
L5a	Sharing state is inflexible	Maintainability (Modifiability, Testability), Portability (Replaceability, Adaptability), Compatibility (Interoperability)
L6	Error handling is difficult	Reliability (Fault tolerance, Recoverability), Maintainability (Analyzability, Testability)

5.3.5 Architectural Pattern Catalog

Architectural patterns as well as their relations to the questions are required as external input for Steps 3 and 5 of our process. Table 5.8 shows an excerpt of the architectural patterns catalog for *Pipes and Filters* and *Blackboard*, including the *type*, *name*, and *identifier* of each pattern, questions related to each pattern separated in questions regarding the context of the pattern and questions regarding the problem each pattern intends to solve. The complete architectural pattern catalog can be found in Appendix B.5.

Table 5.8: Architectural Pattern Description

Pattern			Questions		Consequences	
Type	Name	Identifier	Context	Problem	Benefits	Liabilities
From Mud to Structure	Pipes and Filters	AP2	Q6	Q7	B1, B4, B6, B7, B8A	L5A, L2A, L2B, L6
From Mud to Structure	Blackboard	AP3	Q8	Q7, Q9	B1A, B4, B6A, B9, B10	L7, L8, L9A, L2C

In order to emphasize how all these external inputs are related, we refer to Fig. 5.2. It illustrates the relationship between the artifacts and their use in the selection process from the perspective of the user starting from problem diagrams. In the next section, we describe the process of the architectural pattern selection that makes use of these artifacts.

5.4 The Pattern Selection Process

In this section, we describe our pattern selection process. Figure 5.3 shows an overview of the steps of the pattern selection process.

At first sight, Fig. 5.3 may suggest that an overwhelming amount of input is needed to conduct the proposed process. However, only the *problem diagrams* are specific to the particular software system which is being developed. All other inputs, for example, the *question catalog*, are envisioned to be developed and optimized in a community-driven process. We created first drafts for the external inputs needed for our process in the previous section (see Section 5.3). The external inputs include the *question catalog, relations between problem frames and questions, relations between patterns and questions*, and *relations between consequences and qualities*. For the *problem frames*, reliable sets of frames and their descriptions are already available (cf. [82]). A subset of problem frames is provided in Appendix B.1. For the *architectural patterns*, we made use of architectural patterns described in [62], which provide the starting point for creating external inputs.

Step 1 - Identify matching Problem Frame for each Problem Diagram

For the first step, we assume that the requirements are modeled as *problem diagrams*. Modeling requirements as problem diagrams is described in detail in Chap-

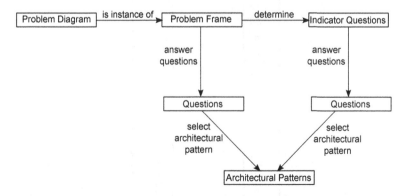

Fig. 5.2: Relations between artifacts for pattern selection from the user perspective

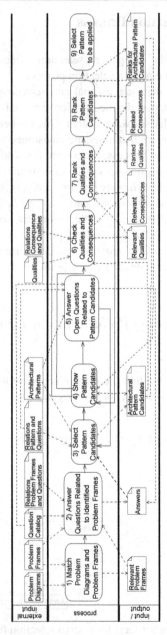

Fig. 5.3: The proposed pattern selection process

ter 4. Problem diagrams can be direct instances of problem frames, but they can also be modeled freely without any problem frame in mind. The step itself is concerned with matching the given problem diagrams to the given *problem frames*. The result of the step is a set of *problem frames* which are *relevant* for the system-to-be.

Step 2 - Answer questions related to identified Problem Frames

In the second step, one starts by answering the set of indicator questions related to the previously identified *relevant problem frames*. The *relation between problem frames and questions* as well as the *question catalog* are external inputs to this step (see Section 5.3.1, Section 5.3.2, and Section 5.3.3). Next, the questions directly bound to problem frames and the questions indicated by the answers to the indicator questions are answered. Note that this way one does not have to answer the full set of questions but only those which are indicated by the problem frames themselves or by the positively answered indicator questions bound to these frames. The result of this step are the questions with corresponding *answers*. Note that within this step only the (indicator) questions are answered which are directly bound to a problem frame which reduces the effort for the initial iteration of the process. The answers to these questions might be already sufficient for selecting an architectural pattern.

Step 3 - Select pattern candidates

Based on the answers and therefore related questions, one can select the *architectural pattern candidates*. A positive answer to a question related to an architectural pattern indicates that this pattern might provide the desired solution. The *architectural patterns* as well as their *relation to the questions* have to be defined beforehand. These relations form the external input for this step (see Section 5.3.5).

Step 4 - Show pattern candidates

Next, the *architectural pattern candidates* are shown to the user. The information shown for each pattern includes the context and problem description of each pattern, the questions which are related to the context and problem description and which have already been answered, the consequences, and the rank of the pattern. The *ranks for the architectural pattern candidates* are only available when the steps six to eight are already conducted. In this step, one can dismiss architectural pattern candidates, which are not of relevance and therefore reduce the set of *architectural pattern candidates*.

In this step, the user has to decide if one of the presented pattern candidates can be selected, i.e. the pattern is applicable for the current problem and context with regard to the system's desired quality attributes. For this purpose, the user may consult the pattern's description, including benefits and liabilities. In this case, Steps 5 to 8 can be skipped and one continues with Step 9. In case no decision is possible (e.g., if there are multiple patterns presented which causes the user to be uncertain), the further process flow depends on the availability of unanswered questions. If there are unanswered questions available, the user continues with Step 5. Otherwise, Step 6 is the next step.

Step 9 - Select pattern to be applied

If there is a pattern candidate which can be selected over the others, the pattern is selected and constitutes the output of the process.

Step 5 - Answer open questions related to pattern candidates

If there are questions, derived from the *pattern catalog*, *related to the architectural pattern candidates*, which have not been answered yet, one answers them now. This might exclude pattern candidates, even if not all the additional answers provide further information for the pattern selection. Note that one does not have to answer all open questions at once. It is also possible to have some iterations between showing candidates and answering open questions left. For example, it might be reasonable to answer only the questions related to the context first. This way, further patterns can be excluded where the context is not met before answering the questions related to the problem.

Step 6 - Check qualities and consequences

In case that no decision is possible and no unanswered questions are left, one has to consider the qualities annotated in the problem diagrams and which consequences might influence the final decision. The *relations between qualities and consequences* serve as external input for this step (see Section 5.3.4). The result of this step are the *relevant qualities and consequences*.

Step 7 - Rank consequences and qualities

Not every quality or consequence has the same importance for the final decision about the pattern chosen. To reflect the different shades of the influences, the qualities and consequences have to be ranked. For evaluating and comparing options among each other, there are several methods known, such as direct scoring [196], the analytic hierarchy process (AHP) [205], or the analytical network process (ANP) [205]. If there is only a small number of pattern candidates and desired qualities, a qualitative investigation and discussion might already be sufficient for this step. The result of this step are the *ranked consequences* and the *ranked qualities*.

Step 8 - Rank pattern candidates

Based on the *ranked consequences* and the *ranked qualities*, the *architectural pattern candidates* are ranked. The result of this step are the *ranks for the architectural pattern candidates*. The next step is *Step 4*, in which pattern candidates are shown to the user and then selected in *Step 9* (see the order of steps in Fig. 5.3).

5.5 Application to the Case Study Smart Grid

In the following, we apply the pattern selection process to the case study *smart grid*. As described in Section 2.6 (see page 43), we consider the use case *Meter Reading for Billing*, which is concerned with gathering, processing, and storing meter readings from smart meters for the billing process. We defined the requirements *R1-R3* to receive, process, and store meter data from smart meters. The requirement *R4* is concerned with submitting meter data to authorized external entities. The gateway shall also provide meter data for consumers for the purpose of checking the billing consistency (*R5*).

Step 1 - Identify matching Problem Frame for each Problem Diagram

In this step, we identify problem frames that match to the problem diagrams for the requirements *R1, R2, R3, R4*, and *R5*.

Requirement R1   The problem diagram *ReceiveMeterData* depicted in Fig. 5.4 contains the causal domain *SmartMeter*, the connection domain *LMN*, and the lexical domain *TemporaryStorage*. The domain *LMN* is a connection domain which can be blinded out for identifying the matching problem frame. The requirement *R1* refers to the causal domain *SmartMeter* and constrains the lexical domain *TemporaryStorage*. This problem diagram represents an instance of the problem frame *Model Building*.

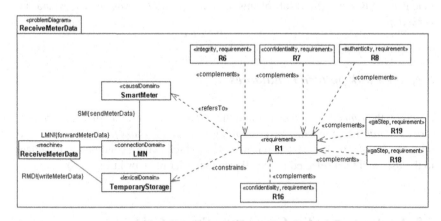

Fig. 5.4: Problem diagram related to functional requirement R1

Requirement R2   The problem diagram *ProcessMeterData* shown in Fig. 5.5 contains the lexical domain *TemporaryStorage*. The requirement *R2* constrains the lexical domain. This problem diagram represents an instance of the problem frame *Transformation*, in which *TemporaryStorage* represents the input as well as the output.

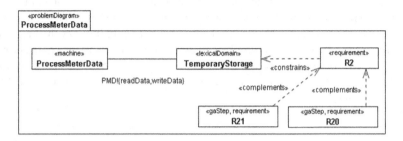

Fig. 5.5: Problem diagram related to functional requirement R2

Requirement R3 The problem diagram *StoreMeterData* depicted in Fig. 5.6 contains two lexical domains *TemporaryStorage* and *MeterData*. The requirement *R3* refers to the lexical domain *TemporaryStorage* and constrains the lexical domain *MeterData*. This problem diagram represents an instance of the problem frame *Transformation*.

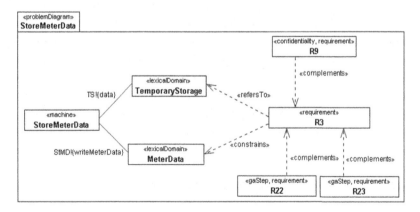

Fig. 5.6: Problem diagram related to functional requirement R3

Requirement R4   The problem diagram *ReceiveMeterData* depicted in Fig. 5.7 contains the lexical domain *MeterData*, the connection domain *WAN*, and the biddable domain *AuthorizedExternalEntities*. The domain *WAN* is a connection domain which can be blinded out for identifying the matching problem frame. The domain *AuthorizedExternalEntities* can be considered as a domain playing the role of a display domain, since the *AuthorizedExternalEntities* shall receive *MeterData*. Therefore, this problem diagram represents an instance of the problem frame *Model Display* as the connection domain *WAN* is not necessary for this problem and the domain *AuthorizedExternalEntities* is considered as a display domain.

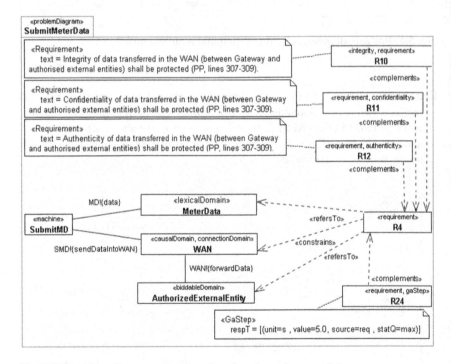

Fig. 5.7: Problem diagram related to functional requirement R4

Requirement R5   The problem diagram *PublishConsumerInfo* depicted in Fig. 5.8 contains the lexical domain *MeterData*, the connection domain *HAN*, the causal domain *UserInterface*, which is connected to the biddable domain *Consumer*.

The domain *HAN* is a connection domain which can be blinded out for identifying the matching problem frame. The domain *UserInterface* can be considered as a display domain that displays the information to the *Consumer*, since a display domain is a special kind of a causal domain. The requirement *R5* refers to the domain *MeterData* and constrains the domain *UserInterface*. This problem diagram represents an instance of the problem frame *Model Display* as the connection domain *HAN* and the biddable domain *Consumer* are not necessary for this problem.

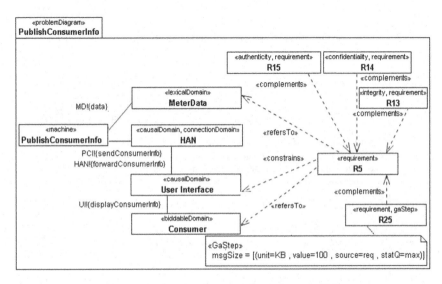

Fig. 5.8: Problem diagram related to functional requirement R5

Step 2 - Answer questions related to identified Problem Frames

For this step, we need several external inputs, namely the question catalog containing the questions and indicator questions. In addition, we need the relations between the problem frames and the questions. Indicator questions for the problem frames *Model Building, Transformation*, and *Model Display* are shown in Table 5.9 - Table 5.11.

As described before, the questions and the indicator questions are related. These tables relate the indicator questions related to the problem frames *Model Building*, *Transformation*, and *Model Display* with the questions. Beside this relation, these tables also contain the information if an indicator question is *domain* or *problem frame specific*. In the first case, the indicator question has only to be answered once, regardless in how many problem diagrams it is contained. In the second case it depends on the problem frame and therefore on the problem diagram. In this case, the indicator question has to be answered for each problem diagram matching the problem frame.

Table 5.9: Indicator Question Properties related to problem frame *Model Building* (external input; used in Step 2)

Identifier	*Indicator Question*	*Indicated Question*	*Problem Frame Specific*	*Domain Specific*
IQ2	Is the functionality provided by **Element1** a low level hardware functionality?	Q3B	No	Yes
IQ4	Is the **Element1** distributed with regards to the machine?	Q10	No	Yes
IQ6	Is the communication between **Element1** and the machine established using multiple (exchangeable) protocols / mechanisms?	Q13A	No	Yes
IQ8	Shall **Element1** be exchangeable at run-time?	Q14B, Q28	No	Yes
IQ10	Can the functionality **Element1** logically be grouped with other functionality?	Q4A	Yes	No
IQ11	Is it possible to handle **Element1** as a stream?	Q7A	No	Yes
IQ14	Will **Element1** be used in another transformation afterward?	Q7B	Yes	No
IQ15	Is it expected that the transformation described by **Element1** will change frequently?	Q7C	Yes	No
IQ21	Is **Element1** expected to change over time?	Q26	Yes	No
IQ22	Is **Element1** likely to change over time?	Q28	No	Yes

As described before in Section 5.2, the indicator questions are formulated as templates. They only refer to **elements** which have to be instantiated for each problem diagram. Table 5.9 - Table 5.11 also contain the information how in the template the **elements** of the indicator questions have to be instantiated. And these tables also relate the questions directly to the problem frame.

Using these inputs, we obtain concrete questions for the requirements *R1-R5* and the related problem frames. These concrete questions are given in Table 5.12 - Table 5.16. We also gather and instantiate the questions indicated by the identified problem frames *Model Building*, *Transformation*, and *Model Display*, and answer them with regards to the given requirements.

Table 5.10: Indicator Question Properties related to problem frame *Transformation* (external input; used in Step 2)

Identifier	Indicator Question	Indicated Question	Problem Frame Specific	Domain Specific
IQ4	Is the **Element1** distributed with regards to the machine?	Q10	No	Yes
IQ6	Is the communication between **Element1** and the machine established using multiple (exchangeable) protocols / mechanisms?	Q13A	No	Yes
IQ8	Shall **Element1** be exchangeable at run-time?	Q14B, Q28	No	Yes
IQ11	Is it possible to handle **Element1** as a stream?	Q7A	No	Yes
IQ13	Has **Element1** been transformed before?	Q7B	Yes	No
IQ14	Will **Element1** be used in another transformation afterward?	Q7B	Yes	No
IQ15	Is it expected that the transformation described by **Element1** will change frequently?	Q7C	Yes	No
IQ21	Is **Element1** expected to change over time?	Q26	Yes	No
IQ22	Is **Element1** likely to change over time?	Q28	No	Yes

Table 5.11: Indicator Question Properties related to problem frame *Model Display* (external input; used in Step 2)

Identifier	Indicator Question	Indicated Question	Problem Frame Specific	Domain Specific
IQ2	Is the functionality provided by **Element1** a low level hardware functionality?	Q3B	No	Yes
IQ4	Is the **Element1** distributed with regards to the machine?	Q10	No	Yes
IQ6	Is the communication between **Element1** and the machine established using multiple (exchangeable) protocols / mechanisms?	Q13A	No	Yes
IQ8	Shall **Element1** be exchangeable at run-time?	Q14B, Q28	No	Yes
IQ10	Can the functionality **Element1** logically be grouped with other functionality?	Q4A	Yes	No
IQ11	Is it possible to handle **Element1** as a stream?	Q7A	No	Yes
IQ13	Has **Element1** been transformed before?	Q7B	Yes	No
IQ15	Is it expected that the transformation described by **Element1** will change frequently?	Q7C	Yes	No
IQ17	Shall **Element1** show multiple views based on **Element2**?	Q17	Yes	No
IQ18	Shall manipulations of **Element2** be reflected immediately on **Element1**?	Q18	Yes	No
IQ21	Is **Element1** expected to change over time?	Q26	Yes	No
IQ22	Is **Element1** likely to change over time?	Q28	No	Yes

Table 5.12: Indicator questions for R1 and Model Building (derived from external inputs and used in Step 2)

Identifier	Question	Answers
IQ2	Is the functionality provided by **Smart Meter** a low level hardware functionality?	Yes, SmartMeter provides low level hardware functionality.
IQ4	Is the **SmartMeter** distributed with regards to the machine?	Yes, SmartMeter is located outside the system-to-be.
IQ4	Is the **TemporaryStorage** distributed with regards to the machine?	No, it is part of the machine.
IQ6	Is the communication between **SmartMeter** and the machine established using multiple (exchangeable) protocols / mechanisms?	No, there is no need for multiple protocols or mechanisms.
IQ6	Is the communication between **TemporaryStorage** and the machine established using multiple (exchangeable) protocols / mechanisms?	No, there is no need for multiple protocols or mechanisms.
IQ8	Shall **SmartMeter** be exchangeable at run-time?	No, there is no need for exchanging SmartMeter at run-time.
IQ8	Shall **TemporaryStorage** be exchangeable at run-time?	No, there is no need for exchanging TemporaryStorage at run-time.
IQ10	Can the functionality **R1** logically be grouped with other functionality?	No, there is no similar functionality that R1 can be grouped with.
IQ11	Is it possible to handle **TemporaryStorage** as a stream?	Yes, it can be handled as a stream of data.
IQ14	Will **TemporaryStorage** be used in another transformation afterward?	Yes, it will be used in R2 and R3.
IQ15	Is it expected that the transformation described by **R1** will change frequently?	No, it is not expected that the transformation changed frequently.
IQ21	Is **R1** expected to change over time?	No, the requirement will not be changed.
IQ22	Is **SmartMeter** likely to change over time?	No, the change of SmartMeter is not expected.
IQ22	Is **TemporaryStorage** likely to change over time?	Yes, TemporaryStorage can change frequently.

Table 5.13: Indicator questions for R2 and Transformation (derived from external inputs and used in Step 2)

Identifier	Question	Answers
IQ13	Has **TemporaryStorage** been transformed before?	Yes, it has been used in R1.
IQ14	Will **TemporaryStorage** be used in another transformation afterward?	Yes, it will be used in R3.
IQ15	Is it expected that the transformation described by **R2** will change frequently?	No, it is not expected that the transformation changed frequently.
IQ21	Is **R2** expected to change over time?	No, the requirement will not be changed.

Table 5.14: Indicator questions for R3 and Transformation (derived from external inputs and used in Step 2)

Identifier	Question	Answers
IQ4	Is the **MeterData** distributed with regards to the machine?	No, MeterData is part of the machine.
IQ6	Is the communication between **MeterData** and the machine established using multiple (exchangeable) protocols / mechanisms?	No, there is no need for multiple protocols or mechanisms.
IQ8	Shall **MeterData** be exchangeable at run-time?	No, there is no need for exchanging MeterData at run-time.
IQ11	Is it possible to handle **MeterData** as a stream?	Yes, it can be handled as a stream of data.
IQ14	Will **MeterData** be used in another transformation afterward?	Yes, it will be transformed into data to be displayed.
IQ15	Is it expected that the transformation described by **R3** will change frequently?	No, it is not expected that the transformation changed frequently.
IQ21	Is **R3** expected to change over time?	No, the requirement will not be changed.
IQ22	Is **MeterData** likely to change over time?	Yes, MeterData can change frequently.

Table 5.17-Table 5.21 show the indicator questions and the answers we assigned to them. Since the indicator questions have to be instantiated with concrete elements from the identified problem frames, the same indicator question may be asked several times. Consequently, a question may have a set of elements for which it is answered positively or negatively, respectively.

We then derive a set of indicated questions by identifying those indicator questions which have been answered positively at least once and gathering its respective indicated questions. This set of indicated questions comprises

- *Q3*, *Q7*, *Q10*, and *Q28* for *R1* (sub questions are mapped to their respective super question, e.g. *Q7A* and *Q7B* is mapped to *Q7* and *Q3B* are mapped to *Q3*). We identify six questions that have to be answered in order to identify relevant pattern candidates for *R1*. While questions *Q3*, *Q7*, *Q10*, and *Q28* are indicated by indicator questions, *Q6* and *Q9* are indicated directly by the extracted problem frame, *Model Building*. Table 5.22 gives an overview of our answers to the indicated questions as well as associated reasoning for *R1*.

- *Q7* and *Q28* for *R2* and *R3* (sub questions were mapped to their respective super question, e.g. *Q7A* and *Q7B* are mapped to *Q7*). We identify four questions that have to be answered in order to identify relevant pattern candidates for *R2* and *R3*. While questions *Q7* and *Q28* are indicated by indicator questions, *Q6* and *Q9* are indicated directly by the extracted problem frames, *Simple Transformation* and *Transformation*. Table 5.23 gives an overview of our answers to the

Table 5.15: Indicator questions for R4 and Model Display (derived from external inputs and used in Step 2)

Identifier	Question	Answers
IQ2	Is the functionality provided by **AuthorizedExternalEntities** a low level hardware functionality?	No, this functionality is no hardware functionality.
IQ4	Is the **AuthorizedExternalEntities** distributed with regards to the machine?	Yes, the system-to-be is connected with the AuthorizedExternalEntities through *WAN*.
IQ6	Is the communication between **AuthorizedExternalEntities** and the machine established using multiple (exchangeable) protocols / mechanisms?	No, there is no need for multiple protocols or mechanisms.
IQ8	Shall **AuthorizedExternalEntities** be exchangeable at run-time?	No, there is no need for exchanging AuthorizedExternalEntities at run-time.
IQ10	Can the functionality **R4** logically be grouped with other functionality?	Yes, it might be grouped with the functionality R5.
IQ13	Has **MeterData** been transformed before?	Yes, MeterData has been transformed before by processing and storing.
IQ15	Is it expected that the transformation described by **R4** will change frequently?	No, it is not expected that the transformation changed frequently.
IQ17	Shall **AuthorizedExternalEntities** show multiple views based on **MeterData**?	No, given the requirement R4, we do not expect multiple views.
IQ18	Shall manipulations of **MeterData** be reflected immediately on **AuthorizedExternalEntities**?	No, there is no need for immediately reflecting the MeterData.
IQ21	Is **R4** expected to change over time?	No, the requirement will not be changed.
IQ22	Is **AuthorizedExternalEntities** likely to change over time?	No, the change of AuthorizedExternalEntities is not expected.

    indicated questions as well as associated reasoning for *R2* and *R3*. We consider indicated questions and answers for *R2* and *R3* in one table as *R2* and *R3* both are concerned with the same problem frame.

- *Q4*, *Q7*, and *Q10* for *R4* and *R5* (sub questions are mapped to their respective super question, e.g. *Q7B* is mapped to *Q7* and *Q4A* is mapped to *Q4*). We identify five questions that have to be answered in order to identify relevant pattern candidates for *R4* and *R5*. While questions *Q4*, *Q7*, and *Q10* are indicated by indicator questions, *Q6*, *Q7*, and *Q9* are indicated directly by the extracted problem frame *Model Display*. Table 5.24 gives an overview of our answers to the indicated questions as well as associated reasoning for *R4* and *R5*.

Table 5.16: Indicator questions for R5 and Model Display (derived from external inputs and used in Step 2)

Identifier	Question	Answers
IQ2	Is the functionality provided by **User Interface** a low level hardware functionality?	No, this functionality is no hardware functionality.
IQ4	Is the **UserInterface** distributed with regards to the machine?	Yes, the system-to-be is connected with the Consumer through *HAN*.
IQ6	Is the communication between **UserInterface** and the machine established using multiple (exchangeable) protocols / mechanisms?	No, there is no need for multiple protocols or mechanisms.
IQ8	Shall **UserInterface** be exchangeable at run-time?	No, there is no need for exchanging UserInterface at run-time.
IQ10	Can the functionality **R5** logically be grouped with other functionality?	Yes, it might be grouped with the functionality R4.
IQ15	Is it expected that the transformation described by **R5** will change frequently?	No, it is not expected that the transformation changed frequently.
IQ17	Shall **UserInterface** show multiple views based on **MeterData**?	No, given the requirement R5, we do not expect multiple views.
IQ18	Shall manipulations of **MeterData** be reflected immediately on **UserInterface**?	No, there is no need for immediately reflecting the MeterData.
IQ21	Is **R5** expected to change over time?	No, the requirement will not be changed.
IQ22	Is **UserInterface** likely to change over time?	No, the change of UserInterface is not expected.

Table 5.17: Indicator Question Answers Overview for R1 (created and used in Step 2)

Indicator Question	Indicated Question	Negatively answered for	Positively answered for
IQ2	Q3B	-	SmartMeter
IQ4	Q10	TemporaryStorage	SmartMeter
IQ6	Q13A	SmartMeter, TemporaryStorage	-
IQ8	Q14B, Q28	SmartMeter, TemporaryStorage	-
IQ10	Q4A	R1	-
IQ11	Q7A	-	TemporaryStorage
IQ14	Q7B	-	TemporaryStorage
IQ15	Q7C	R1	-
IQ21	Q26	R1	-
IQ22	Q28	SmartMeter	TemporaryStorage

Table 5.18: Indicator Question Answers Overview for R2 (created and used in Step 2)

Indicator Question	Indicated Question	Negatively answered for	Positively answered for
IQ13	Q7B	-	TemporaryStorage
IQ14	Q7B	-	TemporaryStorage
IQ15	Q7C	R2	-
IQ21	Q26	R2	-

Table 5.19: Indicator Question Answers Overview for R3 (created and used in Step 2)

Indicator Question	Indicated Question	Negatively answered for	Positively answered for
IQ4	Q10	MeterData	-
IQ6	Q13A	MeterData	-
IQ8	Q14B, Q28	MeterData	-
IQ11	Q7A	-	MeterData
IQ14	Q7B	-	MeterData
IQ15	Q7C	R3	-
IQ21	Q26	R3	-
IQ22	Q28	-	MeterData

Table 5.20: Indicator Question Answers Overview for R4 (created and used in Step 2)

Indicator Question	Indicated Question	Negatively answered for	Positively answered for
IQ2	Q3B	AuthorizedExternalEntities	-
IQ4	Q10	-	AuthorizedExternalEntities
IQ6	Q13A	AuthorizedExternalEntities	-
IQ8	Q14B, Q28	AuthorizedExternalEntities	-
IQ10	Q4A	-	R4
IQ13	Q7B	-	MeterData
IQ15	Q7C	R4	-
IQ17	Q17	R4 (AuthorizedExternalEntities, Meter-Data)	-
IQ18	Q18	R4 (AuthorizedExternalEntities, Meter-Data)	-
IQ21	Q26	R4	-
IQ22	Q28	AuthorizedExternalEntities	-

Table 5.21: Indicator Question Answers Overview for R5 (created and used in Step 2)

Indicator Question	Indicated Question	Negatively answered for	Positively answered for
IQ2	Q3B	UserInterface	-
IQ4	Q10	-	UserInterface
IQ6	Q13A	UserInterface	-
IQ8	Q14B, Q28	UserInterface	-
IQ10	Q4A	-	R5
IQ15	Q7C	R5	-
IQ17	Q17	R5 (UserInterface, MeterData)	-
IQ18	Q18	R5 (UserInterface, MeterData)	-
IQ21	Q26	R5	-
IQ22	Q28	UserInterface	-

Table 5.22: Answers to the indicated questions for *R1* (created in Step 2, used in Step 3)

Question	Answer	Reasoning
Q3	Yes	There might be low level functionality (receiving MeterData from SmartMeter) and high level functionality (processing, storing, and publishing MeterData)
Q6	No	Meter readings of the smart reader shall only be gathered.
Q7	No	Meter readings of smart meter shall be first converted into data to be processed by a software.
Q9	No	The transformations are known.
Q10	No	The system-to-be is not distributed.
Q28	No	There will be no change in the hardware or software.

Table 5.23: Answers to the indicated questions for *R2* and *R3* (created in Step 2, used in Step 3)

Question	Answer	Reasoning
Q6	Yes	TemporaryStorage and MeterData shall be processed as data streams.
Q7	Yes	TemporaryStorage and MeterData shall be transformed from input data to output data streams.
Q9	No	The transformations are known.
Q28	No	There will be no changes in the hardware or software.

Table 5.24: Answers to the indicated questions for *R4* and *R5* (created in Step 2, used in Step 3)

Question	Answer	Reasoning
Q4	Yes	R4 and R5 might be partitioned.
Q6	Yes	MeterData shall be processed.
Q7	Yes	MeterData should be transformed to data to be displayed to the AuthorizedExternalEntities and the Consumer (UserInterface).
Q9	No	The transformations are known.
Q10	No	The system-to-be is not distributed.

Step 3 - Select pattern candidates

As external inputs for this step, we need the architectural patterns and their relations to the questions. Table 5.25 shows the architectural patterns, including the *type*, *name*, and *identifier* of each pattern, questions related to each pattern separated in questions regarding the context of the pattern and questions regarding the problem each pattern intends to solve. The whole architectural pattern catalog is shown in Appendix B.5.

After answering the questions, those patterns that refer to at least one of the questions answered with *Yes* are considered as pattern candidates. The pattern candidates are *Layers* (Q3, Q4), *Pipes and Filters* (Q6, Q7), and *Blackboard* (Q7).

Table 5.25: Excerpt of Architectural Pattern Descriptions

Pattern			Questions		Consequences	
Type	*Name*	*Identifier*	*Context*	*Problem*	*Benefits*	*Liabilities*
From Mud to Structure	Layers	AP1	Q1, Q2	Q3, Q4, Q5	B1, B2, B3, B4	L1, L2, L3, L4
From Mud to Structure	Pipes and Filters	AP2	Q6	Q7	B1, B4, B6, B7, B8A	L5A, L2A, L2B, L6
From Mud to Structure	Blackboard	AP3	Q8	Q7, Q9	B1A, B4, B6A, B9, B10	L7, L8, L9A, L2C

Step 4 - Show pattern candidates

In this step, we show the architectural pattern candidates to the user. It is possible to reduce the set of architectural pattern candidates by dismissing those candidates that are not relevant. In case no decision about the selection of pattern candidates can be made, one has to continue with the process. So, we continue with the next step, as we cannot dismiss any pattern candidate and decide for one candidate.

Step 5 - Answer open questions related to pattern candidates

For this step, we take the architectural patterns and their relations to the questions into account as external input (see Table 5.25). To be able to make well-founded assumptions regarding the appropriateness of the pattern candidates, we gather the unanswered questions which are relevant for the three mentioned patterns, i.e. Q8 (unanswered question relevant for *Blackboard*), and Q1, Q2, and Q5 (unanswered questions relevant for *Layers*). By the architectural pattern *Pipes and Filters* all two questions Q6 and Q7 are already answered. We answer the open questions as stated in Table 5.26.

We answer Q8 with *No*. It addresses the context of the architectural pattern *Blackboard*. As the context of this pattern does not match to our problem, we can exclude this architectural pattern from further consideration. We select the architectural pattern *Pipes and Filters*, as the questions addressing the context and the problem are positively answered. Questions Q1 and Q2 address the context of the *Layers* architectural pattern. We answer both questions with *No*. As our problem description (requirements) does not meet the context of this pattern, we exclude this architectural pattern in this step.

As the architectural patterns *Blackboard* and *Layers* have been excluded in this step, and only the architectural pattern *Pipes and Filters* is left, we could skip Steps 6 to 8 and continue with Step 9. Nevertheless, we continue with Step 6 for qualities and consequences of the selected pattern to show the application of these steps as well.

Step 6 - Check qualities and consequences

Qualities and their relations to the consequences represent the external input of this step (see Tables 5.6 and 5.7 in Section 5.3 for the benefits and liabilities of the

Table 5.26: Unanswered questions referred by pattern candidates (created in Step 5; used in Step 3)

Question	Answer	Reasoning
Q1	No	Smart Metering System is not a large system.
Q2	No	There is no need for decomposing, as Smart Metering System does not have so many components that are not manageable without decomposing.
Q5	No	The mapping is not complex.
Q8	No	From our point of view the *Smart Metering* domain is quite new, however not unknown. Hence, the solution for the problem that the system shall solve is known.

architectural pattern *Pipes and Filters* and Tables B.11 and B.12 in Appendix B.4 for the complete list of benefits and liabilities). We gather and compare the relevant qualities and consequences based on the qualities that are relevant for the smart grid system. Based on the annotations of quality requirements in the problem diagrams, *performance* and *security* are identified as the main qualities being relevant. The quality *security* is not addressed by the architectural patterns. Hence, this should be achieved using specific mechanisms and security patterns. We address this issue later on in Phases 5 and 6 of the QuaDRA framework (see Chapters 8 and 9). The other quality, namely *performance*, is referred to as *efficiency* in ISO/IEC 25010 standard [130]. Therefore, we concentrate on the pattern's consequences targeting *efficiency* in the decision process.

Step 7 - Rank consequences and qualities and Step 8 - Rank pattern candidates

The benefits and liabilities of the *Pipes and Filters* architectural pattern are shown in Table 5.27 and Table 5.28. The *Pipes and Filters* pattern has one benefit targeting *efficiency* (*B8A*) stating that parallel processing is enabled by the pattern and resulting in an efficient resource utilization. On the other hand, the pattern references liability *L2A* states that resource utilization and capability is affected negatively due to expensive state sharing. Since we do not see the need for state sharing in the context of the given requirements, we consider this liability as not severe.

As there is only the *Pipes and Filters* pattern left, no ranking is required and possible.

Table 5.27: An excerpt of the benefits and the related qualities (external input; used in Step 6)

Identifier	Benefit	Related Quality
	Pipes and Filters	
B1	Reuse is improved	Reusability
B4	(Ex)changeability is improved	Maintainability (Modularity, Modifiability), Portability (Replaceability)
B6	Flexibility is improved	Maintainability (Modifiability, Testability), Portability (Replaceability, Adaptability), Compatibility (Interoperability)
B7	Rapid prototyping is possible	Maintainability (Analyzability, Modifiability, Testability)
B8A	Enables parallel processing	Efficiency (Resource utilization)

Table 5.28: An excerpt of the liabilities and the related qualities (external input; used in Step 6)

Identifier	Benefit	Related Quality
	Pipes and Filters	
L2A	Sharing state might be expensive	Effciency (Resource utilization, Capacity)
L2B	Might introduce additional transformation overhead	Effciency (Resource utilization, Capacity)
L5A	Sharing state is inflexible	Maintainability (Modifiability, Testability), Portability (Replaceability, Adaptability), Compatibility (Interoperability)
L6	Error handling is difficult	Reliability (Fault tolerance, Recoverability), Maintainability (Analyzability, Testability)

Step 9 - Select pattern to be applied

We decide for the architectural pattern *Pipes and Filters* as it is the only pattern left. In the next section, we set up an initial architecture which applies this patten.

5.6 Derivation of Initial Architecture

in Section 5.6.1 and Section 5.6.2. According to these design decisions, we return to Phase 1 of the QuaDRA framework and check the subproblems for their appropriateness in Section 5.6.3. Finally, we derive an initial architecture in Section 5.6.4 based on the subproblems.

5.6.1 Design Desicion regarding Architectural Pattern Selection

In the previous section (see Section 5.5), we selected the architectural pattern *Pipes and Filters*. The selected architectural pattern affects the decomposition of the problem diagrams as well as the quality requirements as follows:

Design Decision One: Pipes and Filters for *R2* and *R3*   For designing the requirements *R2* and *R3*, we decided for a *Pipes and Filters* architectural pattern. Currently, we are concerned with two transformation steps, one transformation for processing meter readings to be stored temporarily in the lexical domain *TemporaryStorage* (*R2* in Fig. 5.5) and the second transformation for storing meter readings permanently in the lexical domain *MeterData* (*R3* in Fig. 5.6). These two transformations require the application of two *Pipes and Filters* architectural patterns, which is not efficient due to performance reasons as one additional transformation step should be performed which can be avoided. These two transformations can be merged into one transformation. Therefore, we decide for applying only one *Pipes and Filters* architectural pattern for both requirements. This design decision affects the decomposition of the problem diagrams *ProcessMeterData* and *StoreMeterData* as well as the modeled quality requirements.

Design Decision Two: Pipes and Filters for *R4*   For designing the requirement *R4*, we decided for a *Pipes and Filters* architectural pattern. This design decision affects neither the structure of the subproblems nor the modeled quality requirements.

Design Decision Three: Pipes and Filters for *R5*   For designing the requirement *R5*, we decided for a *Pipes and Filters* architectural pattern. This design decision affects neither the structure of the subproblems nor the modeled quality requirements.

5.6.2 Design Desicion regarding Gateway Physical Boundary

The *Smart Meter* is responsible for collecting the consumption or production data and transmitting this data to the *Gateway*. According to the "*Protection Profile for the Gateway of a Smart Metering System*" [155], the *Gateway* is typically placed in the household or premises of the consumer and enables access to local *Smart Meter*. To ensure the confidentiality, authenticity, and integrity of *Meter Data*, it has to be encrypted and signed before transfer unless the transmission is physically protected. This is the case if the *Smart Meter* and the *Gateway* are being implemented within one device and utilize a wired or optical connection. This is called the *One Box Solution*. It is one physical unit in terms of a sealed box that enables physical protection for the *Gateway*, *Smart Meter*, and the communication channel between them. The advantage of this solution is that there is no need for security mechanisms to protect the communication between the *Gateway* and the *Smart Meter* as the communication happens in the protected area of the box. Hence, we make the following design decision:

Design Decision Four: One Box Solution For the *Smart Meter* and the *Smart Meter Gateway*, we decide for the *One Box Solution*, that is having the *Smart Meter* and the *Smart Meter Gateway* in one physical device. This design decision affects the modeled quality requirements.

5.6.3 Further Iterations - Problem Diagram Splitting

In the previous chapter in Section 4.3 (see Phase 1 on page 124), we described that design decisions might affect the decomposition of the problem diagrams. If this is the case, we should return to that phase and check the appropriateness of the decomposition of the problem diagrams according to the made design decision.

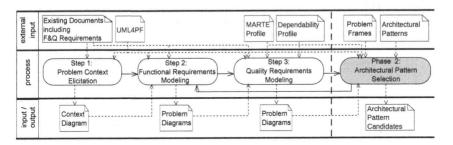

Fig. 5.9: Overview of Phase 1 and its relation to Phase 2

Figure 5.9 shows how the steps of Phase 1 are related to Phase 2 of our QuaDRA framework. We might need to return to *Step 2 - Functional Requirements Modeling* of Phase 1 to decompose or merge subproblems as appropriate according to the selected architectural pattern. Decomposition or merging of functional subproblems might have an impact on quality requirements. Therefore, we need to return to *Step*

3 - Quality Requirements Modeling of Phase 1 as well and check for appropriateness of modeled quality requirements. We perform the second iteration of Phase 1 as follows:

Step 2 - Functional Requirements Modeling (Second Iteration)

Design decision one (*Pipes and Filters* for *R2* and *R3*) affects the decomposition of subproblems for requirements *R2* and *R3*. The other design decisions do not affect the related functional subproblem as the structure of the problem diagrams does not change.

We decided for applying only one *Pipes and Filters* architectural pattern which provides one transformation as two transformations are not efficient due to performance reasons. So, we can avoid one transformation by storing the processed meter readings directly into the lexical domain *MeterData* permanently instead of storing the processed meter readings first into the lexical domain *TemporaryStorage*. To this end, we need to merge the two problem diagrams *ProcessMeterData* and *StoreMeterData* for the requirements *R2* and *R3* in order to apply only one *Pipes and Filters*. The merged problem diagram is shown in Fig. 5.10.

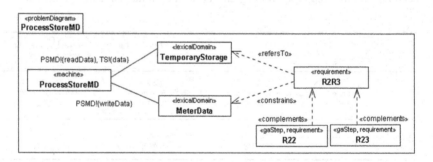

Fig. 5.10: Merged problem diagram related to functional requirements *R2* and *R3*

Step 3 - Quality Requirements Modeling (Second Iteration)

Design decision Four: One Box Solution:
The *Smart Meter* and the *Smart Meter Gateway* are embedded in one box, which

is one physical unit in form of a sealed box/cabinet. This enables that the Gateway and the smart meter communication happens in the protected area of the box. From the security point of view, this solution has the advantage that the communication is protected. Therefore, we can assume that the security requirements *R6*, *R7*, and *R8* are already fulfilled without applying additional security mechanisms. Also the confidentiality requirement *R16* is satisfied as the box is physically protected. Hence, we exclude these quality requirements from further consideration. The confidentiality requirement *R9* related to the functional requirement *R3* is already satisfied due to the same reasons as for the confidentiality requirement *R16*. Hence, we exclude this quality requirement from further consideration as well.

Design decision One: Pipes and Filters for *R2* and *R3*:
We merged the subproblems for the requirements *R2* and *R3*. Therefore, we only consider *R22* and *R23* as performance requirements for the merged subproblem. We exclude the performance requirements *R20* and *R21* from further consideration. Note that this does not mean that we do not consider them at all. It only means that now the performance requirements *R18*, *R22*, and *R24* have to be fulfilled together within 5 seconds and the performance requirements *R19, 23,* and *R25* have to be fulfilled in less than 10 seconds. Beforehand, the performance requirements *R18, R20, R22,* and *R24* had to be fulfilled together within 5 seconds and the performance requirements *R19, R21, 23,* and *R25* had to be fulfilled in less than 10 seconds. It means that excluding the performance requirements *R20* and *R21* is only a modeling decision and does not affect the fulfillment of the desired performance requirements.

5.6.4 Method for Deriving Initial Architecture

After selecting the appropriate architectural patterns and decomposing/merging subproblems according to the selected architectural patterns, we are now able to start designing a software architecture for the machine in the context diagram.

Architecting the software-to-be begins with setting up an initial architecture that we incrementally complete by selecting quality-specific solutions for quality requirements in Chapter 8, applying them in Chapter 9, and deriving implementable architecture alternatives in Chapter 10.

The initial architecture provides a basis to solve the software development problem described by the problem descriptions. It uses the already selected architectural patterns to implement the functional requirements with regard to quality requirements. Figure 5.11 illustrates our method for deriving the initial architecture consisting of four steps. In the following, we describe the steps of our method followed by its application to the smart grid case study.

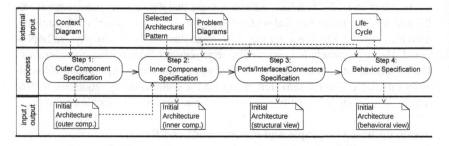

Fig. 5.11: Overview of the method for deriving the initial architecture

Step 1 - Outer Component Specification

The initial architecture consists of one component for the overall machine which builds the outer component of the software-to-be. Constructing the outer component is performed in this step. We represent the initial architecture as a composite structure diagram.

We make use of the UML profile for architecture (see Section 2.3.2 on page 37), which is an extension to UML4PF. The UML profile for architecture allows us to annotate such diagrams with information on components and connectors.

For modeling the machine domain, one has to choose between different stereotypes. If the machine domain represents a distributed system, one uses the stereotype ≪distributed≫. By a local system such as a single computer, the stereotype ≪local≫ is used whereas the stereotypes ≪process≫ and ≪task≫ express a process on a certain platform or a single task within a process. In addition, the stereotype ≪initial_architecture≫ has to be applied to the overall machine to indicate that the architecture is an initial architecture and not yet implementable.

Input for this step is the context diagram. The overall machine component has the same interfaces as described in the context diagram. As an output, one obtains a composite structure diagram containing the outer component and its interfaces to the outside world.

Application of Step 1 - Outer Component Specification

The initial architecture for the smart grid case study is represented as a UML composite structure diagram. For smart grid, we set up one overall component *Smart Meter Gateway* corresponding to the machine in the context diagram. We choose the stereotypes *initial_architecture* and *local* as it is concerned with a single stand-alone system. It has three ports typed with *:PLMN*, *:PHAN*, and *:PWAN*. The ports have a class as a type. This class uses and realizes interfaces. For example, as depicted in Fig. 5.12, the class *PWAN* uses the interface *SMD!{sendDataIntoWAN}* and the class *PLMN* realizes the interface *LMN!{forwardMeterData}*. The ports with the class *PLMN* as a type provide the interface *LMN!{forwardMeterData}* (depicted as a lollipop) and the ports with the class *PWAN* as a type require the interface *SMD!{sendDataIntoWAN}* (depicted as a socket). The complete list of the port types for the initial architecture is given in Appendix B.6. The output of Step 1 is illustrated in Fig. 5.13.

Fig. 5.12: Port types of *PWAN* and *PLMN*

Step 2 - Inner Components Specification

The initial architecture contains one component for each subproblem. Therefore, we use the modeled problem diagrams as an input to this step. The stereotype ≪Component≫ has to be applied to indicate the components in the software architecture. For deriving the components inside the overall machine, we make use of the submachines in the problem diagrams. Each submachine becomes a component to be located inside the outer component. Also the lexical domains as data representations become components in the initial architecture.

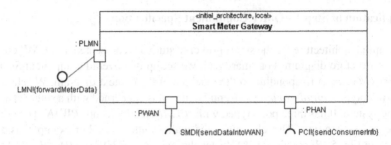

Fig. 5.13: Output of Step 1

By placing the components in the overall machine, one should consider the relevant architectural patterns. The components have to be arranged in a way that they reflect the structure of the relevant architectural style. In some cases new components need to be added to the overall component in order to be able to instantiate the architectural pattern. For example, in order to apply the *Layered* architectural pattern, for each layer a new component needs to be introduced. In contrast, for the architectural pattern *Pipes and Filter* there is no need for introducing new components as the already existing components are used as *Filters*.

Application of Step 2 - Inner Components Specification

Now, we have to place components inside the overall component *Smart Meter Gateway* considering the selected architectural pattern *Pipes and Filters*. For the first component we take the submachine *ReceiveMeterData* in the problem diagram related to the functional requirement *R1*. It becomes a component *ReceiveMeterData* in the initial architecture with the stereotype *Component*. The lexical domain *TemporaryStorage* in the subproblem *ReceiveMeterData* becomes a component as well, which is connected to the component *ReceiveMeterData*.

For the machine *ProcessStoreMD*, we apply the architectural pattern *Pipes and Filters*. The machine *ProcessStoreMD* is mapped to a component in the initial architecture which serves as a *Filter*. The two connections to the component *ProcessStoreMD* serve as *pipes*. The component *TemporaryStorage* serves as a *Pump*, which initiates "pumping" the data into the pipe. The component *MeterData* corresponds to the lexical domain *MeterData* in the subproblem related to the functional requirement *R2R3*. It serves as a *Sink* initiating the final destination of the transformation.

The components *SubmitMD* and *PublishConsumerInfo* with the stereotype *Component* correspond to the submachines in the problem diagrams related to the functional requirements *R4* and *R5*. Also these two components serve as *Filters*. The connections between the component *MeterData* and these two components serve as *Pipes*. The component *MeterData* represents the *Pump*. The two components *SubmitMD* and *PublishConsumerInfo* are connected to the *AuthorizedExternalEntities* and *UseInterface* through two *Pipes*. So, we are concerned with two parallel *Pipes and Filters*. The initial architecture of smart grid is shown in Fig. 5.14. In the next step, we show how the components are connected to each other.

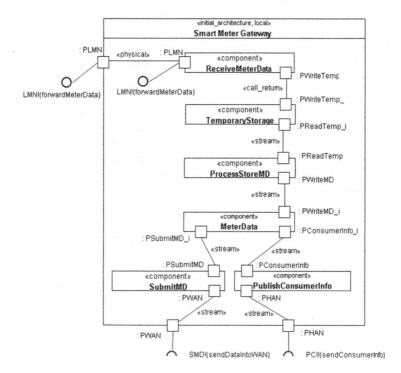

Fig. 5.14: Structural view of the initial architecture of smart grid

5.6.4.1 Step 3 - Ports/Interfaces/Connectors Specification

After specifying the inner components, one needs to specify how the components are connected. To this end, the ports of each component, its interfaces, and connectors have to be specified in this step. The architectural profile for modeling the ports, interfaces, and connectors provides one input. Another input for this step are problem diagrams that provide the basis for the specification of the ports and interfaces.

The components are equipped with ports that correspond to the interfaces in the problem diagrams. The ports should have a type represented as a class with required and provided interfaces. A controlled interface in a problem diagram is mapped to a required interface of the corresponding component in the initial architecture. An observed interface of the machine in the problem diagram is mapped to a provided interface of the corresponding component in the initial architecture. Component ports have to be connected to the ports of the overall machine through connectors. In addition, we specify the connectors between each two components. To this end, we add stereotypes from the UML profile for architecture that describe the technical realization of these connectors. For example, for modeling a physical connector, we make use of the stereotype ≪Physical≫. In a *Pipes and Filters* architectural pattern, the connectors between the *Filters* are *Pipes* expressed with the stereotype ≪Stream≫. The complete set of stereotypes to be used for the connectors can be found in Section 2.3.2 (see page 37). As the output of this step, we obtain the structural view of the initial architecture.

5.6.4.2 Application of Step 3 - Ports/Interfaces/Connectors Specification

The component *ReceiveMeterData* is connected to the *SamrtMeter* with the port *PLMN* by a physical connector expressed with the stereotype ≪Physical≫. The component *TemporaryStorage* is connected to the component *ReceiveMeterData* through a connector with the stereotype ≪call_return≫. The connectors between the components *TemporaryStorage*, *ProcessStoreMD*, *MeterData*, *SubmitMD*, and *PublishConsumerInfor* are *Pipes*. The pipes are expressed with the stereotype ≪Stream≫. The two components *SubmitMD* and *PublishConsumerInfo* are connected to the *AuthorizedExternalEntities* and *UseInterface* through the ports *PWAN* and *PHAN*.

Step 4 - Behavior Specification

To complete the initial software architecture, one needs to specify the behavior of the architecture in addition to its structure. Therefore, this step is concerned with modeling the behavioral view of the initial architecture. As inputs for this step, we make use of the problem diagrams and the life-cycle expressions that enable us to specify the interactions[3] between the components and their order. The life-cycle contains information about the order of interactions described by the requirements. For specifying the behavior, we use UML sequence diagrams. However, any other diagram for modeling the behavior can be used.

Application of Step 4 - Behavior Specification

First, we set up the life-cycle (LC) expressions for our example. The smart grid system has the following life-cycle:

$$LC = ((R1;\ R2R3);\ (R4 \parallel R5))^*$$

At first, the machine of requirement *R1* is executed in LC. That means the meter data are obtained from the smart meter and stored temporarily. Then, the machine for the requirement *R2R3* is executed which processes the temporary stored meter data and stores them persistently. The machines of the requirements *R4* and *R5* are executed concurrently after the execution of the machines for *R1* and *R2R3*. The whole life-cycle can be repeated an arbitrary number of times. By establishing the life-cycle, the order of the interactions between the components is specified.

For specifying the messages exchanging between the components, we make use of the problem diagrams. Figure 5.15 shows the behavioral view of the initial architecture represented as a sequence diagram. It illustrates how the components of the initial architecture interact with each other. The messages represent the phenomena in the problem diagrams. The sequence diagram shows that the meter data is forwarded through the *LMN* to the component *ReceiveMeterData* to be written into the *TemporaryStorage*. The component *ProcessStoreMD* obtains data from *TemporaryStorage* and writes it persistently into *MeterData*. The *par* construct shows the parallel execution of the components *SubmitMD* and *PublishConsumerInfo* after storing the *MeterData* persistently. The component *SubmitMD* receives this data and sends it through *WAN* to the outside world. *WAN* represents one interface to the outside world. The component *PublishConsumerInfo* receives *MeterData* and

---

[3] With interaction in this context we mean the interplay between the components and not the conflicts.

sends it through *LAN* to the consumer. Also *LAN* represents one interface to the outside world.

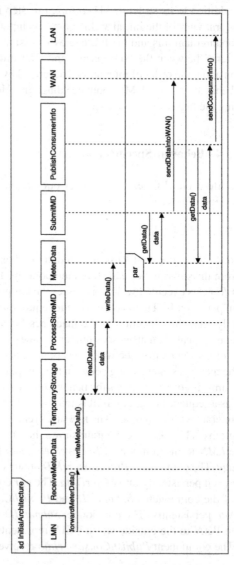

Fig. 5.15: Behavioral view of the initial architecture of smart grid

5.7 Related Work

Zdun [253] proposes a generic pattern language grammar for formalizing patterns and pattern relationships. Using this grammar, sequences of patterns conforming to the pattern language can be derived in order to address a specific design problem. The author analyzes a pattern language consisting of 31 patterns for creating distributed systems. The focus of this work is on describing the relationships and dependencies among patterns in a formal way. There is no structured approach presented on how to use such a pattern language in order to select appropriate patterns. Hence, due to its abstraction level, this work is not meant to be applied directly to concrete software projects. We, in contrast, propose a structured method for selecting appropriate architectural patterns for real-world requirements.

Choppy et al. [69] propose new architectural patterns for basic problem frames to be used in the design phase which are designed to reflect the structure of the problem frames. To create an architectural solution for a concrete problem frame, the relating architectural pattern must be instantiated which provides the starting point for building a software architecture. While our process provides a top-down approach by selecting the architectural patterns for the overall problem, this work is a button-up approach by selecting the architectural patterns for each subproblem. It derives an architecture only based on functional requirements. So, the final architecture does not provide support for achieving quality requirements. From our point of view, this approach can be seen as complementary to ours. So, the overall architectural pattern can be selected through our systematic process. For instantiating the inner components, this work can be used providing a mapping from problem diagrams to the proposed problem frames-based architectural patterns.

Bass and John [46] use a scenario-based approach for selecting architectural design patterns. They identify and classify architecturally significant usability scenarios that describe a user's potential way to interact with a system and discover adequate architectural patterns that support the interaction. Using a matrix, the software architect can identify suitable tactics and benefits from applying the respective tactics for each usability scenario. A hierarchy of architectural patterns is provided that supports the architect to find patterns for implementing a certain tactic. This approach is limited to usability and does not provide support for other quality requirements.

Bosch and Molin [58] propose an iterative method for deriving an architectural design from requirements. First, an initial architecture is created solely based on the functional requirements. Then, a quality estimate for this application architecture is created, whereas the architect may choose from various proposed assessment methods for each quality requirement. If the estimated quality is not in conformance with the set of quality requirements, quality-optimizing architecture transformations are applied to the application and the conformance with quality requirements is estimated again. Otherwise, if the estimated quality meets the quality requirements, the process ends and the final architecture is found. While Bosch and Molin [58] integrate quality requirements after the functionality has been designed, we take quality requirements into account from the very beginning.

5.8 Contributions

In the first part of this chapter, we presented a method for selecting architectural pattern(s) considering quality requirements. We first identify the problem to be solved using problem diagrams which are instances of problem frames. In this stage, we consider the functional requirements in the first place. The architect is presented with questions from a question catalog that are appropriate for the problem identified in the previous step.

Then, we consider and rank benefits and liabilities of the architectural patterns in order to address the quality requirements relevant for the problem annotated in the problem diagrams. This way, we aid the software architect in finding appropriate architectural patterns that solve the problem being addressed taking into account quality requirements. To summarize the contributions of the first part of this chapter, we propose a problem-oriented method that

- selects architectural pattern(s) addressing the functional requirements by mining questions from the *problem* and the *context* of each architectural pattern as well as the quality requirements by relating *liabilities* and *benefits* of each architectural pattern.
- in addition to providing support for software architects in finding suitable architectural pattern(s), provides a reasoning about the appropriateness of the architectural design decisions. The reasoning is provided by a documentation of the relevant questions, the related answers to those questions, and the consequences related to the selected pattern. Consequently the software architects are able to reconstruct the made design decisions later on.

In the second part, we proposed a method for deriving the initial architecture(s) based on the selected architectural pattern(s) as the result of the pattern selection process from the first part. The initial architecture fulfills the functional requirements and takes quality requirements into account by applying the selected architectural pattern(s). It provides a basis for deriving software architecture alternatives to be constructed incrementally by selecting and applying quality-specific solutions for addressing quality requirements in the next chapters.

Chapter 6
Phase 3: Domain Knowledge Analysis

Abstract In requirements engineering, properties of the domains of the environment and assumptions about them are called *domain knowledge*. This chapter outlines the significance of capturing the required domain knowledge when developing software and gives an example of capturing inadequate assumptions about the environment and the resulting consequences. We present a structured method for eliciting, modeling, and using quality-related domain knowledge, which is needed to be captured in addition to exploring the requirements.

6.1 Introduction

The system-to-be comprises the software to be built and its surrounding environment structured as a collection of domains such as people, devices, and existing software [161]. The environment represents the part of the real world into which the software will be integrated. Hence, in requirements engineering, properties of the domains of the environment and assumptions about them, called *domain knowledge*, need to be captured in addition to exploring the requirements [252, 160]. Note that we do not mean *application domain* under the term *domain*, but entities in the environment that are relevant.

Despite the recognition of the significance of capturing the required domain knowledge, it might be missing, left implicit, or be captured inadequately during the software development process [161]. Domain knowledge is often undocumented and tacit in the minds of the people involved in the process of software development [197]. The common ad-hoc nature of gaining domain knowledge is error-prone. Hooks and Farry [127] report on a project where 49% of requirements errors were due to incorrect domain knowledge. Capturing inadequate assumptions about the environment of the flight guidance software led to the crash of a Boeing 757 in Colombia in December 1995 [178].

Several requirements engineering methods exist, e.g., for security. Fabian et al. [94] conclude in their survey about these methods that it is not yet state of the art to consider domain knowledge. The software development process involves knowledge-intensive activities [202]. It is an open research question of *how* to elicit domain knowledge as part of the software development process correctly for effective requirements engineering [181]. van Lamsweerde [161] and Jackson [133] underline the importance of eliciting domain knowledge in addition to the elicitation of requirements to obtain correct specifications. However, there is sparse support in capturing and modeling domain knowledge.

This chapter represents Phase 3 of the QuaDRA framework. In this chapter, we propose a method for capturing implicit domain knowledge, particularly quality-relevant domain knowledge, and making it explicit for reuse in a systematic manner during the software development process. Our approach consists of a meta-process and an object-process which are structured in the steps eliciting, modeling, and using domain knowledge. Both processes are independent from any specific tool or notation. This facilitates the integration of the processes into requirements analysis and design processes.

The meta-process is applied for a given software quality together with a given quality analysis method only once to define how to elicit, model, and use the relevant domain knowledge for the specific software quality and the given analysis method. Results of previous applications of the meta-process for the same software quality together with a different analysis method can be reused. The object-process is applied for a given software project. The domain knowledge is elicited, modeled, and used using the principles that are output of the meta-process for the software quality and quality analysis method under consideration.

We illustrate the application of the meta-process using our QuaRO[1] method [6], which analyzes and detects interactions between security and performance requirements based on pairwise comparisons, and the *PoPeRA* [22] method, which is a method for identifying and analyzing potential performance problems on the requirement analysis level. We illustrate the object-process using the smart grid scenario (see Section 2.6 on page 43) as given application and the QuaRO method as output of the meta-process.

The benefit of our method lies in improving the quality of the requirements engineering process. This is achieved by providing a systematic method that fa-

---

[1] The QuaRO method is a comprehensive method for optimizing requirements according to stakeholders' goals. Through this book, under the *QuaRO* method we understand the part concerning requirements interaction detection.

cilitates the capturing and modeling of implicit domain knowledge as reusable artifacts.

Furthermore, we discuss how domain knowledge affects other artifacts such as requirements and architecture artifacts. We are convinced that during the software development process, domain knowledge is not only used in requirements engineering for obtaining adequate specifications, it also has to be captured during the design phase when selecting patterns and mechanisms or when making design decisions. There exist new assumptions and requirements associated with each pattern and quality-specific solution, which have to be considered when deciding on this solution.

The proposed method in this chapter is based on our work presented in [23]. We are the main author of this work. Rene Meis contributed to eliciting, modeling, and using domain knowledge for privacy as one of the three quality requirements considered in the publication. In this chapter, we introduce the elicitation, modeling, and use of domain knowledge for security and performance. Furthermore, we had valuable discussions with Maritta Heisel and Rene Meis on this work.

In the following, we present the structured meta-process for eliciting, modeling, and using quality-related domain knowledge and its application in Section 6.2. Section 6.3 is devoted to the structured object-process and its application. We discuss related work in Section 6.4 and summarize the contribution of this chapter in Section 6.5.

6.2 Structured Meta-Process

This section describes the meta-process composed of three steps for eliciting, modeling, and using domain knowledge for a specific software quality shown in Fig. 6.1. The starting point is a set of functional and quality requirements that are already modeled. Corresponding requirement models are existing and build the basis for the meta-process. In Chapter 4, we have already described how to build the requirement models.

The meta-process is quality-dependent. That is, it has to be conducted for each software quality once. Once we have elicited and modeled domain knowledge for a specific software quality in steps one and two, we use it in step three by extending an existing method or defining a new one that uses the elicited and modeled domain knowledge for analyzing quality requirements. We consider two methods, namely *QuaRO* [6], which is a method to detect candidates for negative interactions based on pairwise comparisons between quality requirements, and *PoPeRA* [5], which is a method for identifying and analyzing potential performance problems on the

requirements analysis level. For more information, we refer to Chapter 7, in which
the two methods are described.

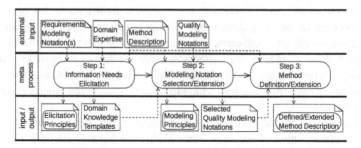

Fig. 6.1: Meta-process for eliciting, modeling, and using domain knowledge

The artifacts in the top of Fig. 6.1 represent the external inputs for the steps of
the method. Those in the bottom of the figure represent the output of the steps providing input for further steps and/or for the object-process (see Section 6.3). In the
following, we describe each step of the meta-process followed by its application
to the software qualities performance and security.

Step 1 - Information Needs Elicitation

This step (see Step 1 in Fig. 6.1) is concerned with eliciting relevant information
needed when dealing with specific software qualities. The source of information
is *domain expertise*. Optionally, *requirements modeling notation(s)* and a *method
description* could be further inputs if existing and needed.

We document the information needs that we elicit for the corresponding software qualities as structured templates called *Domain Knowledge Templates*. Such
templates have to be instantiated separately for each type of software quality in
the first step of the object-process. In addition to the domain knowledge templates,
we provide guidance how to elicit relevant domain knowledge systematically. We
call such guidance *Elicitation Principles*. Domain knowledge templates represent
what domain knowledge has to be elicited, and elicitation principles represent *how*
this domain knowledge has to be elicited. Elicitation principles are used as input
for the first step of the object-process and describe how this step has to be carried
out.

Application of Step 1 - Information Needs Elicitation (for Performance)

We take the UML-based problem frames as the requirements modeling notation. To elicit which domain knowledge the performance analyst requires in order to analyze performance for early software development phases (PoPeRA and QuaRO methods), we make use of domain expertise.

Performance is concerned with the *workload* of the system and the available *resources* to process the workload [47]. The workload is described by triggers of the system, representing requests from outside or inside the system. Workload exhibits the characteristics of the system use. It includes the number of requests (e.g., number of concurrent users) and their arrival pattern (how they are arriving at the system). The arrival pattern can be periodic (e.g. every 10 milliseconds), stochastic (according to a probabilistic distribution), or sporadically (not captured by periodic or stochastic characterization) [44]. Workload of the system represents one of the important issues for resource consumption. In order to answer to the requests, the system has to process the requests, which takes time. Processing the requests requires resources. Each resource has to be expressed by its type in the system, such as CPU, memory, or network, its utilization, and its capacity, such as the transmission speed for a network.

The resulting domain knowledge template for performance is shown in Table 6.1. The columns "Domain Knowledge Description" and "Possible Values" show the domain knowledge to be elicited for performance and its possible values. The column "Value" has to be filled in in the first step of the object-process.

Table 6.1: Domain knowledge template for performance and mapping to the MARTE profile

Quality: Performance				
Domain Knowledge Template				Mapping to MARTE
Domain Knowledge Description	Possible Values		Value	Property
For each Problem Diagram				
Number of concurrent users	Natural			GaWorkloadEvent. pattern. population
Arrival pattern	ArrivalPattern			GaWorkloadEvent. pattern
Data size	DataSize (bit, Byte, KB, MB, GB)			GaStep. msgSize
For each Causal Domain				
Memory	capacity	DataSize (bit, Byte, KB, MB, GB)		HwMemory. memorySize
	latency	Duration (s, ms, min,hr, day)		HwMemory. timing
Network	bandwidth	DataRate (b/s, Kb/s, Mb/s)		HwMedia. bandWidth
	latency	Duration (s, ms, min,hr, day)		HwMedia. packetTime
CPU	speed	Frequency (Hz, kHz, MHz, GHz)		HwProcessor. frequency
	Number of cores	Natural		HwProcessor. nbCores

Once we have captured the *information needs* as domain knowledge templates, we have to give guidance how to elicit them (elicitation principles). The first part of the domain knowledge template for performance contains information relevant for each problem diagram. The second part of the template shows the domain knowledge to be elicited for each causal domain. We iterate over the causal domains in the requirement models (lexical and machine domains are special types of causal domains). By each domain, we have to check if it represents or contains any hardware device that the system is executed on, or any resource that can be consumed by the corresponding performance requirement. Hence, we are concerned with two cases:

- case 1: the domain itself represents a resource such as data storage, memory, network, or software resource.
- case 2: the domain itself does not represent any resource, but it contains hidden resources (resources not modeled yet in the problem diagrams) such as CPU, data storage, memory, network, or software resource.

In the first case, the domain exists in the requirement models. It is a performance-relevant resource, which has to be annotated as such a resource. In the second case, the domain itself represents no resource, but it contains a hidden resource with performance relevant characteristics that is not modeled yet. For example, it contains a CPU, which is relevant when talking about performance issues. For each resource type (CPU, network, memory), we have to state if the resource is already existing in the requirement models or is not modeled yet.

Application of Step 1 - Information Needs Elicitation (for Security)

To guarantee security, we need domain knowledge about the type of possible attackers that influence the restrictiveness of a security requirement. For example, we need to know about the abilities of the attacker, how much resources and effort are available, how much influence security has on the behavior of the overall system-to-be, and which solution to fulfill the requirement has to be chosen. While it is almost impossible to secure a system against an almighty attacker, defending against "script kiddies[2]" can be easily achieved without big impact on the rest of the system.

Different types of attackers can be considered. For example, a software attacker targets at manipulating the software, whereas a network attacker aims at manipulating the network traffic. To describe the attacker we use the properties as de-

---

[2] It refers to an unskilled person who relies on programs or files (scripts) of other people to perform his/her attack (Retrieved from http://www.urbandictionary.com, Oct. 2015).

scribed by the Common Methodology for Information Technology Security Evaluation (CEM) [132] (domain expertise) for vulnerability assessment of the ToE (target of evaluation i.e., system-to-be). The properties to be considered (according to CEM) are [132]:

Elapsed time "Elapsed time is the total amount of time taken by an attacker to identify a particular potential vulnerability ..., to develop an attack method and ... to mount the attack ..." We distinguish between the *preparation time* and the *attack time*.

Specialist expertise "Specialist expertise refers to the level of generic knowledge of the underlying principles, product type or attack methods ...."

Knowledge of the ToE "Knowledge of the ToE refers to specific expertise in relation to the ToE."

Window of opportunity "Identification or exploitation of a vulnerability may require considerable amounts of access to a ToE that may increase the likelihood of detection. ... Access may also need to be continuous, or over a number of sessions."

IT hardware/software or other equipment "... the equipment required to identify or exploit a vulnerability."

The resulting domain knowledge template for security is shown in Table 6.2.

Now, we describe the elicitation principles that support us in capturing domain knowledge. We have to identify attackers for each modeled security requirement. There might exist more than one attacker for a security requirement. It should be checked if such attackers for each security requirement are already identified. If not, we have to identify suitable attackers according to the related security requirement. The domain knowledge template has to be instantiated for each attacker once.

Table 6.2: Domain knowledge template for security and mapping to the dependability profile

Quality: Security			
Domain Knowledge Template			Mapping to profile
Domain Knowledge Description	Possible Values	Value	Property (Dependability profile)
Preparation time	one day, one week, two weeks, ...		Attacker.preparationTime
Attack time	one day, one week, two weeks, ...		Attacker.attackTime
Specialist expertise	laymen, proficient, expert, ...		Attacker.specialistExpertise
Knowledge of the ToE	public, restricted, sensitive, critical		Attacker.knowledge
Window of opportunity	unnecessary/unlimited, easy, ...		Attacker.opportunity
IT hardware/software or other equipment	standard, specialized, bespoke, ...		Attacker.equipment

Step 2 - Modeling Notation Selection/Extension

The aim of this step (see Step 2 in Fig. 6.1) is to select a suitable notation for modeling quality-relevant domain knowledge in a way that it can be used for the requirements analysis. According to the elicited domain knowledge from the previous step, we investigate whether the existing notations are sufficient for integrating domain knowledge in the existing requirement models. In such a case, we select an appropriate notation. Otherwise, we have to extend the existing notations with required artifacts or define a new one. The selected notation will be applied to the requirement models in the object-process in order to support the modeling of domain knowledge. In addition, we obtain *Modeling Principles* as output of this step. They provide guidance for modeling the domain knowledge elicited in the previous step.

Application of Step 2 - Modeling Notation Selection/Extension (for Performance)

We select the MARTE profile [233] for modeling performance-related domain knowledge. For more information regarding the MARTE profile, we refer to Chapter 2 (see page 40). We make use of the stereotypes from the MARTE profile to express the domain knowledge that we elicited in the first step of our method:

GaWorkloadEvent   [3] represents the kind of arrival pattern. A *ClosedPattern* is one kind of arrival pattern. It contains the attribute *population* that represents a fixed number of active users ([233], pages 308 and 503). *Population* expects a value of type *NFP_Integer*, which is a complex data type defined in MARTE containing the attribute *value* expecting an integer number ([233], pages 308 and 506). It initiates system-level behavior using arrival patterns. A *ClosedPattern* is one kind of arrival patterns that contains the parameters necessary to specify a closed Pattern. It is characterized by a fixed number of active or potential users or jobs that cycle between the executing scenario (*population*), and spending an external delay period (sometimes called "think time") outside the system, between the end of one response and the next request (*extDelay*). Other kinds of arrival patterns are *PeriodicPattern* and *AperiodicPattern*. *Population* represents the size of the workload (number of system users) ([233], pages 308 and 503).

HwMemory   contains the attributes *memorySize* that specifies the storage capacity and *timing* that specifies timings of the *HwMemory* ([233], page 597). The

---

[3] Ga ist the abbreviation for Generic Analysis

former expects a value of the type *NFP_DataSize*, which is a complex data type defined in MARTE. It contains the attributes *unit*, which can be selected out of an enumeration (bit, Byte, KB, MB, GB) and *precision*, which is a real number. The latter expects a value of the type *NFP_Duration*, which is a complex data type defined in MARTE. It contains the attributes *unit*, which can be selected out of an enumeration (s, ms, min, hr, day), *clock*, which is a String, *precision*, which is a real number, *worst*, which is a real number representing the worst-case value, and *best*, which is a real number representing the best-case value ([233], page 505). "It is a specialization of *StorageResource*, which represents the different forms of memory. *HwMemory* contains *memorySize* and *timing* as attributes. The former specifies the storage capacity of the *HWMemory*. The latter specifies timings of the *HWMemory*" ([233], page 666).

CommunicationMedia   It represents the means to transport information from one location to another. It contains *capacity* as an attribute ([233], page 597).

HwMedia   is a specialization of *CommunicationMedia*. It contains the attributes *bandWidth* specifying the transfer bandwidth and *packetTime* specifying the time to transmit an element ([233], pages 598 and 665). The former expects a value of the type *NFP_DataTxRate*, which is a complex data type defined in MARTE. It contains the attributes *unit*, which can be selected out of an enumeration (b/s, Kb/s, Mb/s) and *precision*, which is a real number. The latter expects a value of the type *NFP_Duration* ([233], page 505).

ComputingResource   It represents either virtual or physical processing devices capable of storing and executing program code. Hence its fundamental service is to compute ([233], page 598).

HwProcessor   is a generic computing resource symbolizing a processor. It contains the attributes *nbCores*, which specifies the number of cores within the HwProcessor and *frequency* (not contained in the specification, but in the implementation) ([233], page 670). The former expects a value of the type *NFP_Natural*. The latter expects a value of the type *NFP_Frequency*, which is a complex data type defined in MARTE. It contains the attributes *unit*, which can be selected out of an enumeration (Hz, KHz, MHz, GHz, rpm) and *precision*, which is a real number ([233], page 505).

"It is a specialization of *ComputingResource*, which represents either virtual or physical processing devices capable of storing and executing program code. *HwProcessor* is a generic computing resource that symbolizes a processor. It contains as attributes *nbCores*, which specifies the number of cores within the HWProcessor and *frequency* (not contained in the specification, but in the implementation)." ([233], page 670)

GaStep   is a part of a scenario and contains the attribute *msgSize*, which specifies the size of a message to be transmitted by the Step ([233], page 306). It expects a value of the type *NFP_DataSize* ([233], page 505).

The following modeling principles can be used to model performance-relevant domain knowledge. We make use of stereotypes from the MARTE profile to annotate the corresponding domains explicitly as resources. The MARTE profile provides specific stereotypes for each type of resource. To annotate the workload described by triggers of the system, we make use of the stereotype ≪gaWorkloadEvent≫. Its attributes represent the kind of arrival pattern and the number of concurrent users. MARTE defines several arrival patterns such as *periodic* describing periodic interarrival patterns with a deviation (jitter), *aperiodic* describing an unbounded pattern defined by a distribution function, *closed* describing a workload with a fix number of users defined by the attribute *population*, etc.

For data storage, MARTE provides the stereotype ≪storageResource≫. More specifically, the stereotype ≪hwMemory≫ can be used for representing a hardware memory (memory capacity and memory latency). Other possible stereotypes from MARTE are ≪resource≫, ≪deviceResource≫, ≪computingResource≫ and its more specific stereotype ≪hwProcessor≫, ≪communicationResource≫ and its more specific stereotype ≪hwMedia≫. For each resource, we have to capture its capacity and utilization. For example, a storage resource has a *capacity* and a *latency*. For a network resource, MARTE provides the stereotype ≪communicationMedia≫. More specifically, the stereotype ≪hwMedia≫ can be used for representing a network resource (network bandwidth and network latency). The stereotype ≪computingResource≫ and its more specific stereotype ≪hwProcessor≫ are used to model a processor (processor speed and number of processor cores). To model domain knowledge regarding message size and response time, we apply the stereotype ≪gaStep≫ from the GQAM package or ≪paStep≫ from the specialized package PAM. These stereotypes provide the attribute *respT* for annotating such kind of domain knowledge.

In the case that we are concerned with a hidden resource, the hidden resource has to be modeled explicitly as a causal domain. It additionally has to be annotated with a performance relevant stereotype from the MARTE profile representing the kind of resource it provides.

The column "Mapping to MARTE" in Table 6.1 shows how the elicited domain knowledge in step one can be mapped to the MARTE stereotypes and attributes. This mapping is used for modeling domain knowledge.

Application of Step 2 - Modeling Notation Selection/Extension (for Security)

We choose the dependability profile proposed by Hatebur and Heisel [114] for modeling security-related domain knowledge. It provides stereotypes that enable us to express security-relevant domain knowledge identified in the previous step. Specifically, we make use of the stereotype ≪attacker≫ and its attributes to express the attackers and their characteristics that we elicited in the previous step. Each identified attacker has to be modeled explicitly as a biddable domain. The stereotype ≪attacker≫ has to be applied to it. The stereotype ≪attacker≫ contains the attributes *preparationTime*, *attackTime*, *specialistExpertise*, *knowledge*, *opportunity*, and *equipment* to describe the characteristics of the attacker.

The column "Mapping to profile" in Table 6.2 shows how the elicited security-specific domain knowledge can be integrated in the requirement models using the stereotypes and attributes from the dependability profile.

Step 3 - Method Definition/Extension

This step (see Step 3 in Fig. 6.1) aims at defining a new method for requirements analysis such as the QuaRO and POPeRA methods, where quality-relevant domain knowledge has to be considered from the beginning of the analysis process, or extending an existing method with quality-relevant domain knowledge. In case of extending an existing method, the method description has to be considered as input. Additionally, we take the selected quality modeling notations into account for defining a new method or extending an existing one.

Application of Step 3 - Method Definition/Extension (for Performance)

We define the PoPeRA method for detecting potential performance problems and analyzing them. We first identify performance-critical resources that we elicited and modeled as performance-relevant domain knowledge. Next, we identify problem diagrams, where the inbound requests exceed the processing capacity of the performance-critical resource because of the high workload. The resources in such problem diagrams represent potential bottlenecks. The PoPeRa method is described in Section 7.4 (see page 220).

Application of Step 3 - Method Definition/Extension (for Security and Performance)

The QuaRO method uses the structure of problem diagrams to identify the domains, where quality requirements might interact. When the state of a domain can be changed by one or more sub-machines at the same time, their related quality requirements might be in conflict. Modeling domain knowledge regarding security and performance allows us detecting additional domains, where security and performance might conflict. Resources modeled as domain knowledge represent such conflicting domains. The reason is that the achievement of security requirements requires additional resources affecting the achievement of performance requirements negatively. Modeling the attacker and its characteristics determines the strength of the security mechanism to be selected, which affects the resource usage. Therefore, the resource has to be identified and modeled as domain knowledge. To detect interactions we set up tables, in which the columns contain information about quality-relevant domains from the problem diagrams, and the rows contain information about quality requirements under consideration. Whenever the state of a domain can be changed for the achievement of the corresponding quality requirement, we enter a cross in the respective cell. In a stepwise process, we eliminate requirements which are not in conflict. At the end, we obtain a set of security and performance requirements which might be in conflict. The QuaRO method is described in Section 7.3 (see page 210).

6.3 Structured Object-Process

In this section, we describe the object-process composed of the three steps eliciting, modeling, and using domain knowledge for selected software qualities and a specific software application. Once we have annotated the requirement models of a concrete software application with quality requirements, we use the output of the meta-process (see Section 6.2) for applying the object-process.

Figure 6.2 illustrates the steps of the object-process. In the following, we describe each step of the object-process followed by its application to the software qualities performance and security and the concrete software application smart grid.

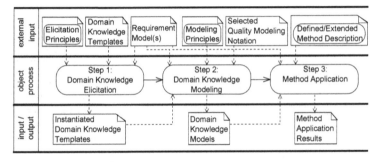

Fig. 6.2: Object-process for eliciting, modeling, and using domain knowledge

Step 1 - Domain Knowledge Elicitation

To elicit quality-relevant domain knowledge for a specific application, we instantiate domain knowledge templates (output of the first step of the meta-process). For the instantiation, we make use of the elicitation principles (also output of the first step of the meta-process) and existing requirement models. The elicitation principles provide guidance for the instantiation of the domain knowledge templates for the given requirement models. As output, we obtain instantiated domain knowledge templates that serve as input for Step 2.

Application of Step 1 - Domain Knowledge Elicitation (for Performance)

For each performance requirement, we instantiate the domain knowledge template for performance (see Table 6.1) according to the information contained in the existing documents for the smart grid application [155, 200]. We exemplify the instantiation of the template for the performance requirement *R24*, which complements the functional requirement *R4* (see Fig. 6.3).

According to the elicitation principles (Step 1 of the meta-process, see Section 6.2), we have to iterate over the causal domains in the requirement models to identify relevant resources. In Fig. 6.3, the causal domain *WAN* represents a performance-specific resource. The machine domain *SubmitMD* contains the hidden resource *CPU*, which is not modeled yet.

For eliciting domain knowledge for the performance requirement *R24*, we need additional information such as *number of concurrent users* that is missing in the Protection Profile [155] and Open Meter [200] documents. Hence, we looked for

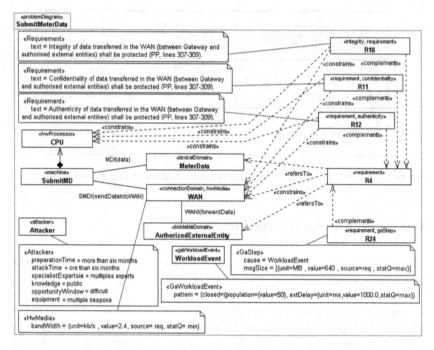

Fig. 6.3: Problem diagram for submitting meter data to external entities

the necessary domain knowledge in the existing literature [4] [87]. Based on this search, we assume the values given in column "Value" in Table 6.3.

For eliciting knowledge about the "number of concurrent users", we have to know the number of electricity providers to which the meter readings have to be sent. There are almost 50 electricity providers in Germany that receive meter readings from the gateway (see the attribute *population* in Fig. 6.3). As the number of concurrent users is not further specified in the documents under consideration, we take the worst case.

"Data size" of meter readings to be transmitted to the gateway can be between 1 KB and 16 MB [87]. It varies according to the period of time, in which meter data has to be sent to authorized external entities. It amounts to 1 KB by immediate sending of meter data after reading and 16 MB by sending meter data every two hours. This would be between 40 KB and 640 MB for 40 smart meters. We set

---

[4] http://www.strom-pfadfinder.de/stromanbieter/

640 MB as value for "data size" (see the attribute *msgSize* in Fig. 6.3). As it is not further specified in the documents under consideration, we take the worst case.

According to the documents from the Open Meter project, for the communication to the outside (*WAN* in Fig. 6.3) a Power Line Communication (PLC) can be used. We take 2.4 Kbps for the "network bandwidth", which is the minimum speed for a reliable communication (see the attribute *bandWidth* in Fig. 6.3). We could not find any information about the latency of PLC to set the value for the "network latency". In the smart meters the "ARM 9 processors" [5] with one core and a speed of 470 MHz can be used. The domain *WAN* is already modeled in the requirement models, whereas the domains *Memory* and *CPU* are not modeled yet (see "Yes" and "No" in Table 6.3). This remark helps us to know which resource has to be modeled explicitly in the next step.

Table 6.3: Instantiated domain knowledge template for performance and mapping to the MARTE profile

Quality: Performance, Requirement: R24				
Domain Knowledge Template				Mapping to MARTE
Domain Knowledge Description		Possible Values	Value	Property
For Problem Diagram *SubmitMeterData*				
Number of concurrent users		Natural	50	GaWorkloadEvent. pattern. population
Arrival pattern		ArrivalPattern	closed	GaWorkloadEvent. pattern
Data size		DataSize (bit, Byte, KB, MB, GB)	640 MB	GaStep. msgSize
For the domain *SubmitMD*				
Memory	-	capacity	DataSize (bit, Byte, KB, MB, GB)	-	HwMemory. memorySize
		latency	Duration (s, ms, min,hr, day)	-	HwMemory. timing
Network	-	bandwidth	DataRate (b/s, Kb/s, Mb/s)	-	HwMedia. bandWidth
		latency	Duration (s, ms, min,hr, day)	-	HwMedia. packetTime
CPU	No	speed	Frequency (Hz, kHz, MHz, GHz)	470 MHz	HwProcessor. frequency
		Number of cores	Natural	1	HwProcessor. nbCores
For the domain *WAN*				
Memory	-	capacity	DataSize (bit, Byte, KB, MB, GB)	-	HwMemory. memorySize
		latency	Duration (s, ms, min,hr, day)	-	HwMemory. timing
Network	Yes	bandwidth	DataRate (b/s, Kb/s, Mb/s)	2.4 Kb/s	HwMedia. bandWidth
		latency	Duration (s, ms, min,hr, day)	-	HwMedia. packetTime
CPU	-	speed	Frequency (Hz, kHz, MHz, GHz)	-	HwProcessor. frequency
		Number of cores	Natural	-	HwProcessor. nbCores

---

[5] http://www.arm.com/markets/embedded/smart-meter.php

Application of Step 1 - Domain Knowledge Elicitation (for Security)

For eliciting security-relevant domain knowledge, we have to instantiate the domain knowledge template for each identified attacker once. We identified one network attacker for three security requirements *R10*, *R11*, and *R12*. The reason is that the *MeterData* to be transmitted through the network *WAN* can be manipulated by a network attacker (see Fig. 6.3). There is no information in the Protection Profile [155] about the attacker that the system must be protected against. Therefore, we assume that the system must be protected against the strongest attacker. Hence, we select for each property the strongest one to obtain values for the column "Value" (see the stereotypes ≪Attacker≫ in Fig. 6.3). Table 6.4 shows the instantiated domain knowledge template for the confidentiality requirement *R11*.

Table 6.4: Instantiated domain knowledge template for security and mapping to the dependability profile

Quality: Security, Requirement: R10, R11, R12			
Domain Knowledge Template			Mapping to profile
Domain Knowledge Description	Possible Values	Value	Property (Dependability profile)
Preparation time	one day, one week, two weeks, ...	more than six months	Attacker.preparationTime
Attack time	one day, one week, two weeks, ...	more than six months	Attacker.attackTime
Specialist expertise	laymen, proficient, expert, ...	multiple experts	Attacker.specialistExpertise
Knowledge of the ToE	public, restricted, sensitive, critical	public	Attacker.knowledge
Window of opportunity	unnecessary/unlimited, easy, ...	difficult	Attacker.opportunity
IT hardware/software or other equipment	standard, specialized, bespoke, ...	multiple bespoke	Attacker.equipment

Step 2 - Domain Knowledge Modeling

In this step (Step 2 in Fig. 6.2), we model the domain knowledge that we elicited in the previous step. For modeling domain knowledge and integrating it in the existing requirement models, we make use of the instantiated domain knowledge templates. By means of modeling principles, we annotate the requirement models with elicited domain knowledge. We use the selected quality modeling notations for annotating requirement models. As a result, we obtain domain knowledge models.

Application of Step 2 - Domain Knowledge Modeling (for Performance)

We make use of the stereotypes ≪gaWorkloadEvent≫, ≪hwMedia≫, ≪hwProcessor≫, and ≪gaStep≫ for modeling performance-specific domain knowledge shown in Table 6.3. The modeled domain knowledge is shown in Fig. 6.3.

Application of Step 2 - Domain Knowledge Modeling (for Security)

In this step, we model the network attacker and its characteristics according to the instantiated domain knowledge template shown in Table 6.4, if it is not modeled yet. We model the network attacker explicitly as a biddable domain for the confidentiality requirement *R11*. Then, we apply the stereotype ≪attacker≫ from the dependability profile we selected in Step 2 of the meta-process. We assign the attributes of the stereotype ≪attacker≫ using the values contained in Table 6.4. The attacker and its properties are shown in Fig. 6.3.

Step 3 - Method Application

The third step is concerned with applying a specific requirements analysis method. Existing requirement models and the domain knowledge models obtained from the previous step are used as input. In addition, we make use of the method description we defined or extended in the third step of the meta-process.

Application of Step 3 - Method Application (for Performance)

By applying the PoPeRA method, we identified *CPU* as a performance-critical resource (see Fig. 6.3). Such resources are modeled as domain knowledge in the problem diagrams where the software might fail to be responsive if related performance requirements are not achieved. Then, using the identified performance-critical resource *CPU*, we analyzed whether the processing capacity of *CPU* suffices to satisfy the performance requirement *R24* and other requirements that have to be achieved using this resource with regard to the existing workload (modeled as domain knowledge). We identified *CPU* as potential bottleneck. After identifying potential bottlenecks that might lead to performance deficiency, we reduce the number of potential conflicts among quality requirements that we obtained as output of the QuaRO method. For each pair of conflicting requirements, we check whether we can mark it as irrelevant according to the identified bottleneck. For more information regarding the PoPeRA method, we refer to Chapter 7. The remaining conflicting requirements have to be resolved later on in Chapter 9.

Application of Step 3 - Method Application (for Security)

By applying the QuaRO method, we identified potential interactions among security and performance requirements. Performance requirement *R24* might be in conflict with security requirements *R10*, *R11*, and *R12* (see Fig. 6.3). The output of the QuaRO method is used as input for the PoPeRA method. For more information regarding QuaRO and PoPeRA, we refer to Chapter 7.

6.4 Related Work

There exist only few approaches dealing with capturing and representing knowledge needed for a successful consideration of software qualities in software development.

Zave and Jackson [252] identify four areas in which the foundation of the requirements engineering discipline seems to be weak. One of these areas is domain knowledge, which supports the refinement of requirements into implementable specifications. The authors explain the terms requirements, domain knowledge, specification, and the relationship between them. Among others, the authors emphasize the importance of capturing domain knowledge for the satisfaction of requirements. However, they do not provide a structured way or a specific notation to model domain knowledge, and they only consider functional requirements.

According to Probst [198], the goal of knowledge management (KM) is the improvement of processes and capabilities by utilizing knowledge resources such as skills, experience, routines, and technologies. The author proposes a KM model that structures the KM process as activities identification, acquisition, development, distribution, preservation, and use of knowledge, called building blocks of KM. The steps of our method can be easily mapped to these building blocks. Knowledge identification identifies which knowledge and expertise exists. This is a prerequisite for conducting our method. It leads to identify the need for capturing, modeling, and using domain knowledge. Knowledge acquisition is concerned with obtaining knowledge from involved stakeholders, domain experts, or using documents. This activity corresponds to the step *information needs elicitation* in our meta-process. Knowledge development aims at producing new knowledge. It can be related to the step *domain knowledge elicitation* in the object-process. The objective of knowledge distribution is to make the knowledge available and usable. This activity corresponds to the step *modeling notation selection* in the meta-process. Knowledge preservation avoids the loss of gained expertise by preserving the knowledge after it has been developed. This building block can be mapped to the step *domain knowledge modeling* which stores the captured domain knowledge in requirement models. Consequently, the knowledge has to be deployed in the production process (knowledge use). This is achieved in our method in the steps *method definition* and *method application*. The mapping of the steps of our method to the KM building blocks shows that we followed successfully the concepts involved in the field of KM.

There exist several approaches for the elicitation of domain knowledge in the field of domain engineering [139, 99]. These approaches focus on the development of reusable software and therefore also on the analysis of the application domain. During the domain analysis phase, domain knowledge is systematically collected and documented. In the field of domain engineering the term "domain" corresponds to the term "system" in Jackson's terminology. In our method, we show how to collect and document domain knowledge in a more fine-grained way which allows us analyzing software quality requirements.

Peng et al. [189] present a method for the analysis of non-functional requirements based on a feature model. This method elicits the domain knowledge before the analysis of non-functional requirements. In contrast, we suggest to elicit the required domain knowledge for a specific software quality. We think that our method leads to a more complete and targeted elicitation of domain knowledge.

A method to derive software architectures from quality requirements is presented in an earlier work [16]. To meet performance requirements, we collect assumptions and facts and them in a domain knowledge diagram for performance. However, in that work, the performance-related domain knowledge is not elicited and modeled systematically.

In the non-functional requirements (NFR) framework [71], knowledge about the particular type of NFR and the domain has to be acquired before using the NFR framework. This knowledge is captured to understand the characteristics of the application domain and to obtain NFR-related information to be used for identifying the important NFR softgoals. Examples of such domain knowledge are organizational priorities or providing terminologies for different types of NFRs. This kind of domain knowledge differs from ours, as it is used as initial information to identify the goals and requirements. The knowledge we capture and model is more fine-grained and is required in addition to the quality requirements. Moreover, we provide a systematic method for capturing and modeling domain knowledge, whereas the NFR framework does not provide any guidelines on how to acquire such domain knowledge.

6.5 Contributions

For an adequate consideration of quality requirements during requirements analysis, we have to identify and take into account the quality-specific domain knowledge for concrete software projects. By means of two different requirement analysis methods, namely PePeRA for performance analysis and QuaRO for requirement interaction detection, we have pointed out the need for eliciting, modeling, and using domain knowledge. To respond to the open research question of *how* to elicit and model domain knowledge correctly, in this chapter, we have proposed a structured method consisting of a meta-process and an object-process for eliciting, modeling, and using quality-specific domain knowledge. It can be summarized as follows:

- The meta-process is quality-dependent. It therefore has to be carried out once for each kind of quality requirement to be considered. To facilitate the reuse of captured and modeled domain knowledge, we provide individual templates and guidelines suitable for each kind of quality requirement. These templates and guidelines are reusable if the same quality shall be considered, but in a different notation or for a different analysis method. We instantiated the meta-process for two kinds of quality requirements, namely performance and security.
- The object-process has to be applied to a concrete software application for selected software qualities. We use the output of the meta-process as the input for the object-process. We showed how the elicited and modeled domain knowledge can be used for performance and security requirements in the two methods PoPeRA and QuaRo.
- Our approach is independent from any specific tool or notation. Hence, it can easily be integrated into existing requirement analysis methods. Our proposed method helps requirements engineers to develop processes for the consideration of quality requirements in a structured way and independently of the tools or notations they use. The results of this chapter are used in *Phase 4: Requirements Interaction Analysis* described in Chapter 7 and *Phase 6: Quality-specific Pattern Selection & Application* described in Chapter 9.

Chapter 7
Phase 4: Requirements Interaction Analysis

Abstract This chapter is divided into four parts for dealing with conflicting requirements. In the first part our structured method for detecting interactions among functional requirements is introduced. In the second part, we propose the *QuaRO* method to identify interaction candidates among quality requirements based on pairwise comparisons. As output, we obtain a set of quality requirements that are potentially interacting. The third part presents the *PoPeRA* method conducting a performance analysis based on *performance domain knowledge* and *security domain knowledge* to identify potential bottlenecks. Using identified bottlenecks, we further reduce the number of potential quality requirement interactions identified by the *QuaRO* method. The fourth part proposes a structured method for resolving the remaining interactions among quality requirements from the previous part by generating alternatives for interacting requirements.

7.1 Introduction

Nowadays, for almost every software system, various stakeholders with diverse interests exist. These interests give rise to different sets of requirements. The combination of these sets may lead to unwanted *interactions* among the requirements. Interactions may not only stem from requirements of different stakeholders, but also from different quality requirements, which are desired by the stakeholders. Quality requirements tend to interfere, conflict, or contradict with each other. Achieving a particular type of quality requirements might hurt the achievement of other types of quality requirements [91, 72]. Therefore, conflicting quality requirements cannot be fulfilled at the same time. For example, enabling a secure communication might conflict with performance requirements. The identification of interactions and inconsistencies in the requirements analysis is essential to avoid costly modifications later on in the software development life cycle and to improve the overall software quality. Nevertheless, such *inconsistencies* among functional as well as quality requirements cannot be detected easily.

In general, the deviation between the intended behavior and structure as formulated by single requirements of a stakeholder and the overall behavior and structure of the resulting system- or software-to-be is called requirement inconsistencies [100, 162]. Such inconsistencies can stem from different sources. The *first source* is the different understanding of terms and different views on the system-to-be of different stakeholders. To this class of inconsistencies also adds missing or misleading information [100, 224]. A *second source* are inconsistencies, which stem from the transformation between different kinds of representations and models [100]. *Another important source* are interactions between requirements, which lead to an unexpected behavior. For functional requirements this source is already known as feature interaction for a long time, e.g. in the domain of telecommunication [63, 64, 162]. For interactions, one can distinguish between unwanted and desirable interactions. The strongest types of interactions are conflicts among requirements, where requirements deny each other, and dependent requirements, where one requirement can be only fulfilled when another requirement is also fulfilled. Between these extremes, there are different shades of negative or positive influences [203, 162]. In this chapter, we treat interactions among functional as well as quality requirements. For functional requirements, we deal with inconsistencies in terms of the third source, namely those interactions which are conflicts, but our method also allows to find other kinds of interactions. For quality requirements, we are concerned with negative influences of requirements on each other.

This chapter represents Phase 4 of our QuaDRA framework. It includes four parts for dealing with conflicting requirements. In the first part, we propose a structured method based on problem frames to identify interactions among functional requirements. In the problem frames approach, functional requirements are described and modeled as problem diagrams. The requirements look like separate models without dependency among each other. But the domains represent the dependencies between separate requirements. Shared domains provide points in the requirement models where requirements might interact. We make use of this information contained in the model to detect interactions among functional requirements. We first start with a full set of requirements represented by subproblems. Then, we incrementally narrow down the set of requirements which might interact in order to obtain a small set of potentially conflicting requirements that can be treated manually. This part is based on our work presented in [13]. The basic idea of our method is developed by the author of this book. We then refined the method jointly with our colleagues Stephan Faßbender and Rene Meis. In [13], we proposed a formalization of our method that can be used as a basis for tool support. The formalization, which is not included in this chapter, has been done by Rene Meis.

In the second part of this chapter, we propose the *QuaRO* method to identify interactions among quality requirements based on pairwise comparisons. The process of detecting candidates of interactions among quality requirements is similar to the process of detecting functional requirement interactions in a way that we analyze shared domains among quality requirements. The general principle of our method is the use of the structure of problem diagrams to identify shared domains where quality requirements might interact. These domains represent *resources* used by conflicting requirements at the same time. Such domains are trade-off points. Applying the *QuaRO* method, we obtain a set of quality requirement pairs which are potentially conflicting. Detecting interactions among quality requirements is one part of our book chapter published in [6]. We are the main author of this part. We had intensive and valuable discussions with Christine Choppy, Stephan Faßbender, and Maritta Heisel on this topic.

In the third part of this chapter, we propose the *PoPeRA* method for analyzing performance problems. The general idea of *PoPeRA* is based on identifying the *resources* that might be used as shared resources between various subproblems, the *workload*, and the *security issues* related to the subproblem. All this information allows us to estimate whether the modeled *performance requirements* can be achieved and, if not, where the potential performance bottlenecks are located. The identified bottlenecks aid in further reducing the set of potentially conflicting quality requirements obtained from the *QuaRO* method. This part is based on our work presented in [22], of which we are the main author.

The straightforward and simple way to resolve the remaining conflicts would be to exclude one of the conflicting requirements from the final set of requirements to be fulfilled for the software-to-be. A more suitable way is making trade-offs among conflicting quality requirements. This way, they can only be satisfied to a certain level [71]. For making trade-offs, we provide alternatives for one or both conflicting requirements which are weaker than the original one. This way, both requirements (alternatives) can be satisficed at the same time. For example, for security requirements there can be certain kinds of attackers we want to be secured against. However, we might not be able to address a strong attacker with certain properties such as the given time and resource limits. Hence, we generate an alternative which is weaker than the original one and might not be conflicting any more. Therefore, in the fourth part of this chapter, we propose a method to generate alternatives for remaining problematic quality requirements. Based on the type of requirement we want to generate alternatives for, there are different properties, which are candidates to be relaxed. Our method identifies those properties and proposes solutions for relaxing them. This part as one part of our book chapter is published in [6]. Stephan Faßbender is the main author of the original method. We however, modified the proposed method to fit in the QuaDRA framework.

The rest of the chapter is organized as follows: Our method to detect interacting functional requirements is described in Section 7.2 while detecting interactions among quality requirements using the *QuaRO* method is proposed in Section 7.3. We introduce our *PoPeRA* method for performance analysis in Section 7.4 and the method for generating requirement alternatives in Section 7.5. Section 7.6 presents related work and Section 7.7 summarizes the contribution of this chapter.

7.2 Functional Requirements Interaction Detection

In this section, we first introduce a sunblind control system as an example in Section 7.2.1. Then, we describe our problem-based functional interaction detection method and its application to the sunblind example in Section 7.2.2.

We applied our method to the smart grid case study. As we did not find any requirement interactions for the use case *Meter Reading for Billing* of the smart grid case study, we chose the sunblind example for illustrating the applicability of our method. We report on the application of our method to the smart grid case study later on in Section 7.2.3.

7.2.1 Sunblind Example

We demonstrate our approach using a sunblind control system. A sunblind is made up of metallic fins, which are attached to the outer side of the window. Additionally, we have a sun sensor, which measures the sun intensity, a wind sensor, which measures the wind speed, and a display, which is suitable to display the current sun intensity and wind speed.

The sunblind is sensitive to sun and wind. A machine shall be built that lowers the sunblind on sunshine and pulls it up on heavy wind. For individual settings it shall be possible to control the sunblind manually, too. The commands for the manual control shall be treated with a higher priority than those ones controlled by the machine. The following requirements are given:

(R1) If there is sunshine for more than one minute, the sun blind will be lowered.
(R2) If there is no sunshine for more than 5 minutes, the sunblind will be pulled up.

(R3) If there is heavy wind for more than 10 seconds, the sunblind will be pulled up, to avoid destruction of the sunblind.

(R4) If the user issues an open/close/stop command, the sunblind will be pulled up/-lowered/stopped.

(R5) If the user interacts with the sunblind, then sunshine and no sunshine are ignored within the next 4 hours.

(R6) If the user activates the holiday mode, the sun blind is pulled up and turned off.

(R7) If the user deactivates the holiday mode, then the sunblind is turned on.

(R8) Sunshine intensity and wind speed shall be displayed on the weather display.

We modeled the requirements as problem diagrams, which are used as input for our method. The problem diagrams for the requirements R1-R8 are shown in Figures 7.1-7.8.

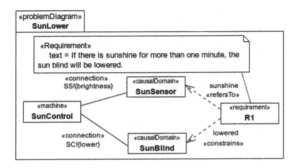

Fig. 7.1: Problem diagram for the requirement R1

To build the overall machine, we have to determine which requirements have to be established in parallel or in sequence. For this purpose, we use the life-cycle expressions introduced in Section 2.4 (see page 42). Our method assumes that this life-cycle is already created. The sunblind system has the following life-cycle:

$$LC = \big(R7;\ (R1 \parallel R2 \parallel R3 \parallel (R4;\ R5) \parallel R8)^* \parallel [R6]\big)^*$$

At first, the machine of requirement R7 is executed in LC. That means the user has to deactivate the holiday mode as first action. Then, the machines for the requirements R1, R2, R3, R8, and the sequential composition of R4 and R5 are executed concurrently an arbitrary number of times. The parallel execution can then be stopped by the machine of requirement R6, which is triggered by the activation of the holiday mode issued by the user. The whole life-cycle can be

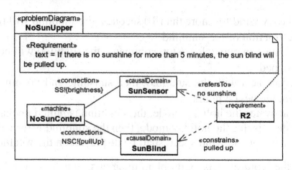

Fig. 7.2: Problem diagram for the requirement R2

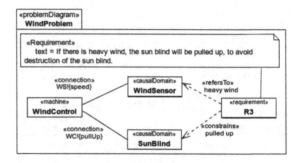

Fig. 7.3: Problem diagram for the requirement R3

repeated an arbitrary number of times. The requirements R4 and R5 are executed sequentially, because after the user issued a command, the system to be built shall preserve the user's configuration of the sunblind for 4 hours.

Throughout this part we refer to this example to describe the proposed method.

7.2.2 Method for Functional Requirements Interaction Detection

Figure 7.9 shows the basic idea of our method consisting of three phases we propose to detect functional requirement interactions.

The method takes the full set of requirements modeled as problem diagrams as input. Based on the information contained in the problem diagrams, Phase 1

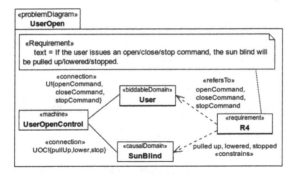

Fig. 7.4: Problem diagram for the requirement R4

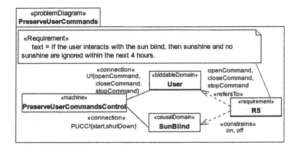

Fig. 7.5: Problem diagram for the requirement R5

(*structure-based pruning*) takes place and removes all requirements for which the structure of problem diagrams already implies that they will not interact. The result is a first set of interaction candidates. In the second phase (*life cycle-based pruning*), those candidates can be further reduced using the information of the life-cycle which contains the information about the sequence of requirements. The life-cycle has to be known beforehand and is an external input to our method. In the third phase (*precondition-based pruning*), those candidates are analyzed further. In this last phase, we identify whether a requirement interaction takes place. In order to keep the effort of this phase manageable, we perform the Phases 1 and 2, which reduce the number of potentially interacting requirements. The overall result is a list of found interactions.

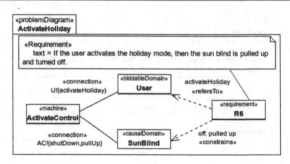

Fig. 7.6: Problem diagram for the requirement R6

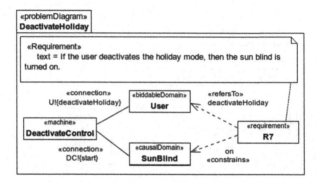

Fig. 7.7: Problem diagram for the requirement R7

Phase 1 - Structure-Based Pruning

In Phase 1, we make use of the structure of the problem diagrams. The steps for
selecting the requirements, which are candidates of a requirements interaction, are
as follows:

Step 1 - Initial Setup
First, we identify for each requirement which domains are referred to or constrained, and which phenomena are controlled or observed by this domain. As
a result, we obtain a table, where a column contains information about a specific
domain and where a row contains the information about a requirement. A cell contains the phenomena controlled or observed by the domain - given by the column

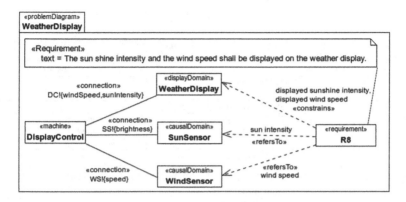

Fig. 7.8: Problem diagram for the requirement R8

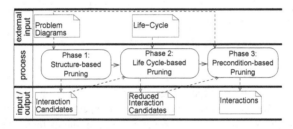

Fig. 7.9: Method for detecting candidates for interactions among functional requirements

- in the problem diagram for a requirement - given by the row. If the domain is constrained in the problem diagram, then it is written in bold font, else in italic font. The result for our example is given in Table 7.1.

Step 2 - Marking Irrelevant Domains
Second, we check for each column, and therefore for each domain, if the domain is constrained at least once and has more than one entry in the corresponding cells (phenomena). If this is not the case, the column (domain) and the corresponding cells (phenomena) are marked as irrelevant. The reason is that interactions only occur on domains which are constrained and target of more than one phenomenon.

From Table 7.1, we can see that no requirements interactions can occur on the *SunSensor*, *WindSensor*, and *User*, because these domains are only referred to by

Table 7.1: Initial requirements interaction table

Requirement / Domain	SunSensor (CausalDomain)	SunBlind (CausalDomain)	WindSensor (CausalDomain)	User (BiddableDomain)	WeatherDisplay (DisplayDomain)
R1	*S-S!*{*brightness*}	**SC!**{**lower**}			
R3		**WC!**{**pullUp**}	*WS!*{*speed*}		
R4		**UOC!**{**pullUp, lower, stop**}		*U!*{*openCommand , closeCommand , stopCommand*}	
R2	*S-S!*{*brightness*}	**NSC!**{**pullUp**}			
R5		**PUCC!**{**start, shutDown**}		*U!*{*openCommand , closeCommand*}	
R6		**AC!**{**shutDown, lower**}		*U!*{*activate-Holiday*}	
R7		**DC!**{**start**}		*U!*{*deactivate-Holiday*}	
R8	*S-S!*{*brightness*}		*WS!*{*speed*}		**DC!**{**wind-Speed, sun-Intensity**}

the requirements in the problem diagrams. Since there is only one requirement constraining the *WeatherDisplay*, we also do not expect any requirements interactions on it. On the *SunBlind* domain we expect requirements interactions from the table, because every requirement except R8 constrains this domain. So, after the second step of Phase 1 we only focus on interactions on the domain *SunBlind*. All other domains are marked as irrelevant (see Table 7.2).

Step 3 - Marking Relevant Phenomena
Third, we have to check for each phenomenon of a column (domain) which is not marked as irrelevant if it is interacting with a combination of phenomena which refer to or constrain the same domain. For each combination, we have to decide whether we can reject the assumption that there is an interaction. If we cannot reject this assumption for sure, we mark all phenomena of the combination as relevant.

For our example, the phenomena of the requirements R4 and R5 are both not interacting with any combination of the other requirements. That is, because the user commands to lower, stop, and pull up the sunblind shall have a higher priority than the other requirements. For all other phenomena, we find combinations of phenomena, such that there is possibly an interaction, and these phenomena are

Table 7.2: Requirements interaction table after Step 2 of Phase 1

Requirement / Domain	~~SunSensor (CausalDomain)~~	SunBlind (CausalDomain)	~~WindSensor (CausalDomain)~~	~~User (BiddableDomain)~~	~~WeatherDisplay (DisplayDomain)~~
R1	~~S- S!{brightness}~~	SC!{lower}			
R3		WC!{pullUp}	~~WS!{speed}~~		
R4		UOC!{pullUp, lower, stop}		~~U!{openCommand, closeCommand, stopCommand}~~	
R2	~~S- S!{brightness}~~	NSC!{pullUp}			
R5		PUCC!{start, shutDown}		~~U!{openCommand, closeCommand}~~	
R6		AC!{shutDown, lower}		~~U!{activateHoliday}~~	
R7		DC!{start}		~~U!{deactivateHoliday}~~	
R8	~~S- S!{brightness}~~		~~WS!{speed}~~		~~DC!{windSpeed, sunIntensity}~~

~~irrelevant~~ <u>relevant</u>

marked as relevant (see Table 7.3).

Step 4 - Pruning

Last, we remove all columns (domains) where all corresponding cells (phenomena) are not marked as relevant. And we remove all rows (requirements) where all corresponding cells (phenomena) left are not marked as relevant.

In our example, we can reduce the requirements interaction table as follows. In Step 2, we saw that the domain *SunBlind* is the only domain relevant for interactions. Hence, the other columns (domains) can be removed. In Step 3, we obtained that R4 and R5 are both not relevant. And also the requirement R8 is not relevant, because it does not operate on the sunblind. Hence, the rows R4, R5, and R8 can be removed from the table (see Table 7.4).

Phase 2 - Life Cycle-Based Pruning

Using the life-cycle, we can further reduce the set of requirements, which are candidates of requirements interaction. The life-cycle contains information about the order of interplays described by the requirements. Besides the life-cycle, the re-

Table 7.3: Requirements interaction table after Step 3 of Phase 1

Requirement / Domain	~~SunSensor (CausalDomain)~~	SunBlind (CausalDomain)	~~WindSensor (CausalDomain)~~	~~User (BiddableDomain)~~	~~Weather rDisplay (DisplayDomain)~~
R1	~~S-S!{brightness}~~	SC!{lower}			
R3		WC!{pullUp}	~~WS!{speed}~~		
R4		~~UOC!{pullUp, lower, stop}~~		~~U!{openCommand, closeCommand, stopCommand}~~	
R2	~~S-S!{brightness}~~	NSC!{pullUp}			
R5		~~PUCC!{start, shutDown}~~		~~U!{openCommand, closeCommand}~~	
R6		AC!{shutDown, lower}		~~U!{activate-Holiday}~~	
R7		DC!{start}		~~U!{deactivate-Holiday}~~	
R8	~~S-S!{brightness}~~		~~WS!{speed}~~		~~DC!{wind-Speed, sun-Intensity}~~

~~irrelevant~~ <u>relevant</u>

Table 7.4: Requirements interaction table after Step 4 of Phase 1

Requirement / Domain	SunBlind(CausalDomain)
R1	SC!{lower}
R3	WC!{pullUp}
R2	NSC!{pullUp}
R6	AC!{shutDown, lower}
R7	DC!{start}

~~irrelevant~~ <u>relevant</u>

duced table, which is the output of Phase 1 (see Table 7.4), serves as input for this phase.

In the sunblind example, we have the following life-cycle:

$$LC = \big(R7; \, (R1 \parallel R2 \parallel R3 \parallel (R4; \, R5) \parallel R8)^{*} \parallel [R6]\big)^{*}$$

At first, the machine of requirement R7 is executed in LC. That means the user has to deactivate the holiday mode as first action. Then, the machines for the requirements R1, R2, R3, R8, and the sequential composition of R4 and R5 are executed concurrently an arbitrary number of times. The parallel execution can then be stopped by the machine of requirement R6, which is triggered by the activation of the holiday mode issued by the user. The whole life-cycle can be repeated an arbitrary number of times. The requirements R4 and R5 are executed sequentially, because after the user issued a command, the system to be built shall preserve the user's configuration of the sunblind for 4 hours.

Step 1 - Reducing Life-Cycle

First, we reduce the life-cycle by removing all requirements which are not part of the reduced table. Then, we obtain a life-cycle which can be handled more easily when evaluating if two requirements happen concurrently or in sequence. And we remove the relevance marker from the cells (phenomena).

The life-cycle LC from the example is reduced by removing all requirements which are not part of the reduced table. By doing this, we obtain the following life-cycle.

$$LC' = \big(R7; \, (R1 \, || \, R2 \, || \, R3)^* \, || \, [R6]\big)^*$$

Step 2 - Marking Relevant Phenomena

Second, we consider for each phenomenon all combinations of phenomena which refer to or constrain the same domain for each column (domain) in the reduced table. For each combination, we check the life-cycle for unwanted sequences of the phenomena at hand. If such a sequence can happen, we mark all phenomena of the combination as relevant.

For our example, we see from the life-cycle that the requirements R7 and R6 are not interacting with the other requirements. This is the case, because they are treated with a higher priority. Furthermore, before the parallel composition of the interplay described by other requirements is started, the sunblind is activated. And if the sunblind is deactivated, it is pulled up, to avoid destruction in the case of heavy wind. The remaining requirements R1, R2, and R3 are executed concurrently in arbitrary sequences. Hence, these phenomena are marked as relevant (see Table 7.5).

Table 7.5: Requirements interaction table after Step 2 of Phase 2

Requirement / Domain	SunBlind(CausalDomain)
R1	**SC!{lower}**
R3	**WC!{pullUp}**
R2	**NSC!{pullUp}**
R6	~~AC!{shutDown, lower}~~
R7	~~DC!{start}~~

~~irrelevant~~ relevant

Step 3 - Pruning
Last, we remove all columns (domains), where all corresponding cells (phenomena) are not marked as relevant. And we remove all rows (requirements), where all corresponding cells (phenomena) left are not marked as relevant.

For our example, we remove the rows R7 and R6 (see Table 7.6).

Table 7.6: Requirements interaction table after Step 3 of Phase 2

Requirement / Domain	SunBlind(CausalDomain)
R1	SC!{lower}
R3	WC!{pullUp}
R2	NSC!{pullUp}

~~irrelevant~~ relevant

Phase 3 - Precondition-based Pruning

We have now a reduced set of possibly interacting requirements. As described in Chapter 6, reasoning about the requirements involves reasoning about the environment and the assumptions made about it (domain knowledge) [68]. According to this, requirements have to be expressed in terms of the environment. Therefore, they are normally written according to the general textual pattern: *"If the environment is like this, then it shall be changed like that."* Hence, a requirement has a pre- and a postcondition, both talking about phenomena of the environment [123]. For example, the requirement R1 states *"If there is sunshine for more than one minute, the sunblind will be lowered."*

For each of the requirement pairs, we investigate whether there is a system state that fulfills the preconditions of both requirements. To determine whether a requirement pair is satisfiable, for each requirement pair we have to check whether their preconditions can occur at the same time. If this is the case, for those requirement pairs we analyze the postconditions for a possible interaction.

For our example, the following requirements are left:

(R1) If there is sunshine for more than one minute, the sunblind will be lowered.

(R2) If there is no sunshine for more than 5 minutes, the sunblind will be pulled up.

(R3) If there is heavy wind for more than 10 seconds, the sunblind will be pulled up, to avoid destruction of the sunblind.

Possible interactions are between the requirement pairs R1 and R2, R1 and R3, and R2 and R3. As we see, the preconditions of the requirements R1 and R2 cannot occur at the same time. Hence, no interaction between the requirements R1 and R2 can happen. For the requirement pair R1 and R3, the preconditions can occur at the same time. We, therefore, have to check the postconditions for a possible interaction. We identify the postconditions as interacting as the sunblind cannot *"be lowered"* and *"be pulled up"* at the same time. Regarding the requirement pair R2 and R3, the preconditions can occur at the same time. Nevertheless, no interaction can take place since the postconditions cannot interact with each other (*"the sunblind will be pulled up"*).

So, we identified only one interaction among the requirements R1 and R3. To cope with this interaction appropriate measures such as prioritization have to be chosen.

In the next section, we report on the application of our method to the smart grid case study.

7.2.3 Application to the Case Study Smart Grid

For the smart grid case study, we refined the 13 minimum uses cases (see Section 2.6 on page 43) to 27 requirements and modeled them as problem diagrams. The problem diagrams modeling the 27 requirements given by the 13 minimum use cases served as an input to Phase 1, Step 1, resulting in 351 possible requirements interactions. The initial requirements interaction table consisted of 19 domains and 27 requirements. A number of 64 phenomena were documented as relevant, because the requirements mentioned them. In the second step, the number of domains on which an interaction could happen was reduced to 4, and 7 requirements were removed from the set of candidates which could cause an interaction. At this point, the number of possible interactions was already reduced by more than fifty percent to 171. The involved number of possibly involved phenomena was cut down to 19. Three of the phenomena were identified as possibly interacting phenomena. As a result, only 1 domain and 5 requirements remained after Step 3. Thus, at the end of Phase 1, we already reduced the number of possible interactions to 10, which makes a reduction by more than 95 percent. Since all of the requirements left may have to be fulfilled in parallel, no further reduction was possible in Phase 2. While checking the preconditions in Phase 3, one more requirement could be rejected to be a candidate for an interaction. In the end, 4 requirements, sources for 6 possible interactions, had to be analyzed in depth.

The analysis revealed that the requirements left caused 2 interactions. One of the original use cases described a process where the energy provider is able to disconnect a household from the grid by ordering the gateway to cut off the electricity supply. One reason could be unpaid bills. On the other hand, the provider can order the gateway to reconnect the household. A second use case describes that the customer is able to define a power consumption threshold. If the threshold is reached by the actual power consumption, the household is also cut off the grid by the gateway. But for this case, the consumer is allowed to override the cut-off manually, reconnecting the household. The two use cases, and therefore also the requirements, did not refer to each other, allowing the customer to override a cut-off ordered by the provider. Or the other way round, the provider could reconnect a household which was taken off the grid on demand of the customer. Hence, we found 2 real interactions.

To sum up, the effort to investigate requirements for interactions in depth was reduced by more than 95 percent. For the interactions left over to the in-depth analysis, the precision was 33 percent (2 real interactions / 6 possible interactions), which is acceptable considering the overall reduction. For calculating the recall, we made a full in depth analysis of all requirements and found no additional interactions which makes a perfect recall of 100 percent. In general, when looking for interactions, it is favorable to have a high recall rather than having a high precision. The reason is that missing one real interaction makes any effort reduction worthless.

For the smart grid case study, especially the effort spent for Phase 1 payed off. Phases 2 and 3 resulted only in a minor reduction of possible interactions. But overall, the effort of executing our method is reasonable with regard to the reduction.

Note that throughout this book, for the case study smart grid we consider the use case *Meter Reading for Billing* (see Section 2.6 on page 43). As we did not find any requirement interactions for the requirements involved in this use case by applying our method, we applied the method to the sunblind example to illustrate its applicability by detecting interactions among functional requirements.

7.3 Method for Quality Requirements Interaction Detection

In this section, we propose the *QuaRO* method to detect candidates for negative interactions between quality requirements based on pairwise comparison of requirements. Figure 7.10 illustrates the phases of our method, the inputs, and the outputs of each phase.

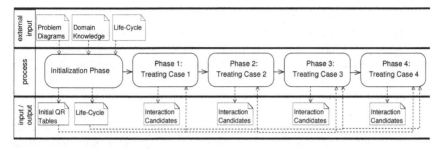

Fig. 7.10: Overview of the *QuaRO* method to detect candidates for quality requirement interactions

To restrict the number of comparisons, we perform an initialization phase, in which we make use of the general relationships among types of quality requirements. We investigate which two types of quality requirements may be in conflict in general. In doing so, we consider different types of quality requirements. The preparation phase results in a table containing all types of quality requirements to be considered. We compare each two types of quality requirements regarding potential conflicts. If there might be conflicts between two quality requirements, we enter a cross in the cell where the two quality requirements cross, otherwise a minus. For example, no interactions between a confidentiality requirement and an integrity requirement are expected. Therefore, the cell crossing these two requirement types in the table contains a minus. In contrast, a confidentiality requirement might be in conflict with a performance requirement. Therefore, the corresponding cell contains a cross. Table 7.7 shows possible interactions among security (confidentiality, integrity, authenticity)[1] and performance requirements in general.

Table 7.7: Possible interactions among types of quality requirements in general

	Confidentiality	Integrity	Authenticity	Performance
Confidentiality	-	-	x	x
Integrity	-	-	-	x
Authenticity	x	-	-	x
Performance	x	x	x	x

---

[1] Table 7.7 illustrates only those quality requirements that are considered in the specification of the smart grid case study

Interactions among quality requirements of different types can occur either between quality requirements related to the same functional requirement or among those related to different functional requirements. We classify quality requirements and their relations to the functional requirements into four cases, see Table 7.8. Case one arises when two quality requirements of the same type are considered that are related to the same functional requirement. The second case is concerned with considering two quality requirements of different types that are related to the same functional requirement. Case three occurs when two quality requirements which are of the same type, but related to different functional requirements, must be achieved in parallel. In the fourth case, two quality requirements which are of different types and related to different functional requirements must be achieved in parallel. We treat each case in a separate phase in the *QuaRO* method. The classification is presented in Table 7.8. The abbreviations FR and QR stand for "Functional Requirement" and "Quality Requirement", respectively.

Table 7.8: Classification table

Case	FR, type of QR	Condition	Row in QR table	QuaRO phase
Case 1	same FR, same type of QR	-	rows related to same FR in same QR table	Phase 1
Case 2	same FR, different types of QR	-	rows related to same FR in different QR tables	Phase 2
Case 3	different FR, same type of QR	in parallel	rows related to different FR in same QR table	Phase 3
Case 4	different FR, different types of QR	in parallel	rows related to different FR in different QR tables	Phase 4

The general principle of the *QuaRO* method for detecting interactions among requirements is using the structure of problem diagrams to identify the domains where quality requirements might interact. Such domains are trade-off points. When the state of a domain can be changed by one or more sub-machines at the same time, their related quality requirements might be in conflict. We express this situation in the problem diagrams by dependencies that constrain such domains. Therefore, to detect interactions we set up tables where the columns contain information about quality-relevant domains (possible trade-off points) from the problem diagrams, and the rows contain information about quality requirements under consideration. We enter crosses in the cells, whenever the state of a domain can be changed for the achievement of the corresponding quality requirement. In the following, we describe the method and its application to the smart grid case study in more detail.

Note that according to the design decisions that we made in Phase 2 of our framework (see *Architectural Pattern Selection* in Chapter 5), we observed that some quality requirements are already fulfilled. Therefore, there is no need for further consideration of these requirements (see Section 4.3 on page 124 for reasoning). These quality requirements include security requirements *R6*, *R7*, *R8*, *R9*, and *R16* and performance requirements *R20* and *R21*. We consider these requirements as fulfilled and, therefore, do not consider them by the application of the *QuaRO* method to the smart grid case study.

Initialization Phase - Initial Setup

In this phase, we make use of the structure of the problem diagrams and domain knowledge regarding quality requirements (see input in Fig. 7.10) to set up the *initial QR tables*. These tables are used for the identification of interactions among quality requirements in later phases. Furthermore, we set up life-cycle expressions that represent the order in which the requirements must be achieved.

Step 1 - Set up Initial Tables

For each type of quality requirement, we identify which domains are constrained by it. This results in *initial QR tables*, where the columns contain information about quality-relevant domains from the problem diagrams, and the rows contain information about quality requirements under consideration. We enter a cross in each cell when a domain – given by the column – is relevant for the quality requirement under consideration – given by the row. For each type of quality requirement, we set up such a table. The second column in each table names the functional requirement related to the quality requirement given in the first column.

When we deal with performance, we need domain knowledge that is necessary to achieve performance requirements. In Chapter 6, we treated eliciting, modeling, and using of quality-specific domain knowledge such as performance-specific and security-specific domain knowledge. We described that performance is concerned with the *workload* of the system and the available *resources* to process the workload. We showed how to model the *workload* and the *resources* using the MARTE profile (see Section 6.2 on page 177 and Section 6.3 on page 186).

Having elicited and modeled the performance-specific domain knowledge, one is now able to set up the initial performance table. In this table, similarly to other initial QR tables, columns contain information about quality-relevant domains from problem diagrams (*resources* in case of performance requirements), and rows contain information about quality requirements under consideration. Table 7.9 presents the initial performance table.

Table 7.9: Initial Performance Table

QR	Related FR	LMN	WAN	HAN	SmartMeter	CPU
R18	R1	x			x	x
R19	R1	x			x	x
R22	R2R3					x
R23	R2R3					x
R24	R4		x			x
R25	R5			x		x

In Chapter 6 in Section 6.2 (see page 177), we argued that resources have to be modeled for security requirements as well. The reason is that the achievement of security requirements requires additional resources that affect the achievement of performance requirements negatively. For example, we have to consider *CPU* as a domain whenever we want to detect interactions among performance and security requirements. The reason is that CPU time is consumed for the achievement of security requirements. Eliciting and modeling resources allows us to set up initial security tables. Initial tables for integrity, authenticity, and confidentiality for our example are given in Table 7.10, Table 7.11, and Table 7.12.

Table 7.10: Initial Integrity Table

QR	Related FR	LMN	WAN	HAN	CPU
R10	R4		x		x
R13	R5			x	x

Table 7.11: Initial Authenticity Table

QR	Related FR	LMN	WAN	HAN	CPU
R12	R4		x		x
R15	R5			x	x

Table 7.12: Initial Confidentiality Table

QR	Related FR	LMN	MeterData	TemporaryStorage	WAN	HAN	CPU
R11	R4				x		x
R14	R5					x	x

Step 2 - Set up Life-cycle

In this step, we set up the life-cycle to describe the relations between the functional requirements of the corresponding subproblems to be achieved to solve the overall problem. The following expression represents the life-cycle for our example:

$$LC = ((R1;\ R2R3);\ (R4\ ||\ R5))^*$$

At first, the machine of requirement *R1* is executed in LC. That means the meter data are obtained from the smart meter and stored temporarily. Then, the machine for the requirement *R2R3* is executed which processes the temporary stored meter data and stores them persistently. The machines of the requirements *R4* and *R5* are executed concurrently after the execution of the machines for *R1* and *R2R3*. The whole life-cycle can be repeated an arbitrary number of times.

Phase 1 - Treating Case 1

In this phase, we compare the rows in each table to identify potential conflicts among quality requirements concerning the first case of Table 7.8. The aim is to detect conflicts among the same type of quality requirements that are related to the same functional requirement. To deal with this case of requirements conflicts, we consider each table separately.

Step 1 - Eliminating Irrelevant Tables

To eliminate irrelevant tables, we make use of the *initial interaction table* (Table 7.7) we set up before. According to this table, interactions among quality requirements of the same type can only happen when considering two performance requirements. Therefore, we mark Table 7.10, Table 7.11, and Table 7.12 as irrelevant for requirements interaction and continue only with Table 7.9 for the treatment of the first case.

Step 2 - Eliminating Irrelevant Rows

In each table under consideration, we perform a pairwise comparison between quality requirements related to the same functional requirement. We check if such quality requirements constrain the same domains (contain crosses in the same columns). We consider the rows related to such quality requirements as relevant and remove the irrelevant rows from Table 7.9. Doing so, we obtain Table 7.13. We also removed the columns *WAN* and *HAN*, because they did not contain any entry after removing irrelevant rows.

Table 7.13: Phase 1, Step 2: reduced performance table

QR	Related FR	LMN	SmartMeter	CPU
R18	R1	x	x	x
R19	R1	x	x	x
R22	R2R3			x
R23	R2R3			x

Step 3 - Detecting Interaction Candidates

Considering the new performance table from the previous step, we look at each two rows sharing the same functional requirement. We determine that the requirements *R18* and *R19* share the same domains *LMN*, *SmartMeter*, and *CPU*. Further, the requirements *R22* and *R23* share the same domain *CPU*. We identify these requirements as candidates for requirement interactions. Table 7.15 summarizes all detected interaction candidates.

Phase 2 - Treating Case 2

This phase is concerned with the second case of Table 7.8, dealing with possible conflicts among different types of quality requirements related to the same functional requirement. Hence, we compare quality requirements related to the same functional requirement in each two tables to identify potential conflicts.

Step 1 - Eliminating Irrelevant Tables

To eliminate irrelevant tables, we make use of the *initial interaction table* (Table 7.7) to determine which two tables should be compared with each other. For our example, we can reduce the number of table comparisons to four: Table 7.10 and Table 7.9, Table 7.12 and Table 7.11, Table 7.12 and Table 7.9, Table 7.11 and Table 7.9.

Note that in each phase we have to consider the initial QR tables such as Table 7.9, and not the new reduced tables such as Table 7.13. The reason is that in each phase we eliminate different rows from the initial QR tables according to Table 7.8.

Step 2 - Detecting Interaction Candidates

To identify interactions among quality requirements related to the same functional requirement, we have to look in different tables at the rows with the same related functional requirement and check if the same domains (columns) contain crosses. Such requirements are candidates for interactions.

This is mostly the case for performance and security requirements. The reason is that solutions for achieving security requirements are time-consuming and this is at the expense of performance. As an example, we describe how we compare Table 7.9 and Table 7.10 . We consider the rows related to the same functional requirement. The rows related to the functional requirement *R4* contain entries in the columns *WAN* and *CPU*. This implies that we might have a conflict between the integrity requirement *R10* and the performance requirement *R24*. Comparing each further two rows results in the following potential conflict: *R13* with *R25*. Table 7.15 summarizes all detected interaction candidates.

Phase 3 - Treating Case 3

In this phase, we deal with case three of Table 7.8, i.e., we consider different functional requirements complemented with the same type of quality requirement. Table 7.7 enables us to eliminate irrelevant tables. Additionally, we make use of the information contained in the life-cycle expression regarding the concurrent achievement of requirements.

Step 1 - Eliminating Irrelevant Tables

According to Table 7.8, we have to consider each table separately. According to Table 7.7, no interactions will occur among different integrity, confidentiality, and authenticity requirements. Hence, we mark Table 7.10, Table 7.11, and Table 7.12 as irrelevant. The only types of quality requirements to be considered are performance requirements as given in Table 7.9.

Step 2 - Eliminating Irrelevant Rows

In each table under consideration, we perform a pairwise comparison between the rows. According to Table 7.8, interactions can only arise when quality requirements must be satisfied in parallel. We make use of the life-cycle expression to identify requirements that must be achieved in parallel.

According to the life-cycle, we can eliminate the rows for the requirements *R18*, *R19*, *R22*, and *R23* in Table 7.9. The reason is that the machines for the requirements *R1* and *R2R3* are executed sequentially. The sequential composition of the requirements *R1* and *R2R3* is executed sequentially with the parallel composition of *R4* and *R5*. The reduced table is given in Table 7.14.

Table 7.14: Phase 3, Step 2: reduced performance table

QR	Related FR	LMN	WAN	HAN	SmartMeter	CPU
R24	R4		x			x
R25	R5			x		x

Step 3 - Detecting Interaction Candidates

In this step, we check if the requirements with parallel satisfaction contain entries in the same column. We see in Table 7.14 that both requirements *R4* and *R5* concern the same domain *CPU*. Therefore, we identify *R24* and *R25* as interaction candidates as given in Table 7.15.

Phase 4 - Treating Case 4

This phase is concerned with case four of Table 7.8, i.e., different functional requirements complemented with different types of quality requirements. Table 7.7 enables us to eliminate irrelevant tables. Additionally, we take the life-cycle expression into account to reduce the number of comparisons within each table.

Step 1 - Eliminating Irrelevant Tables

According to Table 7.7, we can reduce the number of table comparisons to three: Table 7.10 and Table 7.9, Table 7.12 and Table 7.9, Table 7.11 and Table 7.9.

Step 2 - Eliminating Irrelevant Rows

According to the life-cycle, we can reduce the rows for the requirements *R18*, *R19*, *22*, and *R23* in Table 7.9 (see the reasoning in Phase 3, Step 2) and we obtain the same table as shown in Table 7.14.

Step 3 - Detecting Interaction Candidates

According to Table 7.7 and the results obtained from the previous steps, we only have to compare the rows in the following three tables: Table 7.10 and Table 7.14, Table 7.12 and Table 7.14, Table 7.11 and Table 7.14.

We obtain interaction candidates between the integrity and performance requirements, confidentiality and performance requirements, as well as authenticity and performance requirements. Table 7.15 presents the overall result of applying the *QuaRO* method.

Discussion of the results

At this point, we have to check if we can reduce the number of interaction candidates. Looking at the result, we see that most interactions might be among performance and security requirements and among different performance requirements. Additionally, we identified two pairs of interaction candidates among authenticity and confidentiality requirements (Table 7.15, Phase 2). We figure out that the interaction depends on the order of applying confidentiality and authenticity solution

Table 7.15: Candidates of requirements interactions

QuaRO phase	Comparison between tables	Interaction candidates
Phase 1	Table 7.9 with itself	*R18* and *R19*, *R22* and *R23*
Phase 2	Table 7.9 with Table 7.10	*R10* and *R24*, *R13* and *R25*
	Table 7.11 with Table 7.12	~~*R11* and *R12*~~, ~~*R14* and *R15*~~,
	Table 7.9 with Table 7.11	*R12* and *R24*, *R15* and *R25*
	Table 7.12 with Table 7.9	*R11* and *R24*, *R14* and *R25*,
Phase 3	Table 7.14 with itself	*R24* and *R25*
Phase 4	Table 7.10 with Table 7.14	*R10* and *R25*, *R13* and *R24*
	Table 7.12 with Table 7.14	*R11* and *R25*, *R14* and *R24*
	Table 7.11 with Table 7.14	*R12* and *R25*, *R15* and *R24*

mechanisms. If we sign the data first and then encrypt it, we can achieve both confidentiality and authenticity. The other way around, if we encrypted the data first and then signed it, the confidentiality and authenticity requirements would interact with each other. Under this condition, we can exclude interactions among requirement pairs *R11* and *R12*, *R14* and *R15* (crossed out in Table 7.15). Of course, we have to document this condition for the design and implementation phases. All other candidates have to be taken into account for further considerations.

7.4 Method for Performance Requirements Analysis

In this section, we present our method for *problem-oriented performance requirements analysis (PoPeRA)* visualized in Fig. 7.11. Our method is concerned with identifying performance-specific resources, their capacity and utilization, resource usage and resource sharing, and the location of performance problems.

In the previous section (see Section 7.3), we detected a number of potentially conflicting quality requirements. *PoPeRA* supports the requirements engineer in reducing the number of those potential conflicts before applying strategies to resolve the conflicts. To this end, the *PoPeRA* method focuses on identifying potential bottlenecks that might lead to performance deficiencies.

The general idea of *PoPeRA* is based on identifying the *resources* that might be used as shared resources between various subproblems and the *workload* for each subproblem (*Step 1*) as well as identifying the *security related issues* for each subproblem (*Step 2*). This information allows us to qualitatively estimate whether the modeled *performance requirements* can be achieved and, if not, where potential performance bottlenecks are located (*Step 3*). With regard to the identified bottlenecks, the number of potential requirement conflicts is reduced (*Step 4*). In the following, we describe the steps of our method in more detail.

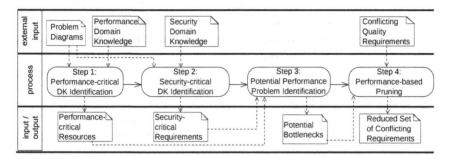

Fig. 7.11: Overview of the *PoPeRA* method

Step 1 - Performance-critical DK Identification

As described in Chapter 6, performance is concerned with the *workload* of the system and the available *resources* to process the workload [44]. Capacity of the resources and the workload are modeled as performance domain knowledge (DK) in Chapter 6.

The goal of this step is to identify whether the available resources are able to master the workload of the system. If the inbound requests exceed the processing capacity of a resource, the resource will be in contention which causes delays for some requests and subsequently to not achieving the performance requirements. Typically, such resources are referred to as *bottlenecks*. Identifying the location of these bottlenecks is critical for the performance of a system. Hence, in this step we check the resources for their processing capacity and their workload.

Application of Step 1 - Performance-critical DK Identification

In Chapter 6 in Section 6.3 (see page 186), we explained detailed how we obtained the performance domain knowledge. Hence, we refer to this chapter for detailed information. Table 7.16 - Table 7.19 show the performance domain knowledge for the performance requirements *R18* and *R19*, *R22* and *R23*, *R24*, and *R25*.

Table 7.16 shows the performance domain knowledge for requirements *R18* and *R19*. The number 74 is an estimated value based on the number of concurrent users as *authorized external entities* which are 50 electricity providers maximum and the number of concurrent users as *consumers* in premises with 8 menages and 3 devices per menage (24 in total). We have to make this assumption as there is no information regarding the number of concurrent users in the Protection Profile [155] and Open Meter [200] documents. The assumption is partially based on the existing literature [2] [87].

"Data size" of meter readings to be transmitted to the gateway can be between 1 KB and 16 MB [87]. It varies according to the period of time, in which meter data has to be sent to authorized external entities. It amounts to 1 KB by immediate sending of meter data after reading and 16 MB by sending meter data every two hours. This would be between 40 KB and 640 MB for 40 smart meters. We set 640 MB as value for "data size". As it is not further specified in the documents under consideration, we take the worst case.

A "CPU" with one core and a speed of 470 MHz can be used. This describes the specification of the "ARM 9 processors" [3] which is used in the smart meters. LMN is the "network" through which meter readings are transferred between the smart meter the machine *ReceiveMeterData*. It has a bandwidth of 250 Kb/s minimum.

Values in other tables (Table 7.17 - Table 7.19) are captured in a similar way.

Step 2 - Security-critical DK Identification

Achieving security requirements requires additional resources such as *CPU* and is time consuming, which is both at the expense of performance. Hence, by analyzing performance problems, security requirements and their satisfaction should be taken into account. In this step, we identify those subproblems which contain *security requirements*.

Additionally, in those identified subproblems we check the related *security domain knowledge*, which is expressed by the attacker and its characteristics as described in Chapter 6. The kind of the attacker and its characteristics such as the time needed for an attack, its equipment, and its knowledge affect the selection of security mechanisms for satisfying the related security requirements. For ex-

---

[2] http://www.strom-pfadfinder.de/stromanbieter/

[3] http://www.arm.com/markets/embedded/smart-meter.php

Table 7.16: Performance domain knowledge for R18, R19

Quality: Performance, Requirement: R18, R19				
Domain Knowledge Template				Mapping to MARTE
Domain Knowledge Description		Possible Values	Value	Property
For Problem Diagram *ReceiveMeterData*				
Number of concurrent users		Natural	74	GaWorkloadEvent. pattern. population
Arrival pattern		ArrivalPattern	closed	GaWorkloadEvent. pattern
Data size		DataSize (bit, Byte, KB, MB, GB)	640 MB	GaStep. msgSize
For the domain *ReceiveMeterData*				
Memory	-	capacity	DataSize (bit, Byte, KB, MB, GB)	-	HwMemory. memorySize
		latency	Duration (s, ms, min,hr, day)	-	HwMemory. timing
Network	-	bandwidth	DataRate (b/s, Kb/s, Mb/s)	-	HwMedia. bandWidth
		latency	Duration (s, ms, min,hr, day)	-	HwMedia. packetTime
CPU	No	speed	Frequency (Hz, kHz, MHz, GHz)	470 MHz	HwProcessor. frequency
		Number of cores	Natural	1	HwProcessor. nbCores
For the domain *LMN*				
Memory	-	capacity	DataSize (bit, Byte, KB, MB, GB)	-	HwMemory. memorySize
		latency	Duration (s, ms, min,hr, day)	-	HwMemory. timing
Network	Yes	bandwidth	DataRate (b/s, Kb/s, Mb/s)	250 Kb/s	HwMedia. bandWidth
		latency	Duration (s, ms, min,hr, day)	-	HwMedia. packetTime
CPU	-	speed	Frequency (Hz, kHz, MHz, GHz)	-	HwProcessor. frequency
		Number of cores	Natural	-	HwProcessor. nbCores

Table 7.17: Performance domain knowledge for R22, R23

Quality: Performance, Requirement: R22, R23				
Domain Knowledge Template				Mapping to MARTE
Domain Knowledge Description		Possible Values	Value	Property
For Problem Diagram *ProcessStoreMD*				
Number of concurrent users		Natural	74	GaWorkloadEvent. pattern. population
Arrival pattern		ArrivalPattern	closed	GaWorkloadEvent. pattern
Data size		DataSize (bit, Byte, KB, MB, GB)	640 MB	GaStep. msgSize
For the domain *ProcessStoreMD*				
Memory	-	capacity	DataSize (bit, Byte, KB, MB, GB)	-	HwMemory. memorySize
		latency	Duration (s, ms, min,hr, day)	-	HwMemory. timing
Network	-	bandwidth	DataRate (b/s, Kb/s, Mb/s)	-	HwMedia. bandWidth
		latency	Duration (s, ms, min,hr, day)	-	HwMedia. packetTime
CPU	No	speed	Frequency (Hz, kHz, MHz, GHz)	470 MHz	HwProcessor. frequency
		Number of cores	Natural	1	HwProcessor. nbCores

Table 7.18: Performance domain knowledge for R24

Quality: Performance, Requirement: R24				
Domain Knowledge Template				Mapping to MARTE
Domain Knowledge Description	Possible Values		Value	Property
For Problem Diagram *SubmitMeterData*				
Number of concurrent users	Natural		50	GaWorkloadEvent. pattern. population
Arrival pattern	ArrivalPattern		closed	GaWorkloadEvent. pattern
Data size	DataSize (bit, Byte, KB, MB, GB)		640 MB	GaStep. msgSize
For the domain *SubmitMD*				
Memory	-	capacity	DataSize (bit, Byte, KB, MB, GB)	-	HwMemory. memorySize
		latency	Duration (s, ms, min,hr, day)	-	HwMemory. timing
Network	-	bandwidth	DataRate (b/s, Kb/s, Mb/s)	-	HwMedia. bandWidth
		latency	Duration (s, ms, min,hr, day)	-	HwMedia. packetTime
CPU	No	speed	Frequency (Hz, kHz, MHz, GHz)	470 MHz	HwProcessor. frequency
		Number of cores	Natural	1	HwProcessor. nbCores
For the domain *WAN*				
Memory	-	capacity	DataSize (bit, Byte, KB, MB, GB)	-	HwMemory. memorySize
		latency	Duration (s, ms, min,hr, day)	-	HwMemory. timing
Network	Yes	bandwidth	DataRate (b/s, Kb/s, Mb/s)	2.4 Kb/s	HwMedia. bandWidth
		latency	Duration (s, ms, min,hr, day)	-	HwMedia. packetTime
CPU	-	speed	Frequency (Hz, kHz, MHz, GHz)	-	HwProcessor. frequency
		Number of cores	Natural	-	HwProcessor. nbCores

ample, to defend against a *layman* attacker with *standard equipment* and only *one day preparation and attack time*, there is no need for strong security mechanisms that affect the satisfaction of performance requirements negatively. Therefore, in addition to the security requirements annotated in each problem diagram, we need the related security domain knowledge in order to be able to estimate the strength of the security solution to achieve the related security requirements.

Application of Step 2 - Security-critical DK Identification

For the smart grid case study, we check the problem diagrams for related security requirements:

R1   For the smart grid case study, we decided for a *One Box Solution* which includes the *Smart Meter* and the *Smart Meter Gateway* in one physical device. It has the advantage that the communication between the *Smart Meter* and the *Smart Meter Gateway* is physically protected (see Section 5.6 on page 161).

Table 7.19: Performance domain knowledge for R25

Quality: Performance, Requirement: R25				
Domain Knowledge Template				Mapping to MARTE
Domain Knowledge Description	Possible Values		Value	Property
For Problem Diagram *PublishConsumerInfo*				
Number of concurrent users	Natural		24	GaWorkloadEvent. pattern. population
Arrival pattern	ArrivalPattern		closed	GaWorkloadEvent. pattern
Data size	DataSize (bit, Byte, KB, MB, GB)		100 KB	GaStep. msgSize
For the domain *PublishConsumerInfo*				
Memory	-	capacity	DataSize (bit, Byte, KB, MB, GB)	-	HwMemory. memorySize
		latency	Duration (s, ms, min,hr, day)	-	HwMemory. timing
Network	-	bandwidth	DataRate (b/s, Kb/s, Mb/s)	-	HwMedia. bandWidth
		latency	Duration (s, ms, min,hr, day)	-	HwMedia. packetTime
CPU	No	speed	Frequency (Hz, kHz, MHz, GHz)	470 MHz	HwProcessor. frequency
		Number of cores	Natural	1	HwProcessor. nbCores
For the domain *HAN*				
Memory	-	capacity	DataSize (bit, Byte, KB, MB, GB)	-	HwMemory. memorySize
		latency	Duration (s, ms, min,hr, day)	-	HwMemory. timing
Network	Yes	bandwidth	DataRate (b/s, Kb/s, Mb/s)	250 Kb/s	HwMedia. bandWidth
		latency	Duration (s, ms, min,hr, day)	-	HwMedia. packetTime
CPU	-	speed	Frequency (Hz, kHz, MHz, GHz)	-	HwProcessor. frequency
		Number of cores	Natural	-	HwProcessor. nbCores

Hence, the security requirements *R6*, *R7*, and *R8* related to the functional requirement *R1* are considered as fulfilled without applying additional security mechanisms and excluded from further consideration. The security requirement *R16* is considered as satisfied as well, due to the same reason. Hence, there is no security requirement related to *R1* to be considered for this step.

R2R3 We decided for merging the subproblems for the requirements *R2* and *R3* (see Section 5.6 on page 161). We have to merge their related quality requirements as well. There is no security requirement for the functional requirement *R2*. The confidentiality requirement *R9* related to the functional requirement *R3* is already satisfied due to the same reasons as for the confidentiality requirement *R16*. Hence, there is no security requirement related to *R2R3* to be considered for this step.

R4 The security requirements *R10*, *R11*, and *R12* are related to the functional requirement *R4* and, therefore, have to be considered for this step.

R5 The security requirements *R13*, *R14*, and *R15* are related to the functional requirement *R5* and, therefore, have to be considered for this step.

Now, we consider the related security domain knowledge. In Chapter 6, we proposed templates for eliciting and documenting security domain knowledge. We identified one network attacker (*WAN attacker*[4]) for the three security requirements *R10*, *R11*, and *R12*. The reason is that the *MeterData* to be transmitted through the network *WAN* can be manipulated by the WAN attacker. According to [155], the *WAN* attacker, which is located in the *WAN*, tries to compromise the confidentiality and/or integrity of the *MeterData* transmitted via the *WAN*. It can also try to conquer a component of the infrastructure (i.e. *SmartMeter* or *Gateway*) via the *WAN* in order to cause damage to the component itself (e.g. by sending forged *MeterData* to an external entity). The *WAN attacker* is characterized according to Table 7.20.

Table 7.20: Security domain knowledge for the requirements *R10*, *R11*, and *R12*

Quality: Security, Requirement: R10, R11, R12			
Domain Knowledge Template			Mapping to profile
Domain Knowledge Description	Possible Values	Value	Property (Dependability profile)
Preparation time	one day, one week, two weeks, ...	more than six months	Attacker.preparationTime
Attack time	one day, one week, two weeks, ...	more than six months	Attacker.attackTime
Specialist expertise	laymen, proficient, expert, ...	multiple experts	Attacker.specialistExpertise
Knowledge of the TOE	public, restricted, sensitive, critical	public	Attacker.knowledge
Window of opportunity	unnecessary/unlimited, easy, ...	difficult	Attacker.opportunity
IT hardware/software or other equipment	standard, specialized, bespoke, ...	multiple bespoke	Attacker.equipment

We identified one *local attacker* for the three security requirements *R13*, *R14*, and *R15*. The reason is that the *MeterData* to be transmitted through the network *HAN* can be manipulated by a local attacker. The network *HAN* is an in-house data communication network that is responsible for interconnecting domestic equipment. It covers a moderately sized geographical area within the premises of the consumer [155]. According to [155], the *local attacker* has less motivation than the *WAN attacker* as a successful attack of a local attacker will always only impact one Gateway. In addition, as this network is not a public one, our assumption is that it cannot be attacked as severely as the *WAN*. The attacker for the requirements *R13*, *R14*, and *R15* is characterized as shown in Table 7.21.

---

[4] The network attacker is a WAN attacker as the meter data corresponding to the requirements *R10*, *R11*, and *R12* are transmitted through a *WAN*.

Table 7.21: Security domain knowledge for the requirements *R13*, *R14*, and *R15*

Quality: Security, Requirement: R13, R14, R15		
Domain Knowledge Template		Mapping to profile
Domain Knowledge Description	Possible Values	Value	Property (Dependability profile)
Preparation time	one day, one week, two weeks, ...	two weeks	Attacker.preparationTime
Attack time	one day, one week, two weeks, ...	two weeks	Attacker.attackTime
Specialist expertise	laymen, proficient, expert, ...	proficient	Attacker.specialistExpertise
Knowledge of the TOE	public, restricted, sensitive, critical	public	Attacker.knowledge
Window of opportunity	unnecessary/unlimited, easy, ...	difficult	Attacker.opportunity
IT hardware/software or other equipment	standard, specialized, bespoke, ...	specialized	Attacker.equipment

Step 3 - Potential Performance Problem Identification

This step has to be supported by a performance analyst to analyze whether the processing capacity of existing resources (output of Step 1) suffices to satisfy performance requirements for each subproblem with regard to the existing workload (output of Step 1) and existing security issues (output of Step 2).

As a result of this step, those resources, in which the inbound requests might exceed the processing capacity of the resource, are identified. That is, from the set of *performance-critical resources* we indicate those resources whose problem diagrams exhibit a high usage. We mark such resources as *bottlenecks* using the stereotype ≪bottleneck≫.

Application of Step 3 - Potential Performance Problem Identification

We go through the subproblems for the requirements *R1*, *R2R3*, *R4*, and *R5* and analyze the outputs of *Step 1* and *Step 2* with regard to the performance requirements. The result of this step is used in the next step for reducing the potential requirement conflicts.

Subproblem *ReceiveMeterData* related to *R1*:

Workload   From the results of *Step 1*, we obtain that the related subproblem for the requirement *R1* exhibits a higher *workload* than the workload for the requirements *R4* and *R5* (see *number of concurrent users* in Table 7.16). The reason is that in a worst case the *consumers* as well as the *authorized external entities* can request the submitting meter data as well as publishing consumer info at the same time. In such a case the machine related to the requirement *R1* has to obtain meter data from the smart meter for all the requests at the same time. Therefore, it must deal with a higher workload than the other requirements. The same holds for the machine related to the requirement *R2R3*. Also, a high amount of data has to be transferred through the *LMN* (see 640 MB for *Data size* in Table 7.16).

Resource   From the results of *Step 1*, we identify two resources *CPU* and *LMN* related to the subproblem *ReceiveMeterData* (see Table 7.16). The network domain *HAN* exhibits a bandwidth of 250 Kb/s, which is much higher than 2.4 Kb/s (in comparison with the bandwidth of *WAN* related to *R4*). Therefore, the network resource *HAN* is no bottleneck for transmitting *MeterData*.

Security DK   According to the results of *Step 2*, for the subproblem *ReceiveMeterData*, there are no security requirements to be considered. Accordingly, there is no security domain knowledge to be considered. Therefore, the performance requirements *R18* and *R19* are not influenced negatively due to the security issues.

Performance requirement   The performance requirement *R19* has to be achieved together with the requirements *R23* and *R25* in less than 10 seconds.

Our estimation   There is a high workload, but an average resource usage, and no security related issues. Hence, we do not expect a potential performance problem regarding *R19*.

For the performance requirement *R18* we expect high workload, average resource usage, and no security issues. Up to this point, we have the same conditions as for the performance requirement *R19*. However, *R18* has to be achieved together with the requirements *R22* and *R24* in less than 5 seconds. Therefore, a potential performance problem for achieving the requirement *R18* might be expected. Hence, we mark the machine *ReceiveMeterData* as a bottleneck.

Subproblem *processStoreMD* related to *R2R3*:

Workload   According to the results of *Step 1*, for the subproblem *ProcessStoreMD* related to *R2R3*, the same workload regarding the *number of concurrent users* applies as for the subproblem *ReceiveMeterData* related to *R1* (see Table 7.17). Also, a high amount of data has to be processed and stored (see 640 MB for *Data size* in Table 7.17).

Resource   According to Table 7.17, we identify *CPU* as the only resource related to the subproblem *ProcessStoreMD*.

Security DK   As the results of *Step 2* for the requirement *R2R3*, we identify no security requirements to be considered for performance analysis. Accordingly, there is no security domain knowledge to be considered. Therefore, the performance requirements *R22* and *R23* are not influenced negatively due to the security issues.

Performance requirement   The performance requirement *R23* has to be achieved together with the requirements *R19* and *R25* in less than 10 seconds.

Our estimation   There is a high workload, but an average resource usage, and no security related issues. Hence, we do not expect a potential performance problem regarding *R23*.

For the performance requirement *R22*, we expect high workload, average resource usage, and no security issues. Up to this point, we have the same conditions as for the performance requirement *R23*. However, *R22* has to be achieved together with the requirements *R18* and *R24* in less than 5 seconds. Therefore, a potential performance problem for achieving the requirement *R22* might be expected. Hence, we mark the machine *ProcessStoreMD* as a bottleneck.

Subproblem *SubmitMeterData* related to *R4*:

Workload   The results of *Step 1* for the subproblem *SubmitMeterData* related to *R4* exhibit a relatively high workload (50 for the *number of concurrent users* in Table 7.18). Also, a high amount of data has to be submitted through the *WAN* (640 MB for *Data size* in Table 7.18). This might influence the achievement of the performance requirement *R24* negatively.

Resource   According to Table 7.18, *CPU* and *WAN (Network)* are considered as resources related to the subproblem *SubmitMeterData*. The network domain *WAN* exhibits a bandwidth of 2.4 Kb/s, which is not much for the amount of data to be transmitted (640 MB) to the *AuthorizedExternalEntities* (in comparison with *HAN* for *R5*). Therefore, *WAN* might cause a bottleneck.

Security DK   According to the results of *Step 2*, for the subproblem *SubmitMeterData*, there are three security requirements *R10*, *R11*, and *R12*. Table 7.20 shows that we are concerned with an attacker with the highest preparation and attack time, *multiple bespoke* equipment, a very high expertise (*multiple experts*), etc. For such a case, we should consider a strong security mechanism that is resource and time consuming accordingly. This might influence the achievement of the performance requirement *R24* negatively.

Performance requirement   The performance requirement *R24* has to be achieved together with the requirements *R18* and *R22* in less than 5 seconds.

Our estimation　According to the high workload, the high resource usage, and the required security mechanisms, we identify a potential performance problem for achieving the requirement *R24*. Hence, we mark the machine *SubmitMeterData* as a bottleneck.

Subproblem *PublishConsumerInfo* related to *R5*:

Workload　The results of *Step 1* for the subproblem *PublishConsumerInfo* related to *R5* exhibit a low workload (24 for the *number of concurrent users* in Table 7.19). Also, the amount of data to be submitted through the *HAN* is not high in comparison to 640 MB for *R4* (100 KB for *Data size* in Table 7.19). Therefore, it is unlikely that this workload affects the achievement of the performance requirement *R25* negatively.

Resource　According to Table 7.19, we identify *CPU* and *HAN* as resources related to the subproblem *SubmitMeterData*. The network domain *HAN* exhibits a bandwidth of 250 Kb/s, which is much higher than 2.4 Kb/s (the bandwidth for *WAN*). Therefore, the network resource *HAN* might not cause a bottleneck for transmitting *MeterData*.

Security DK　According to the results of *Step 2*, for the subproblem *PublishConsumerInfo*, there are three security requirements *R13*, *R14*, and *R15*. Table 7.21 shows that we are concerned with an attacker with a sparse preparation and attack time, *specialized* equipment, a *proficient* expertise, etc. For such a case, there is no need for considering a strong security mechanism (in comparison to security mechanisms for achieving *R10*, *R11*, and *R12*). Therefore, no negative impact for achieving the performance requirement *R25* regarding security issues is expected.

Performance requirement　The performance requirement *R25* has to be achieved together with the requirements *R19* and *R23* in less than 10 seconds.

Our estimation　According to the low workload, the sparse resource usage, and the weak security mechanisms, we do not expect a potential performance problem for achieving the requirement *R25*.

Step 4 - Performance-based Pruning

The goal of this step is to reduce the number of potential conflicts among quality requirements. As the input of this step, we take the output of the *QuaRO* method (see Section 7.3), namely the potential conflicts among performance and security requirements, and the estimation from the previous step into account. For each pair of conflicting requirements, we check whether we can mark it as irrelevant according to the results of the previous step (*Step 3: Potential Performance Problem Identification*). The remaining conflicting requirements have to be resolved later on.

Application of Step 4 - Performance-based Pruning

Table 7.22 shows the output of the *QuaRO* method. In the previous step, we discussed that the requirements *R19*, *R23*, and *R25* can be achieved according to the related workload, resource usage, and related security requirements. Therefore, we can exclude the combination of the security requirements *R13*, *R14*, and *R15* with the performance requirements *R19*, *R23*, and *R25*. They can be considered as not conflicting as no strong security mechanisms are required. Therefore, we can mark the requirement pairs *R13* and *R25*, *R14* and *R25*, and *R15* and*R25* as not conflicting. Table 7.23 shows the excluded and the remaining conflicting requirements.

Table 7.22: Output of the *QuaRO* method

QuaRO phase	Comparison between tables	Interaction candidates
Phase 1	Table 7.9 with itself	*R18* and *R19*, *R22* and *R23*
Phase 2	Table 7.9 with Table 7.10	*R10* and *R24*, *R13* and *R25*
	Table 7.9 with Table 7.11	*R12* and *R24*, *R15* and *R25*
	Table 7.12 with Table 7.9	*R11* and *R24*, *R14* and *R25*,
Phase 3	Table 7.14 with itself	*R24* and *R25*
Phase 4	Table 7.10 with Table 7.14	*R10* and *R25*, *R13* and *R24*
	Table 7.12 with Table 7.14	*R11* and *R25*, *R14* and *R24*
	Table 7.11 with Table 7.14	*R12* and *R25*, *R15* and *R24*

7.5 Method for Generating Requirement Alternatives

In this section, we propose our method for generating alternatives for problematic quality requirements. Based on the type of requirement we want to generate alternatives for, there are different properties, which are candidates to be relaxed. The qualities addressed by different requirements are very different, and as a result, so are the properties, which can be used to relax a requirement. But for particular

Table 7.23: Output of Step 4

QuaRO phase	Comparison between tables	Interaction candidates
Phase 1	Table 7.9 with itself	*R18* and *R19*, *R22* and *R23*
Phase 2	Table 7.9 with Table 7.10	*R10* and *R24*, ~~*R13* and *R25*~~
	Table 7.9 with Table 7.11	*R12* and *R24*, ~~*R15* and *R25*~~
	Table 7.12 with Table 7.9	*R11* and *R24*, ~~*R14* and *R25*~~
Phase 3	Table 7.14 with itself	*R24* and *R25*
Phase 4	Table 7.10 with Table 7.14	*R10* and *R25*, *R13* and *R24*
	Table 7.12 with Table 7.14	*R11* and *R25*, *R14* and *R24*
	Table 7.11 with Table 7.14	*R12* and *R25*, *R15* and *R24*

kinds of qualities those properties are the same. Hence, it is possible to define a property template for a quality, which can be instantiated for a requirement belonging to this quality. The relaxation templates for each type of quality requirements are presented in the following.

Templates for requirement alternatives

We captured in Chapter 6 the properties for each kind of quality requirements as *domain knowledge* and document them in a so-called *Domain Knowledge Template* that has to be instantiated for each specific quality requirement. As we are concerned with the same properties of quality requirements for generating requirement alternatives, we make use of such a template and extend it to document generated requirement alternatives as well. In the domain knowledge templates, we captured the following properties: *Domain Knowledge Description* describing the quality-relevant property, *Possible Values*, describing the range of values the property can take, and *Value* representing the value of property for the original requirement.

We extend the domain knowledge template with one column for *Upper/Lower Bound* describing the lower or upper bound (depending to the property) each property can take when relaxing, and one or more columns for *Value Alt* representing the values of the relaxed properties for requirements alternatives. In Tables 7.24 and 7.25, we present the *Relaxation Templates* for the qualities security and performance before we introduce our method for generating alternatives. We make use of the relaxation templates while we apply our method to generate and document requirement alternatives.

Table 7.24: Relaxation template for performance

Quality: Performance					
Relaxation Template					
Domain Knowledge Description	Possible Values	Value	Upper/ Lower Bound	Value Alt1	Value Alt2
For each Problem Diagram					
Number of concurrent users	Natural				
Arrival pattern	ArrivalPattern				
Data size	DataSize (bit, Byte, KB, MB, GB)				
For each Causal Domain					
Memory	capacity	DataSize (bit, Byte, KB, MB, GB)			
	latency	Duration (s, ms, min,hr, day)			
Network	bandwidth	DataRate (b/s, Kb/s, Mb/s)			
	latency	Duration (s, ms, min,hr, day)			
CPU	speed	Frequency (Hz, kHz, MHz, GHz)			
	Number of cores	Natural			

Table 7.25: Relaxation template for security

Quality: Security					
Relaxation Template					
Domain Knowledge Description	Possible Values	Value	Upper/ Lower Bound	Value Alt1	Value Alt2
Preparation time	one day, one week, two weeks, ...				
Attack time	one day, one week, two weeks, ...				
Specialist expertise	laymen, proficient, expert, ...				
Knowledge of the TOE	public, restricted, sensitive, critical				
Window of opportunity	unnecessary/unlimited, easy, ...				
IT hardware/software or other equipment	standard, specialized, bespoke, ...				

In the following, we describe our method to generate alternatives for interacting requirements. An overview of the steps of this method is shown in Fig. 7.12.

Step 1 - Select pair of conflicting requirements

As the input for the generation of requirement alternatives we select pairs of possibly conflicting quality requirements. We have to analyze each pair for possible requirement alternatives which resolve or relax the interaction.

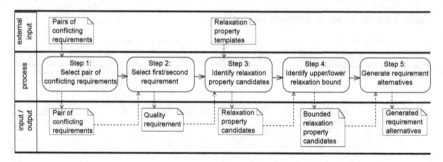

Fig. 7.12: Method for generating alternatives for interacting requirements

Application of Step 1 - Select pair of conflicting requirements

For our example, we make use of Table 7.26, the output of the *PoPeRA* method (see Section 7.4), which serves as the input for this step. We go through the pairs of possibly conflicting requirements and apply the method step by step to them.

Table 7.26: Input for Requirement Alternative Generation

QuaRO phase	Comparison between tables	Interaction candidates
Phase 1	Table 7.9 with itself	*R18* and *R19*, *R22* and *R23*
Phase 2	Table 7.9 with Table 7.10	*R10* and *R24*
	Table 7.9 with Table 7.11	*R12* and *R24*
	Table 7.12 with Table 7.9	*R11* and *R24*
Phase 3	Table 7.14 with itself	*R24* and *R25*
Phase 4	Table 7.10 with Table 7.14	*R10* and *R25*, *R13* and *R24*
	Table 7.12 with Table 7.14	*R11* and *R25*, *R14* and *R24*
	Table 7.11 with Table 7.14	*R12* and *R25*, *R15* and *R24*

Step 2 - Select first/second requirement

In this step, we have to check each of the two requirements for possibilities to resolve the interaction. Hence, we have to execute the next steps for both requirements. Both requirements provide the possibility to be relaxed in order to resolve the interaction.

In Chapter 6, we filled the column "*value*" of the *Domain Knowledge Templates* for all the requirements under consideration. For the *Relaxation Templates* (see Tables 7.24 and 7.25), the column "*value*" remains the same. We have to fill the column *Upper/ Lower Bound* and the columns *Value Alt* for the selected requirement in the next steps.

Application of Step 2 - Select first/second requirement

For our smart grid case study, we aim at generating different alternatives for each requirement in such a way that we have at the end different software architecture candidates with different levels of satisfaction for security and performance.

We decide on generating three different architecture alternatives. For example, we derive one architecture candidate which treats the desired security requirements with a higher priority, one architecture candidate with the best fulfilled performance requirements, and one architecture candidate which provides a compromise of performance and security requirements. The architecture alternative with the best fulfilled performance requirements should satisfy the initial performance requirements and the security requirements alternatives which are weaker than the initial security requirements *R10-R15*. Analogously, for the architecture alternative with the best fulfilled security requirements, we make use of performance requirement alternatives which are weaker than the initial performance requirements *R18-R25* and the initial security requirements. To this end, in this step we need to provide alternatives for all conflicting performance and security requirements to be used in different architecture alternatives.

Tables 7.27 and 7.28 show the relaxation templates for security for the requirements *R10*, *R11*, *R12*, *R13*, *R14*, and *R15*. The relaxation templates for performance for the requirements *R18*, *R19*, *R22*, *R23*, *R24*, and *R25* are given in Table 7.29 - Table 7.32. The templates are already filled in. We describe in the next steps which parts of the templates have to be filled in which step and how.

Step 3 - Identify relaxation property candidates

Based on the type of requirement, there are different properties, which are candidates to be relaxed. These candidates are fixed for each kind of requirement. Hence, we can use predefined templates to identify these properties. For each property the actual value regarding the interacting requirement has to be stated. Next, it has to be decided if this value for the property is a hard constraint, which cannot

Table 7.27: Relaxation template for security requirements *R10, R11, R12*

Quality: Security, Requirements: R10, R11, R12					
Relaxation Template					
Domain Knowledge Description	Possible Values	Value	Upper/ Lower Bound	Value Alt1	Value Alt2
Preparation time	one day, one week, two weeks, ...	more than six months	one month	one month	three months
Attack time	one day, one week, two weeks, ...	more than six months	one month	one month	three months
Specialist expertise	laymen, proficient, expert, ...	multiple experts	proficient	proficient	expert
Knowledge of the ToE	public, restricted, sensitive, critical	public	public	public	public
Window of opportunity	unnecessary/unlimited, easy, ...	difficult	difficult	difficult	difficult
IT hardware/software or other equipment	standard, specialized, bespoke, ...	multiple bespoke	specialized	specialized	bespoke

Table 7.28: Relaxation template for security requirements *R13, R14, R15*

Quality: Security, Requirements: R13, R14, R15					
Relaxation Template					
Domain Knowledge Description	Possible Values	Value	Upper/ Lower Bound	Value Alt1	Value Alt2
Preparation time	one day, one week, two weeks, ...	two weeks	one day	one day	one week
Attack time	one day, one week, two weeks, ...	two weeks	one day	one day	one week
Specialist expertise	laymen, proficient, expert, ...	expert	laymen	laymen	proficient
Knowledge of the ToE	public, restricted, sensitive, critical	public	public	public	public
Window of opportunity	unnecessary/unlimited, easy, ...	difficult	difficult	difficult	difficult
IT hardware/software or other equipment	standard, specialized, bespoke, ...	bespoke	standard	standard	specialized

be changed, or a soft constraint, which might be relaxed. In the second case, we identified a relaxation candidate.

Table 7.29: Relaxation template for performance requirements *R18, R19*

Quality: Performance, Requirements: R18, R19						
		Relaxation Template				
Domain Knowledge Description		Possible Values	Value	Upper/ Lower Bound	Value Alt1	Value Alt2
For Problem Diagram *ReceiveMeterData*						
Number of concurrent users		Natural	74	9	9	36
Arrival pattern		ArrivalPattern	closed	closed	closed	closed
Data size		DataSize (bit, Byte, KB, MB, GB)	640 MB	50 KB	50 KB	1 MB
For Domain *ReceiveMeterData*						
Memory	-	capacity	DataSize (bit, Byte, KB, MB, GB)	Fixed	Fixed	Fixed	Fixed
		latency	Duration (s, ms, min,hr, day)	Fixed	Fixed	Fixed	Fixed
Network	-	bandwidth	DataRate (b/s, Kb/s, Mb/s)	Not relevant	Not relevant	Not relevant	Not relevant
		latency	Duration (s, ms, min,hr, day)	Not relevant	Not relevant	Not relevant	Not relevant
CPU	No	speed	Frequency (Hz, kHz, MHz, GHz)	Fixed	Fixed	Fixed	Fixed
		Number of cores	Natural	Fixed	Fixed	Fixed	Fixed
For Domain *LMN*						
Memory	-	capacity	DataSize (bit, Byte, KB, MB, GB)	Not relevant	Not relevant	Not relevant	Not relevant
		latency	Duration (s, ms, min,hr, day)	Not relevant	Not relevant	Not relevant	Not relevant
Network	Yes	bandwidth	DataRate (b/s, Kb/s, Mb/s)	250 Kb/s	250 Mb/s	250 Mb/s	10 Mb/s
		latency	Duration (s, ms, min,hr, day)	Not known	Not known	Not known	Not known
CPU	-	speed	Frequency (Hz, kHz, MHz, GHz)	Not relevant	Not relevant	Not relevant	Not relevant
		Number of cores	Natural	Not relevant	Not relevant	Not relevant	Not relevant

Application of Step 3 - Identify relaxation property candidates

For the security requirements *R10-R15*, we figure out that the properties "*knowledge of the ToE*" and "*window of opportunity*" are fixed and cannot be relaxed. The rest of properties can be relaxed to generate alternatives for the requirements *R10-R15*. For the performance requirements *R18, R19, R22, R23, R24*, and *R25* the

Table 7.30: Relaxation template for performance requirements *R22, R23*

Quality: Performance, Requirements: R22, R23					
Relaxation Template					
Domain Knowledge Description	Possible Values	Value	Upper/ Lower Bound	Value Alt1	Value Alt2
For Problem Diagram *ProcessStoreMD*					
Number of concurrent users	Natural	74	9	9	36
Arrival pattern	ArrivalPattern	Closed	Closed	Closed	Closed
Data size	DataSize (bit, Byte, KB, MB, GB)	640 MB	50 KB	50 KB	1 MB
For Domain *ProcessStoreMD*					
Memory - capacity	DataSize (bit, Byte, KB, MB, GB)	Fixed	Fixed	Fixed	Fixed
latency	Duration (s, ms, min,hr, day)	Fixed	Fixed	Fixed	Fixed
Network - bandwidth	DataRate (b/s, Kb/s, Mb/s)	Not relevant	Not relevant	Not relevant	Not relevant
latency	Duration (s, ms, min,hr, day)	Not relevant	Not relevant	Not relevant	Not relevant
CPU - speed	Frequency (Hz, kHz, MHz, GHz)	Fixed	Fixed	Fixed	Fixed
Number of cores	Natural	Fixed	Fixed	Fixed	Fixed

characteristics of memory, namely *"Memory capacity"* and *"Memory latency"*, and the characteristics of processor, namely *"CPU speed"* and *"CPU number of cores"* for the gateway are fixed. The rest of the properties can be used for relaxation, if they are known and relevant.

Step 4 - Identify upper/lower relaxation bound

For each property, the upper/lower bound which is still acceptable has to be identified. The upper/lower bounds of all properties form the worst-case scenario, which is still acceptable for a requirement.

Table 7.31: Relaxation template for performance requirement *R24*

Quality: Performance, Requirement: R24						
Relaxation Template						
Domain Knowledge Description		Possible Values	Value	Upper/ Lower Bound	Value Alt1	Value Alt2
For Problem Diagram *SubmitMeterData*						
Number of concurrent users		Natural	50	1	1	20
Arrival pattern		ArrivalPattern	Closed	Closed	Closed	Closed
Data size		DataSize (bit, Byte, KB, MB, GB)	640 MB	40 KB	40 KB	1 MB
For Domain *SubmitMD*						
Memory	-	capacity	DataSize (bit, Byte, KB, MB, GB)	Fixed	Fixed	Fixed	Fixed
		latency	Duration (s, ms, min,hr, day)	Fixed	Fixed	Fixed	Fixed
Network	-	bandwidth	DataRate (b/s, Kb/s, Mb/s)	Not relevant	Not relevant	Not relevant	Not relevant
		latency	Duration (s, ms, min,hr, day)	Not relevant	Not relevant	Not relevant	Not relevant
CPU	No	speed	Frequency (Hz, kHz, MHz, GHz)	Fixed	Fixed	Fixed	Fixed
		Number of cores	Natural	Fixed	Fixed	Fixed	Fixed
For Domain *WAN*						
Memory	-	capacity	DataSize (bit, Byte, KB, MB, GB)	No relevant	No relevant	No relevant	No relevant
		latency	Duration (s, ms, min,hr, day)	No relevant	No relevant	No relevant	No relevant
Network	Yes	bandwidth	DataRate (b/s, Kb/s, Mb/s)	2.4 Kb/s	250 Mb/s	250 Mb/s	10 Mb/s
		latency	Duration (s, ms, min,hr, day)	Not known	Not known	Not known	Not known
CPU	-	speed	Frequency (Hz, kHz, MHz, GHz)	No relevant	No relevant	No relevant	No relevant
		Number of cores	Natural	No relevant	No relevant	No relevant	No relevant

Application of Step 4 - Identify upper/lower relaxation bound

To identify "*upper/lower bound*" for the security requirements *R10*, *R11*, and *R12*, we have to assume values from the possible values, because we have no information about the strength of the *WAN* attacker. Hence, we assume that the system has to be protected at least against a *WAN* attacker who is a "*proficient*", has "*1 month*"

Table 7.32: Relaxation template for performance requirement *R25*

Quality: Performance, Requirement: R25					
Relaxation Template					
Domain Knowledge Description	Possible Values	Value	Upper/ Lower Bound	Value Alt1	Value Alt2
For Problem Diagram *PublishConsumerInfo*					
Number of concurrent users	Natural	24	8	8	16
Arrival pattern	ArrivalPattern	Closed	Closed	Closed	Closed
Data size	DataSize (bit, Byte, KB, MB, GB)	100 KB	10 KB	10 KB	50 KB
For Domain *PublishConsumerInfo*					
Memory	-	capacity	DataSize (bit, Byte, KB, MB, GB)	Fixed	Fixed	Fixed	Fixed
		latency	Duration (s, ms, min,hr, day)	Fixed	Fixed	Fixed	Fixed
Network	-	bandwidth	DataRate (b/s, Kb/s, Mb/s)	Not relevant	Not relevant	Not relevant	Not relevant
		latency	Duration (s, ms, min,hr, day)	Not relevant	Not relevant	Not relevant	Not relevant
CPU	No	speed	Frequency (Hz, kHz, MHz, GHz)	Fixed	Fixed	Fixed	Fixed
		Number of cores	Natural	Fixed	Fixed	Fixed	Fixed
For Domain *HAN*					
Memory	-	capacity	DataSize (bit, Byte, KB, MB, GB)	No relevant	No relevant	No relevant	No relevant
		latency	Duration (s, ms, min,hr, day)	No relevant	No relevant	No relevant	No relevant
Network	Yes	bandwidth	DataRate (b/s, Kb/s, Mb/s)	250 Kb/s	250 Mb/s	250 Mb/s	10 Mb/s
		latency	Duration (s, ms, min,hr, day)	Not known	Not known	Not known	Not known
CPU	-	speed	Frequency (Hz, kHz, MHz, GHz)	No relevant	No relevant	No relevant	No relevant
		Number of cores	Natural	No relevant	No relevant	No relevant	No relevant

for preparing the attack, has "*1 month*" for the attack itself, and has a "*proficient*" equipment for performing the attack (see Table 7.27). The "*upper/lower bound*" for the security requirements *R13*, *R14*, and *R15* is shown in Table 7.28. We assume that the system has to be protected at least against a *HAN* attacker who is "*laymen*", has "*1 day*" for preparing the attack, has "*1 day*" for the attack itself, and has a *"standard"* equipment for performing the attack. The properties *"knowledge of the ToE"* and *"window of opportunity"* are fixed and cannot be relaxed.

As an example for identifying the *"upper/lower bound"*, we take the performance requirement *R24*, which is shown in Table 7.31. We begin with the property *"number of concurrent users"*. For the case that the gateway sends meter readings to the external entities via a concentrator, there is only one user. Hence, we take 1 for the column *"upper/lower bound"*. As *"upper/lower bound"* for the property *"bandwidth"* for the domain *WAN*, we take the bandwidth of Power Line Communication (PLC) that can be up to 250 Mb/s. The *"upper/lower bound"* for the property *"data size"* is assumed to be 40 KB [87]. For the *"upper/lower bound"* for the requirements *R18, R19, R22, R23*, and *R25* see Tables 7.29, 7.30, and 7.32.

Step 5 - Generate requirement alternatives

The first alternative is the requirement realizing the worst-case scenario. Between the original requirement and this lower bound requirement, several other requirements can be generated by varying the relaxation candidates. For each generated requirement this has to be checked, regardless of whether it eliminates the interaction. If it does not, further relaxation is needed.

Application of Step 5 - Generate requirement alternatives

To relax the properties and thus generate alternatives for the requirements *R11* and *R24*, we choose values between the *"value"* and *"upper/lower bound"* for properties that can be relaxed. For example, for the requirement *R24* the properties *"number of concurrent users"*, *"bandwidth"* and *"data size"* can be relaxed. The rest of the properties are either fixed or irrelevant for the corresponding requirement or unknown and thus cannot be considered for the relaxation process. Relaxing possible properties results in requirements alternatives *R11.1* and *R11.2* for the original requirement *R11* and in requirements alternatives *R24.1* and *R24.2* for the original requirement *R24*. In this way, we cannot say that we assuredly resolve interactions between quality requirements, but we can weaken them for sure or even resolve them ideally.

7.6 Related Work

In this section, we discuss related work regarding (functional and quality) requirements interaction in Section 7.6.1 and regarding performance analysis in Section 7.6.2.

7.6.1 Related work with respect to Requirements Interaction

Although the problem of interaction between requirements has been known for a long time and dealing with conflicts among requirements is considered as one important aspect of requirements engineering, little progress has been made to tackle this problem. In this section, we discuss approaches dealing with conflicts among functional requirements as well as quality requirements.

Egyed and Grünbacher [92] introduce an approach based on software quality attributes and dependencies between requirements in order to identify conflicts and cooperations among requirements. They assume that two requirements are conflicting only if their quality attributes are conflicting and there is a dependency between them. In a four-step method, the authors identify conflicts among requirements based on this assumption. After categorizing requirements into software attributes such as security, usability, etc. manually, the authors identify conflicts and cooperations between requirements using dependencies among requirements. In a final step, they filter out requirements, the quality attributes of which are conflicting, but there is no dependency among them. The authors consider the case of conflicting requirements only due to their functionality and not their quality. Our method is similar to this method in a sense that both methods rely on dependencies between requirements. We make use of the existing problem diagrams to find the dependencies by taking the constrained domains into account.

In contrast to our problem-based method, Hausmann et al. [119] introduce a use case-based approach to detect potential inconsistencies between functional requirements. A rule-based specification of pre- and post-conditions is proposed to express functional requirements. The requirements are then formalized in terms of graph transformations that enable expressing the dependencies between requirements. Conflict detection is based on the idea of independence of graph transformations. Similar to our method, the results of the conflict detection method have to be analyzed further manually. Our method detects a set of interaction candidates that need to be analyzed further for real interactions. The approach proposed by Hausmann et al. [119] detects dependencies that represent errors or conflicts to be decided by the modeler. This is due to the incomplete nature of use cases.

Kim et al. [144] propose a process for detecting and managing conflicts between functional requirements expressed in natural language. After identifying, documenting, and prioritizing requirements using goals and scenarios in the first phase, the requirements are classified through the requirements partitioning criteria in the second step. In the third phase, conflicts are detected using a syntactic method to identify candidate conflicts and a semantic method to identify actual conflicts. Step four manages the detected conflicts according to the priorities. Similar to our method, this process reduces the scope of requirements to be considered by performing a syntactic analysis. The semantic analysis is performed manually by the analyst to check and answer a list of questions. As opposed to our method, this method is not formally specified.

Heisel and Souquières [123] developed a formal and heuristic method to detect requirement interactions. Each requirement consists of a pre- and a post-condition. The authors analyze whether the post-conditions are contradictory by sharing common pre-conditions. They also determine post-condition interaction candidates by looking for incompatible post-conditions. As opposed to our approach, the authors formalize the whole set of requirements, which is costly and time-consuming. Our approach utilizes the structure of problem diagrams to reduce the effort for the formalization.

The approach proposed by Alférez et al. [26] finds candidate points of interaction. The authors first analyze the dependencies between use cases to identify potential candidates of conflict. Then they determine whether the detected use cases are related to more than one feature. In contrast to our method, it is not formally defined. Furthermore, this approach is based on use cases, whereas we rely on problem frames.

An approach to detect feature interactions in software product lines (SPL) is proposed by Classen et al. [75]. The authors link feature diagrams used in SPL to the problem frames approach by redefining the notions of *feature* and *feature interaction* based on the entailment relationship $D, S \models R$ [133, 252]. This enables the authors to consider the environment in addition to the requirements, similar to our method. To detect feature interactions, four algorithms are presented based on a set of consistency rules. This work is complementary to our work. Using our approach, the sets of requirements and domains that have to be considered for interactions can be reduced and therefore the modeling and formalization effort is reduced.

van Lamsweerde et al. [162] use different formal techniques for detecting conflicts among goals based on KAOS. One technique to detect conflicts is deriving boundary conditions by backward chaining. Boundary conditions refer to combinations of circumstances causing inconsistency among different goals. Every precondition yields a boundary condition. The other technique is selecting a matching generic pattern. Our method for finding conflicts among requirements can be seen as complementary to this approach that provides techniques for detecting goal conflicts and resolving them. However, to use our method in connection with this approach, requirements as refinement of goals have to be modeled as problem diagrams.

7.6.2 Related work with respect to Performance Analysis

In a software development process, performance solutions are typically considered as architectural decisions to be made in the architecture and design phases. A number of approaches that contributed to software performance development have focused on architectural solutions. Nevertheless, information and knowledge needed for dealing with performance issues, have to be collected and analyzed early in the software development process. Similar to our approach, Williams and Smith [241] explore the information needed to construct and evaluate performance models. This information has to be captured during the analysis and design process. They define a similar set of information required for early life cycle software performance engineering. They use the terms "execution environment" for resource capacity and "resource requirement" for resource utilization and resource type.

In a later work, Smith and Williams [219] present their quantitative approach *software performance engineering (SPE)* to construct software systems with regard to performance objectives and requirements. SPE relies on use cases and scenarios that describe them. In the SPE process, after identifying critical use cases and scenarios, execution graphs are used to determine performance requirements. In further steps, the constructed execution graphs are evaluated to identify performance problems. Although use cases and scenarios build the starting point of the SPE process, it takes in further steps an architectural perspective. While the SPE process uses use cases and scenarios, the POPeRA method is based on problem frames. Problem frames contain more information for the analysis of performance requirements than use cases and scenarios. In contrast to our POPeRA method that focuses on performance requirements analysis, the SPE process requires detailed information regarding system resources that are not available in the early phase of software development, namely requirements engineering. Hence, the SPE process can be used as complementary to the POPeRA method afterwards when performance requirements analysis is performed.

Woodside et al. [246] propose a tool architecture called PUMA. It provides an intermediate model called Core Scenario Model (CSM) that takes a UML model annotated with performance information as input. The UML model is then transformed into performance models after removing the irrelevant design detail.

Tawhid and Petriu [231] propose to generate performance models for a specific product from a software product line (SPL). They aim at choosing a suitable design alternative in the early development phases. The starting point is a UML model that is annotated with performance information using the MARTE profile. Using the Atlas Transformation Language (ATL)[5], an annotated UML model of a product is derived from the annotated UML model of an SPL. In a second transformation a performance model from the annotated UML model of the product is generated using the PUMA transformation approach. These two approaches require design detail that is not available in the requirements analysis phase. However, the PUMA tool can potentially be applied to our annotated requirement models to create performance models. It should be explored whether the resulting performance models provide any useful information to use further.

Bass et al. [47] analyze how architectural mechanisms such as fixed priority scheduling and caching help to achieve performance as one specific quality requirement. They introduce the three strategies resource allocation, resource arbitration, and resource use for the achievement of performance requirements. Each strategy provides a set of performance mechanisms. Fixed priority scheduling that prioritizes processes to a fixed priority uses the strategy resource arbitration. The authors describe two mechanisms that correspond to our comprehensive approach for performance analysis. They do not provide a systematic method on how to identify performance problems and how to apply such mechanisms.

Methods that deal with performance in the early software development mostly use use cases and scenarios for analyzing and understanding requirements. The original problem frames approach does not support quality requirements. Some work has been performed to security requirements analysis [209, 118] and dependability requirements analysis [113, 112] based on problem frames. To the best of our knowledge, there has been no research regarding performance requirements analysis based on problem frames.

7.7 Contributions

In this chapter, we investigated how to detect and resolve requirement interactions among functional as well as quality requirements. This chapter consists of four parts. Our contributions can be summarized as follows:

---

[5] http://www.eclipse.org/atl/

- In the first part, we described a structured method to identify requirement interactions between functional requirements. We first identified and reduced candidates of interactions among a set of requirements modeled as problem diagrams. Then, we showed how to reduce this set of candidates further using life-cycle expressions. In the final phase of our method, we showed the existence of interactions by analyzing the pre- and postconditions.

- In the second part, we presented the *QuaRO* method to detect candidates for negative interactions between quality requirements based on pairwise comparison of requirements. In a preparation phase, to restrict the number of comparisons we made use of general relationships among different types of quality requirements. In further phases, we used the structure of problem diagrams to identify trade-off points. As a result, we obtained a set of pairwise quality requirements which are potentially conflicting.

- In the third part of this chapter, we proposed the *PoPeRA* method, which is based on problem frames for analyzing performance requirements. The *PoPeRA* method helps the performance analyst to identify potential performance problems as early as possible in the software development process using *performance domain knowledge* and *security domain knowledge*. The identified bottlenecks aid in further reducing the set of potentially conflicting quality requirements obtained from the *QuaRO* method. To summarize, the *PoPeRA* method 1) uses the modeled *performance and security domain knowledge* to identify potential bottlenecks, 2) guides the requirements engineer in stepwise analysis of performance requirements, and 3) further reduces the set of potential conflicts among quality requirements.

- In the fourth part, we provided a method for generating alternatives for interacting requirements. This method resolves the remaining conflicts between quality requirements from the *PoPeRA* method by relaxing them. For each original conflicting quality requirement, requirement alternatives are generated. Different sets of quality requirement alternatives lead to different architecture alternatives that fulfill the quality requirements security and performance with different degrees of satisfaction. The generated quality requirement alternatives are addressed in Chapter 9 by selecting and applying appropriate quality-specific solutions.

Chapter 8
Phase 5: Quality-specific Pattern Analysis

Abstract This chapter first introduces the problem-oriented quality patterns for the requirements analysis, which make use of the knowledge located in the design phase such as quality-specific solutions. We then discuss how the selection of quality-specific solutions as design decisions can affect other artifacts such as requirements and domain knowledge. In the third part of this chapter, we propose the *problem-solution diagram* enabling a mapping between the requirements (problem space) and the problem-oriented quality patterns (solution space). This intermediate model provides support for traceability between different model artifacts including the rationale for selecting the architectural solutions.

8.1 Introduction

As described before (see Chapters 2 and 5), patterns describe solutions for commonly recurring problems in software development. They are defined for different software development phases. There exist solutions to performance problems such as performance patterns [220, 96] to be applied during the design and implementation phases. Analogously, there exist security patterns that provide solutions to security problems [211].

We follow the concept of the twin peaks [182] that advocates the concurrent and iterative development of requirements and software architecture descriptions. As described before in this book (see Chapters 1 and 3), according to the twin peaks, requirements accommodated in the problem space and software architecture and design decisions accommodated in the solution space cannot be developed in isolation and should be developed concurrently.

Hence, we aim at refining the requirement models and equipping them with security and performance solution approaches early in the software development process, namely at the requirements level (problem space). To this end, we reuse the existing knowledge at the architectural level (solution space). That is, we use conventional performance and security patterns and adapt them in a way that they can be used in the problem-oriented requirements analysis. We call the adapted patterns *problem-oriented security patterns* and *problem-oriented performance patterns* as we represent them by means of problem diagrams. Refining requirement models with quality issues using architectural knowledge allows us to bridge the gap between quality (security and performance) problems and quality (security and performance) solutions.

This chapter represents Phase 5 of the QuaDRA framework. In the first part, we prepare the architectural knowledge which is located in the solution peak for being reused at the requirement levels by adapting and describing them as *problem-oriented security patterns* and *problem-oriented performance patterns*. In Chapter 9, we move to the problem peak to refine the requirement models by applying the patterns proposed in this chapter. This part is based on our works presented in [20] proposing problem-oriented security patterns and [5] proposing problem-oriented performance patterns.

We discuss how the selection of quality-specific solutions as design decisions can affect other artifacts such as requirements and domain knowledge. This part is based on our work published in [19].

In Chapter 7, we generated alternatives for conflicting requirements. Generating alternatives for quality requirements leads to variability in the problem space. Hence, quality requirements accommodated in the problem space can be considered as drivers that contribute to variability in the solution space. *Problem-oriented quality patterns* as solution alternatives fulfill quality requirements in different ways. We capture such patterns as variabilities in the solution space. To deal with the complexity of variability, we need to 1) explicitly model variability and 2) provide traceability links between variabilities at different levels of abstraction.

To this end, we present a UML-based approach to explicitly model variability in the problem and the solution space by adopting the notion of variability modeling. Then, we provide a mapping of quality requirement alternatives to the *problem-oriented quality patterns*. This mapping, called *problem-solution diagram*, as an intermediate model represents quality-specific solutions as variabilities which are provided with rationales for selecting them. It, therefore, supports the software engineer in the process of decision-making for selecting suitable quality-specific solution variants, reflecting quality concerns, and reasoning about it. This part is based on our work presented in [18]. We are the main author of the publications this chapter is based on. We had useful and valuable discussions with Maritta

Heisel regarding problem-oriented quality patterns and the relation between quality requirements and quality solutions.

The remainder of this chapter is organized as follows. We introduce our problem-oriented security patterns in Section 8.2 while the problem-oriented performance patterns are presented in Section 8.3. Section 8.4 discusses the benefits of the proposed patterns for problem-oriented software development. The problem-solution diagram as a mapping of quality requirements to possible quality-specific solutions is given in Section 8.5. We present related work in Section 8.6. The contribution of this chapter is given in Section 8.7.

8.2 Problem-oriented Security Patterns

According to Clements et al. [78], we require to consider two different concerns for achieving security. The first concern is specifying usage relationships and communication restrictions among different parts of the system. Examples for achieving this are access control such as Role-Based Access Control (RBAC), Message Authentication Code (MAC), and encryption. The other concern is preventing unauthorized intrusion where it does the most damage. This can be achieved by access control such as RBAC. These solutions that address the two concerns are of architectural nature. In the following, we reuse this existing architectural knowledge including patterns and mechanisms and adapt it in a way that it can be expressed as problem diagrams for problem-oriented requirements analysis. We call the adapted patterns *problem-oriented security patterns*. The adaptation allows us to integrate such security-specific solutions early in the requirements engineering phase.

We present five problem-oriented security patterns, namely *symmetric encryption, Message Authentication Code (MAC), Role-Based Access Control (RBAC), digital signature*, and *asymmetric encryption* as examples for achieving confidentiality, integrity, and authenticity. Further problem-oriented security patterns may be extracted from the existing security patterns and mechanisms by software engineers to aid requirements engineers in integrating security solution approaches early in the requirements analysis.

In the following, we first describe an extension of the UML profile UML4PF for modeling problem-oriented security patterns in Section 8.2.1. Then, we describe the structure of the problem-oriented security patterns in Section 8.2.2. Then, we introduce the five problem-oriented security patterns *symmetric encryption* in Section 8.2.3, *MAC* in Section 8.2.4, *RBAC* in Section 8.2.5, *digital signature* in Section 8.2.6, and *asymmetric encryption* in Section 8.2.7.

8.2.1 UML4PF Extension for Problem-oriented Security Patterns

We extend the problem frames notation by introducing new elements for modeling problem-oriented security patterns and their instantiations. Our extension is a UML profile relying on the UML4PF profile (see Section 2.3.1 on page 33). Figure 8.1 shows the stereotypes of this UML profile. In the following, we describe the stereotypes that we used in our profile.

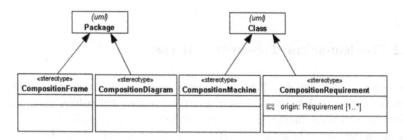

Fig. 8.1: UML4PF Extension for modeling problem-oriented security patterns

One new kind of *UML4PF diagrams* is the *composition frame*. It is expressed by the stereotype ≪CompositionFrame≫. Composition frames deal with the composition of two machines, each of which is described by a problem frame in order to address combined requirements [163]. The other new type of diagrams is the *composition diagram* which represents an instantiation of the composition frame. It is expressed by the stereotype ≪CompositionDiagram≫.

We introduce a new type of requirements, namely *composition requirement* (expressed by the stereotype ≪CompositionRequirement≫). A composition requirement is the requirement corresponding to a composition frame or composition diagram. It represents the combination of two requirements. The attribute *origin* of the stereotype ≪CompositionRequirement≫ indicates the two requirements which build the origin of the composition requirement.

Composition machine is a new type of domains. It represents the machine in a composition frame or composition requirements. It is expressed by the stereotype ≪CompositionMachine≫.

Table 8.1 shows the list of defined stereotypes and their description. Our extension is used in the next sections for modeling problem-oriented security patterns.

Table 8.1: Stereotypes defined for UML4PF extension for modeling the problem-oriented security patterns and their instances

Stereotype, Tagged values	Applies to	Description
≪ConmpositionFrame≫	Package	It represents the composition of two machines, each of which is described by a problem frame.
≪CompositionDiagram≫	Package	It represents an instance of a composition frame.
≪CompositionRequirement≫	Class	It represents the requirement corresponding to the composition frame or composition diagram.
{origin = Origin}	≪CompositionRequirement≫	It represents the requirements building the composition requirement.
≪CompositionMachine≫	Class	It represents the machine in the composition frame or composition diagram.

8.2.2 Structure of the Problem-oriented Security Patterns

A problem-oriented security pattern consists of a *graphical pattern* and a *template*. In the following, we describe the constituents of the pattern.

Graphical pattern:
The graphical pattern involves the following parts:

Functional Problem Frame: During the requirements analysis phase, it is essential to describe and understand the problem explicitly. Hence, setting up a *functional problem diagram* as an instance of the *functional problem frame* is the first step to be performed for describing a specific problem. It captures the structure of the problem explicitly and consists of a generic functional requirement and the involved domains. In order to describe the security problem related to the functional requirement, the functional problem frame contains a specific security requirement, for which we provide a solution approach in the second part. The security requirement is annotated as complement to the functional requirement.

Security Problem Frame: The functional problem frame describes the functional problem and its related security requirement. The second part of a problem-oriented security pattern is a *security problem frame* that describes the particular solution approach for the security requirement annotated in the first part.

Composition Problem Frame: The third part is concerned with composing the *functional problem frame* and *security problem frame* to obtain a solution for the overall problem. Hence, we provide a *composition problem frame* that describes how the *functional problem frame* and the *security problem frame* can be composed to solve the overall problem. To this end, we make use of *Composition Frames* introduced in [163, 24] as a new kind of problem frames. Composition frames deal with the composition of two machines, each of which is described by a problem diagram in order to address combined requirements [163]. We use composition frames to integrate the problem frame for the selected security solution with the functional problem frame. A composition frame includes the domains shared between the functional problem and the security solution, and their corresponding machine domains. For the graphical patterns we use the same notation we use for problem frames.

As an optional part of the graphical pattern, a sequence diagram might be used to illustrate how the functional machine and the security machine interact with each other to solve the overall problem.

Template:

We provide a template consisting of two parts that documents additional information related to the domains in the problem diagrams. Such information is not observable in the graphical pattern. The first part accommodates information about the security mechanism itself such as name (*Name*), purpose (*Purpose*), description (*Brief Description*), and the quality requirement which will be achieved when applying this pattern (*Quality Requirement to be achieved*). Moreover, a security solution may affect the achievement of other quality requirements. For example, improving the security may result in decreasing the performance. Hence, the impact of each security solution on other quality requirements has to be captured in the first part of the template (*Affected Quality Requirement*). A security pattern not only solves a problem, but also produces new functional and quality problems that have to be addressed either as *Requirements* to be elicited or as *Assumptions* needed to be made in the second part of the template. We elicit new functional and quality problems as requirements if the software to be built shall achieve them. Assumptions have to be satisfied by the environment [161]. They are not guaranteed to be true in every case. For the case that we assume the environment (not the machine) takes the responsibility for meeting them, we capture them as assumptions. This should be negotiated with the stakeholders and documented properly.

8.2.3 Problem-oriented Symmetric Encryption Pattern

Symmetric encryption is an important security mechanism to achieve confidentiality. There exists only one *secret key* which is used for encrypting and decrypting a plaintext that has to be kept confidential. *Asymmetric encryption* is a similar means to achieve confidentiality. It, however, uses different keys for the encryption and decryption. One advantage of symmetric encryption is that it is faster than asymmetric encryption. The disadvantage is that both communication parties must know the same key, which has to be distributed securely or negotiated. In asymmetric encryption, there is no key distribution problem, but a trusted third party is needed that issues the key pairs.

We present the *problem-oriented symmetric encryption pattern* by its corresponding graphical pattern depicted in Fig. 8.2 and its corresponding template shown in Table 8.2.

Graphical pattern:

Functional Problem Frame: The graphical pattern first describes the functional problem expressed as the problem frame *GenericProblem*. It describes the functional requirement *FunctionalReq* and the involved domains. The functional requirement is concerned with "sending the data" to be achieved by the machine *FunctionalM*. Data is expressed as the lexical domain *Domain1* in the problem frame. There exist a causal domain *Domain2* such as a network for transforming the data. The confidentiality requirement *ConfidentialityReq* is annotated in the problem frame by complementing the functional requirement. It requires the achievement of the functional requirement in a confidential way. The functional problem frame is depicted at the top of Fig. 8.2. Depending on the functional requirement, the problem frame might contain other domains that are not relevant for the security problem. Hence, they are not represented in the pattern.

Security Problem Frame: The symmetric encryption as a solution for the confidentiality problem is expressed by the problem frame *SymmetricEncryption* shown in the middle of Fig. 8.2. It consists of all domains that are relevant for the solution. The machine *SymEncM* should achieve the confidentiality requirement *ConfidentialityReq* by encrypting the *Domain1* using the *SecretKey* which is part of the machine *SymEncM*.

Composition Problem Frame: The third part of the graphical pattern shown at the bottom of Fig. 8.2 is concerned with combining the *functional problem frame* with the *security problem frame* to obtain the composed problem frame *FunctionalSecComposition*. It consists of the new machine *CompositionM*, both

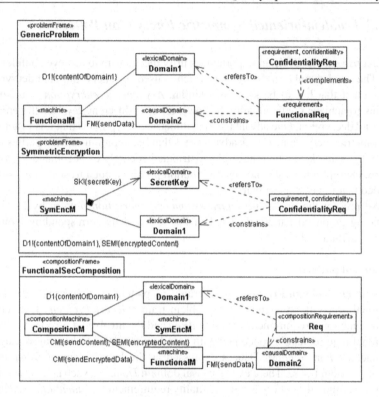

Fig. 8.2: Problem-oriented symmetric encryption pattern (graphical pattern)

machine domains *FunctionalM* and *SymEncM*, and all the domains contained in both problem frames. Note that the lexical domain *SecretKey* is part of the machine *SymEncM* that we made visible as it is of great importance for the encryption mechanism. The machine *CompositionM* is responsible for coordinating the functional machine *FunctionalM* and the solution machine *SymEncM*. The requirement *CompositionReq* shall be achieved by the machine *CompositionM*. It combines the requirements *FunctionalReq* and *ConfidentialityReq*. Figure 8.3 shows how the different machines collaborate with each other in the composed problem diagram *FunctionalSecComposition*. *Domain1* sends its content to the machine *CompositionM*. The machine *CompositionM* sends this content to the machine *SmyEncM* and receives the encrypted content. The encrypted content is sent to the machine*FunctionalM* which sends it further through the causal domain *Domain2*.

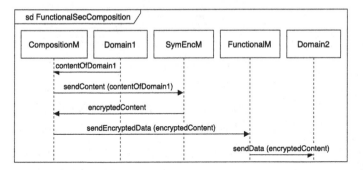

Fig. 8.3: Sequence diagram of the composition problem diagram for Sysmmetric Encryption

We will see in the following by the description of the related template that we need to capture new assumptions and elicit new requirements regarding the secret key.

Template:
The template shown in Table 8.2 represents the additional information corresponding to the graphical part of the problem-oriented pattern *symmetric encryption*. After capturing the basic information in the first part, in the second part we elicit new requirements and capture new assumptions that arise with the solution, such as *secret key shall be/ is distributed*. Eliciting this condition results in thinking about security issues concerned with it, such as *confidentiality and integrity of secret key distribution shall be/is preserved*. Note that the requirements and assumptions are not fixed. Requirements have to be met by the machine (i.e. software-to-be) and assumptions by the environment. If we require that the software we build is responsible for preserving the confidentiality and integrity of the secret key not only during the transmission but also during the storage, we have to capture these as requirements. This is the reason why the necessary conditions are presented as checkboxes to be selected by checking the relevant checkbox as requirement or assumption.

Table 8.2: Problem-oriented Symmetric Encryption pattern (template)

Security Solution	
Name	Symmetric Encryption
Purpose	For *Domain* constrained by the requirement *FunctionalReq*
Brief Description	The plaintext is encrypted using the secret key
Quality Requirement to be achieved	Security (confidentiality) *ConfidentialityReq*
Affected Quality Requirement	Performance *PerformanceReq*, availability *AvailabilityReq*
Necessary Conditions	
Requirement □ Assumption □	Secret key shall be/is distributed.
Requirement □ Assumption □	Confidentiality of secret key distribution shall be/is preserved.
Requirement □ Assumption □	Integrity of secret key distribution shall be/is preserved.
Requirement □ Assumption □	Confidentiality of secret key during transmission shall be/is preserved
Requirement □ Assumption □	Confidentiality of secret key during storage shall be/is preserved.
Requirement □ Assumption □	Integrity of secret key during storage shall be/is preserved.

8.2.4 Problem-oriented MAC Pattern

Message Authentication Code (MAC) is an important means for achieving integrity and authenticity of data. The MAC algorithm uses a secret key and the data to generate a MAC. The verifier uses the same secret key to detect changes to the data as well as to ensure that the data is created by the known sender. The *problem-oriented MAC pattern* is similar to the *problem-oriented symmetric encryption pattern* in a manner that both patterns use a secret key for achieving their goal. Hence, the graphical pattern of MAC is similar to the one of symmetric encryption. Therefore, we do not show the graphical pattern of MAC. Its template is represented in Table 8.3.

Template:
The template shown in Table 8.3 represents the additional information related to the problem-oriented pattern *MAC*. New requirements and assumptions to be considered are represented in the second part of the template.

Table 8.3: Problem-oriented MAC pattern (template)

Security Solution	
Name	Message Authentication Code (MAC)
Purpose	For *Domain* constrained by the requirement *FunctionalReq*
Brief Description	MAC uses a secret key and the data to generate a MAC. The verifier uses the same secret key to detect changes to the data.
Quality Requirement to be achieved	Security (integrity and authenticity) *IntegrityReq*, *AuthenticityReq*
Affected Quality Requirement	Performance *PerformanceReq*
Necessary Conditions	
Requirement □ Assumption □	Secret key shall be/is distributed.
Requirement □ Assumption □	Confidentiality of secret key distribution shall be/is preserved.
Requirement □ Assumption □	Integrity of secret key distribution shall be/is preserved.
Requirement □ Assumption □	Confidentiality of secret key during transmission shall be/is preserved.
Requirement □ Assumption □	Confidentiality of secret key during storage shall be/is preserved.
Requirement □ Assumption □	Integrity of secret key during storage shall be/is preserved.

8.2.5 Problem-oriented RBAC Pattern

Since verifying permission is a frequently recurring problem in security relevant systems, it has been treated in several access control patterns for the design phase [248, 211]. Access control patterns define security constraints regarding access to resources. Role-Based Access Control (RBAC) provides access to resources based on functions of people in an environment, known as *roles*, and the kind of permission they have, known as *rights*.

We present the *problem-oriented RBAC pattern* by its corresponding graphical pattern depicted in Fig. 8.4 and its corresponding template shown in Table 8.4.

Graphical pattern:

Functional Problem Frame: The first part of the graphical pattern, namely the *functional problem frame* expressed by the problem frame *GenericProblem*, is similar to the previous one from the structure point of view. The functional requirement *FunctionalReq* might be "editing data" to be met by the functional machine *FunctionalM*. Data is represented by the lexical domain *Domain*. The functional requirement is complemented by the security requirement *IntegrityReq* demanding "the protection of data against unauthorized access". The functional problem frame is depicted at the top of Fig. 8.4.

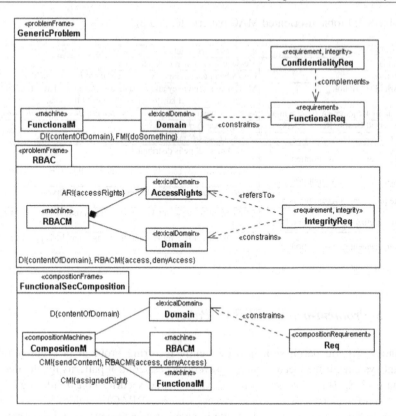

Fig. 8.4: Problem-oriented RBAC pattern (graphical pattern)

Security Problem Frame: The second part provides the domains that are required for applying the *RBAC* pattern, expressed by the problem frame *RBAC* shown in the middle of Fig. 8.4. The lexical domain *AccessRights* represents *user id*, assigned *role(s)* to it, and assigned *right(s)* to the role(s). It is a part of the machine *RBACM* which is responsible for achieving the integrity requirement.

Composition Problem Frame: The third part composes the functional machine *FunctionalM* with the security machine *RBACM* by introducing a new machine *CompositionM* that has to meet the requirement *CompositionReq* composed of the requirements *FuncitonalReq* and *IntegrityReq*. It is depicted at the bottom of Fig. 8.4. Figure 8.5 shows how the different machines collaborate with each other in the composed problem frame *FunctionalSecComposition*. After obtaining the data from the lexical domain *Domain*, the machine *CompositionM* sends this content to the machine *RBACM* and receives the information about accessing or denying the access to data. The assigned rights are then sent to the machine *FunctionalM*.

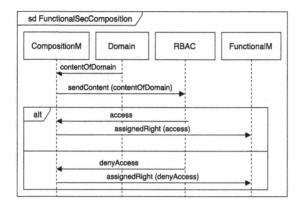

Fig. 8.5: Sequence diagram of the composition problem diagram for RBAC

Note that due to introducing the composition machine *CompositionM* the interfaces of the functional machine *FunctionalM* and the security machine *RBAC* change. The new interfaces are specified at the bottom of Fig. 8.4 and in Fig. 8.5.

The *problem-oriented RBAC pattern* can be used to achieve a confidentiality requirement as well. In Fig. 8.4, we only showed the use of the *problem-oriented RBAC pattern* to achieve the integrity requirement *IntegrityReq* in order to keep the figure clear and readable. One can apply the same pattern and only replace the integrity requirement with the confidentiality requirement to achieve confidentiality.

Template:

The template shown in Table 8.4 represents the additional information corresponding to the graphical part of the problem-oriented pattern *RBAC*. In addition to the basic information regarding the pattern itself, it contains requirements and assumptions to be selected by the requirements engineer. Note that the assumption by applying the problem-oriented RBAC pattern is that all the persons who are authorized to access handle and behave correctly. Note that we do not capture this assumption in Table 8.4 as such kinds of assumptions deal with social engineering and cannot be considered in software development.

Table 8.4: Problem-oriented RBAC pattern (template)

Security Solution	
Name	RBAC
Purpose	For *Domain* constrained by the requirement *FunctionalReq*
Brief Description	It provides access to data based on defined roles and rights captured as access rights.
Quality Requirement to be achieved	Security (confidentiality and integrity during storage) *Confidentiali- tyReq*, *IntegrityReq*
Affected Quality Requirement	Performance *PerformanceReq*, availability *AvailabilityReq*
Necessary Conditions	
Requirement □ Assumption □	Integrity of access rights shall be/is preserved.
Requirement □ Assumption □	Confidentiality of data during storage shall be/is preserved.
Requirement □ Assumption □	Integrity of data during storage shall be/is preserved.

8.2.6 Problem-oriented Digital Signature Pattern

Digital signature is an important means for achieving integrity and authenticity of data. Using the digital signature, a signature is produced using the private key and the data. In order to ensure the authenticity of data, the signature is verified using the public key.

We present the *problem-oriented digital signature pattern* by its corresponding graphical pattern depicted in Fig. 8.6 and its corresponding template shown in Table 8.5.

Graphical pattern:

The structure of the graphical pattern is similar to the structure of the *problem-oriented symmetric encryption pattern*. The difference is that a *private key* is used for signing the data. As we described the structure of the *problem-oriented symmetric encryption pattern* extensively, we do not describe the graphical pattern any more and only refer to Fig. 8.6. The Fig. 8.7 shows how the different machines collaborate with each other in the composed problem diagram *FunctionalSecComposition*.

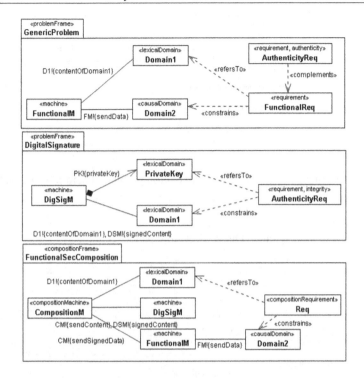

Fig. 8.6: Problem-oriented digital signature pattern (graphical pattern)

Note that the *problem-oriented digital signature pattern* can be used to achieve an integrity requirement as well. In Fig. 8.6, we only showed the use of the *problem-oriented digital signature pattern* to achieve the integrity requirement *AuthenticityReq* in order to keep the figure clear and readable. One can apply the same pattern and only replace the authenticity requirement with the integrity requirement to achieve integrity.

Template:
The template shown in Table 8.5 represents the additional information corresponding to the graphical part of the problem-oriented pattern *digital signature*. New requirements and assumptions to be considered are represented in the second part of the template.

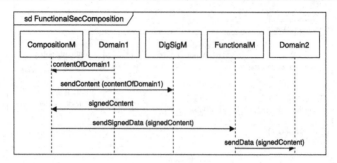

Fig. 8.7: Sequence diagram of the composition problem diagram for Digital Signature

Table 8.5: Problem-oriented Digital Signature pattern (template)

Security Solution	
Name	Digital Signature
Purpose	For *Domain* constrained by the requirement FunctionalReq
Brief Description	Sender produces a signature using the private key and the data.
Quality Requirement to be achieved	Security (integrity and authenticity) *IntegrityReq, AuthenticityReq*
Affected Quality Requirement	Performance *PerformanceReq*
Necessary Conditions	
Requirement □ Assumption □	Integrity of public key during transmission shall be/is preserved.
Requirement □ Assumption □	Confidentiality of private key during transmission shall be/is preserved.
Requirement □ Assumption □	Integrity of private key during transmission shall be/is preserved.
Requirement □ Assumption □	Confidentiality of private key during storage shall be/is preserved.
Requirement □ Assumption □	Integrity of private key during storage shall be/is preserved.
Requirement □ Assumption □	Integrity of public key during storage shall be/is preserved.

8.2.7 Problem-oriented Asymmetric Encryption Pattern

Asymmetric Encryption is an important means for achieving confidentiality of data. Using the asymmetric encryption, the data is encrypted using the public key. Decrypting the data is achieved using its private key. The *problem-oriented asymmetric encryption pattern* is similar to the *problem-oriented symmetric key pattern* in a manner that both patterns are concerned with encrypting data. The difference is that the *problem-oriented symmetric encryption pattern* uses only one *secret key* for encrypting and decrypting data. Therefore, this key must be kept secret. The *problem-oriented asymmetric encryption* uses a *public-private key pair* for achieving its goal. It uses the *public key* for encrypting the data and the corresponding *private key* for decrypting the data. We do not show the graphical pattern of asymmetric encryption as the graphical pattern of the similar pattern symmetric encryption has been described extensively. Its template is represented in Table 8.6.

Template:
The template shown in Table 8.6 represents the additional information related to the problem-oriented pattern *asymmetric encryption*. New requirements and assumptions to be considered are represented in the second part of the template.

Table 8.6: Problem-oriented Asymmetric Encryption Pattern (template)

Security Solution	
Name	Asymmetric Encryption
Purpose	For *Domain* constrained by the requirement *FunctionalReq*
Brief Description	The plaintext is encrypted using the public key and decrypted using the private key.
Quality Requirement to be achieved	Security (confidentiality) *ConfidentialityReq*
Affected quality requirements	Performance *PerformanceReq*, availability *AvailabilityReq*
Necessary Conditions	
Requirement □ Assumption □	Integrity of public key during transmission shall be/is preserved.
Requirement □ Assumption □	Confidentiality of private key during transmission shall be/is preserved.
Requirement □ Assumption □	Integrity of private key during transmission shall be/is preserved.
Requirement □ Assumption □	Confidentiality of private key during storage shall be/is preserved.
Requirement □ Assumption □	Integrity of private key during storage shall be/is preserved.
Requirement □ Assumption □	Integrity of public key during storage shall be/is preserved.

Note that we do not provide a structured method to identify new requirements and assumptions as necessary conditions. However, as mentioned earlier in this section, new requirements and assumptions arise due to introducing the security solution (*Security Problem Frame*). Hence, we can reduce the scope of consideration for identifying new requirements and assumptions to the solution for the security requirement, namely to the *Security Problem Frame*. In this problem frame, we only need to consider the lexical domain, for example the *SecretKey* for the *problem-oriented symmetric encryption pattern* and its related security machine *SymEncM*. For these two domains, we have to think about new problems that might arise and then capture them as new requirements and/or assumptions.

8.3 Problem-oriented Performance Patterns

According to Clements et al. [78], for achieving high performance, we need to consider three different concerns, namely *exploit potential parallelism, manage the
volume of the network communication and frequencies of data access*, and *identify
potential performance bottlenecks*. In the previous chapter (see Chapter 7), we proposed a method for identifying potential performance bottlenecks. For achieving
the other two concerns, we propose *problem-oriented performance patterns* in this
section. These patterns can be applied to problem diagrams containing potential
bottlenecks, which is the topic of the next chapter (see Chapter 9).

For exploiting potential parallelism, the problem-oriented performance patterns
Load Balancer and *Master Worker* can be applied. We make use of the problem-
oriented performance patterns *First Things First* and *Flex Time* for achieving the
second concern, namely managing the volume of the network communication and
frequencies of data access. These patterns provide solutions for the problem situation where an overload of the system is expected.

We make use of a collection of existing performance patterns taken from the
literature [96, 220] in order to adapt them for the requirements analysis phase.
The adaptation allows the use of such performance patterns in the requirements
analysis phase for the analysis of performance problems.

In the following, we first describe the structure of the problem-oriented performance patterns in Section 8.3.2. Then, we introduce four problem-oriented performance patterns *First Things First* in Section 8.3.3, *Flex Time* in Section 8.3.4,
Master Worker in Section 8.3.5, and *Load Balancer* in Section 8.3.6.

8.3.1 UML4PF Extension for Problem-oriented Performance Patterns

We extend the problem frames notation by introducing a new element for modeling
performance problems. Our extension is a UML profile relying on the UML4PF
profile (see Section 2.3.1 on page 33). Figure 8.8 shows the stereotype of the
UML profile extension. In the following, we describe the new stereotype and its
attributes.

For modeling performance problems, we introduce the new stereotype ≪Bottle-
neck≫. It represents potential performance problems. ≪Bottleneck≫ can be applied to the domains that represent resources. In dealing with performance problems, we are concerned with the types of resources, the type of overload, and the

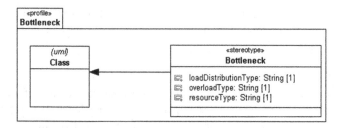

Fig. 8.8: UML4PF Extension for modeling performance problems

type of load distribution. These three different types are represented as attributes of the stereotype ≪Bottleneck≫.

Table 8.7 shows the list of the defined stereotype, its attributes and related descriptions. Our extension is used in the next sections for modeling the potential bottlenecks in the problem-oriented performance patterns.

Table 8.7: Stereotypes defined for UML4PF extension for modeling the performance problems

Stereotype, Tagged values	Applies to	Description
≪Bottleneck≫	Class	It represents a resource that is a bottleneck.
{loadDistributionType = LoadDistribution-Type}	≪Bottleneck≫	It represents the type of the load distribution. It can be *spatial* or *temporal*
{overloadType = OverloadDistributionType}	≪Bottleneck≫	It represents the type of the overload. It can be *permanent* or *temporary*
{resourceType = ResourceType}	≪Bottleneck≫	It represents the type of the resource. It can be *software* or *hardware* or *software/hardware* if there is no matter what is the type of the resource.

8.3.2 Structure of the Problem-oriented Performance Patterns

Each problem-oriented performance pattern encompasses a generic template for describing performance patterns textually. It has to be instantiated for each performance pattern explicitly. In addition to the template, we provide a problem frame that describes the generic structure of the problem. Then, we describe the solution approach by introducing a new problem frame that describes the generic structure of the solution.

Template:

A performance pattern conveys essential performance-specific information and principles for facilitating the reuse of performance knowledge. We propose a template that represents the information contained in the patterns in a way that they can be used on a higher abstraction level than the architecture level, namely on the requirements analysis level.

Our proposed template illustrated in Table 8.8 is inspired by the template for design patterns proposed by Gamma et al. [103]. We modified the template for design patterns to describe and represent performance-specific information. Our template contains additional information for modeling a performance analysis pattern using the UML4PF and MARTE profiles. The proposed template allows software architects to define new performance analysis patterns according to this structure as well.

Table 8.8: Template for problem-oriented performance patterns

1) Name	Name of the pattern
2) Description	Brief description of the pattern
3) Also known as	Other well-known names for the pattern, if any
4) Problem	Situation and structure of the problem
5) Applicability	Conditions under which the pattern can be applied
6) Solution	Structure of the solution using stereotypes from UML4PF and MARTE
7) Collaboration	Behavior Description of solution elements
8) Benefits	Benefits of applying the pattern
9) Consequences	Consequences and hints to be considered when applying the pattern
10) Related patterns	Another pattern related to the pattern

The following information about the characteristics of each mechanism is captured in the template given in Table 8.8: 1) *name* of the pattern, 2) *description* of the pattern, 3) *also known as* representing other well-known names of the pattern, if existing, 4) *problem*, which describes circumstances and structure of the problem, 5) *applicability*, which represents conditions under which the pattern can be applied using stereotypes from the UML profile extension and MARTE 6) *solution*, which represents the structure of the solution using stereotypes from UML4PF and MARTE, 7) *collaboration* describing the behavior of the solution, 8) *benefits* of applying the pattern, 9) *consequences* and additional hints to be considered when applying the pattern, 10) *related patterns* describing other patterns that bear relations to the pattern at hand.

The fields *problem* and *applicability* describe when the pattern can be applied. They represent the pre-conditions for the pattern at hand. The fields *solution, collaboration, benefits*, and *consequences* describe the solution including its elements, their relationships, and their behavior. They represent the post-conditions for the pattern at hand.

Graphical Pattern:
The original performance patterns only describe the principle of the solution. They do not provide any structure of the problem. We provide the structure of the problem as a specific problem frame in addition to the textual description in the template. We call this problem frame the *generic problem structure*.

Note that the problem for all performance patterns presented in this chapter is structured in the same way (see the field *problem* in the template). The reason is that the lack of resources is the essence of most performance problems. This is the case when more requests have to be processed at the same time than the resources can process. Hence, there is only one problem frame describing the generic problem structure. Nevertheless, the conditions under which the patterns can be applied are different (see the field *applicability* in the template).

Similar to the problem frame for describing the problem structure, we provide a problem frame for describing the structure of the solution which we call *generic solution structure*. Again, the structure of the solution is similar for all patterns presented in this chapter. Nevertheless, the patterns behave differently to solve problems that have the same structure but different applicability conditions. The two generic problem frames have to be instantiated for each pattern separately.

Generic problem structure   At the top of Fig. 8.9 is the problem frame describing the *generic problem structure* illustrated. Domains contained in this problem frame are:

- One domain *Machine*, which is a machine domain. It represents a resource expressed by the stereotype ≪resource≫ responsible for responding to the requests. The resource is expected to be the bottleneck which cannot complete all inbound requests (see the stereotype ≪bottleneck≫ in the problem frame *GenericProblem* in Fig. 8.9).
- One *Domain1* domain, which transmits the requests to the machine domain *Machine*. Note that the concrete problem diagram can contain more domains, which are not relevant for the performance problem at hand.

- One *Domain2* domain, which represents an arbitrary domain that might be required for processing the requests by the *Machine*. Note that this domain does not need to be instantiated.
- One *Requirement*, which describes the functional requirement to be satisfied. It requires the processing of the requests.
- One *PerformanceReq*, which describes the performance requirement to be satisfied. It requires the satisfaction of the functional requirement *Requirement* within a specific time.

Generic solution structure   At the bottom of Fig. 8.9, the problem frame describing the *generic solution structure* is shown. It is a *composition frame* that composes several subproblems using a newly introduced machine domain. We introduce the new machine domain *FTF/FT/MW/LB* to compose several machine domains that are bottlenecks (see machine domain *Machine* at the bottom of Fig. 8.9) in order to prevent an overload for each single machine domain. There exists only one machine domain *Machine* for the performance analysis patterns *FTF* and *FT* and at least two machine domains *Machine* of the same type for the performance analysis patterns *LB* and *MW*. Domains contained in this problem frame are:

- One domain *FTF/FT/MW/LB* as a machine domain and as a resource with the stereotypes «machine» and «resource».
- At least one domain as machine domain and as resource (stereotypes «machine» and «resource») responsible for responding to the requests (see *Machine* in the problem frame *GenericSolution* in Fig. 8.9).
- One domain *Domain1* with the stereotype «domain», which transmits the requests to the machine domain *Machine*.
- One domain *Domain2* with the stereotype «domain» required for processing the requests by the machine domain *Machine*.
- One functional requirement *Requirement* with the stereotype «requirement» to be satisfied by the machine domains *Machine* (at least one machine domain).
- One *PerformanceReq* with the stereotypes «requirement» and «paStep» to be satisfied by the machine domains *Machine* (at least one machine domain).

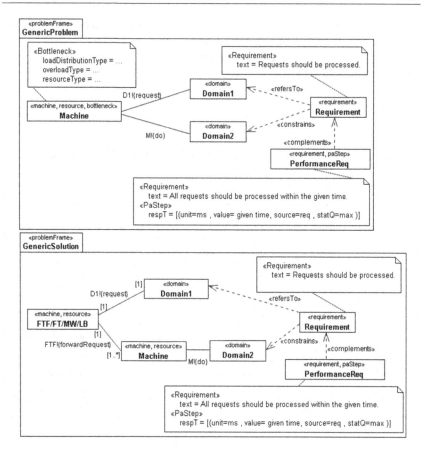

Fig. 8.9: Problem frames describing the structure of the generic problem and the generic solution

8.3.3 Problem-oriented First Things First (FTF) Pattern

The *First Things First* pattern ensures that the most important tasks will be processed if not every task can be processed. The problem that this pattern aims at solving is that a temporary overload of inbound requests is expected. This situation may overwhelm the processing capacity of a specific resource. The First Things First pattern uses the strategy of prioritizing tasks and performing the important tasks with a high priority first. In the case of a permanent overload, applying this pattern would cause the starving of the low priority tasks [220].

The instantiation of the template given in Table 8.8 for the First Things First pattern is shown in Table 8.9.

Table 8.9: First Things First Pattern

1) Name	First Things First (FTF)
2) Description	FTF ensures that the most important tasks will be processed if not every task can be processed.
3) Also known as	-
4) Problem	A temporary overload of inbound requests is expected. This situation may overwhelm the processing capacity of a specific resource (see the generic problem frame in Fig. 8.9).
5) Applicability	FTF pattern is only applicable when there is a temporary overload. That is, the attribute *overloadType* of the stereotype ≪bottleneck≫ in the generic problem frame (see Fig. 8.9) should have the value *temporary*.
6) Solution	The solution uses the strategy of prioritizing tasks and performing the important tasks with a high priority first. A new machine is introduced that takes the responsibility for prioritizing the tasks and assigning them to corresponding domains.
7) Collaboration	When requests are issued, they arrive through *Domain1* at the newly introduced machine domain *FTF*, which takes the responsibility to prioritize the requests and forward them to the corresponding machine that performs the requests using the domain *Domain2*. Note that there exists only one machine domain *Machine* (see the sequence diagram in Fig. 8.10).
8) Benefits	FTF reduces the contention delay for high-priority tasks.
9) Consequences	In the case of a permanent overload, applying this pattern would cause the starving of low-priority tasks.
10) Related patterns	LB and MW patterns can be used to improve the processing capacity if the overload is not temporary.

8.3.4 Problem-oriented Flex Time (FT) Pattern

The *Flex Time* pattern reduces the load of the system by spreading the load temporally. That is, it moves the load to a different period of time where the inbound requests do not exceed the processing capacity of the resource. The problem that this pattern solves is that an overload of the system is expected. The inbound requests exceed the processing capacity of a specific resource. Flex Time is only applicable when some tasks can be performed at a different period of time [220]. Table 8.10 illustrates the instantiation of the template for the Flex Time pattern.

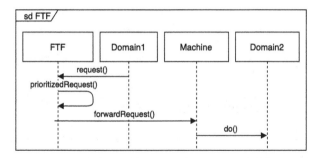

Fig. 8.10: Sequence diagram describing the behavior of the FTF pattern

Table 8.10: Flex Time Pattern

1) Name	Flex Time (FT)
2) Description	FT moves the load to a different period of time where the inbound requests do not exceed the processing capacity of the resource.
3) Also known as	-
4) Problem	An overload of the system is expected. The inbound requests exceed the processing capacity of a specific resource (see the generic problem frame in Fig. 8.9).
5) Applicability	FT is only applicable when some tasks can be performed at a different period of time. That is, the attributes *loadDistributionType* and *overloadType* of the stereotype ≪bottleneck≫ in the generic problem frame in Fig. 8.9 have the values *temporal* and *permanent*.
6) Solution	The solution uses the strategy of spreading the load at a different period of time. A new machine is introduced that takes the responsibility for modifying the processing time of the tasks and assigning them to corresponding domains for processing in the specified time.
7) Collaboration	When requests are issued, they arrive through *Domain1* at the newly introduced machine *FT*, which takes the responsibility to spread the requests at a different period of time to be processed by the corresponding machine using the domain *Domain2*. Note that there exists only one machine domain *Machine* (see the sequence diagram in Fig. 8.11).
8) Benefits	FT pattern reduces the load of the system by spreading it temporally.
9) Consequences	The order of satisfying requirements will be changed. It has to be checked that this modification does not cause new bottlenecks.
10) Related patterns	LB and MW patterns can be used to reduce the load if the tasks cannot be performed at a different period of time.

8.3.5 Problem-oriented Master-Worker (MW) Pattern

The *Master-Worker* pattern makes it possible to serve requests in parallel, similarly to load balancing. In contrast to load balancing that uses hardware com-

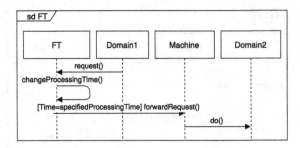

Fig. 8.11: Sequence diagram describing the behavior of the FT pattern

ponents, the master-worker pattern provides a software solution. It consists of a software component called Master and two or more other software components, called Worker. The machine *FTF/FT/MW/LB* in Fig. 8.9 represents the Master and two or more machine domains *Machine* represent the Workers. The task of the master is to divide the request into parallel tasks and to forward them to the workers, which manage the smaller tasks [96]. We instantiate the presented template for the Master-Worker pattern. The result is shown in Table 8.11.

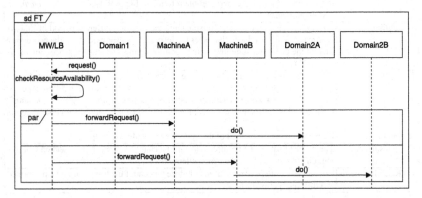

Fig. 8.12: Sequence diagram describing the behavior of the MW and LB patterns

Table 8.11: Master-Worker Pattern

1) Name	Master-Worker (MW)
2) Description	The MW pattern makes it possible to serve requests in parallel. It distributes the load over two or more software resources. The MW pattern consists of a software resource called master and two or more other software resources, called worker. The task of the master is to divide the request into parallel tasks and to forward them to the workers, which manage the smaller tasks. The task should be divisible into parallel smaller tasks.
3) Also known as	Computation replicating
4) Problem	An overload of the system is expected. The inbound requests exceed the processing capacity of a specific resource (see the generic problem frame in Fig. 8.9).
5) Applicability	The MW pattern is applicable when the resource, which is the bottleneck, is a software resource, the overload is permanent, and the load can be spread spatially. That is, the attributes *loadDistributionType* and *overloadType*, and *resourceType* of the stereotype ≪bottleneck≫ in the generic problem frame in Fig. 8.9 have the values *spatial, permanent,* and *software*.
6) Solution	The solution uses the strategy of spreading the load over several software resources.
7) Collaboration	When requests are issued, they arrive through *Domain1* at the newly introduced machine *MW/LB*, which takes the responsibility to forward the request to the corresponding machines which have available resources and can process the request. Fig. 8.12 exemplifies the MW and LB patterns in which the load is distributed between the two machines *MachineA* and *MachineB*. The machines process the request and send the response using the domains *Domain2A* and *Domain2B*. Note that there exist at least two machine domains of the same type. More than two machines can be used if required dependent on the load of the system.
8) Benefits	The MW pattern reduces the load of the system by spreading it spatially.
9) Consequences	Efficient algorithm for allocating the requests to responders is required to ensure that the newly introduced machine does not become the new bottleneck.
10) Related patterns	The LB pattern can be used to reduce the load if the bottleneck is a hardware resource. The FT pattern can be used if the tasks can be performed at a different period of time. The FTF pattern can be used when there is a temporary overload.

8.3.6 Problem-oriented Load Balancer (LB) Pattern

The *Load Balancer* pattern provides a mechanism that is used to distribute computational load evenly over two or more components. The load balancing pattern consists of a component called Load Balancer, and multiple components that implement the same functionality. The machine *FTF/FT/MW/LB* in Fig. 8.9 represents the load balancer. The load balancer can be realized as a hardware or a software component [96]. Table 8.12 presents the instantiation of the template for the Load Balancer pattern.

Table 8.12: Load Balancer Pattern

1) Name	Load Balancer (LB)
2) Description	The LB pattern is used to distribute computational load evenly over two or more resources. It consists of a load balancer, and multiple resources that implement the same functionality. The load balancer can be realized as a hardware or a software component.
3) Also known as	-
4) Problem	An overload of the system is expected. The inbound requests exceed the processing capacity of a specific resource (see the generic problem frame in Fig. 8.9).
5) Applicability	The LB pattern is applicable when the overload is permanent and the load can be spread spatially. That is, the attributes *loadDistributionType* and *overloadType* of the stereotype ≪bottleneck≫ in the generic problem frame in Fig. 8.9 have the values *spatial* and *permanent*.
6) Solution	The solution uses the strategy of spreading the load over several resources.
7) Collaboration	When requests are issued, they arrive through *Domain1* at the newly introduced machine *MW/LB*, which takes the responsibility to forward the request to the corresponding machines which have available resources and can process the request. Fig. 8.12 exemplifies the MW and LB patterns in which the load is distributed between two machines *MachineA* and *MachineB*. The machines process the request and send the response using the domains *Domain2A* and *Domain2B*. Note that there exist at least two machine domains of the same type. More than two machines can be used if required dependent on the load of the system.
8) Benefits	The LB pattern reduces the load of the system by spreading it spatially.
9) Consequences	Efficient algorithm for allocating the requests to responders is required to ensure that the newly introduced *LBMachine* does not become the new bottleneck.
10) Related patterns	The MW pattern can be used to reduce the load if the bottleneck is a software resource. Note that in a MW pattern the task should be divisible into parallel smaller tasks. The FT pattern can be used if the tasks can be performed at a different period of time. The FTF pattern can be used when there is a temporary overload.

8.4 Discussion

In the previous sections, we proposed problem-oriented security and performance patterns to be applied in the requirements engineering phase to the requirement models. In this section, we discuss the benefits of these patterns.

Refining requirement models:
The proposed problem-oriented quality-specific patterns allow software engineers not only to think about security problems as early as possible in the software development life cycle, but also to think about approaches solving such quality-specific problems. By exploring the solution space, we find appropriate solution mechanisms, which can be used for refining security and performance requirement models in the requirement engineering phase. We treat the refinement of requirement models with problem-oriented security and performance patterns in Chapter 9,

where we move to the problem peak.

Bridging the gap:

Problem-oriented security and performance patterns are located in the problem space, aiming at structuring and elaborating security and performance problems. These patterns in the requirements engineering phase represent the counterpart to the "classical" security and performance patterns in the design phase. The elaborated requirement models can easily be transformed into a particular security or performance pattern at the design level. Thus, problem-oriented security patterns support bridging the gap between quality-specific problems and quality-specific solutions.

Impact of design decisions:

Problem-oriented quality-specific patterns represent solution candidates for achieving quality requirements. By exploring the solution space for achieving quality requirements, the software architect requires to know which assumptions and facts have to be considered, and which new functional and quality requirements have to be elicited when making a design decision regarding a specific type of quality requirement. Generally speaking, all information that can affect the requirements and related domain knowledge by making design decisions has to be documented.

The proposed templates for problem-oriented security patterns represent consequences of applying solution approaches by providing new assumptions and/or requirements to be considered when deciding on a specific pattern. Such a template helps the software engineer when selecting a particular solution candidate to keep track of changes in the requirements and domain knowledge. It also supports inexperienced architects in understanding the impact of design decisions on the entire system, particularly on the achievement of quality requirements.

Resolving requirement interactions:

The proposed templates for problem-oriented security patterns can be used for resolving interactions among quality requirements. In Chapter 7, we showed how conflicts among requirements can be resolved by relaxing the requirements and relaxing or strengthening the domain knowledge. Another option for resolving interactions is making trade-offs between corresponding quality-specific solutions. To this end, one or both corresponding quality-specific solutions have to be relaxed. Making such design decisions requires eliciting or updating domain knowledge and requirements associated with the particular solution. For example, selecting a *symmetric encryption* for achieving a confidentiality requirement instead of an *asymmetric encryption* demands different assumptions and requirements with respect to the required keys and key distribution as shown in the corresponding Templates 8.13 and 8.14.

Table 8.13: Problem-oriented Asymmetric Encryption Pattern (template)

Security Solution	
Name	Asymmetric Encryption
Purpose	For *Domain* constrained by the requirement *FunctionalReq*
Brief Description	The plaintext is encrypted using the public key and decrypted using the private key.
Quality Requirement to be achieved	Security (confidentiality) *ConfidentialityReq*
Affected quality requirements	Performance *PerformanceReq*, availability *AvailabilityReq*
Necessary Conditions	
Requirement □ Assumption □	Integrity of public key during transmission shall be/is preserved.
Requirement □ Assumption □	Confidentiality of private key during transmission shall be/is preserved.
Requirement □ Assumption □	Integrity of private key during transmission shall be/is preserved.
Requirement □ Assumption □	Confidentiality of private key during storage shall be/is preserved.
Requirement □ Assumption □	Integrity of private key during storage shall be/is preserved.
Requirement □ Assumption □	Integrity of public key during storage shall be/is preserved.

To demonstrate this idea, we consider the *asymmetric encryption* as the initial security-specific solution, which is selected for satisfying the security requirement *R11* from the case study smart grid, which we introduced in Section 2.6 (see page 43). *R11* is concerned with transmitting meter data through the WAN in a confidential way (see Table 8.15).

Asymmetric encryption provides sufficient protection during transmitting meter data through the WAN so that the confidentiality requirement can be achieved. However, we detected a conflict with the performance requirement *R24* by applying our method for detecting requirement interactions from the previous Chapter (see Chapter 7). Hence, *R24* cannot be achieved in less than 5 seconds when keeping the security-specific solution *asymmetric encryption* for meeting the security requirement *RQ11*. We have to decide for a strategy to resolve the conflict. The possible strategies might be:

- Relaxing the performance requirement by increasing the response time.
- Strengthening or relaxing the performance-related domain knowledge for example by raising the *network bandwidth* or by decreasing the *data size*.

Table 8.14: Problem-oriented Symmetric Encryption Pattern (template)

Security Solution	
Name	Symmetric Encryption
Purpose	For *Domain* constrained by the requirement *FunctionalReq*
Brief Description	The plaintext is encrypted using the secret key
Quality Requirement to be achieved	Security (confidentiality) *ConfidentialityReq*
Affected Quality Requirement	Performance *PerformanceReq*, availability *AvailabilityReq*
Necessary Conditions	
Requirement □ Assumption □	Secret key shall be/is distributed.
Requirement □ Assumption □	Confidentiality of secret key distribution shall be/is preserved.
Requirement □ Assumption □	Integrity of secret key distribution shall be/is preserved.
Requirement □ Assumption □	Confidentiality of secret key during transmission shall be/is preserved
Requirement □ Assumption □	Confidentiality of secret key during storage shall be/is preserved.
Requirement □ Assumption □	Integrity of secret key during storage shall be/is preserved.

Table 8.15: Requirements *R11* and *R24* for smart metering

Quality Requirement	Description
R11	Confidentiality of data transferred in the WAN shall be protected
R24	The time to retrieve meter data from the smart meter and publish it through WAN shall be less than 5 seconds (together with R18, R20, R22)

Such strategies are at the cost of performance requirement *R24* and can only be used if the security requirement *R11* has a higher priority. Here, we assume that the performance requirement *R24* has a higher priority. Hence, we have to make a trade-off by relaxing the security-specific solution. This can be achieved by selecting another security-specific solution, which is faster. We decide on *symmetric encryption* instead of *asymmetric encryption*. Symmetric encryption is faster than the asymmetric encryption. It, however, demands other requirements and domain knowledge. For example, we have to care about the key distribution. Hence, this design decision leads to changes in the requirements as well as in the domain knowledge as shown in Table 8.14.

8.5 Mapping Requirements to Quality Solutions

In this section, we first introduce an extension of the UML profile UML4PF in Section 8.5.1, which is used for modeling the *problem-solution diagram*. Then, we propose the *problem-solution diagram* in Section 8.5.2, which provides a mapping from generated quality requirement alternatives in Chapter 7 to *problem-oriented quality patterns*.

8.5.1 *UML4PF Extension for Mapping Requirements to their Solution Alternatives*

We extend the problem frames notation by introducing new elements for modeling alternatives for quality requirements and their corresponding solutions. Our extension is a UML profile relying on the UML4PF profile (see Section 2.3.1 on page 33). The profile extension allows the creation of new diagram types, statements, and dependencies. Figure 8.13 shows the stereotypes of this UML profile. In the following, we describe the stereotypes that we used in our profile.

New types of diagrams

One new kind of UML4PF diagrams is the *problem-solution diagram*. It is expressed by the stereotype ≪ProblemSolutionDiagram≫. A problem solution diagram consists of two parts for modeling different levels of abstraction. Each part represents a layer. The concept of layers in a feature model is introduced in FODA[1] [140] and FORM[2] [141]. We define the stereotypes ≪ProblemSpace≫ and ≪SolutionSpace≫ for packages representing those layers. The problem space captures requirements, particularly quality requirements. The solution space encompasses solution alternatives for addressing the requirements. The *configura-*

---

[1] Feature-Oriented Domain Analysis
[2] Feature-Oriented Reuse Method

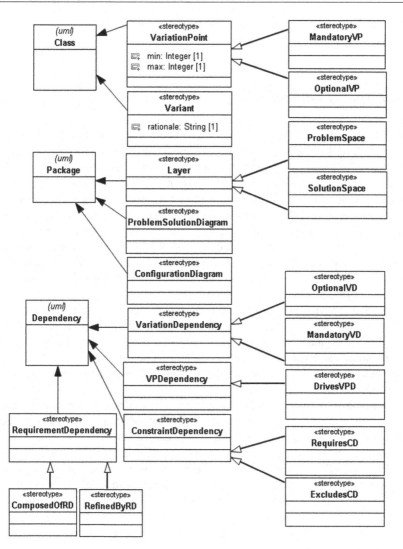

Fig. 8.13: UML4PF Extension for mapping requirements to solution alternatives

tion diagram expressed by the stereotype ≪ConfigurationDiagram≫ is the other
new kind of *UML4PF diagrams*. It represents all the requirements to be addressed

in an architecture alternative as well as their corresponding quality-specific solutions.

New types of statements

We introduce two new types of *statement*, namely *variant* (expressed by the stereotype ≪Variant≫) and *variation point* (expressed by the stereotype ≪Variation-Point≫). Variation points represent locations where variability occurs (see Section 2.5 on page 42). Therefore, they describe variability. Each variation point accommodates different variants. Each variant represents one way of realizing the variability at the specific variation point. Therefore, variation points represent decisions for selecting or not selecting a variant. Variants are connected by dependencies to their corresponding variation point. When deriving candidate architectures, decisions have to be made for each variation point. One can distinguish between *mandatory variation point* (≪MandatoryVP≫) and *optional variation point* (≪OptionalVP≫).

Related to variation points are *variants*, which can represent an *optional variation* or a *mandatory variation*. A variation point indicates by its *min* and *max* properties how many of the variants have to be chosen for the variation point. Each variant can be annotated with a rationale for selecting it. It is indicated by a *rationale* attribute. Using this attribute, reasons for the selection or not selection of a specific variant can be given.

The type of variation relation is indicated by a *variation dependency* (≪Variation-Dependency≫) which can be optional (≪OptionalVD≫) or mandatory (≪MandatoryVD≫). Variants and variation points can be related by a *constraint dependency*. The relation can be an *excludes* (≪ExcludesCD≫) or a *requires* (≪RequiresCD≫) dependency. Requirements can be related by a *requirement dependency* which can be *composed of* (≪ComposedOfRD≫) or *refined by* (≪RefinedByRD≫). Two variation points can be related by a *variation point dependency* (≪VPDependency≫). The stereotype ≪DrivesVPD≫ is a specialization of a variation point dependency. It represents that the source variation point causes the target variation point.

Table 8.16 shows the list of defined stereotypes and their description. The detailed usage of the stereotypes will be explained in the next section.

Table 8.16: Stereotypes defined for UML4PF extension for modeling the mapping of quality requirements and their corresponding solution alternatives

Stereotype, Tagged values	Applies to	Description
≪ConfigurationDiagram≫	Package	It represents all the components contained in an architecture alternative as well as the corresponding requirements.
≪ProblemSolutionDiagram≫	Package	It represents requirements, solutions alternatives, and their mappings.
≪ProblemSpace≫	Package	It captures the requirements.
≪SolutionSpace≫	Package	It captures solutions alternatives on the architecture level.
≪VariationPoint≫	Class	It represents the *Statement*, where variability may exist.
≪Variant≫	Class	It represents a variation.
{rationale = Rationale}	≪Variant≫	It captures the reasoning for selecting a variant.
≪MandatoryVP≫	Class	It represents a variation point that must always be selected.
≪OptionalVP≫	Class	It represents a variation point that may be selected.
≪ConstraintDependency≫	Dependency	It represents a dependency between two variants (classes with stereotype ≪Variant≫)
≪ExcludesCD≫	Dependency	It represents a dependency from a source variant (class with stereotype ≪Variant≫) to a target variant (class with stereotype ≪Variant≫) and prevents selecting the target variant if the source variant has been selected.
≪RequiresCD≫	Dependency	It represents a dependency from a source variant (class with stereotype ≪Variant≫) to a target variant (class with stereotype ≪Variant≫) and requires the target variant to be selected if the source variant has been selected.
≪VPDependency≫	Dependency	It represents a dependency from a source variant point (class with stereotype ≪VariationPoint≫ or ≪MandatoryVP≫ or ≪OptionalVP≫) to a target variation point (class with stereotype ≪VariationPoint≫ or ≪MandatoryVP≫ or ≪OptionalVP≫).
≪DrivesVPD≫	Dependency	It is a specialization of the dependency with the stereotype ≪VPDependency≫ meaning that the source variation point (class with stereotype ≪VariationPoint≫) causes the target variation point (class with stereotype ≪VariationPoint≫).
≪VariationDependency≫	Dependency	It represents a dependency providing a link from a variation point (class with stereotype ≪VariationPoint≫)) to its variants (class with stereotype ≪Variant≫).
≪MandatoryVD≫	Dependency	It points to a variant that must always be selected.
≪OptionalVD≫	Dependency	It points to a variant that may be selected.
≪RequirementDependency≫	Dependency	It represents a dependency between two requirements.
≪ComposedOfRD≫	Dependency	It represents a dependency from a source requirement to a target requirement and captures the decomposition relationships between requirements.
≪RefeindByRD≫	Dependency	It represents a dependency from a source requirement to a target requirement and captures the decomposition relationships between requirements.

8.5.2 Problem-Solution Diagram

In this section, we describe how to provide a mapping of quality requirements to their potential solution alternatives by setting up a problem-solution diagram. It uses the already modeled problem diagrams (see Chapter 4) and problem-oriented quality-specific patterns (see Sections 8.2 and 8.3) and provides a mapping between them. The problem-solution diagram provides a basis for selecting appropriate quality-specific solution mechanisms in the next chapter (see Chapter 9).

For modeling the problem-solution diagram, we use the UML profile extension we introduced in the previous section (see Section 8.5.1). The problem-solution diagram consists of one package for representing the overall mapping between the problem and the solution space. The stereotype ≪ProblemSolutionDiagram≫ has to be applied to this overall package to represent the problem-solution diagram. It consists of two layers to be expressed by the stereotypes ≪ProblemSpace≫ and ≪SolutionSpace≫ to represent the space of requirements as well as the space of solution alternatives.

For modeling the problem space, one uses functional as well as quality requirements from problem diagrams. The problem space can be designed in a flexible way. One can decide for modeling only quality requirements or for modeling both functional and quality requirements. In addition, one can model the decomposition relationships among functional requirements using the stereotypes ≪ComposedOfRD≫ and ≪RefinedByRD≫. Quality requirements represent the variation points as different solution alternatives can be chosen for addressing them on the architecture level. Hence, for each quality requirement and its alternatives (generated in Section 7.5 on page 231), one variation point has to be created (expressed by the stereotype ≪VariationPoint≫). In case one wants to restrict the number of quality requirements related to one variation point, the attributes *min* and *max* can be used. Quality requirements and their generated alternatives represent the variants of one variation point expressed by the stereotype ≪Variant≫.

For modeling the solution space, one uses the problem-oriented security and performance patterns as solution alternatives for achieving quality requirements. The set of patterns provide the variation points and each single problem-oriented security and performance pattern represents a variant. Since these solution alternatives are accommodated in the design space and are used later on as components in the architecture, they are additionally annotated with the stereotype ≪Component≫ from the UML profile for architecture (see Section 2.3.2 on page 37). Note that the solution space is not specific to the smart grid in contrast to the problem space. It represents the set of possible quality-specific patterns and not their instantiations. The reason is that the selection of appropriate quality-specific patterns and their instantiation is achieved in the next chapter. Instantiating patterns that might not be selected in the next chapter would cause a high and unnecessary modeling effort. We avoid this by using the patterns as possible quality-specific solutions in the solution space.

The variation points in the problem space are linked to the variation points in the solution space by a dependency with the stereotype ≪VPDependency≫. Variants in the problem space as well as variants in the solution space are linked by a dependency with the stereotype ≪VariationDependency≫.

The problem-solution diagram for the smart grid case study is shown in Fig. 8.14. The problem-solution diagram *SmartGridPS* is represented by an overall package with the stereotype ≪ProblemSolutionDiagram≫. It consists of the *SmartGridRequirements* representing the problem space (expressed by the stereotype ≪ProblemSpace≫) and the *SmartGridSolutionAlternatives* representing the solution space (expressed by the stereotype ≪SolutionSpace≫).

For the problem space, we make use of all the requirements, functional as well as quality requirements that are already available in the problem diagrams. The requirements *R1*, *R2R3*, *R4*, and *R5* represent the functional requirements. The UML profile extension provides the possibility to model the merging of requirements *R2* and *R3* into the requirement *R2R3*. To this end, one might use the stereotype ≪ComposedOfRD≫ (not shown in Fig. 8.14). A variation point is created for each quality requirement and its generated alternatives. For example, *R18VP* expressed by the stereotype ≪MandatoryVP≫ is a mandatory variation point for the performance requirement *R18* and its generated alternatives *R18.1* and *R18.2* which represent variants (expressed by the stereotype ≪Variant≫). The mandatory variation point *R18VP* has as attributes *min=1* and *max=1* which means that exactly one variant of the three variants must be selected for an architecture alternative. This holds for all mandatory variation points in the problem space. It is only shown for *R18VP* in Fig. 8.14. Other quality requirements have to be modeled in a similar way.

For the solution space, we create one variation point for the problem-oriented performance patterns and one variation point for the problem-oriented security patterns. Each of the problem-oriented performance patterns *LB*, *MW*, *FT*, and *FTF* are modeled as variants and components (stereotypes ≪Variant≫ and ≪Component≫). Also the problem-oriented security patterns *SymEnc*, *AsymEnc*, *RBAC*, *DigSig*, and *MAC* have to be modeled as components and variants. Variation points in the problem space are linked to their corresponding variation points in the solution space using dependencies with the stereotype ≪VPDependency≫. Problem-oriented quality pattern variants are annotated with *rationales* which facilitates the selection of the pattern variants.

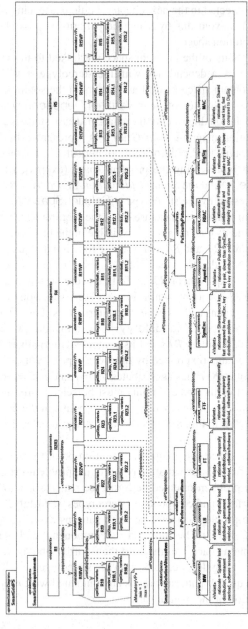

Fig. 8.14: Problem-Solution diagram for smart grid

8.6 Related Work

In this section, we discuss related work with respect to security and performance in Section 8.6.1 and with respect to variability in Section 8.6.2.

8.6.1 Related work with respect to Security and Performance

There has been a number of research works that proposed patterns for different areas of software engineering and other application domains. We mainly discuss here patterns that are related to the problem frames approach.

Beckers et al. [49] propose a meta model for describing context patterns for various kinds of domain knowledge. The meta model is based on a number of context patterns for different areas of domain knowledge such as Peer-to-Peer, cloud computing, and the legal domain developed in the past by the authors. To improve the understanding of the context and eliciting required information, these patterns can be integrated into existing software development methods. The domain knowledge required for the software engineering can be captured by instantiating such context patterns. Similar to our patterns, the context patterns are provided for the requirements engineering phase. However, they differ from our problem-oriented security patterns as they elicit and analyze the context supporting the elicitation of requirements while we focus on finding solution approaches for already elicited security requirements.

Hatebur et al. [116] propose security problem frames and concretized security problem frames. Security problem frames represent special kinds of problem frames which address security problems. Security problem frames do not take into account a solution. They have to be transformed into concretized security problem frames which address a solution using generic security mechanisms. Similar to this approach, we make use of the problem frames approach as a basis for providing security patterns. The first part of our graphical pattern, namely the generic problem diagram, corresponds to the security problem frames proposed in [116]. The second part of our graphical pattern represents a generic security mechanism, while the third part corresponds to the concretized security problem frames. In addition, we provide a template for each pattern including meta information and necessary conditions that need to be considered when applying a specific pattern.

The same authors present a pattern system in a further work [117] based on security problem frames and their counterparts concretized security problem frames. In this work, the relationships and dependencies between different frames are represented explicitly in a pattern system. The pattern system should support the security engineer by choosing the appropriate concretized security problem frame for an identified security problem frame.

A pattern language for security risk analysis of web applications is proposed by Li et al. [166], which can be used to support conducting a risk analysis in the early phase of the software development life cycle. The authors introduce three basic pattern types, namely security requirement patterns, web application architecture design patterns, and risk analysis model patterns that can be combined to build security risk analysis composite patterns. A security requirement pattern is defined according to the problem frames notation. An instantiation of the security requirement pattern, namely a security requirement, represents the input for the web application architecture design pattern representing the architecture design for a specific web application. Our problem-oriented security patterns can be used as an intermediate step between the security requirement patterns and web application architecture design patterns to facilitate the transformation of security requirement patterns in the requirement analysis phase into the web application architecture design patterns in the design phase. In addition, our patterns help identifying new assumptions / requirements that need to be considered when applying a specific security pattern.

Composition frames used in this chapter for problem-oriented performance patterns are used in some other work as well. Laney et al. [163] propose a systematic method to resolve inconsistencies in the problem frames. The authors introduce composition frames in order to deal with composing conflicting requirements. Composition frames are also used in our work on aspect-oriented requirements engineering based on problem frames to restructure requirement models using security patterns [24]. Composition frames in our previous work serve as a means to weave security aspects into the functional structures. In our current work, we use composition frames in a different way. A composition frame in our approach represents the generic solution structure for performance analysis patterns. We use composition frames to apply performance analysis patterns to problem diagrams containing performance problems.

8.6.2 Related work with respect to Variability

One related research topic aims at adopting the notion of variability modeling to generate software architectures. A feature-based method is proposed by Bruijn and van Vliet [60] to generate software architectures with respect to functional and non-functional requirements. The authors treat functional and non-functional requirements separately, constructing two branches in the feature graph. Bruijn and van Vliet generate design alternatives by using *Use Case Maps (UCM)* as a scenario-based architectural description language, which is not model- and pattern-based in contrast to our work.

To treat variability in the requirements analysis and consequently generate a customizable software design, Hui et al. [128] propose a framework for identifying requirements (user goals, user skills, user preferences) from a user perspective. However, this work focuses on the early stage of requirements analysis by choosing goals to represent and analyze variability. This work can be seen as complementary to our approach as our work deals with requirements and specification.

There are a number of UML extensions to model variability. A UML profile is proposed by Clauß [76]. This profile supports only the UML 1.4 and not the current UML version. Also Ziadi et al. [255] introduce a UML profile. We found some differences regarding the modeling of relationships between features or variants. Also modeling of variants in terms of optional or alternative variants is performed in a different way. We customized our UML profile for variability in a way that it can serve our specific needs regarding the coverage of both requirement space and design space.

Another research topic is concerned with connecting problem frames with variability modeling. Zuo et al. [257] introduce an extension of the problem frames notation that provides support for product line engineering using the notion of feature analysis. While Ali et al. [27] propose a method to treat variability of context (conditions in the operating environment influencing the behaviour of the system) in requirements, we take a step forward and connect functional and quality requirements to commonality and variability in the solution space, expressed by alternative solutions. A method for integrating software product line engineering and the problem frames concept considering domain concerns is proposed by Dao et al. [86]. In this work a feature model is mapped to a problem frames model. A goal model is adopted to represent various concerns and variable quality requirements. The mapping between these different models is complicated and time-consuming, hence requires a tool support.

There are works concerning the modeling of quality properties in the context of variability modeling. Yu et al. [250] relate stakeholder goals including quality properties captured as goal models to a feature model by introducing a mapping between goals and features. Lee and Kang [164] consider the usage context as the primary driver for feature selection. The authors present three variability models for the usage context, quality attributes, and the product as well as three mappings between them to derive a product configuration.

8.7 Contributions

In the first part of this chapter, we adapted security and performance architectural patterns in a way that they can be used in the requirements engineering phase for the analysis of security and performance problems. The adapted patterns, the *problem-oriented security patterns* as well as *problem-oriented performance patterns*, are provided using a systematic structure. This part can be summarized as follows:

- Problem-oriented security patterns consist of a three-part graphical pattern and a template describing the effect of the security pattern on requirements when applied.
- We presented five examples of problem-oriented security patterns to address confidentiality, integrity, and authenticity problems on the requirement level.
- Problem-oriented performance patterns consist of a template and two new problem frames describing the generic structure of the problem and the solution.
- We provided four examples of problem-oriented performance patterns.
- Other security and performance patterns and mechanisms located in the solution space can easily be transformed into the problem space analogously, using the proposed structure for problem-oriented security and performance patterns. Necessary for such a transformation is the knowledge about the patterns and/or mechanisms, their structure, and their constituents to build the problem-oriented security and performance patterns.

In a further part of this chapter, we connected the generated quality requirement alternatives from Chapter 7 and the quality-specific solutions. To this end, we introduced the *problem-solution diagram*, which

- provides a mapping of (quality) requirements to problem-oriented quality patterns. Quality requirements drive the variability in the solution space and serve as selection criteria.
- enables the annotation of quality solutions in the solution space with rationales for choosing among alternatives. Thus, the problem-solution diagram represents a "decision space" and provides a good starting point to identify solution candidates for quality requirements.
- supports maintaining traceability between model artifacts, namely between the requirements and the architectural solutions addressing those requirements, including the rationale for selecting the architectural solutions.

The results of this chapter are used in the next chapter for selecting *problem-oriented quality patterns* and applying them to the requirement models.

Chapter 9
Phase 6: Quality-specific Pattern Selection & Application

Abstract In this chapter, we propose a structured method that selects appropriate problem-oriented security and performance patterns introduced in the previous chapter. The method applies such patterns to the requirement models in order to address the quality requirements security and performance early in the software development. This way, we refine the requirement models and bridge the gap between quality problems and quality solutions.

9.1 Introduction

After relaxing the conflicting quality requirements and generating requirement alternatives (see Chapter 7), we have to select appropriate quality-specific solution mechanisms and apply them to achieve the requirement alternatives. To this end, we introduced *problem-oriented performance patterns* and *problem-oriented security patterns* in Chapter 8 as solutions for achieving the quality requirements performance and security.

This chapter represents Phase 6 of the QuaDRA framework. In this chapter, we propose a structured method that selects appropriate *problem-oriented quality patterns* and applies them to requirement models. Doing this, the quality-specific solutions are integrated into the software development process to refine the requirement models and bridge the gap between security and performance problems, and security and performance solutions. The instantiations of the patterns provide a basis for a seamless transition from requirement analysis to architectural design, which is achieved in the next chapter.

This chapter is based on our works presented in [21] proposing the application of problem-oriented security patterns and [22] proposing the application of problem-oriented performance patterns. We are the main author of these works. We had useful and valuable discussions with Maritta Heisel regarding quality-specific solution candidates.

The remainder of this chapter is organized as follows. Our method for selecting and applying problem-oriented quality patterns in presented in Section 9.2. The contribution of this chapter is given in Section 9.3. Note that this chapter does not contain a related work section, as we extensively discussed related work regarding security and performance solution approaches in Chapter 8 (see Section 8.6 on page 285).

9.2 Method for Selecting & Applying Quality-specific Patterns

In this section, we propose a method to select and apply *problem-oriented performance patterns* and *problem-oriented security patterns* in a structured way. The output of this method is a set of problem diagrams containing solution mechanisms for achieving quality requirements. This set of problem diagrams provides the basis for deriving an architecture alternative in the next chapter. For deriving different architecture alternatives, different sets of quality-specific problem diagrams have to be created. To this end, one needs to apply the method iteratively. For example, for producing input for three different software architecture alternatives, one needs to iterate three times over the steps of this method.

In the following, we describe our method to select and apply *problem-oriented quality-specific patterns*. An overview of the steps of the method is shown in Fig. 9.1.

Step 1 - Prioritize quality requirements

In the first step, one needs to prioritize quality requirements for the target software architecture alternative. For deriving each architecture alternative, a new prioritization of quality requirements is needed. Therefore, we require the quality requirements relevant for our purpose as the input for this step.

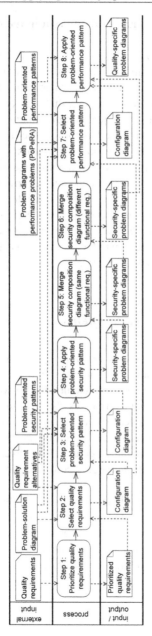

Fig. 9.1: Method for selecting and applying quality-specific patterns

Application of Step 1 - Prioritize quality requirements

In Chapter 7 (see Section 7.5 on page 231), we described that we aim at deriving three different software architecture alternatives with different levels of satisfaction for security and performance for our smart grid case study. As security and performance requirements are interacting, the three architecture alternatives provide trade-offs between these two quality requirements.

The first architecture alternative has to treat the desired performance requirements with the highest priority (*architecture alternative 1*), the second one has to rank the security requirements first (*architecture alternative 2*), and the third one has to provide a trade-off of performance and security requirements with similar priorities (*architecture alternative 3*). This architecture alternative fulfills neither the security requirements nor the performance requirements to the best degree of satisfaction. It, however, *satisfices* both quality requirements with a trade-off which treats both quality requirements with the same priority. We apply the next steps for all three software architecture alternatives.

Step 2 - Select quality requirements

As the input of this step, we take the generated quality requirement alternatives (see Section 7.5 on page 231) and the problem-solution diagram (see Section 8.5 on page 278) into account. For each architecture alternative, one has to select among the sets of quality requirement alternatives. To this end, for each variation point in the problem space of the problem-solution diagram, one quality requirement variant has to be selected. This way, one decides on the requirements to be addressed in the corresponding software architecture alternative. A configuration diagram which corresponds to the selected architecture alternative is created as the output of this step.

Note that the configuration diagram cannot be fully created in this step as the quality-specific solutions are not selected yet. Hence, the configuration diagram in this step contains only the requirements to be addressed in the selected architecture alternative. It has to be completed in the next steps when deciding on quality-specific solutions for each architecture alternative.

Application of Step 2 - Select quality requirements

Architecture Alternative 1

For the smart grid case study, we decided on three architecture alternatives. For the *architecture alternative 1*, we select the following performance requirement variants: *R18, R19, R22, R23, R24,* and *R25*. These performance requirements are the original performance requirements and hence not weakened. As the architecture alternative 1 has to provide a trade-off with the best performance, we need to select the weaker security requirement alternatives than the original ones. To this end, we select the following security requirement variants: *R10.1, R11.1, R12.1, R13.1, R14.1,* and *R15.1* (see Tables 7.27 and 7.28 on page 236 for the requirement alternatives). Figure 9.2 shows the configuration diagram for the architecture alternative 1.

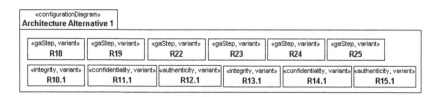

Fig. 9.2: Configuration diagram (only requirements) for the architecture alternative 1

Architecture Alternative 2

For the *architecture alternative 2*, we decide for the strongest security requirements, namely the original ones *R10, R11, R12, R13, R14,* and *R15*. In contrast to the security requirements, we decide for the weakest generated performance requirements that are still acceptable, namely *R18.1, R19.1, R22.1, R23.1, R24.1,* and *R25.1* (see Tables 7.29 - Table 7.32 on page 237 for the requirement alternatives). Figure 9.3 shows the configuration diagram for the architecture alternative 2.

Architecture Alternative 3

The *architecture alternative 3* has to provide a trade-off between performance and security requirements with similar priorities. To this end, we decide on the security requirement alternatives *R10.2, R11.2, R12.2, R13.2, R14.2,* and *R15.2* and perfor-

«configurationDiagram» **Architecture Alternative 2**					
«variant, gaStep» **R18.1**	«gaStep, variant» **R19.1**	«gaStep, variant» **R22.1**	«gaStep, variant» **R23.1**	«gaStep, variant» **R24.1**	«gaStep, variant» **R25.1**
«integrity, variant» **R10**	«confidentiality, variant» **R11**	«authenticity, variant» **R12**	«integrity, variant» **R13**	«confidentiality, variant» **R14**	«authenticity, variant» **R15**

Fig. 9.3: Configuration diagram (only requirements) for the architecture alternative 2

mance requirement alternatives *R18.2, R19.2, R22.2, R23.2, R24.2,* and *R25.2* (see Tables 7.27 - Table 7.32 on page 236 for the requirement alternatives). Figure 9.4 shows the configuration diagram for the architecture alternative 3. Table 9.1 gives an overview of the selected quality requirement variants for all three architecture alternatives.

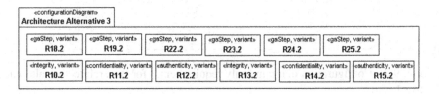

«configurationDiagram» **Architecture Alternative 3**					
«gaStep, variant» **R18.2**	«gaStep, variant» **R19.2**	«gaStep, variant» **R22.2**	«gaStep, variant» **R23.2**	«gaStep, variant» **R24.2**	«gaStep, variant» **R25.2**
«integrity, variant» **R10.2**	«confidentiality, variant» **R11.2**	«authenticity, variant» **R12.2**	«integrity, variant» **R13.2**	«confidentiality, variant» **R14.2**	«authenticity, variant» **R15.2**

Fig. 9.4: Configuration diagram (only requirements) for the architecture alternative 3

Step 3 - Select problem-oriented security patterns

The proposed *problem-oriented security patterns* in Section 8.2 (see page 249) have to be selected in this step for addressing security requirements. According to the strength of the generated security requirement alternatives, it has to be decided on the problem-oriented security patterns. In the previous chapter (see Section 8.5 on page 278), we provided the possibility to annotate the problem-oriented security pattern variants in the *problem-solution diagram* with rationales (see the problem

Table 9.1: Quality Requirement Variants for the Corresponding Architecture Alternatives

Problem-Solution Diagram	Arch. Alternative 1	Arch. Alternative 2	Arch. Alternative 3
Variation Point	Variant	Variant	Variant
R18VP	R18	R18.1	R18.2
R19VP	R19	R19.1	R19.2
R22VP	R22	R22.1	R22.2
R23VP	R23	R23.1	R23.2
R24VP	R24	R24.1	R24.2
R25VP	R25	R25.1	R25.2
R10VP	R10.1	R10	R10.2
R11VP	R11.1	R11	R11.2
R12VP	R12.1	R12	R12.2
R13VP	R13.1	R13	R13.2
R14VP	R14.1	R14	R14.2
R15VP	R15.1	R15	R15.2

space in Fig. 8.14 on page 284). Such rationales should support the selection of those pattern variants. In addition to the problem-oriented security patterns and the problem-solution diagram, we require the *quality requirement alternatives* and the *configuration diagrams* as the input for this step.

Application of Step 3 - Select problem-oriented security patterns

Architecture Alternative 1

For the architecture alternative 1, we selected the weakest security requirements *R10.1*, *R11.1*, and *R12.1* (related to the functional requirement *R4*) and *R13.1*, *R14.1*, and *R15.1* (related to the functional requirement *R5*). According to Table 7.27 (see Section 7.5 on page 231), for the requirements *R10.1, R11.1, R12.1*, we are concerned with a *WAN attacker*, who has *one month* preparation time, *one month* attack time, a *proficient* expertise, and a *specialized* equipment. As we are not concerned with the strongest attacker, the confidentiality requirement *R11.1* is satisfied by selecting the problem-oriented security pattern *symmetric encryption*. Symmetric encryption is fast when compared with other types of encryption such as asymmetric encryption. To achieve the integrity and authenticity requirements *R10.1* and *R12.1*, we select the problem-oriented security pattern *MAC*. MAC uses symmetric keys (only one secret key). This implies that MAC is also faster than the alternative solution *digital signature* which uses asymmetric keys (public-private key pair).

According to Table 7.28 (see Section 7.5 on page 231), for the requirements *R13.1, R14.1, R15.1*, the *HAN attacker* has only *one day* preparation time, *one day* attack time, a *laymen* expertise, and a *standard* equipment. Hence, we are concerned with an attacker with the weakest attacker profile targeting a not public network (*HAN*). According to this and considering the lower priority of security requirements for the architecture alternative 1, we decide for not selecting a security mechanism for the requirements *R13.1, R14.1, R15.1* as the remaining risk for being attacked by such an attacker is low.

Architecture Alternative 2
For the architecture alternative 2, we selected the original security requirements *R10, R11*, and *R12* (related to the functional requirement *R4*) and *R13, R14*, and *R15* (related to the functional requirement *R5*) in order to meet the security requirements the best. For the confidentiality requirements *R11* and *R14*, we select the problem-oriented security pattern *asymmetric encryption* which does not have the key distribution problem compared to its alternative *symmetric encryption* due to the usage of public-private key pair instead of a shared secret key. For the integrity requirements *R10* and *R13* and the authenticity requirements *R12* and *R15* we choose the problem-oriented security pattern *digital signature* due to the same reason as for the *asymmetric encryption*. It uses a public-private key pair instead of a shared secret key used in *MAC*.

Architecture Alternative 3
For the architecture alternative 3, we selected the security requirements *R10.2*, *R11.2*, and *R12.2* (related to the functional requirement *R4*) and *R13.2, R14.2*, and *R15.2* (related to the functional requirement *R5*). These security requirements are not as weak as the security requirements to be addressed by the first architecture alternatives nor as strong as the security requirements related to the second architecture alternatives. Hence, we select the problem-oriented security pattern *symmetric encryption* for the confidentiality requirements *R11.2* and *R14.2*. For the integrity requirements *R10.2* and *R13.2* and for the authenticity requirements *R12.2* and *R15.2* we decide on the problem oriented security pattern *MAC* which provides integrity as well as authenticity.

As we can observe, for the architecture alternative 3 for achieving the security requirements related to the functional requirement *R4* we selected the same problem-oriented security patterns as for the architecture alternative 1. As the security requirements to be addressed in the architecture alternative 3 are stronger than those ones to be addressed in the architecture alternative 1, the corresponding problem-oriented security pattern symmetric encryption for the architecture alternative 3 has to use a stronger encryption algorithm or a stronger key than the ones for the architecture alternative 1. This can be captured as an annotation using the *rationale* attribute of the stereotype ≪Variant≫ for the design phase. The complete configuration diagrams are shown in the next step after selecting the problem-oriented performance patterns.

Step 4 - Apply problem-oriented security patterns

In this step, we apply the problem-oriented security patterns selected in Step 3. As the input, we take the problem-oriented security patterns (see Section 8.2 on page 249) and the created configuration diagrams for each architecture alternative from the previous step into account. To each problem diagram, the selected security mechanism has to be applied by instantiating the problem-oriented security patterns. As described in Section 8.2 (see page 249), the graphical pattern involves the three parts *functional problem diagram*, which is the problem diagram annotated with security requirements, *security problem diagram*, which is the problem diagram describing the particular solution approach for the security requirement annotated in the functional problem diagram, and the *composition problem diagram*, which is the problem diagram composing the first and second part for achieving both functional and security requirements.

As described previously in Section 8.2 (see page 249), new requirements and assumptions arise due to introducing the security solutions. Hence, we have to think about new problems that might arise and then capture them as new requirements and/or assumptions. To this end, we introduced specific templates that represent additional information corresponding to the graphical part of each problem-oriented security pattern. These templates have to be instantiated in this step for each security requirement, for which we introduce a problem-oriented security pattern.

Application of Step 4 - Apply problem-oriented security patterns

Architecture Alternative 1
For the smart grid case study, according to the configuration diagram for the architecture alternative 1 illustrated in Fig. 9.21, we selected the problem-oriented security pattern *symmetric encryption* (see Fig. 8.2 in on page 254) for achieving the confidentiality requirement *R11.1* and the problem-oriented security pattern *MAC* for achieving the integrity and authenticity requirements *R10.1* and *R12.1* related to the functional requirement *R4*.

The functional problem diagram in our case study is the problem diagram *SubmitMeterData* for the functional requirement *R4* shown in Fig. 9.5. Symmetric encryption as the selected solution for the confidentiality problem is expressed by the problem diagram *SymEnc_R4* shown at the top of Fig. 9.6. It contains the machine *SymEncM*, which is responsible for achieving the confidentiality requirement *R11.1* by encrypting the lexical domain *MeterData* using the lexical domain *SecretKey*, which is part of the machine *SymEncM*.

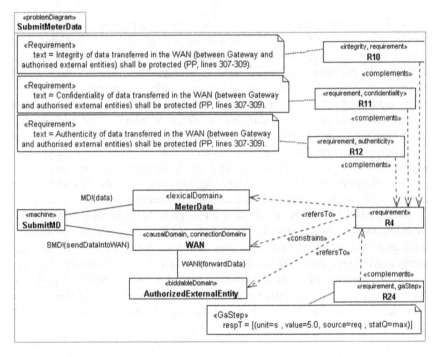

Fig. 9.5: Problem diagram related to functional requirement *R4* and its corresponding quality requirements

The composition problem diagram *R4_SymEnc_Composition* shown at the bottom of Fig. 9.6 combines the functional problem diagram with the security problem diagram. It consists of the new machine *EncryptionManager_R4*, both machine domains *SubmitMD* and *SymEncM*, and the domains of both problem diagrams. Consider that the lexical domain *SecretKey* is part of the machine *SymEncM* and hence is not shown in the composition problem diagram. The machine *EncryptionManager_R4* is responsible for coordinating the functional machine *SubmitMD* and the security solution machine *SecretKey*. It is responsible for obtaining *MeterData*, encrypting it using *SymEncM* and sending it to the *AuthorizedExternalEntities* using *SubmitM*. The requirement *ComposedR4R11.1* consists of the requirements *R4* and *R11.1*. It shall be achieved by the machine *EncryptionManager_R4*.

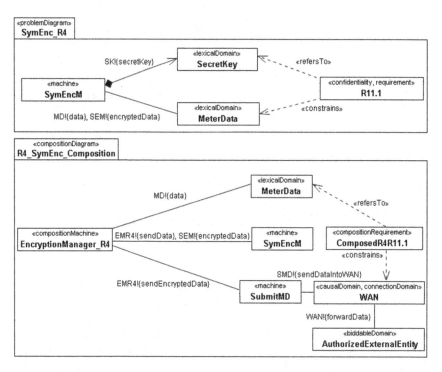

Fig. 9.6: Instantiated problem-oriented security pattern *symmetric encryption* for the confidentiality requirement *R11.1*

Table 9.2 provides an instantiation of the problem-oriented symmetric encryption pattern template shown in Table 8.2 (see page 256). The instantiation is for the confidentiality requirement *R11.1*. In the second part of this template, one needs to decide whether the new conditions have to be treated as assumptions or new requirements. Here, we assume that these necessary conditions hold. We only show the template instantiation for the confidentiality requirement *R11.1*. The complete set of template instantiations is shown in Appendix C.

Table 9.2: Problem-oriented Symmetric Encryption pattern template for the confidentiality requirement *R11.1*

Security Solution for the Confidentiality Requirement *R11.1*	
Name	Symmetric Encryption
Purpose	For *MeterData* constrained by the requirement *R4*
Brief Description	The plaintext is encrypted using the secret key
Quality Requirement to be achieved	Security (confidentiality) *R11.1*
Affected Quality Requirement	Performance *R18*, *R19*, *R22*, *R23*, *R24*, *R25*
Necessary Conditions	
Requirement □ Assumption ☑	Secret key shall be/is distributed.
Requirement □ Assumption ☑	Confidentiality of secret key distribution shall be/is preserved.
Requirement □ Assumption ☑	Integrity of secret key distribution shall be/is preserved.
Requirement □ Assumption ☑	Confidentiality of secret key during transmission shall be/is preserved
Requirement □ Assumption ☑	Confidentiality of secret key during storage shall be/is preserved.
Requirement □ Assumption ☑	Integrity of secret key during storage shall be/is preserved.
Requirement □ Assumption ☑	Confidentiality of encryption machine shall be/is preserved.
Requirement □ Assumption ☑	Integrity of encryption machine shall be/is preserved.

MAC as the selected solution for the integrity and authenticity problem is expressed by the problem diagram *MAC_R4* shown at the top of Fig. 9.7. It contains the machine *MACM*, which is responsible for achieving the integrity and authenticity requirements *R10.1* and *R12.1*. Similar to symmetric encryption, the MAC mechanism uses a shared *SecretKey*, which is part of the machine *MACM*. The composition problem diagram *R4_MAC_Composition* shown at the bottom of Fig. 9.7 combines the functional problem diagram *SubmitMeterData* with the security problem diagram *MAC_R4*. We do not describe it in detail as it is very similar to the composition diagram of the symmetric encryption pattern. In this case, the MAC algorithm of the machine *MACManager_R4* calculates a MAC value which allows the verifier (in our case study the *AuthorizedExternalEntities*) to detect any changes to the *MeterData*. The *AuthorizedExternalEntities* possess the same *SecretKey* for verifying *MeterData*.

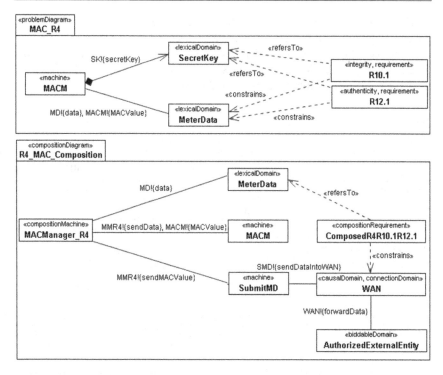

Fig. 9.7: Instantiated problem-oriented security pattern *MAC* for the integrity and authenticity requirements *R10.1* and *R12.1*

Architecture Alternative 2

According to the configuration diagram for the architecture alternative 2 illustrated in Fig. 9.22[1] , we selected the problem-oriented security pattern *asymmetric encryption* for achieving the confidentiality requirements *R11* (related to the functional requirement *R4*) and *R14* (related to the functional requirement *R5*) and the problem-oriented security pattern *digital signature* for achieving the integrity and authenticity requirements *R10* and *R12* (related to the functional requirement *R4*) and *R13* and *R15* (related to the functional requirement *R5*).

---

[1] The dependency ≪RequiresCD≫ is a specialization of the dependency ≪ConstraintDependency≫ between two variants. It requires the target variant to be selected if the source variant has been selected (see Section 8.5.1 on page 278 for more information).

The instantiated asymmetric encryption problem diagram *AsymEnc_R4_R5* for
the confidentiality requirements *R11* and *R14* is shown at the top of Fig. 9.8. The
machine *AsymEncM* uses the *PublicKey* to encrypt *MeterData*. The *PrivateKey*
used for decryption at the receiver side is not shown in this figure as it only shows
the sender side responsible for encrypting the data.

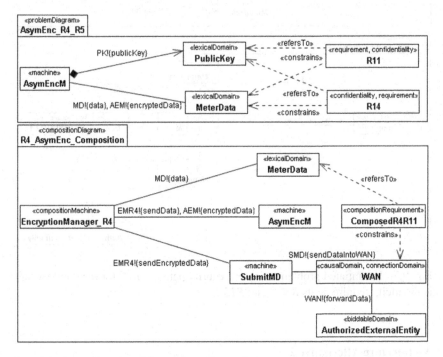

Fig. 9.8: Instantiated problem-oriented security pattern asymmetric encryption for
the confidentiality requirements *R11*

The composition problem diagram *R4_AsymEnc_Composition* shown at the
bottom of Fig. 9.8 combines the functional problem diagram *SubmitMD* with the
security problem diagram *AsymEnc_R4_R5* shown at the top of Fig. 9.8. It consists
of the new machine *EncryptionManager_R4*, both machine domains *SubmitMD*
and *AsymEncM*, and the domains of both problem diagrams. The machine *En-
cryptionManager_R4* is responsible for obtaining *MeterData*, encrypting it using
AsymEncM and sending it to the *AuthorizedExternalEntities* using *SubmitM*. The

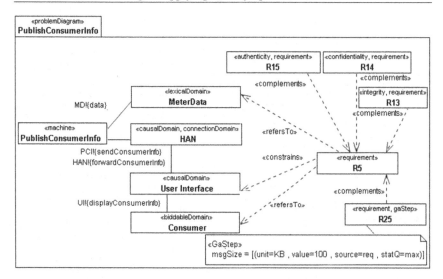

Fig. 9.9: Problem diagram related to functional requirement *R5* and its corresponding quality requirements

requirement *ComposedR4R11* consisting of the requirements *R4* and *R11* shall be achieved by the machine *EncryptionManager_R4*.

The functional problem diagram related to the functional requirement *R5* is the problem diagram *PublishConsumerInfo* shown in Fig. 9.9. The composition problem diagram *R5_AsymEnc_Composition* shown at the bottom of Fig. 9.10 combines the functional problem diagram *PublishConsumerInfo* with the security problem diagram *AsymEnc_R4_R5* shown at the top of Fig. 9.10. The new machine *EncryptionManager_R5* is responsible for obtaining *MeterData*, encrypting it using the asymmetric encryption algorithm of the machine *AsymEncM* and sending it to the *Consumer* using the functional machine *PublishConsumerInfo*.

On the top of Fig. 9.11, the instantiated digital signature problem diagram *DigSig_R4_R5* for the integrity and authenticity requirements *R10, R12, R13*, and *R15* (related to the functional requirements *R4* and *R5*) is illustrated. The machine *DigSigM* uses the *PrivateKey* to sign *MeterData*. The *PublicKey* used for verifying at the receiver side is not shown in this figure as it only shows the sender side responsible for signing the data.

The composition problem diagram *R4_DigSig_Composition* shown in the middle of Fig. 9.11 combines the functional problem diagram *SubmitMeterData*

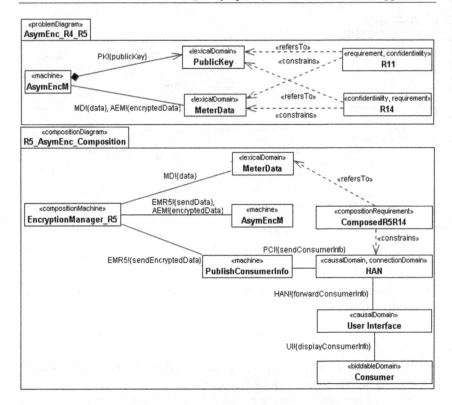

Fig. 9.10: Instantiated problem-oriented security pattern asymmetric encryption for the confidentiality requirements *R14*

(related to the functional requirement *R4*) with the security problem diagram *DigSig_R4_R5*. The machine *SignatureManager_R4* obtains *MeterData*, signs it using the machine *DigSigM*, and sends the signed *MeterData* using the machine *SubmitMD* to the *AuthorizedExternalEntities* which verify the signed *MeterData* using the corresponding public key.

The composition problem diagram *R5_DigSig_Composition* shown at the bottom of Fig. 9.11 combines the functional problem diagram *PublishConsumer-Info* (related to the functional requirement *R5*) with the security problem diagram *DigSig_R4_R5*. It is constructed in a similar way to the composition problem diagram *R4_DigSig_Composition* (related to the functional requirement *R4*) shown previously.

Architecture Alternative 3

For the smart grid case study, according to the configuration diagram for the architecture alternative 3 illustrated in Fig. 9.23, we selected the problem-oriented security pattern *symmetric encryption* for achieving the confidentiality requirements *R11.2* and *R14.2* (related to the functional requirements *R4* and *R5*), and the problem-oriented security pattern *MAC* for achieving the integrity and authenticity requirements *R10.2* and *R12.2* (related to the functional requirement *R4*), and *R13.2* and *R15.2* (related to the functional requirement *R5*). As the instantiation of the selected problem-oriented security patterns is similar to the ones for the architecture alternative 1, we only show the instantiations and do not describe them further. The application of the problem-oriented symmetric encryption pattern is shown in Fig. 9.12 while Fig. 9.13 shows the application of the problem-oriented MAC pattern.

Step 5 - Merge security composition diagrams related to the same functional requirement

The idea of this step and the next step is to merge the created composition diagrams step by step in order to obtain a new composition diagram which contains all relevant security-specific solutions. In this step, we merge the created composition diagrams which are related to the same functionality (same functional requirement). As the input for this step, we make use of the diagrams resulted from the previous step. In the next step, those composition diagrams are merged that are related to different functionalities.

Each composition diagram contains one security manager machine. For merging two composition diagrams, a new composition diagram is created which contains a new composition machine and the domains from both composition diagrams. The new composition machine is composed of the two composition machines from the composition diagrams to be merged. All the phenomena from both composition diagrams are also contained in the new composition diagram.

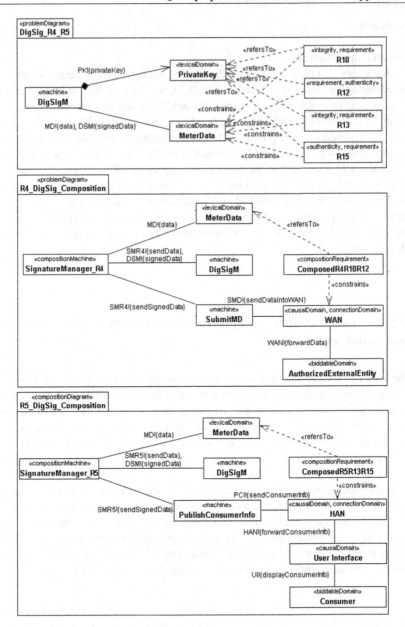

Fig. 9.11: Instantiated problem-oriented digital signature pattern for the integrity and authenticity requirements *R10*, *R12*, *R13*, and *R15*

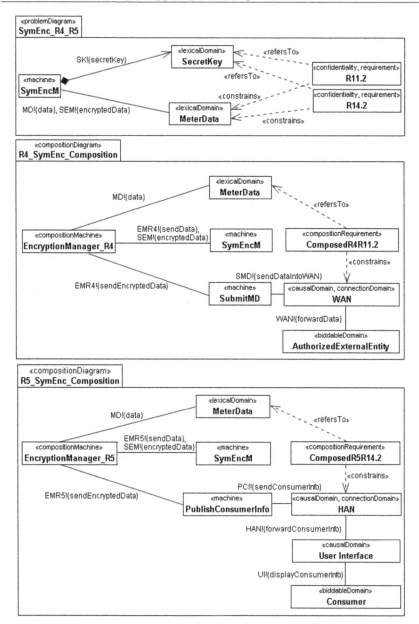

Fig. 9.12: Instantiated problem-oriented symmetric encryption pattern for the confidentiality requirements *R11.2* and *R14.2*

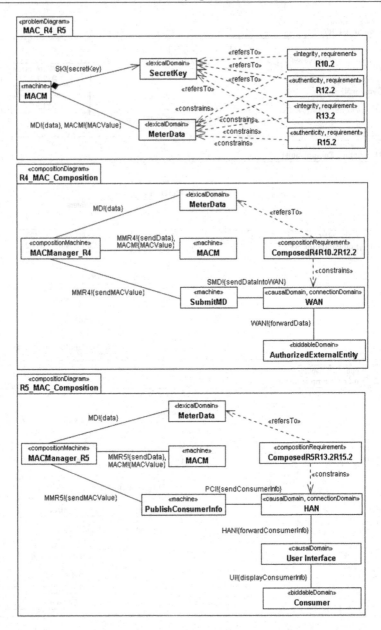

Fig. 9.13: Instantiated problem-oriented MAC pattern for the integrity and authenticity requirements *R10.2*, *R12.2*, *R13.2*, and *R14.2*

Application of Step 5 - Merge security composition diagrams related to the same functional requirement

Architecture Alternative 1

For the architecture alternative 1, we selected symmetric encryption and MAC for achieving confidentiality requirement *R11.1*, integrity requirement *R10.1*, and authenticity requirement *R12.1* related to the functional requirement *R4*. For merging the composition diagrams *R4_SymEncComposition* (see Fig. 9.6) and *R4_MAC_Composition* (see Fig. 9.7), one creates the new composition diagram *R4_Merge_SymEnc_MAC* which contains the new composition machine *SecManager_Sym_MAC_R4* and the domains contained in both composition diagrams, namely *MeterData*, *SymEncM*, *MACM*, *SubmitM*, *WAN*, and *AuthorizedExternalEntity*. The new composition machine *SecManager_Sym_MAC_R4* is composed of the composition machines *EncryptionManager_R4* and *MACManager_R4*. All the phenomena from both composition diagrams are also contained in the new composition diagram. Figure 9.14 illustrates the new composition diagram *R4_Merge_SymEnc_MAC*. The new composition machine *SecManager_Sym_MAC_R4* is in charge of coordinating the order of performing encryption and authentication using MAC. Krawczyk [154] identifies three types of combining encryption with authentication using MAC for protecting communications over an insecure network. These three types are

1. Encrypt then Authenticate (known as *EtA*). It is used in IPsec. The cleartext is encrypted first. Then, a MAC value is computed on the ciphertext. The MAC value is then appended to the ciphertext.
2. Authenticate then Encrypt (known as *AtE*). It is used in Secure Sockets Layer (SSL). In this case, the MAC value is computed on the cleartext and appended to the data. Then, the whole is encrypted.
3. Encrypt and Authenticate (known as *E&A*). It is used in SSH. Here, the MAC value is computed on the cleartext. The cleartext is encrypted. The MAC value is then appended at the end of the ciphertext.

Although *AtE* and *E&A* are common methods for composing encryption and authentication, they might be subject of attacks. Krawczyk shows that only *EtA* is the most secure way in general.

Architecture Alternative 2

For the architecture alternative 2, we selected asymmetric encryption and digital signature for achieving confidentiality requirements *R11* and *R14*, integrity requirements *R10* and *R13*, and authenticity requirements *R12* and *R15* related to the functional requirements *R4* and *R5*. Hence, we are concerned with two merges.

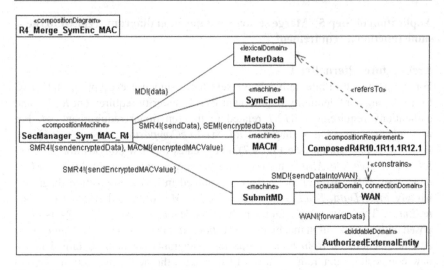

Fig. 9.14: Merged composition diagrams related to the functional requirement *R4* for the architecture alternative 1

First, we merge the composition diagrams *R4_AsymEnc_Composition* (see the diagram at the bottom of Fig. 9.8) and *R4_DigSig_Composition* (see the middle diagram in Fig. 9.11), both related to the functional requirement *R4*. To this end, we create the new composition diagram *R4_Merge_DigSig_AsymEnc* containing the new composition machine *SecManager_Sig_Asym_R4* and the domains contained in both composition diagrams. The new composition machine is composed of the composition machines *EncryptionManager_R4* and *Signature-Manager_R4*. All the phenomena from both composition diagrams are also contained in the new composition diagram. Figure 9.15 illustrates the new composition diagram *R4_Merge_DigSig_AsymEnc*. The new composition machine *Sec-Manager_Sig_Asym_R4* is in charge of coordinating the order of encrypting and signing. Also here, three types of combining encryption and signature for protecting the communication over insecure networks are possible, namely 1) sign-then-encrypt, 2) encrypt-then-sign, and 3) encrypt-and-sign. Although encrypt-then-sign and encrypt-and-sign could provide enough security in most cases, there are, however, subtle attacks for these two cases that might not necessarily cause a problem in all scenarios. Therefore, it is recommended to use sign-then-encrypt.

Second, we merge the composition diagrams *R5_AsymEnc_Composition* (see the diagram at the bottom of Fig. 9.10) and *R5_DigSig_Composition* (see the third

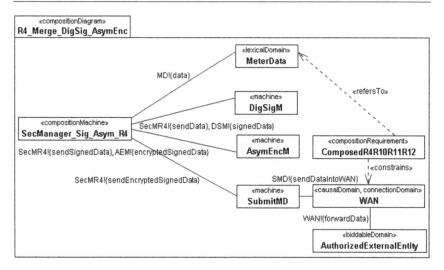

Fig. 9.15: Merged composition diagrams related to the functional requirement *R4* for the architecture alternative 2

diagram in Fig. 9.11), both related to the functional requirement *R5*. To this end, we create the new composition diagram *R5_Merge_DigSig_AsymEnc* containing the new composition machine *SecManager_Sig_Asym_R5* and the domains contained in both composition diagrams. The new composition machine is composed of the composition machines *EncryptionManager_R5* and *SignatureManager_R5*. All the phenomena from both composition diagrams are also contained in the new composition diagram. Figure 9.16 illustrates the new composition diagram *R4_Merge_DigSig_AsymEnc*. Also here, the new composition machine *SecManager_Sig_Asym_R5* is in charge of coordinating the order of encrypting and signing.

Architecture Alternative 3

For the architecture alternative 3, we selected symmetric encryption and MAC for achieving confidentiality requirements *R11.2* and *R14.2*, integrity requirements *R10.2* and *R13.2*, and authenticity requirements *R12.2* and *R15.2* related to the functional requirements *R4* and *R5*. Here, we are concerned with two merges as well.

First, we merge the composition diagrams *R4_SymEnc_Composition* (see the second diagram in Fig. 9.12) and *R4_MAC_Composition* (see the second diagram

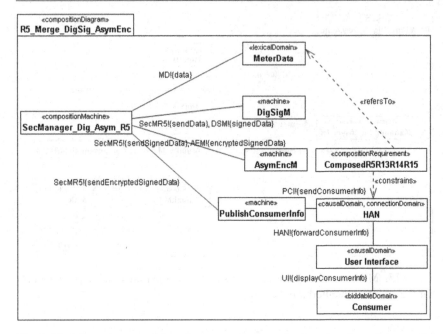

Fig. 9.16: Merged composition diagrams related to the functional requirement *R5* for the architecture alternative 2

in Fig. 9.13), both related to the functional requirement *R4*. To this end, we create the new composition diagram *R4_Merge_SymEnc_MAC* containing the new composition machine *SecManager_Sym_MAC_R4* and the domains contained in both composition diagrams. The new composition machine is composed of the composition machines *EncryptionManager_R4* and *MACManager_R4*. All the phenomena from both composition diagrams are also contained in the new composition diagram. Figure 9.17 illustrates the new composition diagram *R4_Merge_SymEnc_-MAC*. The new composition machine *SecManager_Sym_MAC_R4* is in charge of coordinating the order of performing encryption and authentication using MAC as described for the architecture alternative 1.

Second, we merge the composition diagrams *R5_SymEnc_Composition* (see the third diagram in Fig. 9.12) and *R5_MAC_Composition* (see the third diagram in Fig. 9.13), both related to the functional requirement *R5*. To this end, we create the new composition diagram *R5_Merge_SymEnc_MAC* containing the new composition machine *SecManager_Sym_MAC_R5* and the domains contained in both

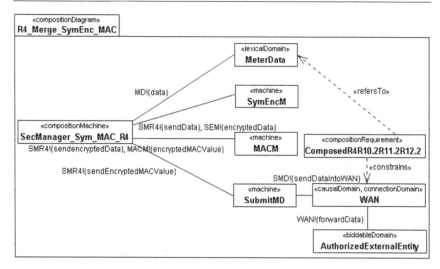

Fig. 9.17: Merged composition diagrams related to the functional requirement *R4* for the architecture alternative 3

composition diagrams. The new composition machine is composed of the composition machines *EncryptionManager_R5* and *MACManager_R5*. All the phenomena from both composition diagrams are also contained in the new composition diagram. Figure 9.18 illustrates the new composition diagram *R5_Merge_SymEnc_MAC*. Also here, the new composition machine *SecManager_Sym_MAC_R5* is in charge of coordinating the order of performing encryption and authentication using MAC.

Step 6 - Merge security composition diagrams related to different functional requirements

In this step, we merge the created composition diagrams relating to different functional requirements from the previous step. We use the resulted security-specific diagrams as an input to Step 8 of our method for applying performance-specific patterns.

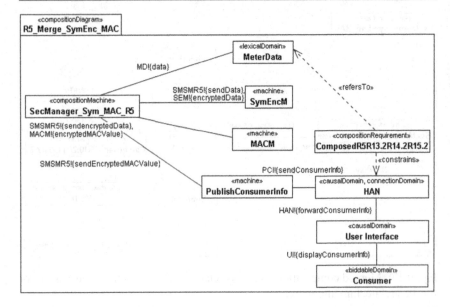

Fig. 9.18: Merged composition diagrams related to the functional requirement *R5* for the architecture alternative 3

The procedure is similar to the one from the previous step. Each composition diagram contains one security manager machine. For merging two composition diagrams, a new composition diagram is created which contains a new composition machine and the domains from both composition diagrams. The new composition machine is composed of the two composition machines from the composition diagrams to be merged. All the phenomena from both composition diagrams are also contained in the new composition diagram.

Application of Step 6 - Merge security composition diagrams related to different functional requirements

Architecture Alternative 1
This step cannot be applied to the diagrams for the architecture alternative 1, as it only addresses security requirements complementing the functional requirement *R4*.

Architecture Alternative 2

For the architecture alternative 2, we merge the composition diagrams *R4_Merge_-DigSig_AsymEnc* (see Fig. 9.15) and *R5_Merge_DigSig_AsymEnc* (see Fig. 9.16). The new composition diagram *Merge_R4_R5_DigSig_AsymEnc* contains the new composition machine *SecManager_Sig_Asym_R4_R5* and the domains from both composition diagrams to be merged. The new composition machine composes the composition machines *SecManager_Sig_Asym_R4* and *SecManager_Sig_Asym_R5*. All the phenomena from both composition diagrams are also contained in the new composition diagram. Figure 9.19 illustrates the new composition diagram.

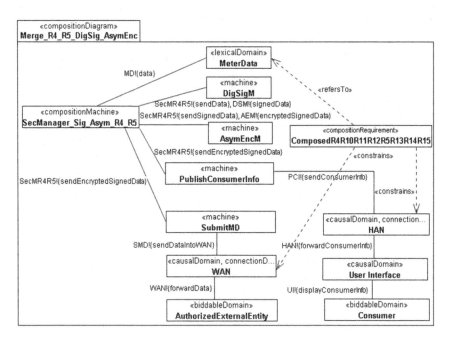

Fig. 9.19: Merged composition diagrams related to the functional requirements *R4* and *R5* for the architecture alternative 2

Architecture Alternative 3

For the architecture alternative 3, we merge the composition diagrams *R4_Merge_-SymEnc_MAC* (see Fig. 9.17) and *R5_Merge_SymEnc_MAC* (see Fig. 9.18). The new composition diagram *Merge_R4_R5_SymEnc_MAC* contains the new composition machine *SecManager_Sym_MAC_R4_R5* and the domains from both composition diagrams to be merged. The new composition machine composes the composition machines *SecManager_Sym_MAC_R4* and *SecManager_Sym_MAC_R5* All the phenomena from both composition diagrams are also contained in the new composition diagram. Figure 9.20 illustrates the new composition diagram.

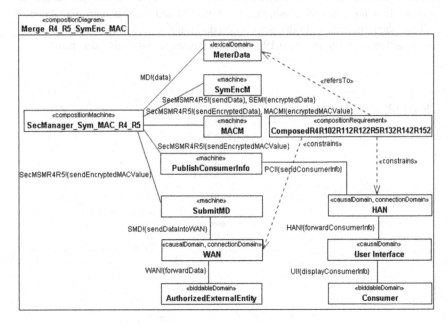

Fig. 9.20: Merged composition diagrams related to the functional requirements *R4* and *R5* for the architecture alternative 3

Step 7 - Select problem-oriented performance patterns

In this step, we select appropriate problem-oriented performance patterns. As input in addition to the *problem-oriented performance patterns, performance require-ment alternatives, problem-solution diagram*, and the *configuration diagrams*, one needs the problem diagrams identified as problematic from the performance per-

Table 9.3: Performance analysis patterns and their selection criteria

	Selection Criteria		
	Type of load distribution	Type of overload	Type of resource
First Things First (FTF)	spatial / temporal	temporary	software / hardware
Flex Time (FT)	temporal	permanent	software / hardware
Load Balancer (LB)	spatial	permanent	software / hardware
Master-Worker (MW)	spatial	permanent	software

spective. Such subproblems have been identified using our performance requirement analysis method PoPeRA (see Section 7.4 on page 220).

Problem-oriented performance patterns are introduced in Chapter 8 (see Section 8.3 on page 264). The field *applicability* in the template for problem-oriented performance patterns (see Table 8.8 in Section 8.3.2 on page 266) represents the pre-conditions each subproblem has to fulfill before applying the specific performance pattern. In order to systematically select the appropriate problem-oriented performance patterns, for each subproblem with identified potential performance problems we have to determine whether the specific subproblem fulfills the required pre-conditions by answering the questions 1) *does the subproblem exhibit a permanent or a temporary high usage?*, 2) *does the subproblem exhibit a spatial or temporal load distribution?*, and 3) *does the involved resource provide a software or a hardware resource?*

Table 9.3 shows the conditions under which the problem-oriented performance patterns can be applied. It provides support in selecting the appropriate patterns. As an example, the problem-oriented performance pattern *Flex Time (FT)* can be applied if the resource is a hardware or a software component, the subproblem can be satisfied to a different period of time (temporal), and a permanent overload of the subproblem is expected.

Application of Step 7 - Select problem-oriented performance patterns

Architecture Alternative 1
According to our performance requirement analysis method PoPeRA (see Section 7.4 on page 220), we expect high workload and average resource usage for the performance requirements *R18* and *R19* related to the functional requirement *R1*. In addition, the performance requirement *R18* has to be achieved together with the performance requirements *R22* and *R24* in less than 5 seconds. Therefore, a potential performance problem due to the requirement *R18* for the subproblem *ReceiveMeterData* is expected.

Also for the performance requirements *R22* and *R23*, related to the functional requirement *R2R3*, we expect high workload and average resource usage. In addition, the performance requirement *R22* has to be achieved together with the performance requirements *R18* and *R24* in less than 5 seconds. Therefore, a potential performance problem for the subproblem *PrcessStoreMD* is expected due to the requirement *R22*.

According to the high workload, the high resource usage, and the strong security requirements *R10.1*, *R11.1*, and *R12.1* (according to the *WAN* attacker profile) for the subproblem *SubmitMeterData*, we identify a potential performance problem for achieving the performance requirement *R24*.

For the subproblem *PublishConsumerInfo* we expect low workload and sparse resource usage. In addition, we did not select any security mechanisms for the corresponding security requirements *R13.1*, *R14.1*, and *R15.1* as we have weak security requirements (according to the *HAN* attacker profile). Therefore, we do not expect a potential performance problem for achieving the performance requirement *R25*. Hence, there is no need for selecting problem-oriented performance requirements for this subproblem.

Now, we have to select the appropriate problem-oriented performance patterns for the subproblems with performance problems, namely the subproblems *ReceiveMeterData* related to the functional requirement *R1*, *PrcessStoreMD* related to the functional requirement *R2R3*, and *SubmitMeterData* related to the functional requirement *R4*. To this end, we make use of Table 9.3.

For all three subproblems, we have a spatial load distribution and a software resource. This is annotated using the attributes *loadDistributionTypes* and *resourceType* of the stereotype ≪bottleneck≫. The overload is temporary as the system faces overload only when requesting *MeterData*. This is annotated using the attribute *overloadType* of the stereotype ≪bottleneck≫ (see Fig. 9.24).

According to this, we could select the *First Things First* pattern that can provide a prioritization of requests. For example, for the subproblem *ReceiveMeterData*, it can assign a higher priority to the requests related to the requirement *R18* and a lower priority to the requests related to the requirement *R19*. This solution might solve the problem for the performance requirement *R18*, it however might cause problems for the performance requirement *R19* as it is treated with a lower priority. As we aim at providing the best performance for the architecture alternative 1, we select the *Load Balancer* pattern that is usually applied by *permanent overload*. With this solution, the problem of starving requests related to the requirement *R19* does not arise.

Also for the subproblems *ProcessStoreMD* related to the functional requirement *R2R3* and *SubmitMeterData* related to the functional requirement *R4*, we select the *Load Balancer* pattern for the same reason. Figure 9.21 shows the configuration diagram for the architecture alternative 1.

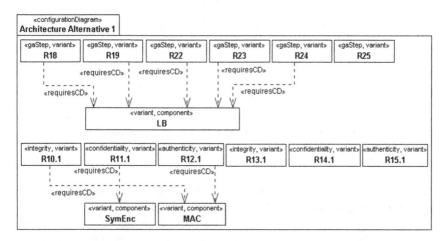

Fig. 9.21: Configuration diagram for the architecture alternative 1

Architecture Alternative 2

The architecture alternative 2 should provide the best security. Performance is considered with a lower priority. For this architecture alternative, the performance requirement alternatives *R18.1, R19.1, R22.1, R23.1, R24.1,* and *R25.1* are selected. These requirements are relaxed in a way that there is no need for applying performance patterns to achieve them. For example, the *number of concurrent users* is reduced, the *network bandwidth* and the *CPU frequency* are increased so that performance problems cannot arise (see Table 7.29 for performance requirement alternatives *R18.1* and *R19.1* on page 237, Table 7.30 for performance requirement alternatives *R22.1* and *R23.1* on page 238, Table 7.31 for performance requirement alternative *R24.1* on page 239, and Table 7.32 for performance requirement alternative *R25.1* on page 240 in Section 7.5). Figure 9.22 shows the configuration diagram for the architecture alternative 2.

Architecture Alternative 3

For architecture alternative 3, we consider performance and security with the same priority. To this end, we relaxed all quality requirements in a way that they can be achieved together using appropriate problem-oriented performance and security patterns. As we are concerned with relaxed performance requirements, a performance solution such as *Load Balancer* is not required. Performance requirements

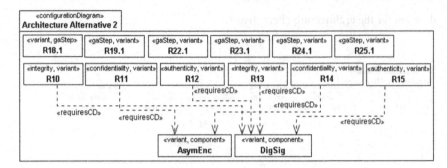

Fig. 9.22: Configuration diagram for the architecture alternative 2

R19.2, R23.2, and *R25.2* should be achieved in less than 10 seconds whereas performance requirements *R18.2, R22.2*, and *R24.2* should be achieved in less than 5 seconds. All requirements with relaxed domain knowledge are shown in Table 7.29 - Table 7.32 (see page 237). According to this, we select the *First Things First* pattern for all performance requirements. It assigns performance requirements *R18.2, R22.2*, and *R24.2* a higher priority than performance requirements *R19.2, R23.2*, and *R25.2*. By doing this, all performance requirements can be fulfilled. Figure 9.23 shows the configuration diagram for the architecture alternative 3.

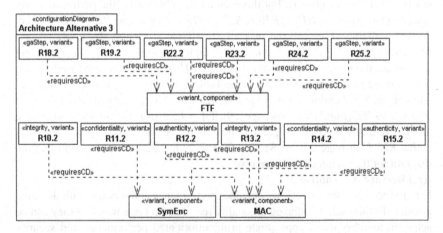

Fig. 9.23: Configuration diagram for the architecture alternative 3

Step 8 - Apply Problem-oriented Performance Patterns

In this step, selected problem-oriented performance patterns have to be applied to the corresponding subproblems. These subproblems have to be instances of the problem frame describing the *generic problem structure* introduced in Section 8.3.2 (see the generic problem frame in Figure 8.9 on page 269). The fields *solution* and *collaboration* in the template for problem-oriented performance patterns (see Table 8.8 in Section 8.3.2 on page 266) describe how the selected pattern can be applied. The *generic solution structure* shown at the bottom of Fig. 8.9 in Section 8.3.2 (see page 269) exemplifies the composition of subproblems as a problem frame describing the *generic solution structure*. Several patterns can be applied to a subproblem if the subproblem fulfills the required pre-conditions shown in Table 9.3.

Application of Step 8 - Apply problem-oriented performance pattern

Architecture Alternative 1
We can apply patterns to the subproblems only when subproblems are valid instances of the problem frame describing the generic problem structure given in Section 8.3.2 (see the top of Fig. 8.9 on page 269). We can apply the *Load Balancer* pattern to the subproblem *ReceiveMeterData* (see Fig. 9.24), as it represents a valid instance of the problem frame describing the generic problem structure. The instance contains the following elements:

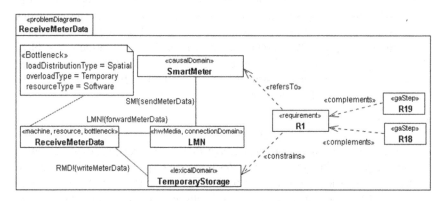

Fig. 9.24: Subproblem *ReceiveMeterData* related to functional requirement *R1*

- One machine domain *ReceiveMeterData* corresponding to the domain *Machine* in the *generic problem structure* (see the top of Fig. 8.9 on page 269). It represents a resource expressed by the stereotype ≪resource≫ which is expected to be the bottleneck expressed with the stereotype ≪bottleneck≫. The machine domain is responsible for responding to the requests. The machine domain is a software resource.
- One domain *LMN* corresponding to the domain *Domain1* in the *generic problem structure*. It transmits the requests to the machine domain *ReceiveMeterData*. Note that the domain *SmartMeter* is an additional domain not relevant for the performance problem at hand.
- One domain *TemporaryStorage* corresponding to the domain *Domain2* in the *generic problem structure*. It is required for processing the requests by the machine domain *ReceiveMeterData*.
- One requirement *R1*, which describes the functional requirement.
- Two performance requirements *R18* and *R19*, which describe the performance requirements corresponding to the functional requirement *R1*.

Subproblems *ProcessStoreMD* and *SubmitMeterData* represent valid instances of the problem frame describing the generic problem structure similar to the subproblem *ReceiveMeterData*. Furthermore, each specific pattern can be applied to a subproblem, if the subproblem fulfills the pre-conditions of the specific pattern given in the field applicability of the pattern template. In the previous step, we specified the characteristics of each problematic subproblem using *load distribution type*, *overload type*, and *resource type*, which correspond to the pre-conditions for the application of the problem-oriented performance pattern *Load Balancer*.

Figure 9.25 shows the application of *Load Balancer* to the subproblems *ReceiveMeterData*, *ProcessStoreMD*, and *SubmitMeterData* which are instantiations of the *generic solution structure* shown at the bottom of Fig. 8.9 (see page 269).

On the top of Fig. 9.25, the application of *Load Balancer* to the subproblem *ReceiveMeterData* is shown. It represents a valid instance of the problem frame describing the generic solution structure (see the bottom of Fig. 8.9 on page 269). The instance contains the following elements:

- One domain *LB* as a machine domain and as a resource with the stereotypes ≪machine≫ and ≪resource≫.
- At least one domain as machine domain *ReceiveMeterData* and as a resource (stereotypes ≪machine≫ and ≪resource≫) responsible for responding to the requests. The new machine *LB* obtains meter readings from *SmartMeter* through *LMN* and distributes the request between several machines *ReceiveMeterData* (see the multiplicity 1..* in Fig. 9.25) that are responsible for temporarily storing meter readings into *TemporaryStorage*.

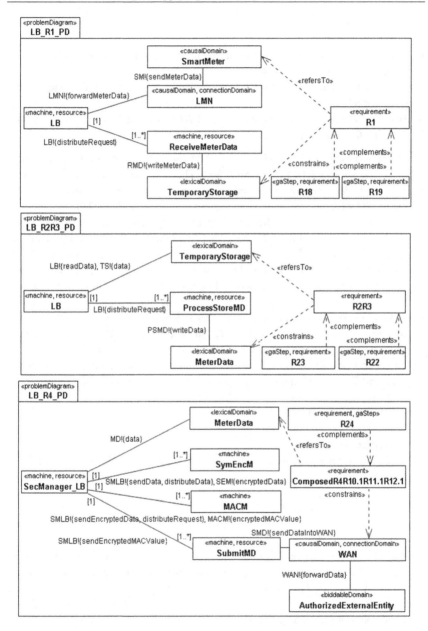

Fig. 9.25: Application of *Load Balancer* to subproblems related to functional requirements *R1*, *R2R3*, and *R4*

- One domain *LMN*, which transmits the requests to the machine domain *ReceiveMeterData*.
- One domain *TemporaryStorage* required for processing the requests by the machine domain *ReceiveMeterData*.
- One functional requirement *R1* to be satisfied by the machine domains *ReceiveMeterData*.
- Two performance requirements *R18* and *R19* to be satisfied by the machine domains *ReceiveMeterData*.

The subproblem in the middle of Fig. 9.25 shows the application of *Load Balancer* to the subproblem *ProcessStoreMD*. The new machine *LB* obtains meter readings from *TemporaryStorage* and distributes it between several machines *ProcessStoreMD* which persistently store meter readings into *MeterData*.

The application of *Load Balancer* to the subproblem *SubmitMeterData* is shown at the bottom of Fig. 9.25. Note that *Load Balancer* is applied to the composition diagram containing the problem-oriented security patterns *symmetric encryption* and *MAC*. In this subproblem, the security manager functionality is extended with the load balancing functionality, instead of introducing a new machine *LB*. The reason is that a security manager machine and a load balancer machine both are in charge of coordinating the other machines. Hence, they can be combined into one machine *SecManager_LB* in order to prevent introducing a new machine domain. For this subproblem, the load balancer distributes the load between several machines *SymEnc*, *MAC*, and *SubmitMD* as required. Introducing only several *SubmitMD* machines does not solve the problem of potentially overloading the encryption machine *SymEnc* or the MAC machine *MACM* as these actions are time consuming.

Architecture Alternative 2
No problem-oriented performance patterns are selected for the architecture alternative 2.

Architecture Alternative 3
For the architecture alternative 3, we do not show that the problem diagrams are a valid instance of the generic problem structure described in Section 8.3.2 (see the top of Fig. 8.9 on page 269) as this is shown once for the architecture alternative 1. In the previous step, we specified the characteristics of each problematic subproblem using *load distribution type*, *overload type*, and *resource type*, which correspond to the pre-conditions for the application of the problem-oriented performance pattern *First Things First*.

Figure 9.26 shows the application of *First Things First* to subproblems *ReceiveMeterData* and *ProcessStoreMD* which are instantiations of the *generic so-*

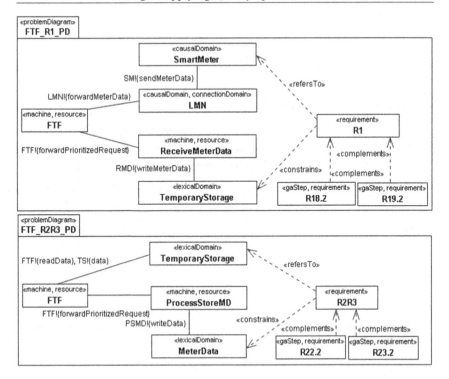

Fig. 9.26: Application of *FTF* to subproblems related to functional requirements *R1* and *R2R3*

lution structure shown at the bottom of Fig. 8.9 (see page 269). On the top of Fig. 9.26, the application of *First Things First* to the subproblem *ReceiveMeterData* is shown. The new machine *FTF* obtains meter readings from *SmartMeter* through *LMN* and forwards meter readings to the machine *ReceiveMeterData* according to the priority of the meter readings. Here, we deal with two kinds of meter readings, meter readings that should be processed, stored, and submitted to the authorized external entities within 5 seconds (related to requirement *R18.2*) and meter readings that should be processed, stored, and submitted to the consumer within 10 seconds (related to requirement *R19.2*). The new machine *FTF* forwards the first kind of meter readings with a higher priority than the second kind of meter readings. The second problem diagram in Fig. 9.26 shows the application of *First Things First* to the subproblem *ProcessStoreMD*. Also here, the requests related to

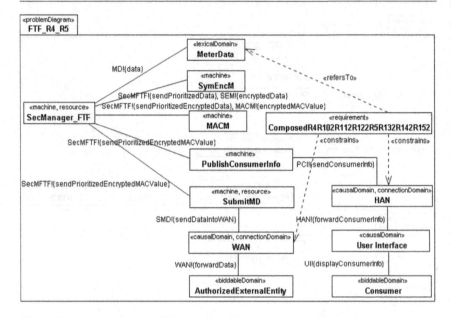

Fig. 9.27: Application of *FTF* to subproblems related to functional requirements *R4* and *R5*

the requirement *R22.2* are treated with a higher priority than the requests related to performance requirement *R23.2*.

Figure 9.27 shows the application of *First Things First* to the subproblems *SubmitMeterData* and *PublishConsumerInfo*. Also here, we apply *First Things First* to the composition diagram which contains already the applied problem-oriented security patterns *symmetric encryption* and *MAC*. The new machine *FTF* is combined with the existing security manager machine *SecManager* to the machine *SecManager_FTF* which coordinates the order of sending requests to the *SymEncM* and *MACM*. In addition, it assigns priorities to the requests and forwards the requests related to performance requirement *R24.2* with higher priority than those requests related to performance requirement *R25.2*.

9.3 Contributions

In this chapter, we bridged the quality requirements with corresponding solution alternatives for achieving them by proposing a comprehensive method. It can be summarized as follows:

- Our method supports the selection of appropriate *problem-oriented quality patterns* and the application of the selected patterns to the requirement models in order to address the quality requirements security and performance. It provides guidance for refining security and performance problems located in the problem space using *problem-oriented quality patterns.*
- The application of our method results in alternatives for the requirement models enriched with quality-specific solutions according to the defined priorities of quality requirements. Our method supports less experienced software engineers in selecting and applying different solution approaches early in the requirements engineering phase in a systematic manner. The enriched requirement model alternatives differ in solutions selected for achieving quality requirements. Such alternatives in requirement models allow us to derive software architecture alternatives that achieve quality requirements in different ways. The derivation of software architecture alternatives is achieved in the next chapter.

Chapter 10
Phase 7: Software Architecture Alternatives Derivation

Abstract In the previous chapter, we systematically incorporated quality-specific mechanisms into requirement models in order to address quality requirements. This chapter proposes a systematic method for deriving implementable software architecture alternatives based on the requirement models. Such requirement models are enriched with quality-specific solutions. The derived implementable software architecture alternatives fulfill quality requirements with different levels of satisfaction.

10.1 Introduction

In Chapter 5, we described how to derive the initial software architecture that is oriented on the decomposition of the overall software development problem into subproblems. It uses the already selected architectural patterns to implement the functional requirements with regard to quality requirements. As a consequence, the derived initial software architecture contributes to the achievement of quality requirements. It, however, does not involve quality-specific solutions to specifically address quality requirements.

In order to incorporate quality-specific solutions into a software architecture, we have introduced *problem-oriented quality patterns* in Chapter 8 and applied them systematically to the requirement models in Chapter 9. We developed alternatives for the requirement models enriched with quality-specific solutions according to the defined priorities of quality requirements. Such alternatives in requirement models allow the derivation of software architecture alternatives.

This chapter describes Phase 7 of our QuaDRA framework. In this chapter, we transform the initial software architecture into implementable software architecture alternatives. The implementable architecture alternatives extend the initial architecture with additional components that address quality requirements. To this end, we use the requirement models containing problem-oriented quality-specific patterns as well as the initial architecture. Application of different quality-specific solutions leads to the derivation of architecture alternatives that fulfill quality requirements in different ways. We propose a systematic method for deriving implementable architecture alternatives.

This chapter is based on our works presented in [16, 7, 150]. In [7], we systematically derive a software architecture from a given problem description based on problem frames. The derived software architecture considers only functional requirements. My colleague Denis Hatebur made the main contribution to this work. We contributed to this work with intensive discussions and feedback together with Isabelle Côté, Maritta Heisel, and Christine Choppy.

We extended this approach by addressing quality requirements in order to derive quality-based software architectures in [16][1] We are the main author of this work. With Denis Hatebur and Maritta Heisel, we had helpful and constructive discussions.

The work presented in [150] uses our quality-based software architecture derivation method presented in [16] as one part of a comprehensive method for deriving and evaluating architecture alternatives. This work has been developed jointly in the context of a research project collaboration with our project partners Marco Konersmann and Benjamin Kersten. Michael Goedicke and Maritta Heisel provided valuable feedback on our work.

The remainder of this chapter is organized as follows. We describe how to systematically derive architecture alternatives from the quality-based requirement models in Section 10.2. Along with the description of software architecture derivation, we show its application to the smart grid. Section 10.3 presents related work, while Section 10.4 concludes this chapter and summarizes the contribution.

10.2 Method for Deriving Implementable Architecture Alternatives

In this section, we propose a systematic method for deriving implementable architecture alternatives. For modeling the implementable architecture alternatives,

---

[1] This work was done after the work in [7]. However, it was published earlier.

we proceed similarly to the modeling of the initial architecture (see Section 5.6 on page 161). Implementable architectures are represented as composite structure diagrams. For modeling these architectures, we use the UML profile for architectures (see Section 2.3.2 on page 37). It allows us to annotate composite structure diagrams with information on components and connectors.

Figure 10.1 illustrates our method for deriving the implementable architecture alternatives consisting of five steps. In the following, we describe the steps of the method followed by its application to the smart grid case study.

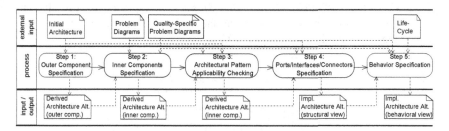

Fig. 10.1: Overview of the method for deriving the implementable architecture alternatives

Step 1 - Outer Component Specification

The implementable architecture consists of one component for the overall machine that is the outer component, similar to the initial architecture. As the input for this step, we require the *initial architecture* (see Step 1 in Fig. 10.1).

The same stereotypes used for modeling the initial architecture (see Section 5.6 on page 161) are used for annotating the outer component and the connectors. To this end, we use the *architecture profile* (see Section 2.3.2 on page 37).

In the initial architecture, the outer component, its type, and its interfaces are specified. For the implementable architecture these elements can be re-used. However, for the outer component in the implementable architecture, one has to apply the stereotype ≪implementable_architecture≫ to indicate that this architecture is an implementable architecture. The ports of the overall machine remain the same as those in the initial architecture. As the output, we obtain the *outer component* of the implementable architecture alternatives, its ports, and interfaces to the outside world.

Application of Step 1 - Outer Component Specification

For the architecture alternatives, we set up one outer component for each architecture alternative. The overall components for the three architecture alternatives are called *Smart Meter Gateway (Alternative 1)*, *Smart Meter Gateway (Alternative 2)*, and *Smart Meter Gateway (Alternative 3)*. They correspond to the overall component in the initial architecture. The initial architecture derived in Phase 2 (see Chapter 5) is again illustrated in Fig. 10.2.

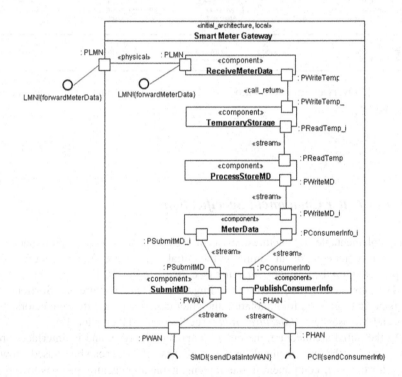

Fig. 10.2: Structural view of the initial architecture of smart grid

For the overall component, we choose the stereotypes *implementable_architecture* to indicate that the architecture is an implementable one and *local* to indicate that we are concerned with a single stand-alone system. Similar to the initial architecture, the implementable architecture has three ports typed with *:PLMN*, *:PHAN*, and *:PWAN* which have a class as a type. This class uses and realizes interfaces. The port with the class *PLMN* as a type provides the interface *LMN!{forwardMeterData}* (depicted as a lollipop) and the ports with the classes *PWAN* and *PHAN* as a type require the interfaces *SMD!{sendDataIntoWAN}* as well as *PCI!{sendConsumerInfo}* (depicted as a socket).

Step 2 - Inner Components Selection

Inner components are those components placed inside the outer component. The aim of this step is to select the inner components. Note that the ports, interfaces, and connectors between these components are specified later on in Step 4. As the first input for this step, we require the *outer component* from the previous step. Similar to the initial architecture, the implementable architecture contains one component for each subproblem expressed with the stereotype ≪Component≫ to indicate the components in the software architecture. Hence, the other input for this step are the initial *problem diagrams* (see Step 2 in Fig. 10.1). These components are also contained in the initial architecture.

In addition, the implementable architecture contains new components for addressing the quality requirements. For deriving those components inside the outer component, we make use of the *quality-specific problem diagrams* from the previous chapter as a further input of this step (see Section 9.2 on page 290). Each submachine in such problem diagrams becomes a component to be located inside the outer component. Also the lexical domains as data representations become components in the implementable architecture, similar to the initial architecture.

Application of Step 2 - Inner Components Selection

Architecture Alternative 1
The implementable architecture alternatives for the smart grid case study are represented as UML composite structure diagrams shown in Figures 10.3 - 10.5. The components highlighted in gray are the new components addressing quality requirements not existing in the initial architecture. In the following, we describe how we derive the inner components of these architecture alternatives.

In this step, one has to select components to be placed inside the outer component *Smart Meter Gateway (Alternative 1)*. To this end, we consider the problem diagrams enriched with problem-specific solutions from the previous phase (see Fig. 9.25 in Section 9.2 on page 323).

Problem diagram related to functional requirement *R1*: From the subproblem *LB_R1_PD*, we take the machines *LB1* and *ReceiveMeterData* and the lexical domain *TemporaryStorage* as components for the implementable architecture expressed with the stereotype *Component*. Note that we might have more instances of the component *ReceiveMeterData* if needed. This is shown in Fig. 10.3 by the port multiplicity [1..*] related to the component *ReceiveMeterData*.

Problem diagram related to functional requirement *R2R3*: The new subproblem related to the functional requirement *R2R3* is the problem diagram *LB_R2R3_PD* which contains the new machine *LB2* in addition to the functional machine *ProcessStoreMD*. Hence, *LB2* and *ProcessStoreMD* become components in the implementable architecture. In addition, the lexical domain *MeterData* is mapped to a component in the architecture. Also here, we might have more instances of the component *ProcessStoreMD* dependent on the current load (see the multiplicity [1..*] of the port related to the component *ProcessStoreMD* in Fig. 10.3).

Problem diagram related to functional requirement *R4*: The new subproblem related to the functional requirement *R4* is the problem diagram *LB_R4_PD* which contains three new machines *SecManager_LB*, *SymEncM*, and *MACM* being represented as components in the implementable architecture in addition to the component *SubmitMD*. More than one instance of the components *SymEncM* and *MACM* is possible if needed (see the port multiplicity [1..*] related to the components *SymEncM* and *MACM* in Fig. 10.3).

Problem diagram related to functional requirement *R5*: The initial problem diagram *PublishConsumerInfo* serves as a basis for the implementable architecture alternative 1 as we did not apply any quality-specific solution to it. Hence, the machine *PublishConsumerInfo* becomes a component in the implementable architecture.

Architecture Alternative 2

In the previous chapter (see Section 9.2 on page 290), we applied problem-oriented security patterns only to the problem diagrams related to the functional requirements *R4* and *R5*. Hence, for the functional requirements *R1* and *R2R3*, we take

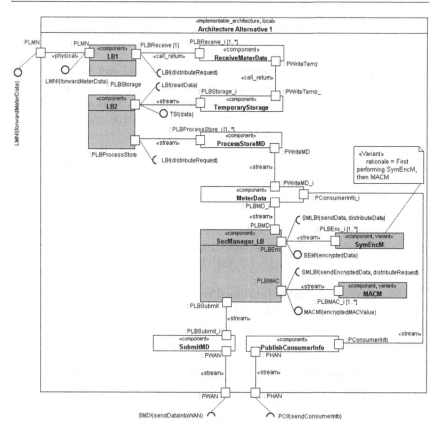

Fig. 10.3: Structural view of the implementable architecture of smart grid (alternative 1)

the initial functional problem diagrams *ReceiveMeterData* and *ProcessStoreMD* as a basis for the implementable architecture. Therefore, modeling the implementable architecture for these two subproblems is similar to the modeling of the initial architecture.

Problem diagram related to functional requirements *R1* and *R2R3*: Considering the problem diagram related to the functional requirement *R1*, the machine *ReceiveMeterData* and the lexical domain *TemporaryStorage* become components in the implementable architecture alternative 2. Considering the problem diagram related to the functional requirement *R2R3*, the machine *ProcessStoreMD* and the lexical domain *MeterData* are mapped to components as well.

Problem diagram related to functional requirements *R4* and *R5*: For the subproblems related to the functional requirements *R4* and *R5*, we consider the composition problem diagram *Merge_R4R5_DigSig_AsymEnc* shown in Fig. 9.19 in Section 9.2 (see page 315). Here, we are concerned with three new machines *SecManager_Sig_Asym_R4_R5*, *DigSigM*, and *AsymEncM* that become components in the implementable architecture alternative 2. In addition, the machines *SubmitMD* and *PublishConsumerInfo* become components in the implementable architecture expressed with the stereotype ≪Component≫.

Architecture Alternative 3

For the architecture alternative 3, we consider the composition problem diagrams enriched with problem-specific solutions from the previous phase (see Figures 9.26 and 9.27 in Section 9.2 on pages 325 and 326).

Problem diagram related to functional requirement *R1*: From the subproblem *FTF_R1_PD*, we take the machines *FTF1* and *ReceiveMeterData*, and the lexical domain *TemporaryStorage* as components for the implementable architecture expressed with the stereotype *Component*.

Problem diagram related to functional requirement *R2R3*: The new subproblem related to the functional requirement *R2R3* is the problem diagram *FTF_R2R3_PD* which contains the new machine *FTF2* in addition to the functional problem diagram *ProcessStoreMD*. Similar to the architecture alternatives 1 and 2, the lexical domain *MeterData* becomes a component in the architecture alternative 3.

Problem diagram related to functional requirements *R4* and *R5*: For the subproblems related to the functional requirements *R4* and *R5*, we consider the composition problem diagram shown in Fig. 9.27 in Section 9.2 (see page 326). Here, we are concerned with three new machines *SecManager_FTF*, *SymEncM*, and *MACM* that become components in the architecture alternative 3. In addition, the machines *SubmitMD* and *PublishConsumerInfo* become components in the architecture alternative 3 expressed with the stereotype ≪Component≫.

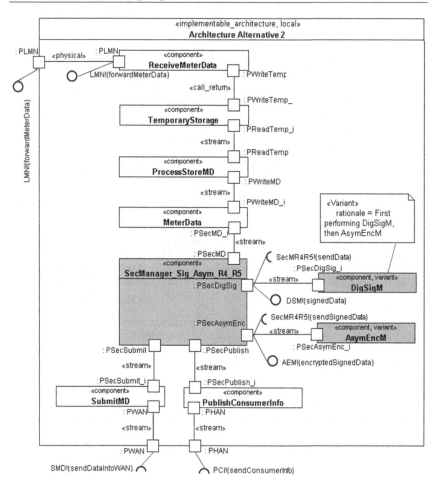

Fig. 10.4: Structural view of the implementable architecture of smart grid (alternative 2)

Step 3 - Architectural Pattern Applicability Checking

In Phase 2 of our framework (see Chapter 5), we selected the architectural pattern with regard to functional requirements. The selected architectural pattern contributes to the achievement of quality requirements as well.

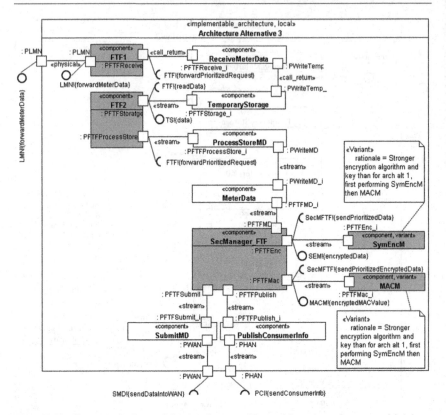

Fig. 10.5: Structural view of the implementable architecture of smart grid (alternative 3)

Applying problem-oriented quality patterns does not influence the overall structure of the architecture and the already applied architectural patterns. The reason is that the essence of the problem diagrams, namely the functional requirements, remains unmodified. The problem-oriented quality patterns provide a local solution to specific parts of the architecture in contrast to architectural patterns which specify the overall structure of the software architecture. Therefore, the selected architectural patterns still fit to the new problem diagrams containing quality specific solutions. Hence, they can be easily integrated into the existing initial architecture without changing the overall structure of the existing architecture.

In the previous phase, we added new machines to the initial problem diagrams in order to achieve quality requirements. Under the consideration of the new machines, we need to take the new components corresponding those machines into account as one part of the architectural pattern. Therefore, as inputs of this step, we consider the *quality-specific problem diagrams*, the *initial architecture*, and the *derived architecture* from the previous step (see Step 3 in Fig. 10.1). As the output of this step, we obtain the derived architecture including the selected architectural pattern. This architecture has to be completed in the next step by specifying the interfaces between the components.

Application of Step 3 - Architectural Pattern Applicability Checking

Architecture Alternative 1
Problem diagram related to functional requirement *R2R3*: To the subproblem *ReceiveMeterData* related to the functional requirement *R1*, we did not apply any architectural pattern. To the subproblem *ProcessStoreMD*, we applied the architectural pattern *Pipes and Filters* in the initial architecture. Before applying this architectural pattern to the architecture, we have to specify the possible changes due to introducing new components in the architecture.

The new subproblem related to the functional requirement *R2R3* is the problem diagram *LB_R2R3_PD* which contains the new machine *LB2* in addition to the functional problem diagram *ProcessStoreMD*. We observe that we are able to apply the architectural pattern *Pipes and Filters* to the problem diagram *LB_R2R3_PD* as the new machine *LB2* can serve as a new *Filter*. Hence, we are concerned with two *Filters LB2* and *ProcessStoreMD*. The connections to the component*LB2*, between the components *LB2* and *ProcessStoreMD*, and the connection out of the component *ProcessStoreMD* serve as *pipes*. The component *TemporaryStorage* serves as a *Source* and the component *MeterData* serves as a *Sink* initiating the final destination of the transformation.

Problem diagram related to functional requirement *R4*: We applied the architectural pattern *Pipes and Filters* also to the subproblem *SubmitMD* in the initial architecture. The quality-specific problem diagram *LB_R4_PD* corresponds to the functional subproblem *SubmitMD*. The new components *SecManager_LB*, *SymEncM*, and *MACM* serve as new *Filters* as they are responsible for transforming *MeterData* from a plaintext to ciphertext. The component *SubmitMD* serves as a *Filter* similar to the initial architecture.

Problem diagram related to functional requirement R5: We did not apply any quality-specific solution to the subproblem *PublishConsumerInfo*. Therefore, the applicability of the architectural pattern *Pipes and Filters* to the subproblem *PublishConsumerInfo* does not need to be checked. The component *PublishConsumerInfo* serves as a *Filter* similar to the initial architecture.

Architecture Alternative 2

Problem diagram related to functional requirement R2R3: To the subproblem *ReceiveMeterData* related to the functional requirement *R1*, we did not apply any architectural pattern. To the subproblem *ProcessStoreMD*, we apply the architectural pattern *Pipes and Filters*. As we did not use any quality-specific solutions for this subproblem, the application of the architectural pattern remains the same as in the initial architecture. So, there is no need for checking its applicability. The component *ProcessStoreMD* serves as a *Filter* and the components *TemporaryStorage* and *MeterData* serve as a *Source* as well as a *Sink*.

Problem diagram related to functional requirements R4 and R5: To the subproblem *Merge_R4R5_DigSig_AsymEnc* related to the functional requirements *R4* and *R5*, the architectural pattern *Pipes and Filters* can be applied. All machines in this subproblem can serve as *Filters*.

Architecture Alternative 3

Problem diagram related to functional requirements R2R3: To the subproblem *ReceiveMeterData* related to the functional requirement *R1*, we did not apply any architectural pattern. To the subproblem *ProcessStoreMD*, we applied the architectural pattern *Pipes and Filters* in the initial architecture. The architectural pattern *Pipes and Filters* can be applied to the implementable architecture, as well as the new machine *FTF2* in the problem diagram *FTF_R2R3_PD* can serve as a new *Filter*. Hence, we are concerned with two *Filters FTF2* and *ProcessStoreMD*. The component *TemporaryStorage* serves as a *Source* and the component *MeterData* serves as a *Sink* initiating the final destination of the transformation.

Problem diagram related to functional requirements R4 and R5: The architectural pattern *Pipes and Filters* applied in the initial architecture can also be applied to the quality-specific problem diagram related to the functional requirements *R4* and *R5*. The components *SecManager_FTF*, *SymEncM*, and *MACM* serve as the new *Filters* as they are responsible for transforming *MeterData* from a plaintext to a ciphertext. The components *SubmitMD* and *PublishConsumerInfo* serve as *Fil-*

ters similar to the initial architecture. The component *MeterData* represents the *Source*.

Step 4 - Ports/Interfaces/Connectors Specification

After selecting the inner components and the architectural pattern, one needs to specify how the components are connected. To this end, the ports of each component, its interfaces, and connectors have to be specified in this step. As the inputs for this step, we consider the *derived architecture* from the previous step, the initial *problem diagrams* and the *quality-specific problem diagrams* that provide the basis for the specification of the ports and interfaces (see Step 4 in Fig. 10.1).

The components are equipped with ports that correspond to the interfaces in the quality-specific problem diagrams. For the case that no quality-specific problem diagram is available, the ports in the initial problem diagrams are used. The ports should have a type represented as a class with required and provided interfaces. A controlled interface in a quality-specific problem diagram or an initial problem diagram is mapped to a required interface of the corresponding component in the implementable architecture. An observed interface of the machine in the quality-specific problem diagram or the initial problem diagram is mapped to a provided interface of the corresponding component in the implementable architecture. Component ports have to be connected to the ports of the outer component. The ports of the outer component remain the same as those in the initial architecture. In addition, we add stereotypes that describe the technical realization of these connectors. The complete set of stereotypes to be used for the connections can be found in Section 2.3.2 (see page 37).

Application of Step 4 - Ports/Interfaces/Connectors Specification

Architecture Alternative 1
Problem diagram related to functional requirement R1: The component *LB1* is connected to the *SamrtMeter* with the port *PLMN* by a physical connector expressed with the stereotype ≪Physical≫. It is also connected to the component *ReceiveMeterData* using a connector with the stereotype *call_return*. The component *LB1* provides the interface *LMN!{forwardMeterData}* and requires the interface *LB!{distributeRequest}*. The component *TemporaryStorage* is connected to the component *ReceiveMeterData* using a connector with the stereotype *call_return*. Note that we do not use the stereotype ≪stream≫ for this connector

as we did not apply the architectural pattern *Pipes and Filters* to this problem diagram.

Problem diagram related to functional requirement *R2R3*: The component *LB2* is connected to the component *TemporaryStorage* with one required and one provided interface and to the component *ProcessStoreMD* with one required interface. The connectors between these components are represented with the stereotype ≪Stream≫ as they provide *Pipes* in the architectural pattern *Pipes and Filters*. Also the connector between the components *ProcessStoreMD* and *MeterData* is a *Pipe* expressed with the stereotype *Stream*.

Problem diagram related to functional requirements *R4* and *R5*: The connectors between the component *SecManager_LB* and other connected components serve as *Pipes* and are expressed with the stereotype ≪Stream≫. The component *SubmitMD* is connected to the *AuthorizedExternalEntities* through the port *PWAN*. This connector serves as a *Pipe*, as well, expressed with the stereotype ≪Stream≫.

The connector between the component *MeterData* and the component *PublishConsumerInfo* serves as a *Pipe* expressed with the stereotype ≪Stream≫. The component *PublishConsumerInfo* is connected to the *UserInterface* through the port *PHAN*. This connector serves as a *Pipe*, as well, expressed with the stereotype ≪Stream≫.

Architecture Alternative 2
Problem diagram related to functional requirements *R1* and *R2R3*: The components *ReceiveMeterData*, *TemporaryStorage*, *ProcessStoreMD*, and *MeterData* are connected similarly to the initial architecture. The component *ReceiveMeterData* is connected to the *SmartMeter* with the port *PLMN* by a physical connection expressed with the stereotype ≪Physical≫. The component *TemporaryStorage* is connected to the component *ReceiveMeterData* using a connection with the stereotype *call_return*. The two connections to the component *ProcessStoreMD* serve as *pipes*. The pipes are expressed with the stereotype ≪Stream≫.

Problem diagram related to functional requirements *R4* and *R5*: The connectors between the component *SecManager_Sym_Asym_R4_R5* and other connected components serve as *Pipes* and are expressed with the stereotype ≪Stream≫. The component *SecManager_Sym_Asym_R4_R5* has one provided interface and a required one to the component *DigSigM*. It has also one provided interface and one required interface to the component *AsymEncM*. The components *SubmitMD* and *PublishConsumerInfo* are connected to the *AuthorizedExternalEntities* as well as *Consumer* through the ports *PWAN* and *LHAN*. These connections serve as *Pipes*, as well, expressed with the stereotype ≪Stream≫.

Architecture Alternative 3

Problem diagram related to functional requirement *R1*: The component *FTF1* is connected to the *SamrtMeter* with the port *PLMN* by a physical connection expressed with the stereotype ≪Physical≫. It is also connected to the component *ReceiveMeterData* with one required interface *FTF!{forwardPrioritizedRequest}* using a connection with the stereotype *call_return*. The component *TemporaryStorage* is connected to the component *ReceiveMeterData* using a connection with the stereotype *call_return*.

Problem diagram related to functional requirement *R2R3*: The connections to the component*FTF2*, between the components *FTF2* and *ProcessStoreMD*, and the connection out of the component *ProcessStoreMD* serve as *pipes*. The pipes are expressed with the stereotype ≪Stream≫. *FTF2* is connected to *TemporaryStorage* with one required and one provided interface. It is connected to the component *ProcessStoreMD* with one required interface.

Problem diagram related to functional requirements *R4* and *R5*: The connections between the component *SecManager_FTF* and other connected components serve as *Pipes* expressed with the stereotype ≪Stream≫. *SecManager_FTF* has one provided and one required interface to the component *SymEncM*. To the component *MACM* are also one provided and one required interface available. The components *SubmitMD* and *PublishConsumerInfo* are connected to the *AuthorizedExternalEntities* and *Consumer* through the ports *PWAN* and *PHAN*. These connections serve as *Pipes*, as well, expressed with the sterotype ≪Stream≫.

Step 5 - Behavior Specification

To complete the implementable architecture, one needs to specify the behavior of the architecture alternatives in addition to their structural view. Therefore, this step is concerned with modeling the behavioral view of the implementable architecture alternatives. As inputs for this step, we make use of the initial *problem diagrams*, *quality-specific problem diagrams* and the life-cycle expressions that enable us to specify the interactions[2] between the components and their order (see Step 5 in Fig. 10.1). The life-cycle contains information about the order of interactions described by the requirements. For specifying the behavior, we use UML sequence diagrams. However, any other diagram for modeling the behavior can be used. For more information regarding creating sequence diagrams from problem diagrams, we refer to [112].

Application of Step 5 - Behavior Specification

Architecture Alternative 1

Figure 10.6 shows the behavioral view of the implementable architecture alternative 1 represented as a sequence diagram. The messages represent the phenomena in the problem diagrams as well as in the quality-specific problem diagrams. LC shown below represents the life-cycle of the smart grid also used for illustrating the behavioral view of the initial architecture.

$$LC = ((R1;\ R2R3);\ (R4\ ||\ R5))^*$$

The same life-cycle is used here for representing the behavioral view of the architecture alternatives. Instead of functional problem diagrams, we use quality-specific problem diagrams. Only for the case that no quality-specific problem diagram exists, we make use of the initial problem diagrams. For achieving the requirement $R1$, the quality-specific problem diagram LB_R1_PD is relevant. The quality-specific problem diagram LB_R2R3_PD is related to the requirement $R2R3$. For the requirement $R4$, we use the quality-specific problem diagram LB_R4_PD. As we did not apply any quality-specific solution related to the requirement $R5$, we make use of the initial problem diagram $PublishConsumerInfo$ for this requirement.

The sequence diagram in Fig. 10.6 shows that the meter data is forwarded through the LMN to the component $LB1$, which forwards the request to the component $ReceiveMeterData$. Meter data is then temporarily stored into $TemporaryStorage$. The component $LB2$ obtains data from $TemporaryStorage$ and forwards it to the component $ProcessStoreMD$, which writes it persistently into $MeterData$. The components $LB1$ and $LB2$ in this case only forward the request to the next component. It is possible to have several components $ReceiveMeterData$ as well as $ProcessStoreMD$. This is marked in the structural view of the architecture alternative 1 shown in Fig. 10.3 by a port multiplicity related to the components

---

[2] With interaction in this context we mean the interplay between the components.

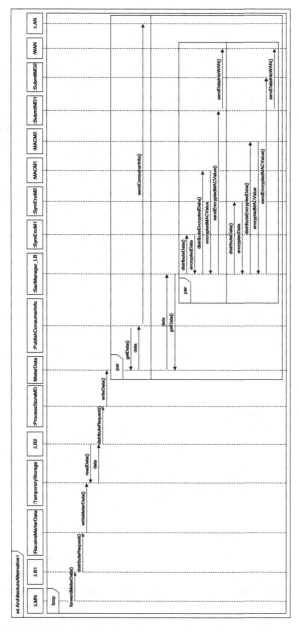

Fig. 10.6: Behavioral view of the implementable architecture (alternative 1)

ReceiveMeterData and *ProcessMeterData*. In such a case the components *LB1* and *LB2* are responsible for distributing the request between these components.

The *par* construct shows the parallel execution of the components related to the functional requirements *R4* and *R5* after storing the *MeterData* persistently. The component *PublishConsumerInfo* receives *MeterData* and sends it through *LAN* to the consumer. *LAN* represents one interface to the outside world. In parallel, the component *SecManager_LB* obtains meter data and distributes it between the two components *SymEncM1* and *SymencM2* responsible for encrypting meter data. We decided for having two instances of the component *SymEncM* (see the port multiplicity related to the component *SymEncM* in Fig. 10.3). More instances are possible. Having encrypted the meter data, it is sent to the components *MACM1* and *MACM2*, where a MAC value of the encrypted meter data is built. Also here, we decided for having two instances of the component *MACM*, called *MACM1* and *MACM2*, in the sequence diagram. The result is sent to the components *SubmitMD1* and *SubmitMD2* to be sent through *WAN* to the authorized external entities. The same applies for the component *SubmitMD* with the two instances *SubmitMD1* and *SubmitMD2*.

The component *SecManager_LB* is responsible for distributing the load between each two components *SymEncM1* and *SymEncM2* for encrypting meter data, *MACM1* and *MACM2* for building a MAC value, and *SubmitMD1* and *SubmitMD2* for sending meter data to the outside world.

For representing the components in the sequence diagram, we used *objects* instead of *classes* as we are concerned with more than one instance for some components.

Architecture Alternative 2

Figure 10.7 shows the behavioral view of the implementable architecture 2 represented as a sequence diagram. Here we are concerned with the same components for achieving the requirements *R1* and *R2R3* as in the initial architecture. The additional components related to the requirements *R4* and *R5* are *SecManager_Sig_Asym_R4_R5*, *DigSigM*, and *AsymEncM* to be taken from the quality-specific problem diagram *Merge_R4R5_DigSig_AsymEnc*.

The sequence diagram shows that the meter data is forwarded through the *LMN* to the component *ReceiveMeterData* to be written into the *TemporaryStorage*. The component *ProcessStoreMD* obtains data from *TemporaryStorage* and writes it persistently into *MeterData*. The components *SecManager_Sig_Asym_R4_R5*, *DigSigM*, and *AsymEncM* must be executed sequentially before sending meter data to the consumer using the component *PublishConsumerInfo* through *LAN* as well as sending meter data to the authorized external entities using the component *SubmitMD* through *WAN*. Sending meter data to the consumer and to the authorized

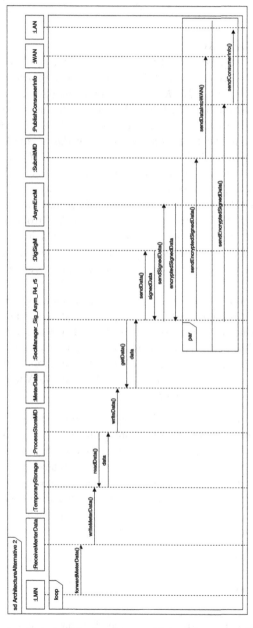

Fig. 10.7: Behavioral view of the implementable architecture (alternative 2)

external entities is executed in parallel.

Architecture Alternative 3
Figure 10.8 shows the behavioral view of the implementable architecture 3 represented as a sequence diagram. Relevant for the requirement *R1* is the quality-specific problem diagram *FTF_R1_PD* and for the requirement *R2R3* the quality-specific problem diagram *FTF_R2R3_PD*. For the requirements *R4* and *R5*, we make use of the quality-specific problem diagram *FTF_R4_R5* which contains the quality-specific components *SecManager_FTF*, *SymEncM*, and *MACM* in addition to the initial components *SubmitMD* and *PublishConsumerInfo*.

The sequence diagram in Fig. 10.8 shows that the meter data is forwarded through the *LMN* to the component *FTF1*, which forwards the prioritized request to the component *ReceiveMeterData*. Meter data is then temporarily stored into *TemporaryStorage*. The component *FTF2* obtains data from *TemporaryStorage* and forwards it to the component *ProcessStoreMD*, which writes it persistently into *MeterData*. The components *FTF1* and *FTF2* are responsible for forwarding the requests with higher priority in case not all requests can be processed at the same time.

The component *SecManager_FTF* obtains meter data and sends it to the components *SymEncM* responsible for encrypting meter data. Having encrypted meter data, it is sent to the component *MACM*, where a MAC value of the encrypted meter data is built. The *par* construct shows the parallel execution of the components related to the functional requirements *R4* and *R5*. The components *SubmitMD* and *PublishConsumerInfo* send the result through *WAN* and *LAN* to the authorized external entities and to the consumer.

In a systematic way, we showed how to derive implementable architecture alternatives from the problem diagrams containing quality solutions for achieving quality requirements. We applied the architectural patterns that we selected in Phase 2 of QuaDRA . Each architecture alternatives is represented by a structural as well as a behavioral view. We applied the proposed method to the case study smart grid and derived three different implementable architecture alternatives that vary in the level of achievement of quality requirements. The derived architecture alternatives are evaluated in the next chapter with regard to quality requirements.

10.3 Related Work

In this section, we consider those works related to constructing architectures based on problem frames. Schmidt and Wentzlaff [210] propose a problem frames-based

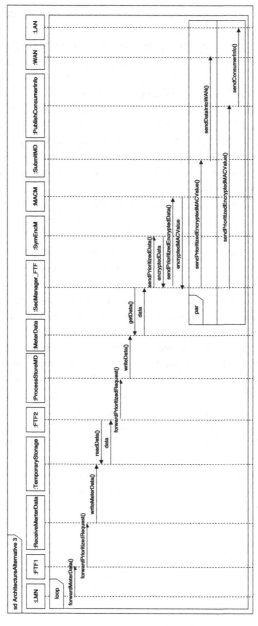

Fig. 10.8: Behavioral view of the implementable architecture (alternative 3)

method by providing a mapping of requirements to architecture design considering usability and security requirements. After understanding the problem and decomposing it to simple subproblems using the problem frames approach, the authors identify different roles existing in the problem diagrams such as the *operator* (user) and *display* (display). The identified roles are then mapped to the artifacts of an architectural pattern such as the *Model View Controller*. By way of an example, the authors show how to balance security and usability requirements. In this paper, there is no systematic approach given for selecting the architectural patterns. It seems that the method is rather a high-level approach relying on the expertise of the method user for applying it and selecting appropriate architectural patterns. Furthermore, there is no specification of the interfaces between the components and the related ports given.

Choppy et al. [70] propose a systematic derivation of software architectures from problem descriptions. After setting up an initial architecture containing one component for each subproblem, the authors apply different design patterns to the initial architecture to obtain an intermediate architecture. In a final step, the components of the intermediate architecture are re-arranged to construct a layered architecture. The first and second steps of our method are inspired by this method. So, the procedure of the first two steps is similar to setting up the initial architecture in this work. The further steps, however, are different. In this work, only functional requirements are considered. So, the final architecture does not provide any systematic support for addressing quality requirements. Moreover, there is no systematic selection of architectural patterns. The final step of this work constructs always a software architecture using the layered architectural pattern.

Choppy et al. [69] propose new architectural patterns for basic problem frames to be used in the design phase which are designed to reflect the structure of the problem frames. To create an architectural solution for a concrete problem frame, the relating architectural pattern must be instantiated which provides the starting point for building a software architecture. In contrast, we make use of the existing architectural patterns. The approach proposed by Choppy et al. derives the architecture only based on functional requirements. So, the final architecture does not provide support for achieving quality requirements. There is also no consideration of reusable knowledge on the architecture level such as existing architectural patterns.

10.4 Contributions

In this chapter, we derive implementable architecture alternatives represented as the structural view using composite structure diagrams and as the behavioral view using sequence diagrams. The implementable architecture extends the initial architecture with additional components that address quality requirements. For the software architecture, we use problem diagrams that instantiate problem-oriented quality patterns in order to incorporate quality-specific solutions into the architecture. To summarize the contributions of this chapter, our approach

- provides a seamless transition from requirements analysis to architectural design. It uses the structure of problem diagrams as a basis to derive software architectures.
- explicitly addresses quality requirements (in particular, security and performance) by applying quality-specific solutions in a systematic way.
- derives software architecture alternatives aiming at satisfying quality requirements to different levels.

Chapter 11
Phase 8: Software Architecture Alternatives Evaluation

Abstract In order to investigate whether a candidate architecture is suitable to achieve its functional as well as quality requirements, candidate architectures have to be evaluated by applying a software architecture evaluation method. This chapter provides a structured overview of existing architecture evaluation methods. We review the secondary literature in a systematic way in order to gather the state-of-the-art in the area of software architecture evaluation methods. Then, we select one method according to the defined selection criteria. The selected architecture evaluation method is used for evaluating the resulting architecture alternatives using the QuaDRA framework from the previous chapter.

11.1 Introduction

To choose an appropriate candidate architecture which achieves functional requirements as well as quality requirements with a particular level of satisfaction, the resulting candidate architectures have to be evaluated. Architecture evaluation aids to address the following concerns [169]:

- Understanding the software architecture
- Verifying that all requirements are addressed in the software architecture
- Making sure that the software will have the desired quality attributes
- Identifying problems with the software architecture

Architecture evaluation methods focus on evaluating a software architecture to determine if and where in the software architecture there might occur problems. The aim of architecture evaluation is not to provide scalar results, but qualitative results. Precisely characterizing quality requirements in terms of measurements at an early stage of design is not useful as such parameters are often implementation dependent. The architecture evaluation analyzes if an architecture is suitable with respect to a set of quality requirements and problematic with respect to another set of requirements.

In this chapter, we aim at evaluating the derived architecture alternatives that we created using the QuaDRA framework. We first provide a structured overview of existing software architecture evaluation methods. We review the secondary literature in a systematic way in order to gather the state-of-the-art in the area of software architecture evaluation methods. Then, we select one evaluation method according to defined selection criteria.

It is crucial to perform the selection by means of a systematic approach considering all relevant criteria. Hence, we develop a structured framework by means of the defined selection criteria. The framework draws upon various sources for accurate selection of the components, elements, and evaluation questions [136, 88, 35, 34, 173]. Our framework aids in deciding which architecture evaluation method is best suited for evaluating the derived architecture alternatives. The selected method is then applied for evaluation and identification of the problematic concerns in the created architecture alternatives.

The remainder of this chapter is organized as follows. We provide an overview of the state-of-the-art in the context of software architecture evaluation methods in Section 11.2. Section 11.3 provides a framework for selecting an appropriate software architecture evaluation method while in Section 11.4 we select the most suitable evaluation method using the developed framework. We evaluate software architecture alternatives using the selected method in Section 11.5. Section 11.6 presents related work and Section 11.7 concludes this chapter and summarizes its contributions.

11.2 Identification of Software Architecture Evaluation Methods

In this section, we aim at finding the state-of-the-art methods with regard to architecture evaluation. To this end, we define the following research question:

"Which methods are reported for evaluating architectures?"

To respond to this question, we searched secondary studies such as surveys, reviews, and mapping studies. Our objective was to find out whether there exists already a systematic review that provides an extensive overview of existing methods regarding architecture evaluation. In the following, we describe our research method for finding secondary studies in Section 11.2.1 and the results in Section 11.2.2.

11.2.1 Research Method

For finding relevant studies, we performed automated and "snowball" search. We conducted the automated search between 2005 and 2015. As a basis for constructing the search strings for the manual search, we used the defined research question. The main search terms were linked with the Boolean operator "AND" and the synonyms and alternative spellings with the Boolean operator "OR" as shown in Table 11.1. Doing this, we obtained the search string *"SS1 AND SS2 AND SS3"* which is composed of search strings from Table 11.1.

Table 11.1: Search strings

Search string
SS1: "software architecture"
SS2: "evaluation" **OR** "assessment" **OR** "analysis"
SS3: "survey" **OR** "SLR" **OR** "mapping study" **OR** "systematic review" **OR** "literature review" **OR** "comparison" **OR** "comparative"

We defined exclusion and inclusion criteria (EC, IC) as given in Table 11.2. We excluded studies according to the exclusion criterion EC1. We included studies according to the inclusion criteria IC1–IC5 linked with the boolean operator "AND". These criteria guided the researcher in the decision whether to include or exclude studies.

Table 11.2: Exclusion and Inclusion Criteria

Exclusion Criteria
EC1: Published as keynote, road map
Inclusion Criteria
IC1: Focus on architecture evaluation methods
IC2: Publishing time between 1/2005 and 4/2015
IC3: In the form of conference, journal papers
IC4: Subject area: computer science
IC5: Language: English

We performed the selection process for automated search in three rounds as follows:

- First round: In this round, we scanned the studies by "title and abstract" to remove irrelevant papers according to the selection criteria. In case a paper was considered completely irrelevant, the researcher did not protocol it at all. The studies, in which the researcher was not sure about their relevance have been included in the set of candidate studies for the second round.
- Second round: The candidate studies from the first round have been further investigated in the second round according to the selection criteria. For this round, we included additional sections of the papers, namely "introduction, discussion, and conclusion". Again, the studies, in which the researcher still was not sure about their relevance, have been included in the set of candidate studies for the next round.
- Third round: The candidate studies from the second round have been scanned by their full text according to the selection criteria. The remaining studies build the search results from automated search.

In addition to the automated search, we performed a snowball search. For the "snowball" search, we did not take the time span into account to be able to find relevant studies published before 2005 as well. In the snowball search, we scanned the references in the selected papers obtained from automated search. The final set of relevant studies is composed of search results from automated search and snowball search.

11.2.2 Results

We scanned 258 papers for the automated search and selected 5 papers. In addition, we selected 2 papers from the snowball search. Table 11.3 shows the final list of 7 secondary studies. The selected studies provide a comprehensive overview of the state-of-the-art regarding architecture evaluation methods. They respond to our research question. Therefore, there is no need for conducting a systematic literature review for finding the primary studies.

From the 7 selected secondary studies, we extracted 16 architecture evaluation methods. A short description of the 16 methods is given in Appendix E. In the next section, we propose a comparative framework for comparing these methods with regard to their properties. The properties serve as selection criteria for selecting the most appropriate architecture evaluation method. Depending on the software project at hand, different architecture evaluation methods can be selected.

Table 11.3: Secondary studies regarding architecture evaluation methods

#	Title	Reference	Kind of search
1	A systematic mapping study on architectural analysis	[66]	Automated
2	Sustainability evaluation of software architectures: A systematic review	[153]	Automated
3	A ten-year survey of software architecture	[67]	Automated
4	Evaluation approaches for software architecture documentation: A systematic review	[43]	Automated
5	A survey on software architecture evaluation methods	[188]	Automated
6	A survey on software architecture analysis methods	[88]	Snowball
7	Comparison of scenario-based software architecture evaluation methods	[34]	Snowball

11.3 Comparative Framework for Software Architecture Evaluation Methods

In this section, we introduce our comparative framework as a selection tool. We use this framework for comparing architecture evaluation methods extracted from the secondary studies in the previous section. Thereby, we focus on their similarities and differences.

The evaluation framework is shown in Table 11.4. We make use of the NIM-SAD framework (see Chapter 3 on page 70) for the overall structure of the framework, similar to our evaluation framework proposed in Chapter 3 for the comparative evaluation of the state-of-the-art methods with regard to the derived meta-requirements. The framework investigates the architecture evaluation methods from the point of view of *method context, method user, method content,* and *validation* taken from the NIMSAD framework. These four facets comprise the *components* of our framework.

Each component consists of *elements*, and the related *evaluation questions*. We make use of various sources for accurate selection of the elements of the framework. To this end, we investigate the secondary studies from the previous section. Some of these studies provide also a comparison of architecture evaluation methods. Based on these studies, we define selection criteria to be embedded in the NIMSAD framework as *elements*. We distinguish between *essential* and *beneficial* selection criteria. The former are concerned with those criteria that *must* be addressed for the appropriate selection of an evaluation method. For example, *quality requirements* is an *essential* selection criteria. The quality requirements that addressed in the software architecture to be evaluated must be covered by the evaluation method. *Beneficial* selection criteria are those that need not necessarily be addressed. It, however, exhibits a benefit if they are supported by the evaluation method. For example, consider the *beneficial* selection criteria *process support*. Detailed guidance on how to perform the evaluation method helps the evaluator by conducting the evaluation task. Therefore, it is *beneficial* if the evaluation method covers support for performing the process.

In Table 11.4, the column "elements" represents the selection criteria. The column "evaluation questions" contains questions specifying the selection criteria to be answered by each evaluation method. The answers to the evaluation questions must comply with the demands related to the software architecture to be evaluated (see Section 11.4.1). The column "classification" specifies whether the selection criterion is "*essential*" or "*beneficial*".

Table 11.4: The components and elements of the comparison framework and the related questions

Component	Elements	Evaluation Questions	Classification
Context	Specific goal	What is the specific goal of the method?	Essential
	Quality requirements	Which quality attributes are treated by the method?	Essential
	SA design phase	For which SA sub-phase is the method applicable?	Essential
	Method input	What are the required inputs for the method? In which form has the software architecture description to be available?	Essential
User	Involved stakeholder	Which stakeholders participate in the evaluation process?	Beneficial
	Process support	How much support is provided for the user while applying the method?	Beneficial
	Required effort	How much effort is required for the user for applying the method?	Beneficial
Content	Tool support	Are there tools that support the evaluation process?	Beneficial
	Reusable knowledge	Does the evaluation method produce and make use of reusable knowledge?	Beneficial
Validation	Method maturity	Has the method been validated in industrial case studies?	Beneficial

In the following, we give reasoning for integrating these criteria in the comparative framework.

Specific goal: Software architecture evaluation methods have the common goal of evaluating the potential of an architecture to achieve or fail to achieve the required quality requirements. However, most of them are optimized for achieving a specific goal, such as risk assessment, trade-off analysis, architecture comparison, etc. In order to benefit best from an evaluation process, the goal of the evaluation has to be specified [35]. The specific goal of the evaluation method must be in accordance with the requirements for such a method.

Quality requirements: Most of the architecture evaluation methods deal with evaluating only one kind of quality requirements. For example, ALMA[1] aims at

---
[1] Architecture Level Modifiability Analysis

evaluating the architecture with regard to modifiability. However, some software systems require the evaluation of multiple attributes. In order to select the proper architecture evaluation method, the considered quality requirements in a software architecture to be evaluated must be covered by the evaluation method.

SA design phase: Traditionally, software architecture evaluation has to be conducted after specifying the software architecture and before the implementation phase [35]. However, software architecture can be evaluated at any stage with different goals in mind [169]. In addition to the traditional software architecture evaluation, there are two other variations with regard to the stage of application, namely early and late evaluation. In the early evaluation, there is no need for waiting until the full specification of the architecture is completed. The objective of early evaluation is to examine those architectural decisions that are already taken and select among those options that are pending. It is commonly based on the experiences and reasoning of software developers [227]. In the late evaluation, not only the architecture, but also the implementation is available and complete. This might be the case when an organization inherits a legacy system. In this case, the stakeholders are interested in understanding the system and whether it meets its requirements [80]. We conclude that the stage in which an evaluation method evaluates a software architecture must be in accordance with the stage in which the software architecture is.

Method input: One criteria for selecting a suitable architecture evaluation method is the input that is required by the evaluation method. Evaluation methods might require different artifacts as input for their successful application. Therefore, it is essential to know what architecture artifacts are needed as input. The input required by an evaluation method must be in accordance with the artifacts represented as a software architecture. As an example, consider an architecture evaluation method requiring a deployment view of the software architecture as input, but the software architecture to be evaluated can only be represented by a structural view. In this case, the evaluation method cannot be selected for evaluating the software architecture at hand.

Involved stakeholder: A stakeholder is a person or organisational representative who has an interest in a system [157]. The evaluation methods vary in the categories of stakeholders that are required to be involved for the evaluation process. It is beneficial that the categories of the stakeholders required by an evaluation method to be involved is in accordance with the categories of the stakeholders that are available by the evaluation process.

Process support: For deciding on an architecture evaluation method, it might be beneficial to know how much support and guidance for conducting the evaluation method is available. A coarse-grained description might be available by all the evaluation methods. However, detailed guidance is mostly missing by those methods [34]. Therefore, it is beneficial that the process support provided by an evaluation method covers the process support that is needed for conducting the architecture evaluation.

Required effort: Providing explicit information regarding the effort in terms of the number of person days required for performing the evaluation is beneficial for selecting an evaluation method. Particularly for large systems, evaluating software architectures is a complicated task that requires substantial resources [44]. It is beneficial that the effort required for applying an evaluation method is in accordance with the effort that can be offered for evaluating the architecture at hand.

Tool support: The software architecture community emphasizes the need for automating the tasks of software architecture evaluation as far as possible. The reason is that these tasks are concerned with collecting, managing, and documenting relevant information which are tedious and error-prone. A tool can support the evaluator by evaluating the outcome, measurement, and administrative information [35]. Therefore, it has to be specified whether the architecture evaluation method has to provide a tool for evaluating the software architecture at hand.

Reusable knowledge: In the software engineering domain, the idea of reusability has long been acknowledged as a means for improving productivity, quality and cost effectiveness [31]. To prevent each evaluation starting from scratch, the reusable knowledge from previous activities and projects has to be incorporated in the software evaluation methods. It has to be specified whether the evaluation method makes use of reusable knowledge by the evaluation process.

Method maturity: It is important that the evaluation methods are validated and applied to numerous software-intensive applications and in different application domains to show that they are generally applicable [35]. Therefore, it is beneficial that the maturity of an evaluation method complies with the method maturity that is needed for evaluating the software architecture at hand.

11.4 Selection of Software Architecture Evaluation Methods

This section deals with comparing the evaluation methods we extracted from the secondary studies with regard to the selection criteria we defined in the previous section. We aim at selecting the most appropriate evaluation method for evaluating the three architecture alternatives developed using the QuaDRA framework. Depending on the architecture to be evaluated and the requirements for an evaluation method, different evaluated methods can be appropriate. First, we define our requirements on an evaluation method in Section 11.4.1. Then, we apply the comparative framework to the methods we extracted before in Section 11.4.2.

11.4.1 Requirements on the Evaluation Method

We first define the requirements on an evaluation method in order to be able to evaluate our derived software architectures. These requirements are mapped to the *essential* selection criteria in the comparison framework. Table 11.5 shows the requirements to be fulfilled by the evaluation method to be selected for our purpose.

As the *specific goal* we define "evaluating and analyzing the architecture with regard to defined quality requirements". We keep the specific goal intentionally generic as every kind of architecture evaluation can provide us with insights regarding the architecture and the fulfillment of quality requirements. An evaluation method must be able to evaluate the *quality requirements* "performance and security" at least in order to be taken into consideration. The evaluation method must be able to evaluate software architectures after producing the "final version of the software architecture and before starting with the detailed design". We are able to provide the "problem description, requirements description, and the software architecture description" to the evaluation method. The evaluation method must require as input these provided artifacts or a subset of them, but no more artifacts than the provided ones. Using these requirements as *essential* selection criteria, we select an evaluation method in the next section by applying the comparison framework.

Table 11.5: Requirements for the evaluation method to be selected for evaluating the architecture alternatives created by the QuaDRA framework

Elements	Requirements
Specific goal	Evaluating and analyzing the architecture with regard to defined quality requirements
Quality requirements	Performance, security
SA design phase	Final version of SA, but prior to detailed design
Method input	Problem description, requirements description, SA description

11.4.2 Application of the Comparative Framework

Tables 11.6 - 11.9 show the application of the comparative framework to the 16 methods we have extracted from the secondary studies. These tables illustrate the properties of the extracted evaluation methods. A short description of the 16 methods is given in Appendix E. Our objective of the comparative evaluation is to select the most appropriate method that fulfills the requirements defined in Table 11.5. To reduce the effort of applying the framework to all 16 methods, we first partially compare the methods by applying the *essential* selection criteria. Those methods that fulfill all *essential* selection criteria are further investigated by applying the *beneficial* selection criteria.

Application of the framework has shown that only three methods *ATAM*, *SAEM*, and *SACAM* meet our defined requirements. Most of the methods have been excluded from further consideration since they deal with other quality requirements than performance and security.

SAAM, *ESAAMI*, *SAAMCS*, *SAAMER*, and *ASAAM* do not fulfill the *essential* selection criterion *quality requirements*. *SAAM*, *ESAAMI*, and *ASAAM* consider each quality requirement in isolation. They cannot analyze an architecture considering two or more quality requirements at the same time. *SAAMCS* and *SAAMER* provide variants of *SAAM* for the quality requirements *flexibility* as well as *evolution* and *reusability*.

SBAR fulfills the *essential* selection criterion *quality requirements*. It, however, does not meet the *essential* selection criterion *method input* as it requires an implemented architecture as input (see Table 11.7). Regarding the *essential* selection criterion *specific goal*, we do not restrict our requirement to a specific goal as any kind of architecture evaluation provides us with insights regarding the weaknesses of the developed architecture alternatives.

The architecture evaluation methods *ALPSM*, *ALMA*, *PASA*, *ALRRA*, *SAR*, *SAAF*, and *ARID* are excluded because they do not fulfill the *essential* selection criterion *quality requirements*. *ALPSM* and *ALMA* analyze *maintainability* of a software system, while *PASA* and *ALRRA* analyze *performance* as well as *reliability* related risks. *SAR* evaluates the architecture with regard to *evolution* and *confiability*. *SAAF* considers only *flexibility* and *ARID* validates the software architecture from the *suitability* point of view.

Table 11.6: Framework application for *essential* selection criteria- part 1

Elements	SAAM[2]	SAAMCS[3]	ESAAMI[4]	SAAMER[5]
Specific goal	Identifying risks and analyzing suitability	Predicting flexibility, assessing risks	Identifying risks and analyzing suitability in a domain-specific and reuse-based development process	Assessing SA for reuse and evolution
Quality requirements	Any single quality requirement to be considered in isolation	Flexibility[6]	Any single quality requirement to be considered in isolation	Evolution, Reusability
SA design phase	Final version of SA	Final version of SA	Final version of SA	Final version of SA
Method input	Problem description, requirements description, SA description (static and dynamic representation of SA, allocation of function to structure)	Categories of complex scenarios, SA description divided into macroarchitecture and microarchitecture	Requirements description, SA description	Requirements description, SA description

---

[2] Scenario-based Architecture Analysis Method

[3] SAAM founded on Complex Scenarios

[4] Extending SAAM by Integration in the Domain

[5] SAAM for Evolution and Reusability

[6] According to ISO 25010 [130], flexibility represents the "degree to which a product or system can be used with effectiveness, efficiency, freedom from risk and satisfaction in contexts beyond those initially specified in the requirements".

[7] Aspectual SAAM

[8] Architecture Trade-off Analysis Method

[9] Scenario-based Architecture Reengineering

[10] Architecture Level Prediction for Software Maintenance

[11] Software Architecture Evaluation Model

[12] Architecture Level Modifiability Analysis

[13] Performance Assessment of Software Architecture

[14] Architecture Level Reliability Risk Analysis

Table 11.7: Framework application for *essential* selection criteria- part 2

Elements	ASAAM[7]	ATAM[8]	SBAR[9]	ALPSM[10]
Specific goal	Evaluating the quality of the architecture using aspects and refactoring concepts	ATAM: Identifying and analyzing sensitivity and trade-off points	Estimating the ability of SA for achieving quality requirements	Analyzing maintainability of the software system
Quality requirements	Any single quality requirement to be considered in isolation	Multiple quality requirements	Multiple quality requirements	Maintainability
SA design phase	Final version of SA	Final version of SA / During SA design and analysis	System Extension or reengineering stage (applied iteratively)	Final version of SA
Method input	Requirements description, SA description	Requirements description, SA description	Implemented architecture	Requirements description, SA description, historical maintenance data, expertise from software engineers

Table 11.8: Framework application for *essential* selection criteria- part 3

Elements	SAEM[11]	ALMA[12]	PASA[13]	ALRRA[14]
Specific goal	Evaluating and predicting the final system quality	Predicting maintenance effort (Union of ALPSM and SAAF)	Identifying and mitigating performance related risks	Analyzing reliability related risks
Quality requirements	Internal and external quality attributes based on a quality model	Maintainability	Performance	Reliability
SA design phase	Final version of SA (intermediate product of the design process)	Final version of SA	Final version of SA, post-deployment, during upgrade of legacy system	Final version of SA
Method input	Software architecture from the developer and user view	Requirements description, SA description	Various view of the SA description	SA description

---

[15] Software Architecture Comparison Analysis Method

[16] Software Review Architecture

[17] Software Architecture Analysis of Flexibility

[18] Active Reviews for Intermediate Design

[19] According to ISO 25010 [130] "this characteristic represents the degree to which a product or system provides functions that meet stated and implied needs when used under specified con-

Table 11.9: Framework application for *essential* selection criteria- part 4

Elements	SACAM[15]	SAR[16]	SAAF[17]	ARID[18]
Specific goal	Selecting architecture by comparing different candidate architectures	Evaluating the architecture regarding evolution and confiability	Identifying high complexity scenarios	Validating design visibility
Quality requirements	Multiple quality requirements	Evolution and confiability	Flexibility	Suitability[19]
SA design phase	During design phase	Final version of SA	Final version of SA	Intermediate Architecture
Method input	Available documentation for architecture candidates, business goals/comparison criteria	Requirements description, SA description	Problem description, requirements description, SA description (static and dynamic representation of SA, allocation of function to structure)	Detailed design of the components

Table 11.10 shows the application of the comparative framework to the methods *ATAM*, *SAEM*, and *SACAM* with regard to *beneficial* selection criteria.

ATAM is a comprehensive method that brings together all major stakeholders of a project and involves them into the evaluation process. SAEM requires knowledge of experts and some data for the evaluation. It, however, is not clear whether and to what extent any stakeholder is involved in evaluation. SACAM makes use of those stakeholders who are relevant for comparing different architecture candidates.

Regarding process support, only ATAM provides a comprehensive guidance published as a book including different case studies [80] and as technical reports describing the application of ATAM in different application domains systems [101, 138, 79, 41]. The two other methods either provide sparse guidance on how to apply them without introducing any application example or describe the application of methods with only small examples.

For a small-size evaluation, ATAM requires the stakeholders such as the architect and the project manager to be available for 11 days whereas the evaluation team needs 15 person-days for conducting the evaluation. The approximate effort for a medium-size evaluation is, however, higher. It amounts to 13 person-days for the stakeholders and 25 person-days for the evaluation team. SAEM provides no information regarding the required effort for the application. 11 days are required for performing an architecture comparison and evaluation using SACAM. This, however, is not further specified in terms of the size of the project to be evaluated

---

ditions. This characteristic is composed of the subcharacteristics completeness, correctness, and appropriateness".

and the number of persons to be involved. As the available information regarding the required effort of evaluation is not complete, it makes a comparison of methods for this selection criteria difficult.

None of the three methods provides any tool for supporting the evaluation process. All methods apply the evaluation in a manual manner. Regarding reusable knowledge, ATAM pays explicit attention in reusing the experience of an evaluation in further projects. To this end, ATAM provides templates for different steps for documenting the results and capturing the identified scenarios, quality requirements, and risks in a structured way. This is not supported by SAEM. SACAM provides an evaluation framework that can be reused for comparing architectures.

Regarding method maturity, we observe that ATAM is the most mature method which is continuously being validated by application to various real projects and case studies [101, 138, 79, 41]. SAEM is not validated yet. To the best of our knowledge, there exist no examples and case studies that apply this evaluation method. There exist small examples that apply SACAM which can be taken as proof of concept. However, there are no real case studies known.

Taken the results of comparing these three methods as a whole, we notice that ATAM fulfills more *beneficial* selection criteria that the other two methods. Therefore, we select ATAM for evaluating the architecture alternatives derived by QuaDRA .

Table 11.10: Framework application for *beneficial* selection criteria

Elements	ATAM	SAEM	SACAM
Involved stakeholder	All major stakeholders	Experts' knowledge and company's accumulated data are required for the evaluation	Designer, comparison stakeholders, candidate stakeholders
Process support	Comprehensively covered	No guidance (no details of the process, no examples)	Moderate guidance (two small examples)
Required effort	11/15 person days	Not specified	11 days
Tool support	Not available	Not available	Not available
Reusable knowledge	Explicitly incorporated in the evaluation process	Not considered	Comparison framework can be reused for an application domain
Method maturity	Continuously being validated	Not validated on any software system	Proof of concept

11.5 Evaluation of Architecture Alternatives using ATAM

The application of our comparative framework in Section 11.4 has shown that ATAM fulfills all *essential* selection criteria. It also provides better results regarding the *beneficial* selection criteria compared to *SAEM* and *SACAM*. Therefore, we selected *ATAM* for evaluating the architecture alternatives created by the QuaDRA framework. We describe its application to the three architecture alternatives in Section 11.5.1. A discussion regarding the application of ATAM and the results is given in Section 11.5.2.

11.5.1 Application of ATAM to Smart Grid's Architecture Alternatives

In this section, we apply ATAM to our case study. We give a description of each ATAM step followed by its application.

Step 1 - Present the ATAM

The first step is concerned with presenting the steps of the evaluation method, the techniques used in ATAM, and the output of ATAM to the stakeholders by the architecture evaluator or the architecture evaluation team. The aim of this step is to build a consensus regarding the understanding and the expectation of the method as well as to clarify any obscurities.

Application of Step 1 - Present the ATAM

We skip this step as in our case we take the role of the architect as a stakeholder as well as the role of the method evaluator.

Step 2 - Present the business drivers

The business goals and the primary architectural drivers are presented by the project manager in order to build a homogeneous understanding. The presentation contains the main functions of the system, possible restrictions, business goals, and architectural drivers.

Application of Step 2 - Present the business drivers

The developed architectures for the smart metering system include five main functions, namely *receiving the meter data from the smart meter (R1), processing meter data (R2), storing meter data (R3), submitting the stored data to external entities (R4)*, and *providing the stored data to the consumer (R5)*.

The objective of a software system is to realize the defined business goals. Business goals exist in various forms and different levels of abstraction. Kazmann and Bass [143] categorize the business goals into five categories *reduce total cost of ownership, improve capability/quality of system, improve market position, support improved business processes*, and *improve confidence in and perception of the system*. The business goal in our case is to *improve the quality of system*. Quality in this context mainly means security and performance. These two quality requirements represent the architectural drivers as well.

Step 3 - Present the architecture

In this step, the leading architect presents the architecture of the system containing technical restrictions, interacting systems, and architectural approaches that have been used for fulfilling the quality requirements.

Application of Step 3 - Present the architecture

Relevant documents for presenting the architecture are

1. the complete list of functional as well as quality requirements (see Chapter 2, page 43),
2. the context view defining the scope of the software, the scope of the environment, and the relations between the software and its environment. The context view was the first document that we produced. It is represented as a context diagram (see Chapter 4, page 114),
3. the problem diagrams describing functional and quality requirements (see Chapter 4, page 118),
4. the requirements view providing a mapping between the requirements and the architecture. It shows that the architecture addresses the quality requirements

and no important requirement has been forgotten. We describe the requirements view by setting up the problem-solution diagram providing the traceability between the quality requirements that shaped the architecture as the main architectural drivers and the quality-specific solutions addressing those requirements in the architecture (see Chapter 8, page 278),

5. the structural and behavioral views of the final software architecture alternatives (see Chapter 11, Figures 10.3- 10.8).

Step 4 - Identify the architectural approaches

In this step, the architecture is viewed by the evaluator team in order to identify the applied architectural approaches. Architectural approaches represent early design decisions made by the architect. They provide the main means for achieving the goal of an architecture. They determine how the system handles changes, responds to attacks, or interacts with other systems.

Application of Step 4 - Identify the architectural approaches

In this step, we identify architectural approaches and mechanisms that we used for achieving security and performance requirements for each architecture alternative. For a detailed description of the architecture alternatives and the applied architectural approaches, we refer to Chapter 10 (see Section 10.2 on page 330). In the following, we briefly show the list of the applied architectural approaches to the architecture alternatives:

Architecture alternative 1:

- Pipes & Filters
- Load Balancer (LB) to achieve performance requirements (for distributing the load by receiving, storing, processing, and submitting meter data)
- Symmetric encryption to achieve confidentiality requirements (to protect the confidentiality of data transferred through WAN)
- Message Authentication Code (MAC) to achieve integrity and authenticity requirements (to protect the integrity and authenticity of data transferred through WAN)

Architecture alternative 2:

- Pipes & Filters

- Asymmetric encryption to achieve confidentiality requirements (to protect the confidentiality of data transferred through WAN and HAN)
- Digital signature to achieve integrity and authenticity requirements (to protect the integrity and authenticity of data transferred through WAN and HAN)

Architecture alternative 3:

- Pipes & Filters
- First Things First (FTF) to achieve performance requirements (for forwarding the requests with higher priority prior to other requests)
- Symmetric encryption to achieve confidentiality requirements (to protect the confidentiality of data transferred through WAN and HAN)
- Message Authentication Code (MAC) to achieve integrity and authenticity requirements (to protect the integrity and authenticity of data transferred through WAN and HAN)

Step 5 - Generate the quality attribute utility tree

In this step, priorities and the most important quality requirements are determined. This step provides guidance for the evaluation team as well as for the stakeholders to reflect on the system requirements. In order to identify the key requirements, a *utility tree* has to be constructed. It guides the stakeholders by defining the concrete quality requirements and prioritizing them.

Figure 11.1 provides an example for the utility tree taken from [80]. It starts with *Utility* as the root node and is subdivided into the categories of quality requirements, which are further refined into their sub-categories. For example, *security* is refined into *data confidentiality* and *data integrity*. The final level is achieved by further division of sub-categories in order to analyze and prioritize the quality requirements in a more precise way. This level provides the concrete scenarios[20] (or requirements). For example *data confidentiality* is further refined into *credit card transactions are secure 99.999% of the time* and *customer DB authorization works 99.999% of the time*. Prioritization is achieved by assigning *High (H)*, *Medium (M)*, and *Low (L)* to the concrete requirements. The tuple in Fig. 11.1 on each leaf represents the prioritization of two dimensions. The first dimension states the importance of the requirement's success while the second one expresses the difficulty to achieve this requirement.

The utility tree as the output of Step 5 points out where to focus on and where to examine the architectural approaches. Constructing such a utility tree helps to

---

[20] Requirements in the context of the QuaDRA framework can be considered as scenarios in the context of ATAM, as they are represented in the same level of granularity

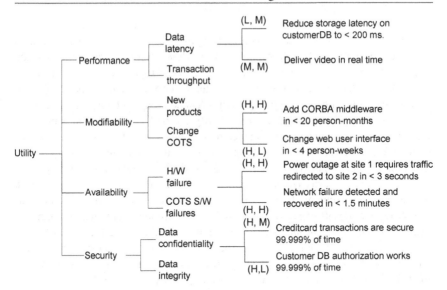

Fig. 11.1: An Example of the *utility tree*

decide on those scenarios (requirements) that need to be focused on according to the defined prioritization. ATAM suggests to select those scenarios containing at least one *H* and one *M* in their prioritization. The reason is that these scenarios have a higher impact on the overall achievement of quality requirements for the system.

Application of Step 5 - Generate the quality attribute utility tree

We set up the utility tree for our example shown in Table 11.11. The two quality requirement categories are *security* and *performance* (see column *Quality require- ment category*) that are refined into *confidentiality, authenticity, integrity* as well as *response time* (see column *Quality requirement sub-category*). The final refine- ment of quality requirements is achieved by precisely describing each requirement (see column *Quality requirement refinement*).

As an example, we take the category *security* and its sub-category *confidential- ity*. The requirement *R7* states that "the gateway shall provide the protection of confidentiality when receiving meter data from a meter via the LMN."

A prioritization of requirements is required in this step which allows us to select and analyze those requirements with higher priorities in further steps. We assign priorities by defining the *importance* and the *difficulty* of achievement for each requirement and each architecture alternative. *A1-A3* represent architecture alternative 1 - architecture alternative 3. In Chapter 9 (see Section 9.2 on page 290), we described that we aim at deriving three different software architecture alternatives with different levels of satisfaction for security and performance for our smart grid case study. As security and performance requirements are interacting, the three architecture alternatives provide trade-offs between these two quality requirements. The first architecture alternative has to treat the desired performance requirements with the highest priority (*architecture alternative 1*), the second one has to rank the security requirements first (*architecture alternative 2*), and the third one has to provide a trade-off of performance and security requirements with similar priorities (*architecture alternative 3*). This architecture alternative fulfills neither the security requirements nor the performance requirements to the best degree of satisfaction. It, however, satisfices both quality requirements with a trade-off which treats both quality requirements with a similar priority.

Table 11.11: Utility tree for smart grid

Quality requirement category	Quality requirement sub-category	Quality requirement refinement	Importance	Difficulty
Security	Confidentiality	The gateway shall provide the protection of confidentiality when receiving meter data from a meter via the LMN (R7).	A1:L	A1:L
			A2:H	A2:L
			A3:M	A3:L
		Data shall be protected from unauthorized disclosure while persistently stored in the gateway (R9).	A1:L	A1:L
			A2:H	A2:L
			A3:M	A3:L
		Confidentiality of data transferred in the WAN shall be protected (R11).	A1:L	A1:M
			A2:H	A2:H
			A3:M	A3:M
		The gateway shall provide the protection of confidentiality when transmitting processed meter data locally within the LAN (R14).	A1:L	A1:L
			A2:H	A2:L
			A3:M	A3:L

		Data shall be protected from unauthorized disclosure while temporarily stored in the gateway (R16).	A1:L	A1:L
			A2:H	A2:L
			A3:M	A3:L
	Authenticity	The gateway shall provide the protection of authenticity when receiving meter data from a meter via the LMN (R8).	A1:L	A1:L
			A2:H	A2:L
			A3:M	A3:L
		Authenticity of data transferred in the WAN shall be protected (R12).	A1:L	A1:M
			A2:H	A2:H
			A3:M	A3:M
		The gateway shall provide the protection of authenticity when transmitting processed meter data locally within the LAN (R15).	A1:L	A1:L
			A2:H	A2:L
			A3:M	A3:L
	Integrity	The gateway shall provide the protection of integrity when receiving meter data from a meter via the LMN (R6).	A1:L	A1:L
			A2:H	A2:L
			A3:M	A3:L
		Integrity of data transferred in the WAN shall be protected (R10).	A1:L	A1:M
			A2:H	A2:H
			A3:M	A3:M
		The gateway shall provide the protection of integrity when transmitting processed meter data locally within the LAN (R13).	A1:L	A1:L
			A2:H	A2:L
			A3:M	A3:L
Performance	Response Time	The time to retrieve meter data from the smart meter and publish it through the WAN shall be less than 5 seconds (R18, R20, R22, R24)	A1:H	A1:H
			A2:L	A2:L
			A3:M	A3:M
		The time to retrieve meter data from the smart meter and publish it through the HAN shall be less than 10 seconds (R19, R21, R23, R25)	A1:H	A1:M
			A2:L	A2:L
			A3:M	A3:L

Therefore, we set the *importance* of all security requirements as *L* and for all performance requirements as *H* for the architecture alternative *A1* as we treat performance for this architecture alternative with higher priority than security. The same reasoning holds for the *importance* of architecture alternatives *A2* and *A3*. So, we set the *importance* of all security requirements as *H* and for all performance requirements as *L* for the architecture alternative *A2*. For the architecture alternative *A3*, we set the *importance* of all security and performance requirements as *M*.

As we can see in Table 11.11, the *difficulty* of all three architecture alternatives for the requirements *R6*, *R7*, *R9*, and *R16* is set as *L*. The reason for this is due to the design decision *One Box Solution* we made in Chapter 5 (see Section 5.6 on page 161). For the *Smart Meter* and the *Smart Meter Gateway*, we decided for the *One Box Solution*, that is having the *Smart Meter* and the *Smart Meter Gateway* in one physical device in form of a sealed box/cabinet. This enables that the Gateway and the smart meter communication happens in the protected area of the box. From the security point of view, this solution has the advantage that the communication is protected. Therefore, we assume that the security requirements *R6*, *R7*, and *R8* are already fulfilled without applying additional security mechanisms. Also the confidentiality requirements *R9* and *R16* are satisfied as the box is physically protected. Therefore, the *difficulty* of achieving these requirements is set as *L*.

The security requirements *R10*, *R11*, and *R12* are related to the same functional requirement *R4* which requires *submitting of meter data to authorized external entities through WAN*. According to the security analysis in Chapter 7 (see Section 7.4 on page 222), for architecture alternative 2 (*A2*) we are concerned with a *WAN attacker* with the highest preparation and attack time, *multiple bespoke* equipment, a very high expertise (*multiple experts*), etc. To this end, we decide on high difficulty (*H*). For *A1* and *A3*, we are concerned with a *WAN attacker*, who is less experienced and has less equipment available. Hence, we decide on medium difficulty (*M*).

The security requirements *R13*, *R14*, and *R15* are related to the same functional requirement *R5* which requires *publishing consumer info for the consumer through HAN*. According to the security analysis in Chapter 7 (see Section 7.4 on pages 222 and 227), for architecture alternative 2 (*A2*) we are concerned with a *HAN attacker* with a sparse preparation and attack time, *specialized* equipment, a *proficient* expertise, etc. To this end, we decide on low difficulty (*L*). For *A1* and *A3*, the *HAN attacker* has even less experience and equipment available. Also in this case, we decide on low difficulty (*L*).

At this point, we have to decide on those scenarios (requirements) that need to be focused on according to the defined prioritization. According to the ATAM suggestion for selecting scenarios containing at least one *H* and one *M* in their prioritization, we select those scenarios with the combinations (H, M), (M, H), or (H, H). To this end, we select the scenarios for *R10*, *R11*, and *R12* for *A2* to further investigation (see the fields highlighted in gray in Table 11.11).

For the category *performance*, we capture the requirements *R18*, *R20*, *R22*, and *R24* as one scenario as the response time is only available for all 4 requirements together. The same holds for the requirements *R19*, *R21*, *R23*, and *R25*.

According to the performance analysis in Chapter 7 (see Section 7.4 on pages 222 and 227), for the requirements *R18*, *R20*, and *R22*, we expect a high workload and average resource usage while for the requirement *R24* a high workload and a high resource usage are expected. In addition, for this requirement, the security requirements *R10*, *R11*, and *R12* have to be achieved at the same time. To this end, we set the difficulty of achievement for the requirements *R18*, *R20*, *R22*, and *R24* for *A1* as high (*H*). For *A2* and *A3*, we relaxed the performance-related domain knowledge as a conflict resolution strategy (see Chapter 7). Hence, we can achieve them with low (*L*) and medium (*M*) difficulty.

According to the performance analysis in Chapter 7 (see Section 7.4 on pages 222 and 227), for the requirements *R19*, *R21*, and *R23*, we expect a high workload and average resource usage while for the requirement *R25* a low workload and a sparse resource usage are expected. In addition, for this requirement, we are concerned with weak security mechanisms. To this end, we set the difficulty of achievement for the requirements *R19*, *R21*, *R23*, and *R25* for *A1* as medium (*M*). For *A2* and *A3*, we relaxed the performance-related domain knowledge as a conflict resolution strategy (see Chapter 7). Hence, we can achieve them with low (*L*) difficulty.

Due to ATAM suggestion for scenario selection, we select both performance scenarios for *A1* to further investigation (see the fields highlighted in gray in Table 11.11). Note that no scenarios for *A3* have been selected considering the ATAM suggestion for selecting scenarios.

Step 6 - Analyze the architectural approaches

After capturing the architectural approaches and collecting the set of quality requirements, in this step the evaluator team examines to what extent the applied architectural approaches meet the quality requirements. In this step, risks, nonrisks, sensitivity points, and trade-off points are identified.

According to Clements et al. [80], *risks* refer to those architectural decisions that are potentially problematic. *Nonrisks* represent good design decisions based on assumptions that are often implicit in the software architecture.

An architectural decision that is critical for achieving a particular quality requirement is called *sensitivity point*. It may involve one or more architectural components. Sensitivity points are those locations in the architecture that the architect has to pay attention to when analyzing the achievement of a quality requirement. An architectural decision that affects more than one quality requirement and represents a sensitivity point for more than one quality requirement is a *trade-off point*.

ATAM provides a template for structuring the analysis of architectural approaches shown in Fig. 11.2 (taken from [80]). The template has to be instantiated for specifying one scenario. The template supports the evaluator team in particularly identifying the sensitivity points, trade-off points, risks, and nonrisks for the selected scenarios of the utility tree. Sensitivity and trade-off points are later specified as either risks or nonrisks.

Analysis of Architectural Approach				
Scenario #:Number	Scenario: Text of scenario from utility tree			
Attribute(s)	Quality attributes with which this scenario is concerned			
Environment	Relevant assumptions about the environment in which the system resides, and the relevant conditions when the scenario is carried out			
Stimulus	A precise statement of the quality attribute stimulus (e.g. function invoked, failure, threat, modification) embodied by the scenario			
Response	A precise statement of the quality attribute response (e.g. response time, measure of difficulty of modification)			
Architectural Decisions	Sensitivity	Tradeoffs	Risk	Nonrisks
Architectural decisions relevant to this scenario that affect quality attribute response	Sensitivity point #	Tradeoff point #	Risk #	Nonrisk #
...	...	...	...	...
...	...	...	...	...
Reasoning	Qualitative and/or quantitative rationale for why the list of architectural decisions contributes to meeting each quality attribute requirement expressed by the scenario			
Architectural Diagram	Diagram or diagrams of architectural views annotated with architectural information to support the above reasoning, accompanied by explanatory text if desired			

Fig. 11.2: Template for the analysis of architectural approaches

Figure 11.3 (taken from [80]) provides an example of applying the template for the scenario *A12: detect and recover from HW failure of a primary CPU* and the quality requirement *availability*. This scenario can happen in the "normal operation" of the system (*environment*) when "one of the CPUs fails" (*stimulus*). In this case the system has to provide "0.999999 availability of the switch" (*response*). Architectural decisions that have been made so far are "backup CPUs", "no backup data channel", "watchdog", "heartbeat", and "failover routing". The evaluator team analyzes these architectural decisions and identifies all these architectural approaches as sensitivity points. "No backup data channel" is identified as a trade-off point. The further analysis of these architectural decisions shows that "backup CPUs" and "no backup data channel" provide risks to the architecture whereas "watchdog", "heartbeat" and "failover routing" are nonrisks. The template provides also the option to give a reasoning for the analysis and also to draw an architectural diagram if needed.

Application of Step 6 - Analyze the architectural approaches

For the analysis, we use the template shown in Fig. 11.2. We instantiate this template for the integrity requirement *R10* and the authenticity requirement *R12* for the architecture alternative *A2* (see the instantiated template in Fig. 11.4). The architectural approach (architectural decision (AD) in Fig. 11.4) that has been applied in the architecture alternative *A2* in order to achieve these requirements is the *digital signature*. This scenario shown in Fig. 11.4 happens in the "normal operation" (*environment*), "while transferring" (*stimulus*), and the system has to achieve the "integrity and authenticity of data" as a *response* to the *stimulus*. For achieving the requirements *R10* and *R12*, we only applied *digital signature* as an *architectural decision*. It is a *sensitivity point (S1))* as it affects the security of the architecture. We identified one *risk (R1)* associated with *digital signature*. The risk is that an attacker might be able to forge signatures or misuse signatures, if the process of digital signing is not secure[21]. As a *reasoning* for the architectural decision *digital signature*, we refer to the description of the problem-oriented digital signature pattern given in Section 8.2.6 on page 260. It describes why digital signature contributes to achieving the integrity and authenticity requirements. As an *architectural diagram*, we refer to the structural view of the architecture alternative 2 (*A2*) given in Fig. 10.4 on page 337.

The architectural approach *asymmetric encryption* has been applied in the architecture alternative *A2* in order to achieve the confidentiality requirement *R11*

---

[21] https://www.thales-esecurity.com/solutions/by-technology-focus/digital-signatures

Analysis of Architectural Approach				
Scenario #: 12	Scenario: Detect and recover from HW failure of a primary CPU			
Attribute(s)	Aailability			
Environment	Normal operations			
Stimulus	One of the CPU fails			
Response	0.999999 availability of the switch			
Architectural Decisions	Sensitivity	Tradeoffs	Risk	Nonrisks
Backup CPUs	S2		R8	
No backup data channel	S3	T3	R9	
Watchdog	S4			N12
Heartbeat	S5			N13
Failover routing	S6			N14
Reasoning	- Ensures no common mode failure by using different hardware and operating system (see Risk 8) - Worst-case roll over is accomplished in 4 seconds as computing slate takes that long at worst - Garanteed to detect failure with 2 seconds based on rates of heartbeat and watchdog - Watchdog is simple and proven reliable - Availability requirement might be at risk due to lack of backup data channel (see Risk 9)			
Architectural Diagram				

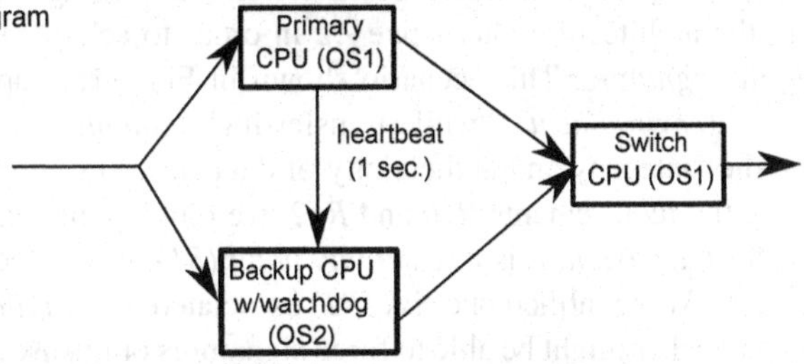

Fig. 11.3: An Example for the analysis of architectural approaches

(see the instantiated template in Fig. 11.5). The scenario happens in the "normal operation" (*environment*), "while transferring" (*stimulus*), and the system has to achieve the "confidentiality of data" as a *response* to the *stimulus*. For achieving the requirement *R11*, we only applied the *asymmetric encryption* as the *architectural decision (AD2)*. It is a *sensitivity point* as it affects security of the system.

	Analysis of Architectural Approach			
Scenario #: R10 / R12	Scenario: Integrity and authenticity of data transferred in the WAN shall be protected.			
Attribute(s)	Security (integrity, authenticity)			
Environment	Normal operation			
Stimulus	While transferring			
Response	Integrity and authenticity of data			
Architectural Decisions	Sensitivity	Tradeoffs	Risk	Nonrisks
AD1 - digital signature	S1		R1	
Reasoning	See problem-oriented digital signature pattern in Chapter 8 (Section 8.2.5 on page 186)			
Architectural Diagram	See A2 in Figure 10.4 in Section 10.2 on page 242			

Fig. 11.4: Analysis of the scenarios *R10* and *R12* for *A2*

As a *reasoning* for the architectural decision *asymmetric encryption*, we refer to the description of the problem-oriented asymmetric encryption pattern given in Section 8.2.7 on page 262. It describes why asymmetric encryption contributes to achieving the confidentiality requirement. As an *architectural diagram*, we refer to the structural view of the architecture alternative 2 (*A2*) given in Fig. 10.4 on page 337.

The architectural approach *load balancer* has been applied in the architecture alternative *A1* in order to achieve the response time requirements *R18-R25* (see the instantiated template in Fig. 11.6). The scenario happens in a "normal operation" (*environment*), "while receiving, processing, storing, submitting" (*stimulus*), and the system has to respond "in less than 5 sec for requirements *R18, R20, R22, R24* and in less than 10 sec for requirements *R19, R21, R23, R25*" as a *response* to the *stimulus*.

For achieving these requirements, we applied the *load balancer* as the *architectural decision (AD3)*. It is a *sensitivity point (S3)* as introducing a load balancer might affect the performance of the system itself. It is not a *trade-off point* as it does not affect the security of the system. For *A1* three load balancers are placed. At this stage of the software architecture, it is hard to assess whether all three load balancers are required. Further performance analysis might be required later on if the detailed design is built and there exist more details regarding the deployment of the software components on the hardware components. For now, we can mark the load balancer as a *risk (R3)* which has to be investigated further.

Analysis of Architectural Approach				
Scenario #: R11	Scenario: Confidentiality of data transferred in the WAN shall be protected.			
Attribute(s)	Security (confidentiality)			
Environment	Normal operation			
Stimulus	While transferring			
Response	Confidentiality of data			
Architectural Decisions	Sensitivity	Tradeoffs	Risk	Nonrisks
AD2 - asymmetric encryption	S2			
Reasoning	See problem-oriented asymmetric encryption pattern in Chapter 8 (Section 8.2.6 on page 186)			
Architectural Diagram	See A2 in Figure 10.4 in Section 10.2 on page 242			

Fig. 11.5: Analysis of the scenario *R11* for *A2*

The other architectural decision is *symmetric encryption* which contributes to the achievement of security (confidentiality). Therefore, it is a *sensitivity point (S4)*. It might take some time due to the required computation time and, therefore, affect the achievement of the performance requirements. Hence, it represents a *trade-off point (T4)* to be taken into account as an *architectural decision (AD4* in Fig. 11.6). We argue that this might not be a problem related to performance in *A1* as we only use this mechanism for encrypting meter data that are submitted to the outside world, namely to the *authorized external entities* (related to *R4*). For meter data related to *R5*, we do not use the encryption mechanism due to performance reasons. Therefore, it does not represent a risk for achieving performance requirements *R18 - R25*.

The other architectural decision is *MAC* which contributes to the achievement of security (integrity and authenticity). Therefore, it is a *sensitivity point (S5)*. Also this mechanism takes some time due to its computation and, therefore, affects the fulfillment of the performance requirements. Hence, it represents a *trade-off point (T5)* to be considered as an *architectural decision (AD5* in Fig. 11.6). For this architectural decision, we argue similarly to the previous architectural decision. It might not cause a problem for performance in *A1* as we only use this mechanism for achieving security related to *R4*. Similar to the reasoning for the architectural approach *symmetric encryption*, the architectural approach *MAC* does not provide a risk for achieving performance requirements.

	Analysis of Architectural Approach			
Scenario #: R18-R25	Scenario: The time to retrieve meter data from the smart meter and publish it through the WAN shall be less than 5 seconds (R18, R20, R22, R24). The time to retrieve meter data from the smart meter and publish it through the HAN shall be less than 10 seconds (R19, R21, R23, R25).			
Attribute(s)	Performance (response time)			
Environment	Normal operation			
Stimulus	Receive, process, store, and submit			
Response	Response time in less than 5 sec/response time in less than 10 sec			
Architectural Decisions	Sensitivity	Tradeoffs	Risk	Nonrisks
AD3 - LB	S3		R3	
AD4 - symmetric encryption	S4	T4		
AD5 - MAC	S5	T5		
Reasoning	See problem-oriented load balancer pattern in Chapter 8 (Section 8.3 on page 188)			
Architectural Diagram	See A1 in Figure 10.3 in Section 10.2			

Fig. 11.6: Analysis of the scenarios *R18-R25* for *A1*

Step 7 - Brainstorm and prioritize scenarios

In this step, other stakeholders than the architect brainstorm for identifying scenarios in order to revisit those scenarios from Step 5. The list of identified scenarios by the other stakeholders has to be compared with the scenarios contained in the utility tree from Step 5 to examine whether new scenarios have been identified. The purpose of this step is to find a consensus between the architect and other stakeholders regarding the scenarios and their prioritization. For the case that new scenarios have been identified by other stakeholders, they have to be added to the utility tree.

Application of Step 7 - Brainstorm and prioritize scenarios

We skip this step as in our case our position as the architect makes us the only stakeholder.

Step 8 - Analyze the architectural approaches

In this step, the same activities as in Step 6 have to be performed by the evaluator. The new scenarios from the previous step have to be taken into account. The architect explains to the stakeholders whether and to what extent the applied architectural approaches contribute to the satisfaction of new scenarios.

Application of Step 8 - Analyze the architectural approaches

We skip this step due to skipping Step 7.

Step 9 - Present the results

The evaluator team presents the gained information and results of applying ATAM to the stakeholders. The architecture, quality requirements, and the collected information from each step are summarized. The main outputs of ATAM, namely 1) the prioritized scenarios, 2) the catalog of architectural approaches used, 3) mapping of architectural approaches to quality requirements, 4) risks and nonrisks, and 5) sensitivity and trade-off points are presented to the stakeholders.

Application of Step 9 - Present the results

We presented the application of each ATAM step in detail. We selected scenarios to be further analyzed for the architecture alternatives *A1* and *A2*. According to the selection criteria suggested by ATAM, we did not select any scenarios related to the architecture alternative *A3*. Hence, it is considered as not critical.

Regarding the architecture alternative *A1*, we identified three architectural decisions *load balancer*, *symmetric encryption*, and *MAC*. *Load balancer* has been identified as a potential *risk* to be further analyzed in the detailed design. *Symmetric encryption* and *MAC* represent *trade-off points*. We, however, did not identify a risk regarding these two architectural approaches.

Regarding the architecture alternative *A2*, we identified two architectural decisions *digital signature* and *asymmetric encryption* for the scenarios *R10*, *R11*, and *R12*. Digital signature has been identified as a potential *risk* to be taken into account during the detailed design and implementation.

11.5.2 Discussion of the results

In this step, we discuss our experience of applying ATAM.

Architecture evaluation experience

We observed that ATAM provides a guideline on the steps of the evaluation and the order of applying the steps. It, however, does not explicitly state how to apply each step. For example, Step 6 of ATAM is concerned with analyzing the architectural approaches. ATAM provides a template for this step. However, there is no clear guidance on how to analyze the architectural approaches, and identify the risks and nonrisks in a detailed and systematic manner. A challenge that we have faced during the application of ATAM was that experience and intuition of the evaluators play an essential role in how expressive and convincing the results are. ATAM is a strong experience-based approach for architecture evaluation. This holds for other methods developed by the Software Engineering Institute (SEI)[22], such as ADD[23], as well [102].

Experienced evaluators use the instantiated templates as output of Step 6 to decide which architectural decisions might be problematic based on their experience. Beside the templates that support the collection of the right information in a structured way for the evaluator, Step 6 does not provide any systematic support on how to identify the problematic decisions.

Reliability of the results

By applying ATAM, we played the role of the software architect as a stakeholder as well as the role of the evaluator at the same time. This might have biased the results of the evaluation. To mitigate this bias, we allocated a master thesis on this topic using the same case study in order to gain a different and external perspective regarding the evaluation task. The results obtained from the master thesis are not much different as also in this case there was a lack of experience in evaluating software architectures. This supports our view of ATAM being an experience-based method.

---

[22] http://www.sei.cmu.edu/
[23] Attribute Driven Design

Benefits of the architecture evaluation

The main and obvious benefit of architecture evaluation is identifying architectural problems and risks. In addition, there are the other benefits that contribute to the success of a software project. We give an overview of these benefits in the following [80]:

Put stakeholders in the same room is considered as one additional benefit of applying ATAM. In most cases, an architecture evaluation is the first time that stakeholders gather together in order to explain their goals and motivations and to communicate with each other.

Forces an articulation of specific quality goals is another additional benefit of ATAM given by its authors. Often quality goals and requirements are not captured in the requirement documents or only documented in a vague and an ambiguous manner. ATAM supports the explicit and precise capturing of quality requirements by establishing a utility tree which forces the stakeholders to think about their desired goals and requirements. Also this benefit does not apply in our case as we documented quality requirements in a systematic and methodical manner in Phase 1 of QuaDRA .

Results in the prioritization of conflicting goals ATAM helps resolving conflicting goals and requirements by prioritizing them if they cannot all be satisfied. Also this additional benefit does not provide an added value as we provide methods for systematically detecting and resolving conflicting requirements in Phase 4 of QuaDRA described in Chapter 7.

Forces a clear explication of the architecture The architect has to explain the architecture to the stakeholders that were not privy to the architecture creation process and to make them understand it. As explained before, we as the only stakeholder in the evaluation process do not benefit from this force.

Improves the quality of architectural documentation Often in practice, the architecture documentation has not been prepared well. But, the architecture evaluation requires a full documentation of the software architecture. At the latest when evaluating the architecture, the documentation should be completed. Here, we also observe that we cannot profit much, as documenting all artifacts produced by every phase of the QuaDRA framework is an explicit part of QuaDRA.

Uncovers opportunities for cross-project reuse Stakeholders and evaluators are often involved in other projects. As such, they are in a position to discover components that can be reused in other projects or reuse and import components from other project to the current one. From our point of view, this might be a beneficial issue when working in practice in different projects. However, this benefit could not be explored in our current position in the research and within this book.

Results in improved architecture practices Those organizations that incorporate architecture evaluation into their development process benefit from the improvement in the quality of the developed architectures. The reason is that the architects learn to already address the issues in the architecture development which will be raised later in the architecture evaluation. Also this benefit does not directly apply to our case.

All these benefits do not apply to our current work. However, many projects might profit from these add-ons as often the software architectures created in such organizations lack documentation and explicit consideration of quality requirements. So, they might use one or more of these benefits when evaluating the architecture to obtain a better architecture. A straightforward and right way for obtaining a suitable software architecture is, however, to construct the software architecture from the beginning in a systematic and methodical way. We have shown in this book how to develop such an architecture. After applying ATAM, we observed that most of the benefits of applying ATAM are not applicable to our case, as the software architecture derived using the QuaDRA framework already contains most of the artifacts that are created during ATAM. In the following, we describe which steps of ATAM can be left out when applying QuaDRA for creating architectures.

Benefits of applying QuaDRA

When using QuaDRA for deriving architectures, there is no need for applying all the steps of ATAM for the architecture evaluation. In this case, most of the ATAM steps can be left out.

Step 2 of ATAM is concerned with identifying the main functions of the system, possible restrictions, business goals, and architectural drivers. We treated these issues in Phase 1 of QuaDRA described in Chapter 4.

Steps 3 and 4 of ATAM are concerned with the architecture of the system containing technical restrictions, interacting systems, and architectural approaches that have been used for fulfilling the quality requirements. We treat these issues in different parts of QuaDRA. For example, in Phase 1, we provide the context view defining the scope of the system and the environment. In Phase 3, we select, document, and apply architectural patterns in a systematic way. In Phase 7, we provide the structural and behavioral view of the software architecture. As all these phases are carefully documented, the related steps in ATAM can be left out.

Similar to ATAM, QuaDRA supports the explicit and precise capturing of quality requirements which forces the stakeholders to think about their desired goals and requirements. We documented quality requirements in a systematic and methodical manner in Phase 1 of QuaDRA described in Chapter 4. Therefore, when conducting QuaDRA for deriving quality-based software architecture, the related step in ATAM, namely Step 5, can be left out in a large part. We consider the requirement prioritization part of Step 5 as useful in order to avoid the consideration of all requirements.

Step 6 of ATAM uses the results of the previous steps and structures them in predefined templates. In order to identify risks, nonrisks, sensitivity and trade-off points, applying this step might be useful. However, as we provide methods for identifying conflicts (trade-off points in ATAM) and resolving them in Phase 4 of QuaDRA, not many new insights can be expected as the result of this step. Steps 7 and 8 provide a repetition of Steps 5 and 6 when new scenarios are identified. Step 9 presents the results.

11.6 Related Work

In this section, we review the attempts providing a systematic comparison of the state-of-the-art in the area of architecture evaluation methods. There is little consensus on the criteria that a software architecture evaluation method should fully address. To the best of our knowledge there is a sparse number of works dealing with this topic [88, 34, 35]. All these works propose an explicit framework for comparing architecture evaluation methods.

Dobrica and Niemelä [88] present and discuss eight of the most representative architecture evaluation methods. They propose a comparison framework for comparing these methods including eight comparison elements. Similar to our comparison framework, this work is a qualitative framework which discusses the similarities and differences between the architecture evaluation methods instead of providing a quantitative judgement. In this work, the authors do not provide any explanation on why those particular elements have been selected for their framework. There is also no explanation of the elements of the framework. Furthermore, the authors do not reason why they selected those eight particular evaluation methods.

A framework for comparing and classifying software architecture evaluation methods is proposed by Babar et al. [35]. This framework includes 15 comparison elements. In contrast to the previous work, it provides a detailed explanation of the framework elements. Also this work provides a comparison of eight evaluation methods. This work focuses only on scenario-based architecture evaluation methods. The methods *SAAM*, *SAAMCS*, *SAAMER*, *ATAM*, and *SBAR* are selected in both frameworks for comparison.

Babar and Gorton [34] improve the work proposed in [35] by making some adjustments to the framework. For the new framework, they make use of the NIM-SAD framework for classifying the components of the framework in *context, stakeholders, contents*, and *reliability*. They also extend the comparison elements to 17. In this work, the authors limit their comparative evaluation to only four scenario-based methods *SAAM, ATAM, PASA*, and *ALMA*. All these three frameworks do not report on how they selected the evaluation methods to be compared. In contrast, we conducted a systematic literature review to find the architecture evaluation methods. In our framework, we provide a comparison of 16 architecture evaluation methods.

11.7 Contributions

In order to identify and localize the problems with the derived software architecture alternatives regarding the achievement of quality requirements, we conducted an architecture evaluation in this chapter. Our contributions can be summarized as follows:

- Systematic selection of the state-of-the-art methods by conducting a secondary literature review. We scanned 258 secondary studies by conducting automated and snowball search. As the final result, we selected 7 secondary studies from which we extracted 16 architecture evaluation methods.
- Developing a structured framework and selection criteria for analyzing and comparing the state-of-the-art methods. The framework is structured in *Components, Elements, Evaluation Questions*, and *Classification*. It can be easily modified and extended to desirable features.
- Selecting an architecture evaluation method by applying the developed framework for evaluating the architecture alternatives created by QuaDRA. Only the three methods *ATAM, SAEM*, and *SACAM* fulfilled all the *essential* selection criteria. *ATAM* has been selected as the most suitable method as it fulfills more *beneficial* selection criteria than the other methods.
- Evaluating the derived architecture alternatives by applying ATAM. The aim of ATAM is not to provide a decision regarding the selection of the most suitable architecture alternative with regard to specific quality requirements. It rather focuses on determining if and where in the software architecture there might be problems with regard to specific quality requirements.
- Critically discussing the results of applying ATAM and its benefits to the QuaDRA framework. The architecture evaluation using ATAM showed that the most benefits one could gain from applying ATAM can also be obtained by de-

riving software architectures using the QuaDRA framework. The reason is that almost all the artifacts to be created during the application of ATAM are created during different phases of QuaDRA.

Chapter 12
Validation of the QuaDRA Framework

Abstract At the beginning of this book in Chapter 1, we described the existing gap in research regarding methods for building software architectures based on (quality) requirements. We developed the QuaDRA framework described in Chapters 4 - 11 that aims at bridging this gap. This chapter describes the validation of the QuaDRA framework for quality-aware co-development of requirements and software architecture alternatives. It represents a comparative evaluation of QuaDRA and the state-of-the-art methods. The objective of the comparative evaluation is to figure out whether QuaDRA exhibits a substantial progress over the state-of-the-art methods.

12.1 Introduction

We highlighted two existing challenges in software engineering at the beginning of this book in Chapter 1 that provide the basis for this book: 1) an existing gap in research regarding methods for building software architectures based on (quality) requirements, 2) the intuition-, communication-, and experience-based nature of existing methods for developing requirements and software architectures.

In order to overcome these challenges, we first systematically derived meta-requirements that a method for quality-aware development of requirements and software architecture has to meet in Chapter 3. After classifying the meta-requirements in *essential*, *recommended*, and *optional*, we used them as evaluation criteria in a structured framework that we developed for comparing the state-of-the-art methods. The comparative evaluation has shown that none of the compared methods fulfills all the *essential* and *recommended* meta-requirements or nearly all of them. Our evaluation underlined the lack of methodological support for systematic development of artifacts in both phases with respect to quality requirements in a unified process.

We developed a framework described in Chapters 4 - 11 that aims at remedying this lack by fulfilling the identified meta-requirements. In developing QuaDRA our primary goal was to achieve the *essential* and *recommended* meta-requirements. The *optional* meta-requirements played a secondary role in being achieved by the QuaDRA framework.

The goal of this chapter is to provide a validation of QuaDRA by applying the systematic evaluation framework from Chapter 3. The framework application demonstrates to what extent the QuaDRA framework satisfies the meta-requirements. It allows us to compare our method with the state-of-the-art methods. Our objective of the comparative evaluation is to figure out whether QuaDRA exhibits a substantial progress over the state-of-the-art methods. With this chapter we provide answers for the research question *RQ 4* defined at the beginning of this book.

This chapter is structured as follows. Section 12.2 reviews the evaluation framework that we developed before. Section 12.3 provides an overview of the value assignment schema for making our method comparable with the state-of-the-art methods. In Section 12.4, we validate the QuaDRA framework by applying the developed evaluation framework. We conclude this chapter in Section 12.5.

12.2 Evaluation Framework

We developed an evaluation framework in Chapter 3 as an analysis tool for comparative evaluation of methods bridging the gap between requirements and software architecture with respect to quality requirements (see Section 3.4 on page 73). This evaluation framework uses the meta-requirements that we derived in Section 3.2 (see page 54). The meta-requirements build the *elements* of the framework. We used this framework for evaluating the methods, which we identified by conducting an SLR in Section 3.6 (see page 75). The evaluation framework is shown in Table 12.1.

We divided the meta-requirements into the three categories *"essential"*, *"recommended"*, and *"optional"*:

Essential meta-requirements   are required and must be fulfilled when developing such a method. That is, we cannot speak of a "method supporting the quality-aware development of requirements and software architecture" if not all of the essential meta-requirements are fulfilled.

Table 12.1: The comparative evaluation framework and its constituents

Component	Elements	Evaluation Questions	Classification
Context	Development phase	Which phases are covered by the method?	Method characteristic
	Method input	What are the required inputs for the method?	Method characteristic
	Method output	What are the produced outputs of the method?	Method characteristic
	Application domain	For which application domain is the method developed?	Method characteristic
User	User skill	What specific skills does an inexperienced software engineer require to accomplish tasks required by the method?	Method characteristic
Content	Quality req.	How are quality requirements elicited and documented?	Essential
	Guidance	How much support for applying the method by the user is provided by the reported method?	Essential
	Knowledge reuse	To what extent is making use of reusable knowledge supported?	Essential
	RE descr.	Which RE artifacts are created by the method? Which notation/language is used by the method to represent RE models, diagrams, and other artifacts it creates? Which RE approach is used for creating the artifacts?	Essential
	Design descr.	Which design artifacts are created by the method? Which notation/language is used by the method to represent design models, diagrams, and other artifacts it creates? Which design approach is used for creating the artifacts?	Essential
	Traceability	To what extent is traceability between requirements and design artifacts supported?	Recommended
	Design rationale	To what extent is capturing the rationales behind design decisions supported?	Recommended
	Trade-off analysis	Whether and to what extent is trade-off analysis supported?	Recommended
	Arch. alternatives	To what extent are alternative architectures supported?	Recommended
	Iterative dev.	To what extent is the iterative development of requirements and software architectures supported?	Recommended
	Concurrent co-dev.	To what extent is the intertwining and concurrent co-development of requirements and software architecture supported?	Optional
	Arch. views	Whether and which views are used for representing the RE and design artifacts?	Optional
	Tool support	Are there tools to support the method and its artifacts? Which activities of the methods are supported by the tools?	Optional
Validation	Arch. evaluation	Whether and how does the method evaluate the satisfaction of quality requirements in the produced software architecture?	Recommended

Recommended meta-requirements   are of high interest, but might not be absolutely required. That is, we can still speak of a "method supporting the quality-aware development of requirements and software architecture" if not all recommended meta-requirements are met. In such a case, we are concerned with a method which is not optimal for our purposes but still acceptable.

Optional meta-requirements   represent those meta-requirements that do not need to be necessarily fulfilled for a "method supporting the quality-aware development of requirements and software architecture". Their fulfillment, however, provides additional characteristics that are useful.

In addition to the three categories "*essential*", "*recommended*", and "*optional*" for meta-requirements, we defined the category "*method characteristics*". This category is concerned with those characteristics that every software engineering method exhibits. Examples for such characteristics are *user skill* and *application domain*. We also make use of these characteristics for the comparative evaluation.

12.3 Value Assignment Schema

In Chapter 3, we provided a value assignment schema that we chose for making the selected methods comparable (see Section 3.8.1 on page 97). We decided to use a 3-score scale consisting of +, o, and - for assigning values to the meta-requirements, as it might be easier to handle than other scoring systems.

Table 12.2 shows the value assignment schema for each meta-requirement. The first column of Table 12.2 represents the "*meta-requirement*", the second column gives the possible answers to the evaluation question ("*answer to evaluation question*"), and the third column represents the values we assigned (+, o, -) for making the meta-requirement comparable with other methods ("*assigned value*").

12.4 Comparative Evaluation of the QuaDRA Framework

This section deals with evaluating the QuaDRA framework based on the derived meta-requirements and the developed comparative evaluation framework. We first evaluate the QuaDRA framework by assigning values to the meta-requirements and give reasoning for it in Section 12.4.1. We show the application of the evaluation framework to QuaDRA and then compare the results of evaluation with state-of-the-art methods in Section 12.4.2.

12.4.1 Value Assignment

For each meta-requirement, we ask the *evaluation question* and provide answers for the question (*answer for QuaDRA*).

User skill

Evaluation question: What specific skills does an inexperienced software engineer require to accomplish tasks required by the method?

Answer for QuaDRA: QuaDRA uses problem frames as the basis for requirements engineering. Hence, the only specific skill that the user requires is the knowledge of problem frames. In addition to problem frames, QuaDRA uses UML diagrams for modeling requirement as well as architecture descriptions. However, UML is assumed to be known to the software engineers. Therefore, it is not considered as a specific skill. As a result of evaluation, we assign the value "+" to the *essential meta-requirement user skill* as only 1 specific skill is required for applying the QuaDRA framework.

Quality requirements

Evaluation question: How are quality requirements elicited and documented?

Answer for QuaDRA: In QuaDRA , quality requirements are elicited and documented right from the beginning of the software development process, namely in the requirements engineering. In Phase 1 of QuaDRA (see Chapter 4), we propose a systematic method that elicits quality requirements and documents them in a structured way. By applying this method, quality requirements can be captured and documented as problem diagrams in a structured way. Each problem diagram additionally contains the textual description of quality requirements in natural language. To the *essential meta-requirements quality requirements* we assign the value "+" as the proposed method elicits and documents quality requirements in a structured and systematic way.

Guidance and method structure

Evaluation question: How much support for applying the method by the user is provided by the reported method?

Answer for QuaDRA: The QuaDRA framework provides various structured

Table 12.2: Mapping between meta-requirements and the assigned values

Meta-requirements	Answer to evaluation question	Assigned value
User Skill	4 needed skills	-
	3 needed skills	o
	1-2 needed skills	+
Quality requirements	Structured and systematic elicitation and documentation	+
	Vaguely elicitation and documentation	o
	No elicitation and documentation	-
Guidance and method structure	"Yes" and "step by step"	+
	"Yes" and "relatively detailed"	o
	"No" and "step by step"	o
	"No" and "relatively detailed"	-
Knowledge reuse	"Architectural patterns" and "tactics[1]"	+
	"Only architectural patterns"	o
	"Only tactics"	o
	"No architectural patterns" and "no tactics"	-
RE and design descriptions	"unified language for RE and architecture" and "semi-formal"	+
	"unified language for RE and architecture" and "only natural language"	o
	"different languages for RE and architecture" and "semi-formal"	o
	"different languages for RE and architecture" and "only natural language"	-
Traceability	Yes	+
	Partially	o
	No	-
Design rationale	Yes	+
	Partially	o
	No	-
Trade-off analysis	"Detection" and "resolution"	+
	"Only detection"	o
	"Only resolution"	o
	"No detection" and "no resolution"	-
Architecture alternatives	Yes	+
	Partially	o
	No	-
Iterative development	Yes	+
	No	-
Concurrent co-development	Yes	+
	No	-
Arch. views	"structural" and "behavioral" and "deployment" or "development"	+
	"structural" and "behavioral"	o
	"structural"	-
Tool support	Yes	+
	Partially	o
	No	-
Architecture evaluation	Yes	+
	Partially	o
	No	-

methods for the different phases of co-developing requirements and software architecture alternatives. Each method involves a number of steps to be performed, required inputs and resulting outputs. In addition, it explicitly specifies in which order the different steps have to be executed. All the methods provide a "step by step" guidance in order to support inexperienced software engineers in achieving the goal of the method. That is, our proposed methods do not rely on intuition or experience of software engineers. As an example, our decision making process for selecting architectural patterns is a "step-by-step" and systematic process in contrast to the current state-of-the-art in which the decision making process is often described as an ad-hoc and creative process relying to a large extent on the experience and expertise of the architects [120, 253]. Therefore, we assign the value "+" to the *essential meta-requirement guidance and method structure*.

Knowledge reuse

Evaluation question: To what extent is making use of reusable knowledge supported?

Answer for QuaDRA: A quality-aware software development process covering requirements engineering and software architecture must include step-by-step and systematic ways for finding solutions such as patterns, styles, and tactics to achieve quality requirements. QuaDRA uses architectural patterns for addressing quality requirements in the software architecture. In Phase 2 (see Chapter 5), a systematic pattern selection process is presented which guides the user through the pattern selection and provides support for decision making. In Phase 5 (see Chapter 8) mechanisms (also known as *tactics*) for fulfilling quality requirements are identified and analyzed. Such mechanisms are used in a structured method in Phase 6 (see Chapter 9) for enriching requirement models with quality-specific solutions. The value "+" is assigned to the *essential meta-requirement knowledge reuse* as we use architectural patterns as well as quality-specific mechanisms for achieving quality requirements.

RE and design description

Evaluation question: Which RE and design artifacts are created by the method? Which notation/language is used by the method to represent RE and design models, diagrams, and other artifacts it creates? Which RE and design approach is used for creating the artifacts?

Answer for QuaDRA: We create a context diagram as well as problem diagrams annotated with domain knowledge as RE artifacts (see Chapter 4). As design artifacts we create architecture diagrams containing the structural as well as the behavioral views (see Chapters 5 and 11). The notation and the language that is used in both kinds of artifacts is UML. The context diagrams and the problem diagrams are represented as UML class diagrams. Architecture artifacts contain the structural view of the architecture represented as UML composite structure diagrams and the behavioral view of the architecture represented as UML sequence diagrams. The requirement artifacts as well as the design artifacts are maintained in one unified model. This allows us to keep consistency of the UML artifacts through the two phases requirements engineering and architecture design. As we use UML for representing the RE as well as design artifacts, we are concerned with a unified and semi-formal language. Hence, the value "+" is assigned to the *essential meta-requirement RE and design description.*

Traceability

Evaluation question: To what extent is traceability between requirements and design artifacts supported?

Answer for QuaDRA: We provide the intermediate model *problem-solution diagram* which explicitly provides trace links from quality requirements to the quality-specific solution alternatives (see Chapter 8 on page 278). Furthermore, to create architecture, we map problem diagrams to components in the software architecture. So, it is clear which components are in charge of fulfilling which requirements. Furthermore, we keep the requirements as well as the design artifacts in one unified model. This helps us to find the links between different model artifacts using OCL expressions. So, we assign the value "+" to the *recommended meta-requirement traceability.*

Design rationale

Evaluation question: To what extent is capturing the rationales behind design decisions supported?

Answer for QuaDRA: Our pattern selection process contains structured and transparent decision making steps, which support the software engineer in capturing and tracing the design decisions and the related rationale. It provides a reasoning about the appropriateness of the architectural design decisions. The reasoning is provided by a documentation of the relevant questions, the related answers to those questions, and the consequences related to the selected pattern. Consequently, the software engineers are able to reconstruct the made design decisions later on (see Chapter 5). Also other methods of the QuaDRA framework such as requirement interaction detection methods, performance analysis method, and requirement alternative generation method guide the user in documenting rationales by decision making in a structured way so that other designers can understand them without additional assistance.

In addition, in our developed templates for *problem-oriented quality patterns*, we document the pre-conditions and post-conditions for applying the patterns. The pre-conditions can be annotated in the requirement models using the attributes of the ≪bottleneck≫ stereotype. Thus, we capture the limitations and constraints of the possible options.

Furthermore, the *problem-solution diagram* provides the possibility to document rationales for selecting quality-specific solutions in the *solution space*. Each quality-specific solution alternative can be annotated with a rationale for selecting it. It is indicated by the attribute *rationale* of the stereotype *variant*. Using this attribute reasons for selecting or not selecting a specific quality-specific solution can be annotated in the models. Moreover, in the architecture diagram, we provide the option for documenting rationales for the selected quality-specific solution. This can be captured as an annotation using the attribute *rationale*. By doing this, we keep the documentation for selecting or not selecting an option over another option in the architecture models. Consequently, we assign the value "+" to the *recommended meta-requirement design rationale*.

Trade-off analysis

Evaluation question: Whether and to what extent is trade-off analysis supported? **Answer for QuaDRA:** Trade-off analysis involves the systematic treatment of conflicts among requirements. Most software engineers use common sense practices such as documentation reviews. In the QuaDRA framework, we propose two methods for systematic detection of functional as well as quality requirements (see Chapter 7 on page 198 and 210). To make the conflicting requirements manageable, we narrow down the set of interacting requirement pairs using a structured method (see Chapter 7 on page 220). Another method is proposed to resolve the remaining conflicts among quality requirements by relaxing them and generating requirement alternatives (see Chapter 7 on page 231). So, QuaDRA detects and resolves conflicts between quality requirements. Hence, we assign the value "+" to the *recommended meta-requirement trade-off analysis*.

Architecture alternatives

Evaluation question: To what extent are alternative architectures supported?
Answer for QuaDRA: There might exist various solutions for achieving quality requirements. Such solution might lead to different levels of satisfaction of quality requirements. We make use of architectural patterns (see Chapter 5) as well as quality-specific solutions (see Chapters 8 and 9) to address quality requirements. Selecting different architectural patterns and quality-specific solutions leads to architecture alternatives. In the QuaDRA framework, we propose the systematic derivation of architecture alternatives from requirement descriptions (see Chapter 10). Having supported the creation of architecture alternatives by QuaDRA , we assign the value "+" to the *recommended meta-requirement architecture alternatives*.

Iterative development

Evaluation question: To what extent is the iterative development of requirements and software architectures supported?
Answer for QuaDRA: It is necessary to provide feedback loops in the architecting process to enable the software system to respond to changes in the problem space as well as in the solution space. QuaDRA proposes an iterative and concurrent way of developing requirement and architecture descriptions. The phases of QuaDRA are constructed in such a way that there is forward and backward feedback between the problem and the solution peaks. So, the changes in one peak are considered in the other peak for further development. This way, the artifacts in both phases are developed concurrently and consistently to each other. Hence, we assign the value "+" to the *recommended meta-requirement iterative development*.

Architecture evaluation

Evaluation question: Whether and how does the method evaluate the satisfaction of quality requirements in the produced software architecture?
Answer for QuaDRA: Evaluation of software architecture is essential to ensure whether and to which extent quality requirements have been addressed in the software architecture. In Phase 8 of the QuaDRA framework (see Chapter 11), we provide an evaluation of the created software architecture alternatives using the widely used and established method *ATAM*. The architecture evaluation using ATAM shows that the most benefits one could gain from applying ATAM can also

be obtained by deriving software architectures using the QuaDRA framework. The reason is that almost all the artifacts to be created during the application of ATAM are created during different phases of QuaDRA. Therefore, we can say that the architecture evaluation is already contained in QuaDRA by construction. Hence, we assign the value "+" to the *recommended meta-requirement architecture evaluation*.

Concurrent co-development

Evaluation question: To what extent is the intertwining and concurrent co-development of requirements and software architecture supported?

Answer for QuaDRA: As described above, we not only propose an iterative approach for developing the requirements and software architectures. We also propose the concurrent co-development of the requirement and architecture artifacts. QuaDRA follows the idea of the Twin Peaks model which resulted from the experiences of its author in industrial environments [182]. We assign the value "+" to the *optional meta-requirement concurrent co-development*.

Architecture views

Evaluation question: Whether and which views are used for representing the RE and design artifacts?

Answer for QuaDRA: Different architectural views can be defined for a software architecture, each of which represents a specific perspective of the software architecture design. Since there is no consensus on the number and nature of the architectural views, it can be hardly defined which kinds of architectural views are required. According to Smolander et al. [222], the most appropriate set of architectural views cannot be objectively specified in general. Based on the prevalent situation and characteristics of the organizations and software projects, the architectural views have to be selected.

We found out that all the six selected methods support the *structural view* of the software architecture and most of them provide additionally the *behavioral view* of the software architecture. Two of the selected methods provide the *deployment view* as well. QuaDRA provides four different views. In addition to the *structural view* and the *behavioral view*, we provide two additional views namely the *context view* and the *requirements view*.

The context view proposed by Rozanski and Woods [204, 245] documents the system context. In our context view, we defined the scope of the software, the scope of the environment, and the relations between the software and its environment. The context view was the first document that we produced. It is illustrated as a context diagram.

According to Clements et al. [78], in order to document the software architecture in an appropriate way, it has to be shown that the architecture satisfies the requirements and no important requirement has been forgotten. To this end, a mapping between the requirements and the architecture can be captured in a separate requirements view. We describe the requirements view by setting up the problem-solution diagram providing the traceability between the quality requirements that shaped the architecture as the main architectural drivers and the quality-specific solutions addressing those requirements in the architecture.

We believe that for software projects developing architectures based on quality requirements, these four views are essential. Nevertheless, we assign the value "o" to the *optional meta-requirement architecture views* as we do not provide support for the *deployment view* or *development view*.

Tool support

Evaluation question: Are there tools to support the method and its artifacts? **Answer for QuaDRA:** A tool can provide support for some time-consuming and error-prone tasks of a method. For the QuaDRA framework, we provided tool support based on the UML4PF tool mainly for modeling the required artifacts. We developed various UML profiles that are integrated in the UML4PF tool. Nevertheless, new features for the tool that support the the interactive creation of the *problem-solution diagram*, the *initial architecture*, and the *quality-driven architecture alternatives* in a semi-automated way might be useful. Another useful feature is the identification and implementation of validation conditions in order to check the consistency of artifacts within each model and between different models. Hence, we assign the value "o" to the *optional meta-requirement tool support* as we do not provide tool support for all the activities of the QuaDRA framework.

12.4.2 Comparison of QuaDRA with the State-of-the-Art Methods

Table 12.3 shows the application of the evaluation framework to QuaDRA using the value assignment above. It also illustrates the application of the evaluation framework to the state-of-the-art methods which we presented in Chapter 3 (see page 97). This way, we present a direct comparison of the existing methods with the QuaDRA framework and show to what extent our developed framework fulfills the meta-requirements.

The dark gray rows show the *essential* meta-requirements, which are *quality requirements, guidance, knowledge reuse,* and *RE and design descriptions.* The light gray rows indicate the *recommended* meta-requirements, which include *traceability, design rationale, trade-off analysis, architecture alternatives,* and *iterative development.* The non-colored rows are the *optional* meta-requirements, which are *concurrent co-development, architecture views,* and *tool support.* In addition, we take into account the *method characteristic user skill* for the comparative evaluation, as the number of new skills to learn by a novice software engineer might have an impact on the application of the method.

Table 12.3: Evaluation comparison of QuaDRA with state-of-the-art methods

Elements	ATRIUM	Marew et al.	Sangwan et al.	Ovaska et al.	Sánchez et al.	Tropos	QuaDRA
User skill	-	+	o	+	o	+	+
Quality requirements	+	+	+	+	+	+	+
Guidance and method structure	+	o	o	-	-	o	+
Knowledge reuse	o	o	+	+	o	o	+
RE and design description	o	-	+	+	+	o	+
Traceability	+	o	+	-	-	o	+
Design rationale	+	-	-	-	-	+	+
Trade-off analysis	-	+	+	+	-	-	+
Architecture alternatives	o	-	-	-	o	o	+
Iterative development	+	+	-	+	-	-	+
Concurrent co-development	+	-	-	-	-	-	+
Architecture views	-	+	-	+	o	o	o
Tool support	+	-	-	+	o	-	o
Architecture evaluation	-	-	-	-	-	o	+

In Chapter 3 (see page 104), we discussed the fulfillment of the meta-requirements by the state-of-the-art methods by category. Regarding the category *essential* meta-requirements that are considered as *must have* meta-requirements, we have seen that none of the methods fulfills all four meta-requirements. *Eliciting and documenting meta-requirements in a structured way (quality requirements in Table 12.3)* is fulfilled by all methods whereas *(Guidance and method structure in Table 12.3)* is not satisfied by most of the methods. One reason for this can be that these methods do not place importance on guiding the user providing a step by step method and detailed guidance as they are designed for experienced software engineers and not for novices. QuaDRA, in contrast to the existing methods, fulfills all the *essential* meta-requirements.

Regarding the category *recommended* meta-requirements, we take from Table 12.3 that none of the state-of-the-art methods deals with creating *architecture alternatives*. Some of the methods take alternatives for architectural patterns into account. They, however, do not create alternatives for the final architecture. *Architecture evaluation* is another *recommended* meta-requirement that is fully satisfied by none of the state-of-the-art methods. This means that these methods do not evaluate to what extent the resulting final software architecture meets the elicited and modeled quality requirements. Similar to the category *essential* meta-requirements, QuaDRA is also for the category *recommended* meta-requirements the only method that fulfills all meta-requirements.

Regarding the category *optional* meta-requirements, two of the existing methods satisfy two of three *optional* meta-requirements. QuaDRA satisfies one *optional* meta-requirement fully and the two others from this category are partially satisfied.

According to this evaluation, we showed that QuaDRA is able to address the identified gaps in Chapter 3 and to remedy the lack of methodological support for systematic development of both phases with respect to quality requirements in a unified process.

12.5 Contributions

In this chapter, we applied our structured evaluation framework to the QuaDRA framework. Our objective was to examine to what extent the derived meta-requirements are fulfilled by our developed method. We aimed at examining to what extent QuaDRA can contribute to bridging the existing gap with regard to the quality-aware development of requirements and software architecture alternatives. Our contributions can be captured as follows:

- Evaluation of QuaDRA by applying the developed framework. The evaluation shows that QuaDRA fulfills all the *essential* and *recommended* meta-requirements.
- Comparative evaluation of QuaDRA with the state-of-the-art methods. It demonstrates that QuaDRA exhibits a substantial progress over the state-of-the-art methods.
- Overcoming the lack of systematic and methodological guidelines for development of requirements and software architecture with respect to quality requirements in a unified process.

Chapter 13
Extending Problem-Oriented Requirements Engineering for SPL

Abstract In the QuaDRA framework, we have provided support for developing a single system. In this chapter, we show how to enhance the problem-oriented requirements engineering for supporting a product line development. We extend the problem frames approach with a notation for modeling variability by providing a UML profile. Furthermore, we propose the structured PREVISE method, which conducts requirements engineering in software product lines taking into account quality requirements. Our method covers domain engineering as well as application engineering.

13.1 Introduction

In the QuaDRA framework, we developed a method for deriving design alternatives from quality requirements (Chapters 4 - 11). We investigated how different user preferences and needs regarding security and performance can influence the design of software. In this chapter, we perform a first effort for extending the QuaDRA framework, which supports a single-system development to a product-line development addressing quality requirements.

Software product line engineering (SPLE) represents a paradigm to develop software applications which are tailored to individual customer's needs [194]. The benefits of applying SPLE are the reduction of development cost, enhancement of productivity, reduction of time to market, enhancement of quality, and reduction of maintenance of a software [194].

Software product lines (SPL) involve a set of common features as well as a set of variable ones. The first challenge we are facing is how to utilize and adjust conventional requirements engineering techniques for modeling and engineering product families. Modeling and managing variability is the central concept in SPLE. Beyond the variability which is caused by variable requirements, there exist further variabilities, which might emerge because of changes in the environment in which the software will be located. Such kind of variability should be taken into consideration when developing SPL.

In this chapter, we propose the PREVISE (**PR**obl**E**m-oriented **V**ar**I**ability Re-quirement**S** **E**ngineering) method, which conducts requirements engineering in software product lines considering quality requirements. Our method is composed of four phases. It covers domain engineering (Phases 1 and 2) as well as application engineering (Phases 3 and 4). While Phase 1 is concerned with exploring the variability caused due to entities in the environment of the software, Phase 2 identifies the variability in functional and quality requirements. The configuration for a concrete product is selected in Phase 3. Subsequently, deriving a requirement model for a concrete product is achieved in Phase 4.

The PREVISE method extends Phase 1 of the QuaDRA framework for developing SPL. The benefit of our proposed method is manifold.

- First, it elicits variability and adds it stepwise to the model. One can start from a description of a system-to-be containing no variability. Hence, we do not rely on (complete) knowledge about the variability of a system-to-be.
- Second, it considers all kinds of sources for variability in a structured way. It identifies the variability, which is caused by entities in the environment, the communication shared between the entities and the system-to-be, and variability due to varying behavior of the system-to-be.
- Third, the information regarding variability, environment, functional requirements, and quality requirements are kept in a single model, which facilitates consistency checking, traceability, and tool support. For modeling we rely on UML, which is widely adopted and provides diagrams for all software engineering phases.
- Fourth, our method enables the generation of feature diagrams [140] and Orthogonal Variability Modeling (OVM) [194] diagrams from the model, which enables documentation and supports the analysis of the variability (see Section 2.5 for more information regarding feature modeling and OVM).

This chapter is based on our work presented in [10]. The PREVISE method and the UML profile for variability modeling have been developed jointly with our colleague Stephan Faßbender. The application of the method to the example has been done by Stephan Faßbender. We had valuable and useful discussions with our colleague Martin Filipczyk regarding variability modeling. Michael Goedicke, Maritta Heisel, and Marco Konersmann provided valuable feedback on this work.

The chapter is structured as follows. An alarm system as a running example is introduced in Section 13.2. Section 13.3 describes how we extend problem frames with a notation for variability. We introduce the PREVISE method in Section 13.4. Section 13.5 presents related work. Section 13.6 concludes this chapter, and summarizes the contribution.

13.2 Alarm System Example

As our running example, we have chosen an alarm system. We will not elaborate on a full alarm system, but a very small and simple one, blanking many functionalities that such a system normally embodies. An initial problem description is given as follows:

The *alarm system* is installed within a defined perimeter, such as a building. In this building alarm *buttons* and *signal horns* are installed. Whenever a person in the building witnesses a critical situation such as a fire, he / she shall warn others. A *witness* can *alert* others in the building, using the alarm buttons. The *alarm is given* using the signal horn. The alarm shall be given within one second.

Additionally, every *alarm raised* is forwarded to an *alarm central*. The notification is repeated every 30 seconds. The *broadcast* to the alarm central is optional as not every owner of the alarm system needs or can afford using such an alarm central. When a communication to an alarm central is established, no third party shall be able to tamper with the communication. From this small scenario, we can derive two functional requirements (*R*), one performance requirement (*PR*) and one security requirement (*SR*):

R1   A witness can alert others in a building using the alarm button. The alarm is given using the signal horn.
R2   Every alarm raised is forwarded to an alarm central. The notification is repeated every 30 seconds.
PR1   The alarm shall be given within one second.
SR1   When a communication to an alarm central is established, no third party shall be able to tamper with the communication.

13.3 UML4PF Extension for Modeling Variability

We extend the problem frames notation by introducing new elements for modeling variability in software product lines. We base our extension on the OVM terms (see Section 2.5 for detailed information). Our extension is a UML profile relying on the UML4PF profile (see Section 2.3.1 for detailed information). The profile extension allows the creation of new types of diagrams and statements. Figure 13.1 shows the stereotypes of the problem frames profile for variability.

New types of diagrams

The first new kind of *UML4PF diagrams* is the *variability diagram*. It is expressed by the stereotype ≪VariabilityDiagram≫. A variability diagram captures the actual variation points.

The variability can stem from requirements, domains, and phenomena. Therefore, we define *requirement variability diagram* (expressed by the stereotype ≪RequirementVariabilityDiagram≫), *domain variability diagram* (expressed by the stereotype ≪DoaminVeriabilityDiagram≫), and *phenomenon variability diagram* (expressed by the stereotype ≪PhenomenonVariabilityDiagram≫). One special variability diagram is the *constraint variability diagram* (expressed by the stereotype ≪ConstraintVariabilityDiagram≫) which captures constraints to variability.

We define two new sub-types for the *context diagram*, namely a *variability context diagram* (expressed by the stereotype ≪VariabilityContextDiagram≫) and a *product context diagram* (expressed by the stereotype ≪ProductContext-Diagram≫). A *variability context diagram* describes the context containing the variability. In contrast, a *product context diagram* describes the context regarding a particular product, which is defined by a *configuration*.

The same distinction is made for *problem diagrams*. For problem diagrams we also have *variability problem diagrams* and *product problem diagrams*. The final new type of diagrams is the *configuration diagram* which describes a particular configuration for a product.

New types of statements

To the *statement*, we introduce three new types, namely *variant* (expressed by the stereotype ≪Variant≫), *variation visibility* (expressed by the stereotype ≪VariationVisibility≫), and *variation point* (expressed by the stereotype ≪VariationPoint≫). One can distinguish between *mandatory variation point* (≪MandatoryVP≫) and *optional variation point* (≪OptionalVP≫). A variation point can have

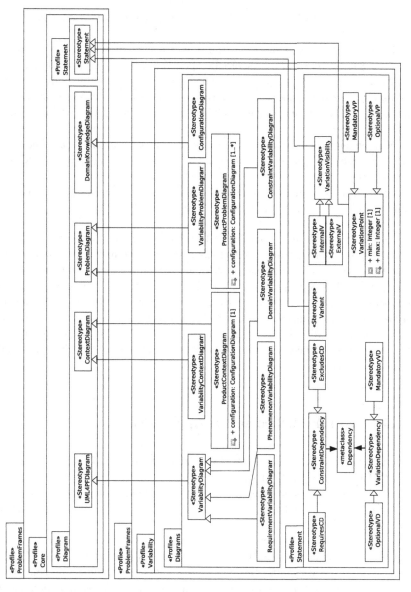

Fig. 13.1: UML4PF Extension for Variability

two different kinds of *variation visibility*, namely the *external* (≪ExternalV≫) and *internal* (≪InternalV≫) visibility.

Related to variation points are *variants*, which can represent an *optional variation* or a *mandatory variation*. A variation point indicates by its *min* and *max* properties how many of the variants have to be chosen for the variation point. The type of variation relation is indicated by a *variation dependency* (≪VariationDependency≫) which can be optional (≪OptionalVD≫) or mandatory (≪MandatoryVD≫).

Variants and variation points can be related by a *constraint dependency*. The relation can be an *excludes* (≪ExcludesCD≫) or a *requires* (≪RequiresCD≫) dependency.

Table 13.1 shows the list of defined stereotypes and their description. The detailed usage of the stereotypes will be explained in Section 13.4.

The UML profile for variability is to a large extent similar to the UML4PF extension for mapping requirements to their solution alternatives proposed in Section 8.5.1 (see page 278) as both profiles are based on the variability notion provided in OVM. It is possible to merge both profiles into one profile. However, we deliberately keep the two profiles separate, so they can be applied independently from each other. In this way, one can only use the QuaDRA framework with its corresponding UML profiles. In case one wants to use the QuaDRA extension for variability as well, the UML4PF extension for variability has to be bound in addition.

13.4 PREVISE Method and its Application

In this section, we present the PREVISE (**PR**obl**Em**-oriented Va**rI**ability Require-ment**S** Engineering) method which defines the activities in Phase 1 of the domain and the application engineering, namely the requirements engineering. We describe how we extend our problem-oriented requirements engineering method described in Chapter 4 for SPL.

Figure 13.2 shows an overview of the PREVISE method for domain engineering. Domain engineering consists of the two phases *Context Variability Elicitation* and *Problem Variability Decomposition*. Application engineering consists of the two phases *Configuration Engineering* and *Deriving a Product Requirements Model*. In the following, we briefly describe the phases of the PREVISE method:

Phase Context Variability Elicitation: This phase comprises four steps. In this phase, we analyze the context of the software to be built and identify the vari-

Table 13.1: Stereotypes defined for UML4PF extension for variability modeling

Stereotype	Applies to	Description
≪VariabilityDiagram≫	Package	It captures the actual variation points.
≪RequirementVariabilityDiagram≫	Package	It captures variability arising from requirements.
≪PhenomenonVariabilityDiagram≫	Package	It captures variability arising from phenomena.
≪DomainVariabilityDiagram≫	Package	It captures variability arising from domains.
≪ConstraintVariabilityDiagram≫	Package	It captures constraints to variability.
≪VariabilityContextDiagram≫	Package	It represents the context containing variability.
≪ProductContextDiagram≫	Package	It represents the context regarding a particular product, which is defined by a *configuration*. This context diagram does not contain variability any more.
≪VariabilityProblemDiagram≫	Package	It represents a problem diagram containing variability.
≪ProductProblemDiagram≫	Package	It represents a problem diagram regarding a particular product, which is defined by a *configuration*. This problem diagram does not contain variability any more.
≪ConfigurationDiagram≫	Package	It describes a particular configuration for a product.
≪Variant≫	Class	It represents a variation.
≪VariationVisibility≫	Class	It represents the visibility of a variation.
≪InternalV≫	Class	It is visible only to the developers.
≪ExternalV≫	Class	It is visible to every stakeholder.
≪VariationPoint≫	Class	It represents a *Statement*, where the product might contain variability.
≪MandatoryVP≫	Class	It represents a variation point that should be selected for every product.
≪OptionalVP≫	Class	It represents a variation point that could be selected for a product.
≪ConstraintDependency≫	Dependency	It represents a dependency between two variants (class with stereotype ≪Variant≫)
≪ExcludesCD≫	Dependency	It represents a dependency from a source variant (class with stereotype ≪Variant≫) to a target variant (class with stereotype ≪Variant≫) and prevents selecting the target variant if the source variant has been selected.
≪RequiresCD≫	Dependency	It represents a dependency from a source variant (class with stereotype ≪Variant≫) to a target variant (class with stereotype ≪Variant≫) and requires the target variant to be selected if the source variant has been selected.
≪VariationDependency≫	Dependency	It represents a dependency providing a link from a variation point (class with stereotype ≪VariationPoint≫)) to its variants (class with stereotype ≪Variant≫).
≪MandatoryVD≫	Dependency	It represents that the variant must be selected for a product.
≪OptionalVD≫	Dependency	It represents that the variant may be selected for a product.

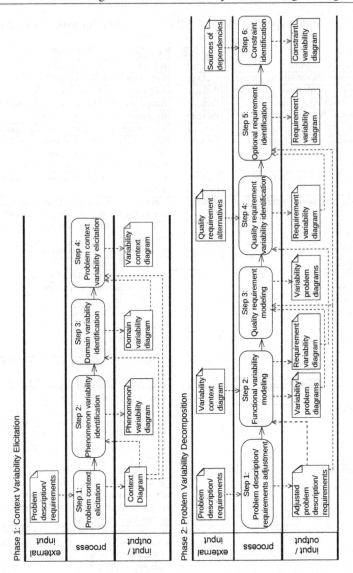

Fig. 13.2: Overview of the PREVISE method for domain engineering

ability originating from the context. In each step we create different types of diagrams that we require later on in the *application engineering*. *Context diagram, phenomenon variability diagram, domain variability diagram,* and *variability context diagram* are the outputs of Steps 1 to 4. This phase is the counterpart to Step 1 (*problem context elicitation*) of Phase 1 for developing single systems introduced in Chapter 4 (see Section 4.3 on page 114).

Phase Problem Variability Decomposition: This phase comprises six steps. In this phase, the overall problem is decomposed into smaller subproblems according to the requirements of the system-to-be. The quality and functional requirements are adjusted in a way that they reflect the variability of the problem. *Variability problem diagram, requirement variability diagram,* and *constraint variability diagram* are the types of diagrams that we produce in this phase. This phase is the counterpart to Steps 2 and 3 (*functional requirements modeling* and *quality requirements modeling*) of Phase 1 for developing single systems introduced in Chapter 4 (see Section 4.3 on page 116 and Section 4.3 on page 118).

Phase Configuration Engineering: This phase comprises four steps. In this phase the configuration for the concrete product is selected. *Configuration diagram* is the output of this phase. It is possible to define more than one configuration. To this end, this phase has to be repeated.

Phase Deriving a Product Requirements Model: This phase comprises three steps. In this phase, the concrete product requirements model is derived based on the configuration produced in the previous phase. For each configuration, one can derive product requirement models.

In the following, we describe each phase and its corresponding steps in detail. After the description of each step, we directly show its application to the example *alarm system*. In Section 13.4.1, we describe the phases of domain engineering and the subsequent steps, in which we create a requirement model for the SPL. Then, we describe the phases of application engineering, in which we derive a concrete SPL product from the SPL requirement model in Section 13.4.2.

13.4.1 Product Line Requirement Model Creation

This section describes the elicitation and modeling of variability contained in the context of the problem as well as the variability contained in the requirements. By doing this, we obtain requirement models for SPL.

Phase 1 - Context Variability Elicitation

In this phase, the context of the system-to-be is analyzed, and variation points in the environment of the machine are identified.

Step 1 - Problem context elicitation

The input of this step is the *problem description/ requirements*. For our method, it is not necessary to have a problem description which already includes variability. Instead, one can start by giving a problem description for one possible product. The variability is identified and added in later steps. Hence, in Step 1 we derive a *context diagram* from the problem description as described in Chapter 4 (see Section 4.3 on page 114).

Application of Step 1 - Problem context elicitation

The context diagram for our example is shown in Fig. 13.3. A biddable domain *Witness* alerts others in the building (*W!alert*) using the causal domain *Button* which requests the machine *AlarmSystem* for raising an alarm (*B!raiseAlarm*). The machine *AlarmSystem* produces an alarm using the causal domain *SignalHorn* (*AS!giveAlarm*). In addition, the machine can broadcast the alarm to the causal domain *AlarmCentral* (*AS!broadcastAlarm*).

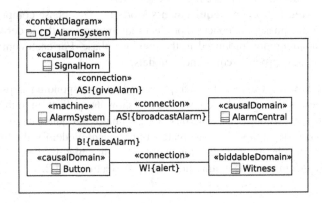

Fig. 13.3: Context diagram for the Alarm System

Step 2 - Phenomenon variability identification

In this step, we analyze the phenomena of the context diagram in order to identify variability in phenomena. Hence, the *context diagram* serves as input for this step. By investigating the phenomena we are faced with two issues. The first issue is regrading the generic phenomena. One case is that the phenomenon at hand is a generic one which has more than one possible concrete instance. The other case is that the phenomenon is a specific one, but there may be other alternatives for the phenomenon at hand. If one of these two cases holds, the generic phenomenon has to be considered as a variation point. The concrete phenomena have to be modeled as variants. Additionally, one has to decide if a variant or a variation point is optional or not.

The second issue is when a phenomenon is shared using a dedicated connection domain. In this case, this connection domain has to be added to the context diagram.

For modeling the variability in phenomena, we make use of the *phenomenon variability diagram* (stereotype ≪PhenomenonVariabilityDiagram≫). A variation point has to be modeled either as *mandatory* (stereotype ≪MandatoryVP≫) or as *optional* (stereotype ≪OptionalVP≫). A variant is expressed by the stereotype ≪Variant≫.

Application of Step 2 - Phenomenon variability identification

For our example, the phenomenon *alert* turns out to be a generic phenomenon, which has two variants. First, one can *push* something to give the alert. Second, one can *shout* to give an alarm, which is a more advanced option for an alarm system. Figure 13.4 shows the resulting *phenomenon variability diagram* named *PVD_Alert*:

Phenomenon alert   is a *mandatory* variation point with two *optional* variants (see *max* in Fig. 13.4) from which at least one (see *min* in Fig. 13.4) has to be chosen.

Phenomenon pushToAlert   is a variant phenomenon. There is an optional variation dependency (stereotype ≪OptionalVD≫) connecting the variation point *alert* to the variant *pushToAlert*.

Phenomenon shoutToAlert   is a variant phenomenon. There is an optional variation dependency (stereotype ≪OptionalVD≫) connecting the variation point *alert* to the variant *shoutToAlert*.

Additionally, we find three connection domains. The *SignalHorn* and the *Button* are connected to the machine via *Wires*. The *AlarmCentral* is connected via the *Internet*. The connection domains have to be modeled in the context diagram. Note that we do not show the refined context diagram containing the connection domains here.

Step 3 - Domain variability identification

Similar to the phenomena, the variability of domains in the context diagram has to be investigated. Hence, the *context diagram* is the input for this step. We have

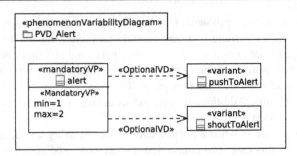

Fig. 13.4: Phenomenon Variability Diagram for alert

to check for variation points and variants. Note that it can occur that a variant is a variation point since it can be further refined to variants.

For modeling the variability in domains, we make use of the *domain variability diagram* (stereotype ≪DomainVariabilityDiagram≫). Variation points and variants have to be modeled as described before.

Application of Step 3 - Domain variability identification
One example for domain variability is shown in Fig. 13.5. The starting domain for this variability is the causal domain *Wire*. It connects the causal domain *Button* with the machine. The domain *Wire* is abstracted to the causal domain *RaiserConnection*, which is a mandatory variation point. The resulting *domain variability diagram* is shown in Fig. 13.5 named *DVD_RaiserConnection*:

Domain RaiserConnection   is a *mandatory* variation point with two *optional* variants (see *max* in Fig. 13.5) from which at least one (see *min* in Fig. 13.5) has to be chosen.

Domain DirectAccess   is a variant domain. There is a mandatory variation dependency (stereotype ≪MandatoryVD≫) connecting the variation point *RaiserConnection* to the variant *DirectAccess*.

Domain IndirectAccess   is a variant domain. There is an optional variation dependency (stereotype ≪OptionalVD≫) connecting the variation point *RaiserConnection* to the variant *IndirectAccess*.

Variants for the domain *DirectAccess* are shown in Fig. 13.6:

Domain DirectAccess   is a *mandatory* variation point with two *optional* variants from which exactly one has to be chosen (see *min* and *max* in Fig. 13.6).

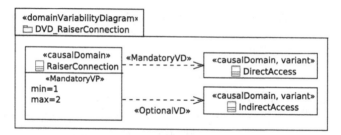

Fig. 13.5: Domain Variability Diagram for the domain *RaiserConnection*

Domain Wire is a variant domain. There is an optional variation dependency (stereotype ≪OptionalVD≫) connecting the variation point *DirectAccess* to the variant *Wire*.

Domain Wireless is a variant domain. There is an optional variation dependency (stereotype ≪OptionalVD≫) connecting the variation point *DirectAccess* to the variant *Wire*.

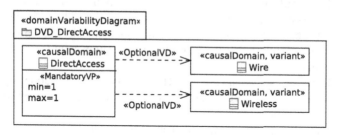

Fig. 13.6: Domain Variability Diagram for the domain *DirectAccess*

The causal domain *Button* is abstracted to the causal domain *Raiser*. Variants for the domain *Raiser* are shown in Fig. 13.7:

Domain Raiser is a *mandatory* variation point with two *optional* variants from which at least one has to be chosen (see *Min* and *max* in Fig. 13.7).

Domain MobileRaiser is a variant domain. There is an optional variation dependency (stereotype ≪OptionalVD≫) connecting the variation point *Raiser* to the variant *MobileRaiser*.

Domain InstalledRaiser is a variant domain. There is an optional variation dependency (stereotype ≪OptionalVD≫) connecting the variation point *Raiser* to the variant *InstalledRaiser*.

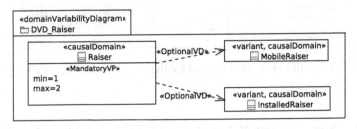

Fig. 13.7: Domain Variability Diagram for the domain *Raiser*

The domain *InstalledRaiser* is a variation point as well. Its variants are shown in Fig. 13.8:

Domain InstalledRaiser is an *optional* variation point with three *optional* variants from which at least one has to be chosen (see *min* and *max* in Fig. 13.8).

Domain Switch is a variant domain. There is an optional variation dependency (stereotype ≪OptionalVD≫) connecting the variation point *InstalledRaiser* to the variant *Switch*.

Domain Button is a variant domain. There is an optional variation dependency (stereotype ≪OptionalVD≫) connecting the variation point *InstalledRaiser* to the variant *Button*.

Domain VoiceSensor is a variant domain. There is an optional variation dependency (stereotype ≪OptionalVD≫) connecting the variation point *VoiceSensor* to the variant *Button*.

The causal domain *SignalHorn* is abstracted to the causal domain *Notifier*. The domain *Notifier* is a variation point as well. Its variants are shown in Fig. 13.9:

Domain Notifier is a *mandatory* variation point with one *optional* variant and one *mandatory* variant from which at least the *mandatory* variant has to be chosen (see *min* and *max* in Fig. 13.9).

Domain SignalHorn is a variant domain. There is a mandatory variation dependency (stereotype ≪MandatoryVD≫) connecting the variation point *Notifier* to the variant *SignalHorn*.

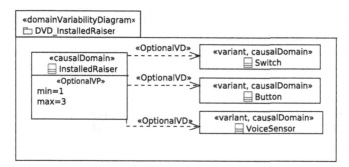

Fig. 13.8: Domain Variability Diagram for the domain *InstalledRaiser*

Domain Display   is a variant domain. There is an optional variation dependency (stereotype ≪OptionalVD≫) connecting the variation point *Notifier* to the variant *Display*.

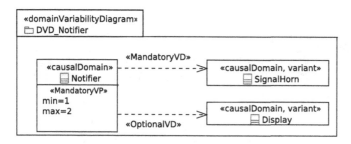

Fig. 13.9: Domain Variability Diagram for the domain *Notifier*

Step 4 - Problem context variability elicitation
In this step, we capture the variability in the context diagram which has to be modeled as *variability context diagram*. The variability context diagram is a specialization of the context diagram. It represents a context diagram for the SPL. The variability context diagram enables us not only to elicit all domains related to the problem to be solved, but also to capture which domains represent variability and which ones commonality.

The structure of the variability context diagram is similar to the context diagram from Step 1. It differs from the context diagram in the way that we represent variation points for the problem domains and phenomena which involve variability. The *context diagram* and the *domain variability diagrams* are used as input to generate the *variability context diagram*. It is possible to generate the variability context diagram automatically using the context diagram and the domain variability diagrams.

For modeling the variability context diagram (stereotype ≪VariabilityContext-Diagram≫), we use the domain stereotypes as usually for a context diagram. In addition, we make use of the stereotypes ≪MandatoryVP≫ and ≪OptionalVP≫ to illustrate the variation points.

Application of Step 4 - Problem context variability elicitation
Figure 13.10 illustrates the resulting variability context diagram for our example. The domains *AlarmSystem,Witness*, and *AlarmCentral* are directly taken from the context diagram as they are not variable. The domain *SignalHorn* is replaced by the variation point *Notifier*. The domain *Button* is replaced by the variation point *Raiser*. Additionally, the connection domains and their abstract variation points *RaiserConnection, NotifierConnection*, and *AlarmCentralConnection* are added to the variability context diagram. Table 13.2 shows an overview of the domains in the context diagram and the variability context diagram.

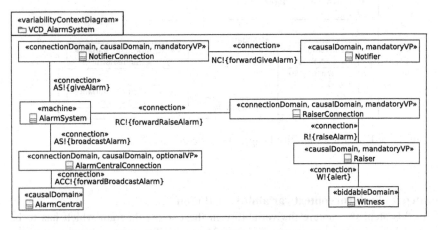

Fig. 13.10: Variability Context Diagram for the Alarm System

Table 13.2: Domains in the context diagram and variability context diagram

Domain in context diagram	Domain in context variability diagram
AlarmSystem	AlarmSystem
Witness	Witness
AlarmCentral	AlarmCentral
SignalHorn	Notifier
Button	Raiser
-	NotifierConnection
-	RaiserConnection
-	AlarmCentralConnection

13.4.1.1 Phase 2 - Problem Variability Decomposition

In this phase, the overall problem is decomposed into smaller subproblems according to the requirements of the system-to-be. The quality requirements and functional requirements are adjusted in a way that they reflect the variability of the problem.

Step 1 - Problem description/ requirements adjustment
In this step, the textual requirements of the machine are derived from the problem description. As the initial problem description does not contain the variability identified in Phase 1, the textual description of the requirements has to be adjusted.

Application of Step 1 - Problem description/ requirements adjustment
In Section 13.2, we already derived the textual requirements from the initial problem description. In this step, the wording has to be adjusted to the variability context diagram. For example, requirement *R1* changes to "*A witness can* [alert] *others in a building using* [raisers]. *The alarm is given using* [notifiers]."

Step 2 - Functional variability modeling
This step is concerned with decomposing the overall problem into subproblems, which accommodate variability. As input, we take the *adjusted problem description / requirements* and the *variability context diagram* into account. Each functional requirement has to be modeled as a problem diagram. Whenever the problem diagram contains at least one variation point, the requirement is variable, too. Such diagram is a specialization of a *problem diagram*. It is called *variability problem diagram*.

But variability in a requirement cannot only stem from the phenomena or domains which are variable. Sometimes requirements contain further variation points, which do not show up in the structure of a problem diagram. One reason might be a variability in behavior, for example in the sequence of phenomena.

Hence, each requirement has to be checked for such variations not visible in the problem diagrams. Such variabilities are represented by a *requirement variability diagram* which represents the requirement as variation point and its alternatives as variants.

Application of Step 2 - Functional variability modeling

For our example, the functional requirement *R2* contains further variability. The repetition of the alarm notification is optional. The according *requirement variability diagram* is shown in Fig. 13.11. Note that the requirement *R2.1* contains further variability regarding the time span between the repetitions. Figure 13.12 shows the *variability problem diagram* for the requirement *R2*.

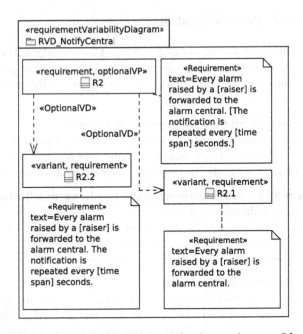

Fig. 13.11: Requirement Variability Diagram for the requirement *R2*

Functional requirement *R1* contains no variability, as it is not a variation point. Figure 13.13 shows the *variability problem diagram* for the requirement *R1*.

Step 3 - Quality requirement modeling

This step is concerned with annotating quality requirements which complement

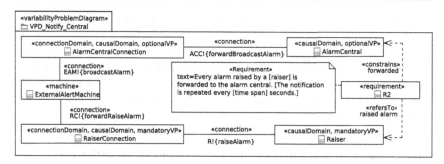

Fig. 13.12: Variability Problem Diagram for the requirement *R2*

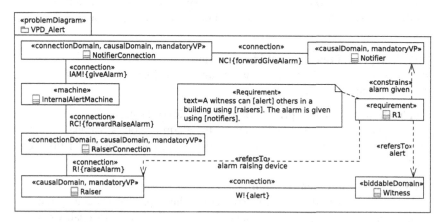

Fig. 13.13: Variability Problem Diagram for the requirement *R1*

functional requirements. In contrast to functional requirements, quality require-ments are not modeled as problem diagrams on their own. Instead, they augment existing functional requirements. Therefore, as input we take *variability problem diagrams* in addition to the *adjusted problem description/ requirements* into ac-count. This step is identical to Step 3 of Phase 1 introduced in Chapter 4 (see Section 4.3 on page 118).

Step 4 - Quality requirement variability identification

This step is concerned with variability in quality requirements. There might be different reasons for causing such a variability. Making trade-offs among quality requirements of different types might be one reason. Such requirements are subject to interactions. Interactions among quality requirements can be detected by applying the method proposed in Phase 4 in Chapter 7 (see Section 7.3 on page 210). To resolve interactions, we generate requirement alternatives by relaxing the original requirement. The generated quality requirement alternatives provide variants for the original requirement. The *requirement variability diagrams* have to be updated according to the results of the method proposed in Phase 4. Sometimes, quality requirements introduce new domains, e.g., an attacker for security, and new phenomena. Thus, one has to check these domains and phenomena for variability, too.

Application of Step 4 - Quality requirement variability identification
For our example, we have the security requirement *SR1*. It complements the functional requirement *R2*. A biddable domain representing an *Attacker* has to be added. The domain *Attacker* represents a variation point as there can be different kinds of attackers distinguished by their abilities (see Chapter 7 for more information).

Step 5 - Optional requirement identification
In this step, we identify the requirements that are optional. They have to be modeled as optional variation point.

Application of Step 5 - Optional requirement identification
For the alarm system, the notification of the alarm central is optional, which is already reflected in Fig. 13.11, as *R2* is annotated as an optional variation point (*optionalVP*).

Step 6 - Constraint identification
This step is concerned with identifying constraint dependencies among requirements, phenomena, and domain variants. Dependencies caused by quality requirements interactions are identified in the method proposed in Phase 4 in Chapter 7 (see Section 7.3 on page 210). For functional requirements, one can use the RIT (Requirements Interaction Tables) as proposed in in Phase 4 in Chapter 7 (see Section 7.2 on page 198). Other kinds of dependencies have to be checked manually.

We distinguish between two types of dependencies, namely *requires* (stereotype ≪RequiresCD≫) in which one variant or variation point requires another variant or variation point for a valid configuration, and *excludes* (stereotype ≪ExcludesCD≫) in which one variant or variation point is not allowed together with another variant or variation point in a valid configuration. Variability in constraints is modeled by the *constraint variability diagram*.

Application of Step 6 - Constraint identification
In our example, the phenomenon *shoutToAlert* requires a *Voice Sensor*. The according *constraint variability diagram* is shown in Fig. 13.14.

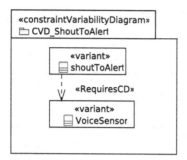

Fig. 13.14: Constraint Variability Diagram for alert to shout

13.4.2 Deriving a Concrete Product Requirement Model

To derive requirements for a concrete SPL product, we make use of the artifacts generated in domain engineering. The aim of the application engineering is to get a coherent subset of requirements for a particular product from the overall set of requirements containing variability. Figure 13.15 shows an overview of the PRE-VISE method for application engineering. The application engineering is divided into two phases, which are explained in the following.

13.4.2.1 Phase 3 - Configuration engineering

In this phase, the configuration for the concrete product is selected. The following steps can be supported by a feature diagram and OVM diagrams (see Section 2.5 on page 42) derived from the domain requirements model. Note that this phase can be repeated to define more than one configuration.

Step 1 - Requirements selection:
The first step towards a configuration is to select the desired requirements among all optional requirements. This selection may reduce the phenomena and domains to select from in the next steps. The reason is that phenomena and domains which are only bound to optional requirements that are not selected can be left out. For all requirements which represent an optional variation point, one has to decide whether to include the requirement or not. Next, one has to select a variant for all requirements which represent a variation point and which are included in the desired set of requirements. The desired set contains the selected optional and

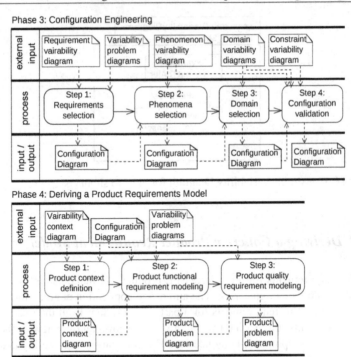

Fig. 13.15: Overview of the PREVISE method for domain engineering

all mandatory requirements. The selected variants have to be documented in a *configuration diagram* (stereotype ≪ConfigurationDiagram≫).

Application of Step 1 - Requirements selection:

For our alarm system product, we decide to leave out the notification of the alarm central. Hence, we also do not have to select any requirement variant, as *R1*, which is the only requirement in our desired set, is no variation point. Consequently, the *configuration diagram* contains no requirement variant. Figure 13.16 shows the (complete) configuration diagram for our example.

Step 2 - Phenomena selection:

The second step is to select the variants for all phenomena that are variation points. To this end, we make use of the *phenomenon variability diagram*. The reason for going first for the phenomena is that phenomena are the starting point of the interaction of end users with the system-to-be. Thus, we have the end user in focus.

Additionally, the selected phenomena often constrain the set of domains to be chosen from. In many cases, specific phenomena exclude or require specific domains.

Application of Step 2 - Phenomena selection:
From the *phenomenon variability diagram* shown in Fig. 13.4, we select the phenomenon *pushToAlert*, which is a variant of the phenomenon *alert*. The basic product of our alarm system will only support the alarm raising by pressing a raiser. Figure 13.16 shows the (complete) configuration diagram for our alarm system product.

Step 3 - Domain selection:
In this step, one has to select for all domain variation points the according desired variants. To this end, we make use of *domain variability diagrams*.

Application of Step 3 - Domain selection:
For the domain *Notifier*, we select the variants *Display* and *SignalHorn* (see Fig. 13.9). For the raiser, we select the *Switch* (see Fig. 13.8). Both are connected via wire to the alarm system (see Fig. 13.6). The selected domains are shown in the configuration diagram in Fig. 13.16.

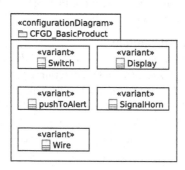

Fig. 13.16: Configuration Diagram for Basic Product

Step 4 - Configuration validation:
Last, we have to check if the constraints defined in the *constraint variability diagrams* are all satisfied. Additionally, we have to check whether the variation dependencies given by the variation diagrams *domain variability diagrams* and *phenomenon variability diagram* and the *min / max* constraints of the variation points are satisfied.

Application of Step 4 - Configuration validation:
For our case, the configuration is valid. For example, the phenomenon *alert* requires at least one variant as shown in Fig. 13.4. We selected the variant *pushToAlert*.

The domain *RaiserConnection* requires at least one variant to be selected (see Fig. 13.5). We see that the *DirectAccess* is mandatory. For the *DirectAccess*, we have to select exactly one variant which is the domain *Wire* in our case (see Fig. 13.6).

The domain *Raiser* demands at least one variant to be selected (see Fig. 13.7). We selected the causal domain *InstalledRaiser*, from which at least one variant has to be selected (see Fig. 13.8). We selected the causal domain *Switch*.

The domain *Notifier* requires at least one variant and two variants maximum. We selected the two variants *SignalHorn* and *Display* (see Fig. 13.9).

13.4.2.2 Phase 4 - Deriving a Product Requirements Model

In this phase, the concrete product requirements model is derived based on a given configuration. Note that one can define more than one configuration at a time and derive product requirement models for them.

Step 1 - Product context definition:
This step is concerned with deriving a *product context diagram* for a concrete product. A *product context diagram* is a context diagram which is tailored to a concrete product. To derive a *product context diagram*, we make use of a *configuration diagram* that defines which requirement variants have to be achieved by the concrete product. Then, we derive the product context diagram from the *variability context diagram*, replacing all variation points by the variants defined by the configuration. Variation points which are not addressed by a variant in the configuration are removed.

Application of Step 1 - Product context definition:
In our case, we combine the *variability context diagram* shown in Fig. 13.10 with the configuration given in Fig. 13.16. The resulting *product context diagram* is shown in Fig. 13.17. The domain *Witness* is no variation point. Therefore, it remains unchanged. For the variation points *NotifierConnection* and *RaiserConnection* we selected the variant *Wire*. For the variation point *Notifier* we selected the variants *SignalHorn* and *Display*. The variant *Switch* has been selected for the variation point *Raiser*. The phenomenon variant *pushToAlert* between the domains *Witness* and *Switch* in the *product context diagram* has been selected for the phe-

nomenon variation point *alert* between the domains *Witness* and *Raiser* in the *variability context diagram*.

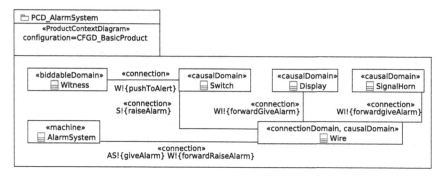

Fig. 13.17: Product Context Diagram for the Alarm System

Step 2 - Product functional requirement modeling:
In this step, we derive *product problem diagrams* for a concrete product. By means of the configuration we know which functional requirements have to be involved in the requirement models for the concrete SPL product. We use the *variability problem diagrams* for deriving the *product problem diagrams*. One additional step is the textual adjustment of the requirements.

Application of Step 2 - Product functional requirement modeling:
We only have one requirement for our basic product configuration. The adjusted text for the requirement *R1* states that *"A witness can push to alert others in a building using a switch. The alarm is given using signal horns and displays."* The according *product problem diagram* is shown in Fig. 13.18.

Step 3 - Product quality requirement modeling:
For the product quality requirement modeling one has to perform the same activities as given for Step 2.

13.5 Related Work

In this section, we report on methods which connect problem frames and variability. They combine problem frames as an early requirements analysis approach with methods or notations for modeling variability to develop product families.

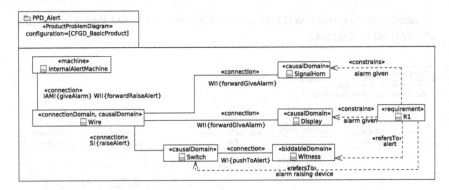

Fig. 13.18: Product Problem Diagram for Alert

Zuo et al. [257] introduce an extension of the problem frames notation that provides support for product line engineering. The extension for problem frames only supports variability in requirements and machines. In contrast to the PRE-VISE method, the authors do not consider the variability, which can be caused by domains and phenomena. Furthermore, the authors provide only a notation for domain engineering. They do not propose a method for conducting domain engineering. Besides, this work does not take application engineering into consideration. That is, there is no methodical support provided on how to derive a product from the SPL.

Ali et al. [28] propose a vision for dealing with variability in requirements caused by the environment. The authors propose an idea for a framework, which relates the three requirements engineering methods goal models, feature diagrams, and problem frames to the environmental context in order to use context information for product derivation. Similar to Phase 1 of our method, namely *context variability elicitation*, this approach proposes to consider the context dimension as it influences the variability at the system level. In contrast, it does not pay attention to the variability which might be caused by the requirements. It relies on existing knowledge about variability. Moreover, it does not introduce any systematic method to conduct SPLE with problem frames.

Variability, which emerges due to changes in the environment (contextual variability), is discussed by Salifu et al. [206]. The authors first set up problem diagrams and then identify a set of variables representing the contextual variations. Using the contextual variables, variant problem diagrams are derived. Contextual variability is taken into account in Phase 1 of our method as well. In their work, the authors provide no systematic approach on how to identify contextual variations in the environment. In contrast, we set up context diagrams and identify contextual variations systematically by identifying variable phenomena and domains involving in the context diagram. Moreover, application engineering is not considered in this work.

An approach for combining SPLE and the problem frames concept is proposed by Dao et al. [86]. The starting point is a feature model, which is mapped to a problem frames model to elicit functional requirements and domain assumptions. To take quality requirements into account, a goal model is adopted. In contrast to our method, which addresses quality requirements by augmenting the existing functional problem diagrams, this approach uses goal models. The three different notations feature models, problem frames, and goal models are used, which might cause consistency problems among different models. In contrast, we provide one single model, which enables consistency checking and tool support.

Similar to our method, the approach proposed by Classen et al. [74] considers variability in requirements and phenomena. However, the authors do not treat variability in domains. Moreover, they do not consider the context diagram and the variability reflected in it due to the variability in domains. Furthermore, quality requirements are not considered.

13.6 Contributions

In this chapter, we have presented an extension of the problem frames notation to enable variability modeling. The notation is available as UML profile in the UML4PF tool suite. The notation extension for variability is accompanied by a method called PREVISE for discovering variability, modeling variability, and deriving products from variability models. The contributions of this work are as follows:

- An OVM-based notation for adding variability to requirements, which are expressed in the problem frames notation (see Section 13.3).
- A method, which can be conducted without any previous knowledge about variability.
- A structured method for conducting domain engineering in the requirements phase, which includes discovering and modeling variability (see Section 13.4.1).
- A structured method for conducting application engineering in the requirements phase, which includes setting up configurations for products and deriving requirement models for products according to the configurations (see Section 13.4.2).

Chapter 14
Conclusions

Abstract This chapter first summarizes the results of this book. Then, we discuss the previously defined research questions and provide a critical review of to what extent the research questions are addressed in this book. Finally, we point out proposals for future research.

14.1 Summary

One challenge in developing requirements and software architecture is the existing gap regarding methods for building software architectures based on requirements. This task is even more challenging when software qualities have to be addressed in the software development. The other challenge is concerned with the ad-hoc nature and experience-based development of software systems which provide difficulties for inexperienced software engineers to follow the current software development methods in practice. The goal of this book is to contribute to the filling of the aforementioned gaps by developing a systematic method that bridges the gap between requirements and software architecture with respect to quality requirements. Before developing such a method, two issues need to be clarified: 1) What are the meta-requirements that a method for quality-aware development of requirements and software architecture should fulfill? 2) Do the existing methods fulfill these meta-requirements? If yes, there is no need for developing such a method.

Chapter 3 provides answers to these questions. We reviewed empirical studies related to quality requirements and software architecture such as interviews, group discussions, and experience reports in order to identify the meta-requirements. These works provide direct evidence from real case studies. Based on the identified meta-requirements, we developed a comprehensive evaluation framework aiming at comparing and analyzing the existing methods. In order to identify the existing methods, we conducted a systematic literature review. As a result, we identified 6 relevant methods. Applying the evaluation framework to the identified methods showed that none of the compared methods fulfills all the meta-requirements or nearly all of them. Our evaluation underlines the lack of methodological support for a systematic development of requirements and software architecture with respect to quality requirements in a unified process.

In order to meet the meta-requirements and fill the identified gap, we developed the comprehensive framework QuaDRA based on problem frames, comprising eight phases proposed in Chapters 4 - 11. QuaDRA provides a structured way for guiding software engineers in quality- and pattern-based co-development of requirements and early software architecture design alternatives in an iterative and concurrent manner.

QuaDRA starts with Phase 1 (see Chapter 4), in which we proposed a structured method for modeling the context as well as modeling the functional and quality requirements. To this end, we extended the UML profile for problem frames with new stereotypes for annotating quality requirements in the problem diagrams.

After that, we developed a process in Phase 2 for the systematic selection of appropriate architectural patterns that contribute to the satisfaction of the modeled quality requirements (see Chapter 5). In our process, we relate problem diagrams to relevant architectural patterns by means of a question catalog. Selecting different architectural patterns provides one way to produce architecture alternatives that achieve quality requirements in different ways. Furthermore, we proposed a systematic method for creating initial architecture(s) based on the selected architectural pattern(s). The created initial architecture(s) provide(s) the basis for the final architecture alternatives.

For Phase 3, we showed a structured method for eliciting and modeling quality-related domain knowledge which is required for detecting and resolving requirement conflicts (see Chapter 6). Our method augments the requirement models with required domain knowledge for performance and security requirements by providing domain knowledge templates.

For the detection and the resolution of potential conflicts among functional as well as quality requirements, we developed a method in Phase 4 of QuaDRA in Chapter 7. Furthermore, we showed how the PoPeRA method can be used for analyzing the conflicting requirements with respect to available resources and usage profiles. Using the PoPeRA method, the set of potential conflicting requirements can be restricted. Moreover, as a resolution strategy, we presented a method that supports the creation of quality requirement alternatives for remaining conflicting requirements in a systematic way.

We developed problem-oriented quality patterns as quality-specific solutions based on problem frames. Such patterns target the achievement of security and performance requirements. Moreover, we proposed an intermediate model, called problem-solution diagram for providing a mapping between the quality requirement alternatives and the quality-specific solution alternatives. The problem-solution diagram can be used for deriving architecture alternatives (see Phase 5 in Chapter 8). By means of a structured method, we showed how the quality-specific patterns can be instantiated and integrated in the requirement models. Our method results in subproblems that contain solution approaches with regard to security and performance (see Phase 6 in Chapter 9).

In Phase 7, we presented a systematic method for deriving architecture alternatives. The requirement models enriched with solution approaches are used for creating the implementable architecture alternatives based on the initial architecture(s) (see Chapter 10). In order to provide an evaluation of the software architecture alternatives, we reviewed the state-of-the-art methods in the area of software architecture evaluation. We developed a framework for the systematic selection of existing architecture evaluation methods. Using our framework, we selected the established evaluation method ATAM that can be applied for evaluating the derived implementable architecture alternatives with regard to security and performance (see Phase 8 in Chapter 11).

The validation of the QuaDRA framework regarding the fulfillment of meta-requirements is achieved in Chapter 12. To this end, we applied our comparative evaluation framework developed in Chapter 3. The analysis showed that all important meta-requirements are fulfilled by the QuaDRA framework. QuaDRA overcomes the lack of systematic and methodological guidelines for development of requirements and software architecture with respect to quality requirements in a unified process.

In addition, we proposed an extension of QuaDRA for supporting SPL. In Chapter 13, we extended the problem frames approach with a notation for modeling variability by providing a UML profile. Furthermore, we conducted requirements engineering in SPL considering quality requirements in a methodical way.

14.2 Answer to Research Questions

After providing a summary of our contributions in the previous section, in this section we explicitly show how the research questions are addressed in our book.

RQ 1 What are the meta-requirements that a systematic method for quality-aware development of requirements and software architecture should fulfill?

Answer After reviewing 11 empirical studies related to quality requirements and software architecture in Chapter 3, we systematically identified meta-requirements for a method bridging the gap between both phases with regard to quality requirements. We classified the identified meta-requirements into the three categories *"essential"*, *"recommended"*, and *"optional"*. *Essential meta-requirements* are required and must be fulfilled when developing such a method. That is, we cannot speak of a "method supporting the quality-aware development of requirements and software architecture" if the essential meta-requirements are not fulfilled. These meta-requirements are:

- Eliciting and documenting quality requirements in a systematic and structured way
- A structured method and extensive guidelines
- Use of unified notations and languages as well as a combination of semi-formal and natural language
- Use of reusable knowledge

Recommended meta-requirements are of high interest, but might not be absolutely required. That is, we can still speak of a "method supporting the quality-aware development of requirements and software architecture" if not all recommended meta-requirements are met. In such a case, we are concerned with a method which is not optimal for our purposes but still acceptable. These meta-requirements are:

- Traceability support between requirements and architecture artifacts
- Capturing and documenting design rationale in a systematic way
- Detecting conflicts and interactions among (quality) requirements as well as resolving such interdependencies
- Supporting architecture alternatives
- Supporting feedback loops between requirements and software architecture
- Support for the evaluation of the software architecture

Optional meta-requirements represent those meta-requirements that do not necessarily have to be fulfilled for a "method supporting the quality-aware development of requirements and software architecture". Their fulfillment, however, provides additional characteristics that are useful. These meta-requirements are:

- Co-development of requirements and software architecture in an iterative and concurrent manner
- Defining architectural views
- Tool support

RQ 2 Is there a lack of methodological support in existing research for fulfilling these metarequirements?

Answer In order to be able to find an answer for this research question, one needs to know the existing methods for quality-aware development of requirements and software architecture. To this end, we conducted a Systematic Literature Review (SLR). We scanned 2304 papers using manual search, automated search, and snowball search. As the final result, we extracted data from 6 papers describing 6 different methods. The next step was to investigate whether these methods fulfill the meta-requirements. To this end, we developed a comparative evaluation framework as an analysis tool by means of the identified meta-requirements. The framework is applied to analyze the identified methods from the SLR. Our evaluation underlines the lack of methodological support for systematic development of both phases with respect to quality requirements in a unified process. It shows that none of the existing methods fulfills all meta-requirements we identified before. The main finding of our review was the identification of a need for a unified method which supports the development of requirements and software architectures with respect to quality requirements.

RQ 3 If yes, how can a new process provide guidance in developing requirements and software architecture with respect to quality requirements considering the identified meta-requirements?

Answer In Chapters 4 - 11 of this work, we provided the comprehensive and structured development framework QuaDRA composed of eight phases based on the problem frames approach. It guides software engineers in co-developing the requirements and early software architecture design alternatives in an iterative and concurrent manner taking into account quality requirements. The QuaDRA framework involves the following structured methods for

- modeling quality requirements (see Chapter 4),
- systematic selection of architectural patterns (see Chapter 5)
- eliciting, modeling, and using quality-related domain knowledge (see Chapter 6).
- detecting potential interactions among functional requirements (see Chapter 7).
- detecting potential interactions among quality requirements (see Chapter 7).
- performance requirements analysis and restricting the set of potential interactions (see Chapter 7).
- resolving requirement conflicts by generating requirement alternatives (see Chapter 7).
- identifying, structuring, and analyzing quality-specific solutions (see Chapter 8).

- selecting and applying quality-specific solutions (see Chapter 9).
- deriving software architecture alternatives (see Chapter 10).
- evaluating software architecture alternatives (see Chapter 11).

RQ 4   Does the new process fulfill the identified meta-requirements? How can this process be validated in a structured way with respect to the identified meta-requirements?

Answer   Chapter 12 of this book provides a validation of the QuaDRA framework. We apply the comparative evaluation framework comprising the *essential, recommended, optional meta-requirements* to QuaDRA in order to examine to what extent these meta-requirements are fulfilled by our method. We compare the results of applying the evaluation framework to QuaDRA with the results of its application to the state-of-the-art methods in Chapter 3. We summarize that

- none of the state-of-the-art methods fulfills all 4 *essential* meta-requirements whereas our QuaDRA framework satisfies all 4 *essential* meta-requirements *quality requirements, guidance and method structure, knowledge reuse, RE and design description.*
- none of the state-of-the-art methods fulfills all *recommended* meta-requirements whereas our QuaDRA framework satisfies all *recommended* meta-requirements *traceability, design rationale, trade-off analysis, architecture alternatives, iterative development,* and *architecture evaluation.*
- *optional* meta-requirements are partially fulfilled by QuaDRA. This is also the case for the state-of-the-art methods. We fully satisfy the *optional* meta-requirement *concurrent co-development,* and partially the meta-requirements *tool support* and *architecture views.*

We conclude that with QuaDRA we achieve our goal for a systematic co-development of requirements and software architecture with regard to quality requirements. Although we do not fully meet the *optional* meta-requirements, this causes no obstacle in achieving our goal, as these meta-requirements provide only additional *nice to have* features for such a method. Thus, we can contribute to closing the identified gap between requirements engineering and software architecture taking into account not only functional but also quality requirements. Software engineers and particularly inexperienced software engineers benefit from our method as it is based on structured steps and systematic guidance as opposed to an ad-hoc, experience- and intuition-based state-of-the-art approach.

RQ 5   How can the new process be extended for supporting important concepts of requirements engineering such as Software Product Lines (SPL)?

Answer   Chapter 13 of this book presents an extension of the the problem frames notation as well as methodical support for SPL. In Chapter 13, we provide the structured PREVISE method as an extension of the QuaDRA framework, which supports a single-system development, to a product-line development addressing quality requirements. PREVISE, which consists of four phases, covers domain engineering (Phases 1 and 2) as well as application engineering (Phases 3 and 4). While Phase 1 is concerned with exploring the variability caused due to entities in the environment of the software, Phase 2 identifies the variability in functional and quality requirements. The configuration for a concrete product is selected in Phase 3. Subsequently, deriving a requirement model for a concrete product is achieved in Phase 4.

14.3 Future Research

This section provides several proposals on how our work can be continued.

14.3.1 Risk Analysis for Deriving Security Requirements

In Phase 1 of the QuaDRA framework (see Chapter 4), we showed how to elicit security requirements from existing documents and incorporated them into requirement models in a systematic way. This procedure might bear the risk that not all relevant security requirements can be considered in the requirement models due to poor documentation of the requirements. In order to improve this situation, we aim at extending the QuaDRA framework with *security risk analysis* as a separate phase to be performed before eliciting and modeling security requirements. We have already performed preliminary work regarding security risk analysis [15, 14] which consists of identifying assets, vulnerabilities and threats, assessing business impact, determining security failures, and estimating risk levels. Finally, security requirements have to be defined for those assets that have an unacceptable risk level. The so defined security requirements are then modeled and integrated into requirement models.

14.3.2 Integrating Tactics into the Process of Architectural Pattern Selection

As described before (see Section 2.2.3 on page 27 and Section 2.2.4 on page 28), while architectural patterns contribute to the fulfillment of several quality requirements positively or negatively in a larger scale, *tactics* aim at improving one specific quality requirement in a more local manner. Hence, when assessing an architectural pattern's appropriateness for fulfilling a quality it is also important to judge whether further tactics regarding a quality are applicable and how much effort one has to spend to integrate them into an architectural pattern. In Chapter 5, we provided a systematic process for selecting architectural patterns. In this process, tactics are not considered yet. In the future, we want to enrich the architectural pattern process with tactics. We have performed preliminary work on this topic in [8]. In this work, we investigate the relationship between several architectural patterns and performance as well as security tactics. We study how easily a tactic can be implemented in an architectural pattern. Based on our investigation, we provide mappings between the architectural patterns and tactics. We aim at using the results of this work for extending our pattern selection process with tactics.

14.3.3 Aspect-oriented Requirements Engineering with Problem Frames

In Chapter 13, we proposed an extension of the QuaDRA framework for supporting SPL. Another important concept in requirements engineering is *Aspect-Oriented Requirements Engineering (AORE)* [199]. It deals with cross-cutting concerns at the requirements level in order to achieve the *separation of concerns*. The cross-cutting concerns are encapsulated into separate modules, known as *aspects*, that can be woven into a base system without altering its structure. This provides support for modularity and maintainability. Quality concerns [71] such as security, performance and usability affect several parts in software systems, and are considered as cross-cutting concerns. We aim to provide a structured method based on problem frames for extending the QuaDRA framework also with AORE and have already performed preliminary work in [24].

14.3.4 Providing Support for SPL in the Architecture Phase

In Chapter 13, we provided the structured PREVISE method as an extension of the QuaDRA framework to support SPL for RE. We aim at extending this method for supporting SPL in the architecture phase considering quality requirements. We had lots of discussions with our colleagues and project partners[1] on this topic. As a result of our discussions, we conclude that taking into account variability on the architecture level with regard to quality requirements appears as a complex or even hardly possible task if using architectural patterns for addressing quality requirements. Hence, we decided to run a workshop in order to bring together researchers and practitioners to share ideas and experiences, discuss open problems, and propose promising solutions with a particular focus on handling variability in software architecture with respect to quality attributes. The VAriability for QUalIties in SofTware Architecture (VAQUITA)[2] workshop was held jointly with ECSA 2015 [11, 12]. During the working group discussion, we discussed about variability and SPL considering quality attributes on the architecture level. We identified that it might be too complex to come up with a (reference) architecture with sufficient commonalities when applying architectural patterns for addressing different quality requirements. The problem identified in this context is that on the one hand quality requirements are mostly conflicting and on the other hand architectural patterns contributing to the satisfaction of those requirements always come with some benefits for one type of quality requirements and liabilities for the other type of quality requirements. This makes the decision about selecting the architectural patterns for a (reference) architecture complex. However, the workshop participants discussed four potential solutions to deal with this dilemma:

Early design decision Early at the architectural level, it should be decided on the satisfaction of only one type of non-conflicting quality requirements. This early design decision allows the selection of an architectural pattern contributing to the satisfaction of the selected quality requirement. This idea, however, is contrasting the variability and product line concepts.

Patterns in application engineering The architectural pattern should not be applied in the domain engineering but in the application engineering phase. This solution might need some refactoring work as it might be late to apply an architectural pattern at this level.

No common architecture There might not exist a (reference) architecture which accommodates the commonalities of all conflicting quality requirements. The

---

[1] GenEDA project. http://www.geneda.org/

[2] http://vaquita-workshop.org/

reason is that quality requirements are considered as architectural drivers. Different conflicting quality requirements might lead to completely different software architectures using different architectural patterns so that no common architecture can exist.

Pattern and tactics An architectural pattern positively contributing to one type of quality requirements and negatively contributing to other types of quality requirements should be applied in domain engineering. In application engineering, tactics should be used to compensate the negative effect of the architectural pattern on one type of quality requirements. This solution also does not provide an optimal solution to the problem at hand.

In the future, we want to investigate these various suggestions in order to select a proper solution for extending the QuaDRA framework to support SPL at the architecture level.

14.3.5 Architecture Views

In Chapter 12, we emphasized that there is no consensus on the number and nature of the architectural views. Therefore, the architectural views have to be selected, based on the prevalent situation and characteristics of the organizations and software projects.

All the six methods selected by our SLR in Chapter 3 support the structural view of the software architecture and most of them provide additionally the behavioral view of the software architecture. Two of the selected methods provide the deployment view as well. We provided four different views for our QuaDRA framework. In addition to the structural view and the behavioral view, we provided two additional views, namely the context view and the requirements view as these views are essential when dealing with quality requirements. In order to provide the deployment view as well, we aim at extending our framework with this architecture view.

14.3.6 Tool Support

In this book, we provided tool support based on the UML4PF tool mainly for modeling the required artifacts. We developed various UML profiles that are integrated in the UML4PF tool. Our UML profiles define the relevant stereotypes for the following tasks:

- modeling quality requirements and incorporating them into requirement models
- modeling problem-solution diagrams
- modeling problem-oriented patterns and integrating them into requirement models
- supporting SPL with problem frames

We want to extend the UML4PF tool with further modules to

- interactively create the required artifacts such as the *problem-solution diagram*, the *initial architecture*, and the *quality-driven architecture alternatives* in a semi-automated way.
- identify and implement validation conditions in order to check the consistency of artifacts within each model and between different models.

Appendix A
OCL Expressions related to the UML profile Extension for Quality Requirements

```
Dependency.allInstances () ->                                                    1
select(a | a.oclAsType(Dependency).getAppliedStereotypes ().name ->              2
includes('constrains')) ->                                                       3
forAll(source.getAppliedStereotypes ().name ->                                   4
includes('FunctionalRequirement') implies not                                    5
target.getAppliedStereotypes ().name->includes('Machine') or                     6
(target.getAppliedStereotypes ().name->includes('CausalDomain') or               7
target.getAppliedStereotypes ().general.name->includes('CausalDomain') or        8
target.getAppliedStereotypes ().general.general.name->includes('CausalDomain')) )9
```

Listing A.1: A **functional** requirement does not constrain a machine domain

We retrieve all dependencies (line 1). After that, we select those dependencies that have the stereotype ≪constrains≫ assigned (lines 2 and 3). It is then necessary to verify that all dependencies originating (keyword source) from a functional requirement (lines 4 and 5) do not point (keyword target) to a machine domain (line 6). The expression also passes if this dependency points to a machine that is also a causal domain or a sub-type (in another subproblem) (lines 7-9).

```
Class.allInstances () ->                                                         1
select ( getAppliedStereotypes ().name ->                                        2
         includes('FunctionalRequirement')) ->
forAll (clientDependency ->                                                      3
collect (r | r.oclAsType(Dependency).getAppliedStereotypes ().name ->            4
includes('constrains'))                                                          5
-> count(true) >= 1)                                                             6
```

Listing A.2: A **functional** requirement has at least one constrains dependency

We collect all classes which have the stereotype ≪FunctionalRequirement≫ (lines 1 and 2). For theses classes, the dependencies of the class (using *clientDependency*, line 3) with the stereotype ≪constrains≫ assigned are collected (lines

3-5). We then check for each of these dependencies that there is at leas one dependency with the stereotype ≪constrains≫ (line 6).

```
Class.allInstances()->                                                          1
select(getAppliedStereotypes().name -> includes('Dependability') or            2
getAppliedStereotypes().general.name -> includes('Dependability') or           3
getAppliedStereotypes().general.general.name -> includes('Dependability')      4
    and
getAppliedStereotypes().name -> includes('QualityRequirement')) ->             5
forAll(clientDependency ->                                                      6
select (d | d.oclAsType(Dependency).getAppliedStereotypes.name ->              7
includes ('complements'))                                                       8
.oclAsType(Dependency).target.getAppliedStereotypes().name ->                 9
includes('FunctionalRequirement')                                              10
-> count(true) >= 1)                                                            11
```

Listing A.3: A dependability requirement always complements a **functional** requirement

We select all classes with the stereotype ≪Dependability≫ or its subtypes (≪Confidentiality≫, ≪Integrity≫, or ≪Availability≫) and additionally the stereotype ≪QualityRequirement≫ (lines 1-5). In all these classes, we check whether their dependencies with the stereotype ≪complements≫ point to at least one class with the stereotype ≪FunctionalRequirement≫.

Appendix B
Architectural Pattern Selection

B.1 Problem Frames Catalog

Fig. B.1: Required Behavior

Fig. B.2: Simple Transformation

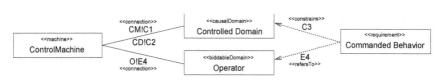

Fig. B.3: Commanded Behavior

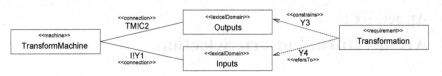

Fig. B.4: Transformation

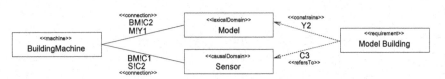

Fig. B.5: Model Building

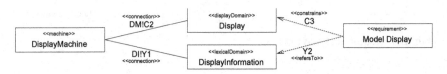

Fig. B.6: Model Display

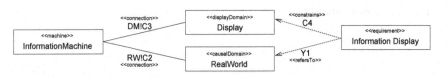

Fig. B.7: Information Display

B.2 Question Catalog

Table B.1: Question Catalog (questions)

Identifier	Question
Q1	Is the system to be developed considered as a large system?
Q2	Shall the system be decomposed?
Q3	Shall the system fulfill functionality on different levels of abstraction?
Q3A	Is there high level (user centric) functionality to be provided by the system?
Q3B	Is there low level (hardware) functionality to be provided by the system?
Q3C	Is there a flow of communication / transformation between functionality on different levels of abstraction?
Q4	Is a partitioning of high level functionality possible?
Q4A	Does a classification scheme separating groups of functionality exist?
Q4B	Is the functionality of a class non interfering with the functionality of other classes?
Q5	Is the mapping between high level functionality and low level functionality complex?
Q6	Is the system-to-be related to processing of data streams?
Q7	Is one key functionality to transform input data to output data?
Q7A	Is it possible to handle the data as a stream?
Q7B	Are there several transformation steps?
Q7C	Is the transformation to be changed frequently?
Q7D	Are steps of the transformation to be carried out by different parties or parts of the system?
Q8	Is the domain of the system-to-be immature and no solution for the problem the system shall solve is known?
Q9	Is there a transformation of data for which the transformation is (partly) unknown?
Q9A	Is it possible to split up the transformation into several steps, where the solution for some transformations is unknown?
Q9B	Is the (best) strategy for combining the transformations unknown?
Q10	Is the environment of the system-to-be or the system-to-be distributed?
Q11	Are there heterogeneous and independent components, which have to cooperate?
Q12	Shall a monolithic system be avoided?
Q12A	Has the system-to-be or parts of it to be distributed?
Q13	Is there heterogeneity, which cannot be avoided?
Q13A	Is there more than one communication mechanism / protocol to be used?
Q13B	Is there more than one technology / platform / framework to be used?
Q13C	Is there more than one programming language to be used?
Q14	Shall the system-to-be provide component encapsulation?
Q14A	Shall the system-to-be hide component specific details from the user / invoker?
Q14B	Shall it be possible to change components at run-time?
Q14C	Shall all component invocations be transparent for the invoker?
Q15	Is the system to be developed an interactive application?
Q16	Are requirements of different users regarding the user interface conflicting in an interactive application and is there a need for several / flexible user interface paradigms?
Q17	Shall the same information in an interactive application be presented differently in multiple views?
Q18	Shall data manipulations of the system to be developed in an interactive application be reflected immediately by the display?
Q19	Shall changes to the user interface in an interactive application be easy and possible even at run-time?
Q20	Is it the case that changes to the user interface / porting the user interface in an interactive application affect code in the core of the application?
Q21	Shall the interactive system be developed with the help of agents?
Q22	Are agents in an interactive system responsible for separate tasks to perform the whole system functionality in a cooperative manner?
Q23	Is the interactive system to be developed a production-planning-system (PPS)?
Q24	Do the agents in an interactive system maintain their own state and data model?

Q25	Do changes to individual agents in an interactive system affect the whole system?
Q26	Is the system-to-be expected to be able to adapt changing system requirements?
Q27	Shall core functionality be encapsulated to enable development of multiple applications building on core functionality?
Q28	Does the system have to cope with a changing software and hardware environment?

Table B.2: Question Catalog (indicator questions)

Identifier	Indicator Question
IQ1	Is the behavior of **Element1** as described by **Element2** dependent on an user functionality on a higher abstraction level?
IQ2	Is the functionality provided by **Element1** a low level hardware functionality?
IQ3	Is the functionality provided to **Element1** translated into a low level functionality executed by **Element2**?
IQ4	Is the **Element1** distributed with regards to the machine?
IQ5	Is the **Element1** distributed with regards to the **Element2**?
IQ6	Is the communication between **Element1** and the machine established using multiple (exchangeable) protocols / mechanisms?
IQ7	Is the communication between **Element1** and **Element2** established using multiple (exchangeable) protocols / mechanisms?
IQ8	Shall **Element1** be exchangeable at run-time?
IQ9	Is the information shown on **Element1** dependent on low level functionality?
IQ10	Can the functionality **Element1** logically be grouped with other functionality?
IQ11	Is it possible to handle **Element1** as a stream?
IQ12	Has **Element1** been transformed before or will **Element1** be used in another transformation afterward?
IQ13	Has **Element1** been transformed before?
IQ14	Will **Element1** be used in another transformation afterward?
IQ15	Is it expected that the transformation described by **Element1** will change frequently?
IQ16	Shall the functionality of **Element1** be hidden from **Element2**?
IQ17	Shall **Element1** show multiple views based on **Element2**?
IQ18	Shall manipulations of **Element2** be reflected immediately on **Element1**?
IQ19	Shall **Element1** show multiple views to **Element2**?
IQ20	Shall several / flexible interface paradigms used for representing information on **Element1** to suffice different needs of **Element2** ?
IQ21	Is **Element1** expected to change over time?
IQ22	Is **Element1** likely to change over time?

B.3 Relations between Problem Frames and Questions

Table B.3: Problem Frame *Required Behavior* and related Indicator Questions

Required Behavior					
<<machine>> ControlMachine	<<connection>> CM!C1 CD!C2		<<causalDomain>> ControlledDomain	<<constrains>> C3	<<requirement>> Required Behavior
Indicator Questions					**Question**
Identifier	*ELEMENTS*				*Identifier*
	ELEMENT	Replacement			
IQ1	ELEMENT1	Controlled Domain			
IQ2	ELEMENT1	Controlled Domain			
IQ4	ELEMENT1	Controlled Domain			
IQ6	ELEMENT1	Controlled Domain			
IQ8	ELEMENT1	Controlled Domain			
IQ21	ELEMENT1	Required Behavior			
IQ22	ELEMENT1	Controlled Domain			

Table B.4: Problem Frame *Simple Transformation* and related Indicator Questions

Simple Transformation					
<<machine>> TransformationMachine	<<connection>> TM!C1 D!Y1		<<lexicalDomain>> Data	<<constrains>> C3	<<requirement>> Simple Transformation
Indicator Questions					**Question**
Identifier	*ELEMENTS*				*Identifier*
	ELEMENT	Replacement			
IQ4	ELEMENT1	Data			
IQ6	ELEMENT1	Data			
IQ8	ELEMENT1	Data			
IQ11	ELEMENT1	Data			Q6, Q9
IQ12	ELEMENT1	Data			
IQ15	ELEMENT1	Simple Transformation			
IQ21	ELEMENT1	Simple Transformation			
IQ22	ELEMENT1	Data			

Table B.5: Problem Frame *Commanded Behavior* and related Indicator Questions

Indicator Questions			Question
Identifier	*ELEMENTS*		*Identifier*
	ELEMENT	*Replacement*	
IQ2	ELEMENT1	Controlled Domain	
IQ3	ELEMENT1	Operator	
	ELEMENT2	Controlled Domain	
IQ4	ELEMENT1	Controlled Domain	
IQ6	ELEMENT1	Controlled Domain	
IQ8	ELEMENT1	Controlled Domain	
IQ10	ELEMENT1	Commanded Behavior	
IQ16	ELEMENT1	Controlled Domain	
	ELEMENT2	Operator	
IQ21	ELEMENT1	Commanded Behavior	
IQ22	ELEMENT1	Controlled Domain	

Table B.6: Problem Frame *Transformation* and related Indicator Questions

Indicator Questions			Question
Identifier	*ELEMENTS*		*Identifier*
	ELEMENT	*Replacement*	
IQ4	ELEMENT1	Inputs	
	ELEMENT1	Outputs	
IQ6	ELEMENT1	Inputs	Q6, Q9
	ELEMENT1	Outputs	
IQ8	ELEMENT1	Inputs	
	ELEMENT1	Outputs	
IQ11	ELEMENT1	Inputs	
	ELEMENT1	Outputs	
IQ13	ELEMENT1	Inputs	
IQ14	ELEMENT1	Outputs	
IQ15	ELEMENT1	Transformation	
IQ21	ELEMENT1	Transformation	
IQ22	ELEMENT1	Inputs	
	ELEMENT1	Outputs	

Table B.7: Problem Frame *Model Building* and related Indicator Questions

Model Building		
<<connection>> BM!C2 M!Y1	<<lexicalDomain>> Model	<<constrains>> Y2
<<machine>> BuildingMachine		<<requirement>> Model Building
BM!C1 S!C2 <<connection>>	<<causalDomain>> Sensor	C3 <<refersTo>>

Indicator Questions			Question
Identifier	ELEMENTS		*Identifier*
	ELEMENT	*Replacement*	
IQ2	ELEMENT1	Sensor	
IQ4	ELEMENT1	Model	
		Sensor	
IQ6	ELEMENT1	Model	Q6, Q9
		Sensor	
IQ8	ELEMENT1	Model	
		Sensor	
IQ10	ELEMENT1	Model Building	
IQ11	ELEMENT1	Model	
IQ14	ELEMENT1	Model	
IQ15	ELEMENT1	Model Building	
IQ21	ELEMENT1	Model Building	
IQ22	ELEMENT1	Model	
		Sensor	

Table B.8: Problem Frame *Model Display* and related Indicator Questions

Model Display

Indicator Questions			Question
Identifier	ELEMENTS		Identifier
	ELEMENT	Replacement	
IQ2	ELEMENT1	Display	
IQ4	ELEMENT1	Display Display Information	
IQ6	ELEMENT1	Display Display Information	
IQ8	ELEMENT1	Display Display Information	
IQ10	ELEMENT1	Model Display	Q6, Q7, Q9
IQ11	ELEMENT1	Display Information	
IQ13	ELEMENT1	Display Information	
IQ15	ELEMENT1	Model Display	
IQ17	ELEMENT1	Display	
	ELEMENT2	Display Information	
IQ18	ELEMENT1	Display	
	ELEMENT2	Display Information	
IQ21	ELEMENT1	Model Display	
IQ22	ELEMENT1	Display Display Information	

Table B.9: Problem Frame *Information Display* and related Indicator Questions

Information Display

Indicator Questions			Question
Identifier	ELEMENTS		Identifier
	ELEMENT	Replacement	
IQ2	ELEMENT1	Real World	
IQ4	ELEMENT1	Display Real World	
IQ6	ELEMENT1	Display Real World	
IQ8	ELEMENT1	Display Real World	
IQ10	ELEMENT1	Information Display	
IQ15	ELEMENT1	Information Display	
IQ21	ELEMENT1	Information Display	
IQ22	ELEMENT1	Display Real World	

Table B.10: Indicator Question Properties (external input; used in Step 2)

Identifier	Indicated Question	Problem Frame Specific	Domain Specific
IQ1	Q3A	Yes	No
IQ2	Q3B	No	Yes
IQ3	Q3C	No	Yes
IQ4	Q10	No	Yes
IQ5	Q10	No	Yes
IQ6	Q13A	No	Yes
IQ7	Q13A	No	Yes
IQ8	Q14B, Q28	No	Yes
IQ9	Q3A	Yes	No
IQ10	Q4A	Yes	No
IQ11	Q7A	No	Yes
IQ12	Q7B	Yes	No
IQ13	Q7B	Yes	No
IQ14	Q7B	Yes	No
IQ15	Q7C	Yes	No
IQ16	Q14C	Yes	No
IQ17	Q17	Yes	No
IQ18	Q18	Yes	No
IQ19	Q17	Yes	No
IQ20	Q16	Yes	No
IQ21	Q26	Yes	No
IQ22	Q28	No	Yes

B.4 Benefits and Liabilities

Table B.12: Liabilities and their relation to qualities

Identifier	Benefit	Quality
L1	Cascading of changing behavior is difficult	Maintainability (Modifiability)
L2	The efficiency might be affected negatively	Efficiency (all)
L2a	Sharing state might be expensive	Efficiency (Resource utilization, Capacity)
L2b	Might introduce additional transformation overhead	Efficiency (Resource utilization, Capacity)
L2c	Cannot be parallelized	Efficiency (Resource utilization)
L2d	Frequently data access in view affects performance	Efficiency (Resource utilization, Time behaviour)
L3	Work might be done several times or completely unnecessary work is done	Efficiency (Resource utilization)
L3a	Potential for excessive number of updates	Efficiency (Resource utilization)
L4	Right granularity of of classification / grouping is hard to find	Development effort[1]
L5	The flexibility might be affected negatively	Maintainability (Modifiability, Testability), Portability (Replaceability, Adaptability), Compatibility (Interoperability)
L5a	Sharing state is inflexible	Maintainability (Modifiability, Testability), Portability (Replaceability, Adaptability), Compatibility (Interoperability)
L6	Error handling is difficult	Reliability (Fault tolerance, Recoverability), Maintainability (Analyzability, Testability)
L7	Testing is difficult	Maintainability (Testability)
L8	Establishing a control strategy is difficult	Maintainability (Analyzability, Testability), Functional suitability (Functional appropriateness), Reliability (Availability)
L9	Effort to be spent is high	Development effort
L9a	Development effort is high	Development effort
L10	Robustness impacted negatively	Reliability (Recoverability, Fault tolerance)
L11	Complexity might be increased	Maintainability (Analyzability, Modifiability, Testability), Efficiency (Capacity)
L11a	Complexity of control components is high	Development effort, Maintainability (Analyzability, Modifiability, Testability)
L11b	Modification on meta level may cause damage	Maintainability (Modifiability, Analyzability)
L11c	Increased number of components	Efficiency (Capacity)
L12	Reusability might be affected negatively	Maintainability (Reusability)
L12a	Individual reuse of view and controller is difficult	Maintainability (Reusability)
L13	View and controller components are closely-coupled	Maintainability (Modifiability), Portability (Replaceability, Adaptability)
L14	Change to view and controller when porting is required	Portability (Replaceability, Adaptability)
L15	Additional wrapping is required when using MVC with modern user-interface tools	Development effort
L16	Similar user interfaces require high maintainability effort	Maintainability
L17	Not all potential changes to the software are supported	Maintainability (Modifiability)

[1] not in ISO 25010

L18	Programming language might not support reflection	-

Table B.11: Benefits and their relation to qualities

Identifier	Benefit	Quality
B1	Reuse is improved	Reusability
B1a	Reusable knowledge source	Reusability
B2	Standardization of task and interfaces improved	Reusability, Portability(Adaptability, Replaceability), Interoperability
B3	Dependencies are kept local	Maintainability (all)
B4	(Ex)changeability is improved	Maintainability (Modularity, Modifiability), Portability (Replaceability)
B5	No intermediate file necessary	Efficiency (Resource utilization)
B6	Flexibility is improved	Maintainability (Modifiability, Testability), Portability (Replaceability, Adaptability), Compatibility (Interoperability)
B6a	Enables experimentation	Maintainability (Modifiability, Testability)
B6b	Portability is improved	Portability (Replaceability, Adaptability)
B6c	Interoperability is improved	Compatibility (Interoperability)
B7	Rapid prototyping is possible	Maintainability (Analyzability, Modifiability, Testability)
B8	Efficiency is improved	Efficiency
B8a	Enables parallel processing	Efficiency (Resource utilization)
B9	Maintainability is improved	Maintainability
B10	Improved robustness	Reiliability (Recoverability, Fault tolerance))
B11	Location transparency	Usability (Accessibility), Portability (Adaptability, Replaceability), Maintainability (all)
B12	Implementing and using multiple views with a single model	Maintainability (all), Portability (Adaptability, Replaceability)
B12a	Synchronizing of views	Maintainability (all), Portability (Adaptability, Replaceability)
B12b	Pluggable views and controllers even at run-time	Portability (Adaptability, Replaceability)
B12c	Exchangeability of "look and feel"	Maintainability (Modifiability), Portability (Adaptability, Replaceability)
B13	Enables building application frameworks	Maintainability (all), Reliability (Maturity)
B14	Enables separation of concerns	Maintainability (all)
B15	Provides support for change and extension	Maintainability (Modularity, Reusability, Analyzability, Modifiability), Portability (Adaptability, Replaceability), Compatibility (Interoperability)
B15a	No explicit source code modifications are needed	Maintainability (Modularity, Reusability, Analyzability, Modifiability), Portability (Adaptability, Replaceability)
B15b	Support for any kind of change	Maintainability (Modularity, Reusability, Analyzability, Modifiability), Portability (Adaptability, Replaceability)
B16	It facilitates multi-tasking and multi-user applications	Usability (Operability), Efficiency (Resource utilization)

B.5 Architectural Pattern Catalog

Table B.13: Architectural Pattern Description

Pattern			Questions		Consequences	
Type	*Name*	*Identifier*	*Context*	*Problem*	*Benefits*	*Liabilities*
From Mud to Structure	Layers	AP1	Q1, Q2	Q3, Q4, Q5	B1, B2, B3, B4	L1, L2, L3, L4
From Mud to Structure	Pipes and Filters	AP2	Q6	Q7	B1, B4, B6, B7, B8A	L5A, L2A, L2B, L6
From Mud to Structure	Blackboard	AP3	Q8	Q7, Q9	B1A, B4, B6A, B9, B10	L7, L8, L9A L2C
Distributed Systems	Broker	AP4	Q10, Q11	Q12, Q13, Q14	B1, B4, B6B, B6C, B11	L2, L10, L7
Interactive Systems	Model-View-Controller	AP5	Q15	Q16, Q17, Q18, Q19, Q20	B12, B13	L2D, L3A, L11, L12A, L13, L14, L15
Interactive Systems	Presentation-Abstraction-Control	AP6	Q15, Q21	Q22, Q23, Q24, Q25	B14, B15, B17	L11, L11A, L2, L16
Adaptable Systems	Microkernel	AP7	Q26, Q27	Q28, Q29	B6B, B9, B15	L2, L11, L9A
Adaptable Systems	Reflection	AP8	Q30	Q26	B15, B16, B16A	L11B, L11C, L2, L17, L18

B.6 Initial Architecture - Port Types

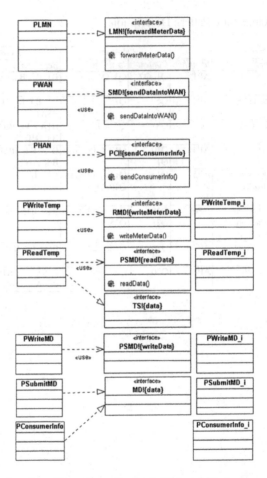

Fig. B.8: Complete list of port types for the initial architecture

Appendix C
Quality-specific Pattern Selection & Application

C.1 Problem-oriented Security Pattern Template for A1

Table C.1: Problem-oriented Symmetric Encryption pattern template for the confidentiality requirement *R11.1*

Security Solution for the Confidentiality Requirement *R11.1*	
Name	Symmetric Encryption
Purpose	For *MeterData* constrained by the requirement *R4*
Brief Description	The plaintext is encrypted using the secret key
Quality Requirement to be achieved	Security (confidentiality) *R11.1*
Affected Quality Requirement	Performance *R18*, *R19*, *R22*, *R23*, *R24*, *R25*
Necessary Conditions	
Requirement □ Assumption ☑	Secret key shall be/is distributed.
Requirement □ Assumption ☑	Confidentiality of secret key distribution shall be/is preserved.
Requirement □ Assumption ☑	Integrity of secret key distribution shall be/is preserved.
Requirement □ Assumption ☑	Confidentiality of secret key during transmission shall be/is preserved
Requirement □ Assumption ☑	Confidentiality of secret key during storage shall be/is preserved.
Requirement □ Assumption ☑	Integrity of secret key during storage shall be/is preserved.
Requirement □ Assumption ☑	Confidentiality of encryption machine shall be/is preserved.
Requirement □ Assumption ☑	Integrity of encryption machine shall be/is preserved.

Table C.2: Problem-oriented MAC pattern template for the integrity and authenticitiy requirements *R10.1* and *12.1*

Security Solution for the Integrity and Authenticity Requirements *R10.1* and *12.1*	
Name	Message Authentication Code (MAC)
Purpose	For *MeterData* constrained by the requirement *R4*
Brief Description	MAC uses a secret key and the data to generate a MAC. The verifier uses the same secret key to detect changes to the data.
Quality Requirement to be achieved	Security (integrity and authenticity) *10.1*, *12.1*
Affected Quality Requirement	Performance *R18*, *R19*, *R22*, *R23*, *R24*, *R25*
Necessary Conditions	
Requirement □ Assumption ☑	Secret key shall be/is distributed.
Requirement □ Assumption ☑	Confidentiality of secret key distribution shall be/is preserved.
Requirement □ Assumption ☑	Integrity of secret key distribution shall be/is preserved.
Requirement □ Assumption ☑	Confidentiality of secret key during transmission shall be/is preserved.
Requirement □ Assumption ☑	Confidentiality of secret key during storage shall be/is preserved.
Requirement □ Assumption ☑	Integrity of secret key during storage shall be/is preserved.
Requirement □ Assumption ☑	Confidentiality of encryption machine shall be/is preserved.
Requirement □ Assumption ☑	Integrity of encryption machine shall be/is preserved.

C.2 Problem-oriented Security Pattern Template for A2

Table C.3: Problem-oriented Asymmetric Encryption Pattern template for the Confidentiality requirement *R14*

Security Solution for Confidentiality requirement *R14*	
Name	Asymmetric Encryption
Purpose	For *MeterData* constrained by the requirement *R5*
Brief Description	The plaintext is encrypted using the public key and decrypted using the private key.
Quality Requirement to be achieved	Security (confidentiality) *R14*
Affected quality requirements	Performance *R18.1, R22.1, R24.1*
Necessary Conditions	
Requirement □ Assumption ☑	Integrity of public key during transmission shall be/is preserved.
Requirement □ Assumption ☑	Confidentiality of private key during transmission shall be/is preserved.
Requirement □ Assumption ☑	Integrity of private key during transmission shall be/is preserved.
Requirement □ Assumption ☑	Confidentiality of private key during storage shall be/is preserved.
Requirement □ Assumption ☑	Integrity of private key during storage shall be/is preserved.
Requirement □ Assumption ☑	Integrity of public key during storage shall be/is preserved.

Table C.4: Problem-oriented Asymmetric Encryption Pattern template for the Confidentiality requirement *R11*

Security Solution for Confidentiality requirement *R11*	
Name	Asymmetric Encryption
Purpose	For *MeterData* constrained by the requirement *R4*
Brief Description	The plaintext is encrypted using the public key and decrypted using the private key.
Quality Requirement to be achieved	Security (confidentiality) *R11*
Affected quality requirements	Performance *R18.1, R19.1, R22.1, R23.1, R24.1, R25.1*
Necessary Conditions	
Requirement □ Assumption ☑	Integrity of public key during transmission shall be/is preserved.
Requirement □ Assumption ☑	Confidentiality of private key during transmission shall be/is preserved.
Requirement □ Assumption ☑	Integrity of private key during transmission shall be/is preserved.
Requirement □ Assumption ☑	Confidentiality of private key during storage shall be/is preserved.
Requirement □ Assumption ☑	Integrity of private key during storage shall be/is preserved.
Requirement □ Assumption ☑	Integrity of public key during storage shall be/is preserved.

Table C.5: Problem-oriented Digital Signature pattern template for the Integrity and Authenticity requirements *R10* and *R12*

Security Solution for Integrity and Authenticity Requirements *R10* and *R12*	
Name	Digital Signature
Purpose	For *MeterData* constrained by the requirement *R4*
Brief Description	Sender produces a signature using the private key and the data.
Quality Requirement to be achieved	Security (integrity and authenticity) *R10, R12*
Affected Quality Requirement	Performance *R18.1, R19.1, R22.1, R23.1, R24.1, R25.1*
Necessary Conditions	
Requirement □ Assumption ☑	Integrity of public key during transmission shall be/is preserved.
Requirement □ Assumption ☑	Confidentiality of private key during transmission shall be/is preserved.
Requirement □ Assumption ☑	Integrity of private key during transmission shall be/is preserved.
Requirement □ Assumption ☑	Confidentiality of private key during storage shall be/is preserved.
Requirement □ Assumption ☑	Integrity of private key during storage shall be/is preserved.
Requirement □ Assumption ☑	Integrity of public key during storage shall be/is preserved.
Requirement □ Assumption ☑	Confidentiality of signature machine shall be/is preserved.
Requirement □ Assumption ☑	Integrity of signature machine shall be/is preserved.

Table C.6: Problem-oriented Digital Signature pattern template for the integrity and authenticity requirements *R13* and *R15*

Security Solution for Integrity and Authenticity Requirements *R13* and *R15*	
Name	Digital Signature
Purpose	For *MeterData* constrained by the requirement *R5*
Brief Description	Sender produces a signature using the private key and the data.
Quality Requirement to be achieved	Security (integrity and authenticity) *R13*, *R15*
Affected Quality Requirement	Performance *R18.1*, *R22.1*, *R24.1*
Necessary Conditions	
Requirement ☐ Assumption ☑	Integrity of public key during transmission shall be/is preserved.
Requirement ☐ Assumption ☑	Confidentiality of private key during transmission shall be/is preserved.
Requirement ☐ Assumption ☑	Integrity of private key during transmission shall be/is preserved.
Requirement ☐ Assumption ☑	Confidentiality of private key during storage shall be/is preserved.
Requirement ☐ Assumption ☑	Integrity of private key during storage shall be/is preserved.
Requirement ☐ Assumption ☑	Integrity of public key during storage shall be/is preserved.
Requirement ☐ Assumption ☑	Confidentiality of signature machine shall be/is preserved.
Requirement ☐ Assumption ☑	Integrity of signature machine shall be/is preserved.

C.3 Problem-oriented Security Pattern Template for A3

Table C.7: Problem-oriented Symmetric Encryption pattern template for the confidentiality requirement *R11.2*

Security Solution for the Confidentiality Requirement *R11.2*	
Name	Symmetric Encryption
Purpose	For *MeterData* constrained by the requirement *R4*
Brief Description	The plaintext is encrypted using the secret key
Quality Requirement to be achieved	Security (confidentiality) *R11.2*
Affected Quality Requirement	Performance *R18.2, R19.2, R22.2, R23.2, R24.2, R25.2*
Necessary Conditions	
Requirement ☐ Assumption ☑	Secret key shall be/is distributed.
Requirement ☐ Assumption ☑	Confidentiality of secret key distribution shall be/is preserved.
Requirement ☐ Assumption ☑	Integrity of secret key distribution shall be/is preserved.
Requirement ☐ Assumption ☑	Confidentiality of secret key during transmission shall be/is preserved
Requirement ☐ Assumption ☑	Confidentiality of secret key during storage shall be/is preserved.
Requirement ☐ Assumption ☑	Integrity of secret key during storage shall be/is preserved.
Requirement ☐ Assumption ☑	Confidentiality of encryption machine shall be/is preserved.
Requirement ☐ Assumption ☑	Integrity of encryption machine shall be/is preserved.

Table C.8: Problem-oriented Symmetric Encryption pattern template for the confidentiality requirement *R14.2*

Security Solution for the Confidentiality Requirement *R14.2*	
Name	Symmetric Encryption
Purpose	For *MeterData* constrained by the requirement *R5*
Brief Description	The plaintext is encrypted using the secret key
Quality Requirement to be achieved	Security (confidentiality) *R14.2*
Affected Quality Requirement	Performance *R18.2, R22.2, R24.2*
Necessary Conditions	
Requirement □ Assumption ☑	Secret key shall be/is distributed.
Requirement □ Assumption ☑	Confidentiality of secret key distribution shall be/is preserved.
Requirement □ Assumption ☑	Integrity of secret key distribution shall be/is preserved.
Requirement □ Assumption ☑	Confidentiality of secret key during transmission shall be/is preserved
Requirement □ Assumption ☑	Confidentiality of secret key during storage shall be/is preserved.
Requirement □ Assumption ☑	Integrity of secret key during storage shall be/is preserved.
Requirement □ Assumption ☑	Confidentiality of encryption machine shall be/is preserved.
Requirement □ Assumption ☑	Integrity of encryption machine shall be/is preserved.

Table C.9: Problem-oriented MAC pattern template for the integrity and authenticitiy requirements *R10.2* and *12.2*

Security Solution Security Solution for the Integrity and Authenticity Requirements *R10.2* and *12.2*	
Name	Message Authentication Code (MAC)
Purpose	For *MeterData* constrained by the requirement *R4*
Brief Description	MAC uses a secret key and the data to generate a MAC. The verifier uses the same secret key to detect changes to the data.
Quality Requirement to be achieved	Security (integrity and authenticity) *R10.2*, *R12.2*
Affected Quality Requirement	Performance *R18.2, R19.2, R22.2, R23.2, R24.2, R25.2*
Necessary Conditions	
Requirement □ Assumption ☑	Secret key shall be/is distributed.
Requirement □ Assumption ☑	Confidentiality of secret key distribution shall be/is preserved.
Requirement □ Assumption ☑	Integrity of secret key distribution shall be/is preserved.
Requirement □ Assumption ☑	Confidentiality of secret key during transmission shall be/is preserved.
Requirement □ Assumption ☑	Confidentiality of secret key during storage shall be/is preserved.
Requirement □ Assumption ☑	Integrity of secret key during storage shall be/is preserved.
Requirement □ Assumption ☑	Confidentiality of encryption machine shall be/is preserved.
Requirement □ Assumption ☑	Integrity of encryption machine shall be/is preserved.

Table C.10: Problem-oriented MAC pattern template for the integrity and authen-ticitiy requirements *R13.2* and *15.2*

Security Solution Security Solution for the Integrity and Authenticity Requirements *R13.2* and *15.2*	
Name	Message Authentication Code (MAC)
Purpose	For *MeterData* constrained by the requirement *R5*
Brief Description	MAC uses a secret key and the data to generate a MAC. The verifier uses the same secret key to detect changes to the data.
Quality Requirement to be achieved	Security (integrity and authenticity) *R13.2*, *R15.2*
Affected Quality Requirement	Performance *R18.2*, *R22.2*, *R24.2*
Necessary Conditions	
Requirement □ Assumption ☑	Secret key shall be/is distributed.
Requirement □ Assumption ☑	Confidentiality of secret key distribution shall be/is preserved.
Requirement □ Assumption ☑	Integrity of secret key distribution shall be/is preserved.
Requirement □ Assumption ☑	Confidentiality of secret key during transmission shall be/is preserved.
Requirement □ Assumption ☑	Confidentiality of secret key during storage shall be/is preserved.
Requirement □ Assumption ☑	Integrity of secret key during storage shall be/is preserved.
Requirement □ Assumption ☑	Confidentiality of encryption machine shall be/is preserved.
Requirement □ Assumption ☑	Integrity of encryption machine shall be/is preserved.

Appendix D
Quality-based Architecture

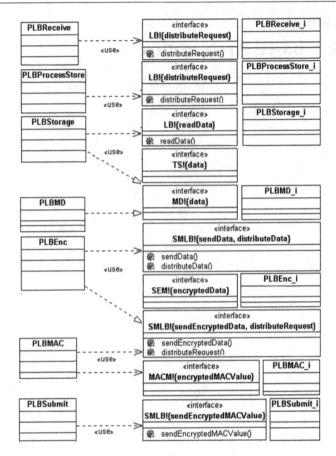

Fig. D.1: List of port types for the quality-based architecture alternative 1

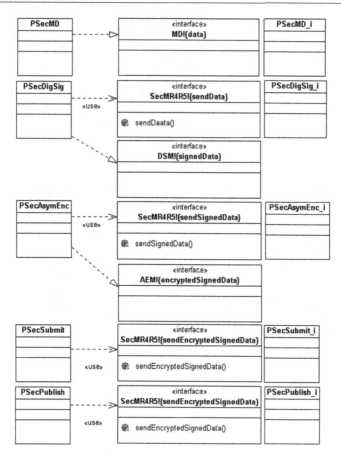

Fig. D.2: List of port types for the quality-based architecture alternative 2

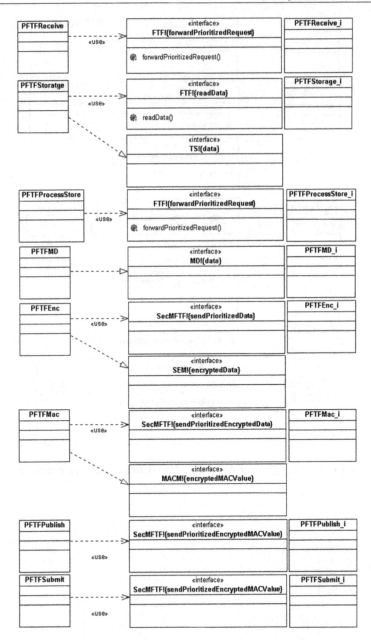

Fig. D.3: List of port types for the quality-based architecture alternative 3

Appendix E
Architecture Evaluation Methods

This section provides an overview of the state-of-the-art of the architecture evaluation methods. For this overview, we used the secondary studies published in [88, 34, 35].

Scenario-based Architecture Analysis Method (SAAM)

SAAM consists of 6 activities. Its goal is to identify and assess the risks inherent to the architecture as well as analyzing the suitability of the architecture with regard to the desired characteristics of a particular system. Any single quality requirement in the form of scenarios can be evaluated by SAAM. SAAM can be applied to the final version of the software architecture and prior to the detailed design. The software architecture to be evaluated has to be presented as structural and behavioral views. Additionally, the allocation of functionality to the structure should be specified.

SAAM founded on Complex Scenarios (SAAMCS)

SAAMCS comprising 3 activities extends SAAM for considering complex scenarios and their impact on the software architecture. Flexibility is the quality requirement that is addressed by SAAMCS. It can be applied to the final version of the software architecture. The software architecture has to be described as macroarchitecture and microarchitecture.

Extending SAAM by Integration in the Domain (ESAAMI)

ESAAMI integrates SAAM in a domain-specific and reuse-bassed development process. ESAAMI requires the similar architecture descriptions used by SAAM. The method activities in ESAAMI are similar to SAAM.

SAAM Evolution and Reusability (SAAMER)

SAAMER comprises 4 activities to be performed iteratively. It provides an extension to SAAM with respect to the quality requirements evolution and reusability. SAAMER can be applied to the final version of the software architecture. It requires the architectural views static, map, dynamic, and resource for assessing the software architectures.

Aspectual SAAM (ASAAM)

ASAAM as an extension to SAAM provides support for evaluating the quality of the software architecture using aspects and refactoring concepts. Similar to SAAM, any quality requirements to be considered in isolation can be addressed by ASAAM. ASAAM can be applied to the final version of the software architecture.

Architecture Trade-off Analysis Method (ATAM)

A comprehensive description of ATAM is given in Chapter 2 (see Section 2.2.7 on page 31) as well as in Chapter 11 (see Section 11.5 on page 367).

Scenario-based Architecture Reeingeering (SBAR)

The goal of SBAR is to estimate the ability of the desigend software architecture for achieving quality requirements. The method comprises 3 activities that have to be performed iteratively. SBAR can be applied to an existing system for system extension or reengineering of the system. Multiple quality requirements are considered in SBAR. An implemented system is required for this method.

Architecture Level Prediction for Software Maintenance (ALPSM)

ALPSM evaluates the maintainability of the software architecture. For predicting the effort needed for adapting the system, it uses the size of changes. ALPSM can be applied to the final version of the software architecture. It consists of 6 activities.

Software Architecture Evaluation Method (SAEM)

The goal of SAEM is to predict the quality of the final system. It considers internal and external quality requirements based on a quality model. The internal quality represents the set of qualities from the developer's view. The external quality represents the set of qualities from the perspective of the user. SAEM can be applied to the final version of the software architecture. As architecture descriptions the two different viewpoints, namely the developer view and the user view are required.

Architecture Level Modifiability Analysis (ALMA)

The goal of ALMA is to analyze the software architecture from the modifiability point of view. The focus of analyzing is on risk assessment, maintenance cost prediction, and software architecture comparison. ALMA consists of 5 activities to be performed sequentially. It can be applied to the final version of the software architecture. As architectural descriptions, several architectural views such as contextual, conceptual, and dynamic are required for ALMA.

Performance Assessment of Software Architecture (PASA)

The goal of PASA is to assess the software architecture with regard to performance. It comprises 10 activities for identifying and mitigating performance related risk on the architecture level. It can be applied to the final version of the software architecture, to the post-deployment stage, and during an upgrade of a legacy system. It requires various views of the software architecture description.

Architecture Level Reliability Risk Analysis (ALRRA)

The goal of ALRRA is to analyze the reliability related risks on the level of software architecture. It is used to identify critical components and connectors. ALRRA consists of 6 activities. It can be applied to the final version of the software architecture [247].

Software Architecture Comparison Analysis Method (SACAM)

The goal of SACAM is to select an architecture by comparing different candidate architectures. It uses business goals of the organization as a basis for the selection criteria. SACAM consists of 6 activities. It can be applied to the final version of the software architecture.

Software Architecture Review (SAR)

The goal of SAR is to evaluate the software architecture with regard to evolution and confiability. It can be applied to the final version of the software architecture.

Software Architecture Analysis of Flexibility (SAAF)

SAAF is very similar to SAAM regarding the evaluation of the software architecture. Additionally, it provides support for idenfiying scenarios with high complexity during the evaluation. SAAF can be applied to the final version of the software architecture.

Active Reviews for Intermediate Design (ARID)

The goal of ARID is to perform a suitability analysis for the intermediate design. It comprises 9 activities to be performed in 2 phases. The suitability of the design is the quality requirement considered in ARID. As the architectural description, ARID needs detailed design of the components.

References

[1] Proceedings of the 1st International Workshop on Twin Peaks of Requirements and Architecture (TwinPeaks). IEEE (2012)

[2] Proceedings of the 2nd International Workshop on the Twin Peaks of Requirements and Architecture (TwinPeaks). IEEE Press (2013)

[3] Proceedings of the 3rd International Workshop on Twin Peaks of Requirements and Architecture (TwinPeaks). IEEE (2013)

[4] Proceedings of the 5th International Workshop on the Twin Peaks of Requirements and Architecture (TwinPeaks), vol. 2 (2015)

[5] Alebrahim, A.: Performance Analysis Patterns for Requirements Analysis. In: Proceedings of Student Research Forum Papers and Posters, the 41st International Conference on Current Trends in Theory and Practice of Computer Science (SOFSEM), *CEUR Workshop Proceedings*, vol. 1326, pp. 54–66. CEUR-WS.org (2015)

[6] Alebrahim, A., Choppy, C., Faßbender, S., Heisel, M.: Optimizing functional and quality requirements according to stakeholders' goals. In: I. Mistrik, R. Bahsoon, P. Eeles, R. Roshandel, M. Stal (eds.) System Quality and Software Architecture (SQSA), chap. 4, pp. 75–120. Elsevier (2014)

[7] Alebrahim, A., Côté, I., Heisel, M., Choppy, C., Hatebur, D.: Designing Architectures from Problem Descriptions by Interactive Model Transformation. In: Proceedings ot the 27th Symposium on Applied Computing (SAC), pp. 1256–1258. ACM (2012)

[8] Alebrahim, A., Fassbender, S., Filipczyk, M., Goedicke, M., Heisel, M.: Towards a Reliable Mapping Between Performance and Security Tactics, and Architectural Patterns. In: Proceedings of the 20th European Conference on Pattern Languages of Programs (EuroPLoP), pp. 39:1–39:43. ACM, New York, NY, USA (2015)

[9] Alebrahim, A., Fassbender, S., Filipczyk, M., Goedicke, M., Heisel, M.: Towards Systematic Selection of Architectural Patterns with Respect to Quality Requirements. In: Proceedings of the 20th European Conference on Pattern Languages of Programs (EuroPLoP), pp. 40:1–40:20. ACM, New York, NY, USA (2015)

[10] Alebrahim, A., Faßbender, S., Filipczyk, M., Goedicke, M., Heisel, M., Konersmann, M.: Towards a Computer-aided Problem-oriented Variability Requirements Engineering Method. In: L. Iliadis, M. Papazoglou, K. Pohl (eds.) Advanced Information Systems Engineering Workshops - CAiSE 2014 International Workshops, LNBI 178, pp. 136–147. Springer (2014)

[11] Alebrahim, A., Faßbender, S., Filipczyk, M., Goedicke, M., Heisel, M., Zdun, U.: 1st Workshop on VAriability for QUalIties in SofTware Architecture (VAQUITA): Workshop Introduction. In: Proceedings of the 2015 European Conference on Software Architecture Workshops, ECSAW '15, pp. 22:1–22:2. ACM (2015)

[12] Alebrahim, A., Faßbender, S., Filipczyk, M., Goedicke, M., Heisel, M., Zdun, U.: Variability for Qualities in Software Architecture. SIGSOFT Software Engineering Notes 41(1), 32–35 (2016)

[13] Alebrahim, A., Faßbender, S., Heisel, M., Meis, R.: Problem-Based Requirements Interaction Analysis. In: Proceedings of the 20th International Working Conference on Requirements Engineering: Foundation for Software Quality (REFSQ), LNCS 8396, pp. 200–215. Springer (2014)

[14] Alebrahim, A., Faßbender, S., Htebur, D., Goeke, L., Côté, I.: A Pattern-Based and Tool-Supported Risk Analysis Method Compliant to ISO 27001 for Cloud Systems. International Journal of Secure Software Engineering (IJSSE) 6(1), 24–46 (2015)

[15] Alebrahim, A., Hatebur, D., Goeke, L.: Pattern-Based and ISO 27001 Compliant Risk Analysis for Cloud Systems. In: Proceedings of the 1st International Workshop on Evolving Security and Privacy Requirements Engineering (ESPRE), pp. 42–47. IEEE (2014)

[16] Alebrahim, A., Hatebur, D., Heisel, M.: A Method to Derive Software Architectures from Quality Requirements. In: T.D. Thu, K. Leung (eds.) Proceedings of the 18th Asia-Pacific Software Engineering Conference (APSEC), pp. 322–330. IEEE Computer Society (2011)

[17] Alebrahim, A., Hatebur, D., Heisel, M.: Towards Systematic Integration of Quality Requirements into Software Architecture. In: I. Crnkovic, V. Gruhn, M. Book (eds.) Proceedings of the 5th European Conference on Software Architecture (ECSA), LNCS 6903, pp. 17–25. Springer (2011)

[18] Alebrahim, A., Heisel, M.: Supporting Quality-Driven Design Decisions by Modeling Variability. In: Proceedings of the 8th International ACM SIG-

SOFT Conference on Quality of Software Architectures, part of Comparch '12 Federated Events on Component-Based Software Engineering and Software Architecture (QoSA), pp. 43–48. ACM (2012)

[19] Alebrahim, A., Heisel, M.: Intertwining Relationship between Requirements, Architecture, and Domain Knowledge. In: Proceedings of the 9th International Conference on Software Engineering Advances (ICSEA), pp. 1–7 (2014)

[20] Alebrahim, A., Heisel, M.: Problem-oriented Security Patterns for Requirements Engineering. In: Proceedings of the 19th European Conference on Pattern Languages of Programs (EuroPLoP), pp. 9:1–9:17. ACM, New York, NY, USA (2014)

[21] Alebrahim, A., Heisel, M.: Towards Developing Secure Software using Problem-oriented Security Patterns. In: Proceedings of the 6th International Cross-Domain Conference on Availability, Reliability, and Security in Information Systems and HCI (CD-ARES), LNCS 8708, pp. 45–62. Springer (2014)

[22] Alebrahim, A., Heisel, M.: Applying Performance Patterns for Requirements Analysis. In: Proceedings of the 20th European Conference on Pattern Languages of Programs (EuroPLoP), pp. 35:1–35:15. ACM, New York, NY, USA (2015)

[23] Alebrahim, A., Heisel, M., Meis, R.: A Structured Approach for Eliciting, Modeling, and Using Quality-Related Domain Knowledge. In: Proceedings of the 14th International Conference on Computational Science and Its Applications (ICCSA), LNCS 8583, pp. 370–386. Springer (2014)

[24] Alebrahim, A., Tun, T.T., Yu, Y., Heisel, M., , Nuseibeh, B.: An Aspect-Oriented Approach to Relating Security Requirements and Access Control. In: Proceedings of the CAiSE'12 Forum at the 24th International Conference on Advanced Information Systems Engineering (CAiSE), *CEUR Workshop Proceedings*, vol. 855, pp. 15–22. CEUR-WS.org (2012)

[25] Alexander, I.: Misuse cases help to elicit non-functional requirements. Computing & Control Engineering Journal pp. 40–45 (2003)

[26] Alférez, M., Moreira, A., Kulesza, U., Araújo, J.a., Mateus, R., Amaral, V.: Detecting feature interactions in SPL requirements analysis models. In: Proceedings of the 1st International Workshop on Feature-Oriented Software Development, FOSD '09, pp. 117–123. ACM (2009)

[27] Ali, R., Yu, Y., Chitchyan, R., Nhlabatsi, A., Giorgini, P.: Towards a Unified Framework for Contextual Variability in Requirements. In: IWSPM'09 (2009)

[28] Ali, R., Yu, Y., Chitchyan, R., Nhlabatsi, A., Giorgini, P.: Towards a Unified Framework for Contextual Variability in Requirements. In: IWSPM '09, pp. 31–34. IEEE (2009)

[29] Almari, H., Boughton, C.: Questionnaire report on matter relating to software architecture evaluation. In: Software Engineering, Artificial Intelligence, Networking and Parallel/Distributed Computing (SNPD), 2014 15th IEEE/ACIS International Conference on, pp. 1–6 (2014)

[30] Ameller, D., Ayala, C., Cabot, J., Franch, X.: How do software architects consider non-functional requirements: An exploratory study. In: Proceedings of the 20th IEEE International Requirements Engineering Conference (RE), pp. 41–50 (2012)

[31] Aurum, A., Jeffery, R., Wohlin, C., Handzic, M.: Managing Software Engineering Knowledge. Springer (2003)

[32] Avgeriou, P., Grundy, J., Hall, J.G., Lago, P., Mistrík, I. (eds.): Relating Software Requirements and Architectures. Springer (2011)

[33] Avgeriou, P., Zdun, U.: Architectural patterns revisited: a pattern language. In: Proceedings of the 10th European Conference on Pattern Languages of Programs (EuroPlop), pp. 1–39 (2005)

[34] Babar, M., Gorton, I.: Comparison of scenario-based software architecture evaluation methods. In: Proceedings of the 11th Asia-Pacific Software Engineering Conference (APSEC), pp. 600–607 (2004)

[35] Babar, M., Zhu, L., Jeffery, R.: A framework for classifying and comparing software architecture evaluation methods. In: Proceedings of the Australian Software Engineering Conference (ASWEC), pp. 309–318 (2004)

[36] Babar, M.A., Zhang, H.: Systematic Literature Reviews in Software Engineering: Preliminary Results from Interviews with Researchers. In: Proceedings of the 3rd International Symposium on Empirical Software Engineering and Measurement (ESEM), pp. 346–355. IEEE Computer Society (2009)

[37] Bachmann, F., Bass, L.: Introduction to the Attribute Driven Design Method. In: Proceedings of the 23rd International Conference on Software Engineering, ICSE '01, pp. 745–746. IEEE Computer Society, Washington, DC, USA (2001)

[38] Bachmann, F., Bass, L., Klein, M.: Moving from quality attribute requirements to architectural decisions. In: STRAW, pp. 122–129 (2003)

[39] Bachmann, F., Bass, L., Klein, M., Shelton, C.: Designing software architectures to achieve quality attribute requirements. Software, IEE Proceedings - **152**(4), 153–165 (2005)

[40] Bajpai, V., Gorthi, R.: On Non-Functional Requirements: A Survey. In: IEEE Students' Conference on Electrical, Electronics and Computer Science (SCEECS), pp. 1–4. IEEE Computer Society (2012)

[41] Barbacci, M., Clements, P., Lattanze, A., Northrop, L., Wood, W.: Using the architecture tradeoff analysis method (atam) to evaluate the software architecture for a product line of avionics systems: A case study. Tech. Rep. CMU/SEI-2003-TN-012, Software Engineering Institute, Carnegie Mellon University (2003)

[42] Barbacci, M., Ellison, R., Weinstock, C., Wood, W.: Quality attribute workshop participants handbook. Tech. rep., Software Engineering Institute (2000)

[43] Barcelos, R., Travassos, G.: Evaluation approaches for Software Architectural Documents: A systematic Review. In: Ibero-American Workshop on Requirements Engineering and Software Environments (IDEAS) (2006)

[44] Bass, L., Clemens, P., Kazman, R.: Software architecture in practice, second edn. Addison-Wesley (2003)

[45] Bass, L., Clements, P., Kazman, R.: Software Architecture in Practice, SEI Series in Software Engineering. Addison Wesley (1998)

[46] Bass, L., John, B.E.: Linking usability to software architecture patterns through general scenarios. Journal of Systems and Software **66**(3), 187 – 197 (2003)

[47] Bass, L., Klein, M., Bachmann, F.: Quality attributes design primitives. Tech. rep., Software Engineering Institute (2000)

[48] Bass, L.J., Klein, M., Bachmann, F.: Quality Attribute Design Primitives and the Attribute Driven Design Method. In: Revised Papers from the 4th International Workshop on Software Product-Family Engineering, PFE '01, pp. 169–186. Springer Verlag, London, UK, UK (2002)

[49] Beckers, K., Faßbender, S., Heisel, M.: A meta-model for context-patterns. In: Proceedings of the 18th European Conference on Pattern Languages of Program (EuroPLoP), pp. 5:1–5:15. ACM (2013)

[50] Berntsson Svensson, R., Gorschek, T., Regnell, B.: Quality requirements in practice: An interview study in requirements engineering for embedded systems. In: M. Glinz, P. Heymans (eds.) Requirements Engineering: Foundation for Software Quality (REFSQ), LNCS 5512, pp. 218–232. Springer Berlin Heidelberg (2009)

[51] Bin, Y., Zhi, J., Xiaohong, C.: An Approach for Selecting Implementation Strategies of Non-functional Requirements. In: Proceedings of the 4th Asia-Pacific Symposium on Internetware, Internetware '12, pp. 20:1–20:7. ACM (2012)

[52] Bode, S., Riebisch, M.: Impact Evaluation for Quality-Oriented Architectural Decisions regarding Evolvability. In: Software Architecture, pp. 182–197. Springer (2010)

[53] de Boer, R.C., van Vliet, H.: Controversy Corner: On the similarity between requirements and architecture. Journal of System and Software **82**(3), 544–550 (2009)

[54] Borg, A., Yong, A., Carlshamre, P., Sandahl, K.: The bad conscience of requirements engineering: An investigation in real-world treatment of non-functional requirements. In: International Conference on Software Engineering Research and Practice (SERP) (2003)

[55] Bosch, J.: Design and use of software architectures. Addison-Weseley (2000)

[56] Bosch, J.: Design and Use of Software Architectures: Adopting and Evolving a Product-line Approach. ACM Press/Addison-Wesley Publishing Co., New York, NY, USA (2000)

[57] Bosch, J.: Software Architecture: The Next Step. In: F. Oquendo, B. Warboys, R. Morrison (eds.) Software Architecture, LNCS 3047, pp. 194–199. Springer Berlin Heidelberg (2004)

[58] Bosch, J., Molin, P.: Software architecture design: evaluation and transformation. In: Proceedings of the International Conference and Workshop on Engineering of Computer-Based Systems (ECBS), pp. 4–10 (1999)

[59] Brereton, P., Kitchenham, B., Budgen, D., Turner, M., Khalil, M.: Lessons from applying the systematic literature review process within the software engineering domain. Journal of Systems and Software **80**(4), 571–583 (2007)

[60] Bruijn, H.d., Vliet, J.C.v.: Scenario-Based Generation and Evaluation of Software Architectures. In: Proceedings of the 3rd International Confrence on Generative and Component-Based Software Engineering (GCSE), pp. 128–139. Springer (2001)

[61] Budgen, D., Turner, M., Brereton, P., Kitchenham, B.: Using Mapping Studies in Software Engineering. In: Proceedings of PPIG 2008, pp. 195–204. Lancaster University (2008)

[62] Buschmann, F., Meunier, R., Rohnert, H., Sommerlad, P., Stal, M.: Pattern-Oriented Software Architecture: A System of Patterns, vol. 1. John Wiley & Sons (1996)

[63] Calder, M., Kolberg, M., Magill, E.H., Reiff-Marganiec, S.: Feature interaction: a critical review and considered forecast. Comput. Netw. **41**, 115–141 (2003)

[64] Cameron, E.J., Velthuijsen, H.: Feature interactions in telecommunications systems. Comm. Mag. **31**(8), 18–23 (1993)

[65] Castro, J., Kolp, M., Mylopoulos, J.: Towards requirements-driven information systems engineering: The tropos project. Inf. Syst. **27**(6), 365–389 (2002)

[66] Catal, C., Atalay, M.: A Systematic Mapping Study on Architectural Analysis. In: Proceedings of the 10th International Conference on Information Technology: New Generations (ITNG), pp. 661–664 (2013)

[67] Chen, Y., Li, X., Yi, L., Liu, D., Tang, L., Yang, H.: A ten-year survey of software architecture. In: IEEE International Conference on Software Engineering and Service Sciences (ICSESS), pp. 729–733 (2010)

[68] Cheng, B.H.C., Atlee, J.M.: Research Directions in Requirements Engineering. In: Future of Software Engineering, FOSE '07, pp. 285–303. IEEE Computer Society (2007)

[69] Choppy, C., Hatebur, D., Heisel, M.: Architectural patterns for problem frames. IEE Proceedings – Software, Special issue on Relating Software Requirements and Architecture **152**(4), 198–208 (2005)

[70] Choppy, C., Hatebur, D., Heisel, M.: Systematic Architectural Design based on Problem Patterns. In: P. Avgeriou, J. Grundy, J. Hall, P. Lago, I. Mistrik (eds.) Relating Software Requirements and Architectures, chap. 9, pp. 133–159. Springer (2011)

[71] Chung, L., Nixon, B., Yu, E., Mylopoulos, J.: Non-functional Requirements in Software Engineering. Kluwer Academic Publishers (2000)

[72] Chung, L., Nixon, B.A., Yu, E., Mylopoulos, J.: Non-functional requirements in software engineering. Klewer Academic (2000)

[73] Chung, L., Sampaio do Prado Leite, J.C.: On Non-Functional Requirements in Software Engineering. In: A. Borgida, V. Chaudhri, P. Giorgini, E. Yu (eds.) Conceptual Modeling: Foundations and Applications, *Lecture Notes in Computer Science*, vol. 5600, pp. 363–379. Springer Berlin Heidelberg (2009)

[74] Classen, A., Heymans, P., Laney, R.C., Nuseibeh, B., Tun, T.T.: On the Structure of Problem Variability: From Feature Diagrams to Problem Frames. In: Proceedings of the 1st International Workshop on Variability Modelling of Software-Intensive Systems (VaMoS), pp. 109–117 (2007)

[75] Classen, A., Heymans, P., Schobbens, P.Y.: What's in a feature: a requirements engineering perspective. In: Proceedings of the Theory and Practice of Software, 11th International Conference on Fundamental Approaches to Software Engineering, FASE'08/ETAPS'08, pp. 16–30. Springer (2008)

[76] Clauß, M.: Modeling variability with UML. In: GCSE – Young Researchers Workshop (2001)

[77] Cleland-Huang, J., Avgeriou, P., Burge, J.E., Franch, X., Galster, M., Mirakhorli, M., Roshandel, R. (eds.): Proceedings of the 4th International Workshop on Twin Peaks of Requirements and Architecture. ACM (2014)

[78] Clements, P., Bachmann, F., Bass, L., Garlan, D., Ivers, J., Little, R., Merson, P., Nord, R., Stafford, J.: Documenting Software Architectures: Views and Beyond, second edn. Addison-Wesley (2011)

[79] Clements, P., Bergey, J., Mason, D.: Using the sei architecture tradeoff analysis method to evaluate win-t: A case study. Tech. Rep. CMU/SEI-2005-TN-027, Software Engineering Institute, Carnegie Mellon University (2005)

[80] Clements, P., Kazman, R., Klein, M.: Evaluating Software Architectures: Methods and Case Studies. Addison-Wesley Professional (2002)

[81] Côté, I., Hatebur, D., Heisel, M., Schmidt, H.: UML4PF – A Tool for Problem-Oriented Requirements Analysis. In: Proceedings of the International Conference on Requirements Engineering (RE), pp. 349–350. IEEE Computer Society (2011)

[82] Côté, I., Hatebur, D., Heisel, M., Schmidt, H., Wentzlaff, I.: A Systematic Account of Problem Frames. In: Proceedings of the European Conference on Pattern Languages of Programs (EuroPLoP), pp. 749–767. Universitätsverlag Konstanz (2008)

[83] Cysneiros, L.M., do Prado Leite, J.C.S.: Using uml to reflect non-functional requirements. In: Proceedings of the 2001 Conference of the Centre for Advanced Studies on Collaborative Research, CASCON '01, pp. 2–. IBM Press (2001)

[84] Cysneiros, L.M., do Prado Leite, J.C.S.: Nonfunctional requirements: From elicitation to conceptual models. IEEE TRANSACTIONS ON SOFTWARE ENGINEERING 30(5), 328–350 (2004)

[85] Daneva, M., Buglione, L., Herrmann, A.: Software architects experiences of quality requirements: What we know and what we do not know? In: J. Doerr, A. Opdahl (eds.) Requirements Engineering: Foundation for Software Quality, LNCS 7830, pp. 1–17. Springer Berlin Heidelberg (2013)

[86] Dao, T.M., Lee, H., Kang, K.C.: Problem frames-based approach to achieving quality attributes in software product line engineering. In: Proceedings of the 15th International Conference on Software Product Lines (SPLC), pp. 175–180. IEEE (2011)

[87] Deconinck, G.: An evaluation of two-way communication means for advanced metering in Flanders (Belgium). In: Instrumentation and Measurement Technology Conference Proceedings (IMTC), pp. 900–905 (2008)

[88] Dobrica, L., Niemelä, E.: A Survey on Software Architecture Analysis Methods. IEEE Transactions on Software Engineering. **28**(7), 638–653 (2002)

[89] Doerr, J., Kerkow, D., Koenig, T., Olsson, T., Suzuki, T.: Non-functional requirements in industry - three case studies adopting an experience-based nfr method. In: Proceedings of the 13th IEEE International Conference on Requirements Engineering (RE), pp. 373–382 (2005)

[90] Durdik, Z., Koziolek, A., Reussner, R.: How the understanding of the effects of design decisions informs requirements engineering. In: Twin Peaks of Requirements and Architecture (TwinPeaks), 2013 2nd International Workshop on the, pp. 14–18 (2013)

[91] Ebert, C.: Putting requirement management into praxis: dealing with nonfunctional requirements. Information and Software Technology **40**(3), 175 – 185 (1998)

[92] Egyed, A., Grunbacher, P.: Identifying requirements conflicts and cooperation: How quality attributes and automated traceability can help. IEEE Softw. **21**(6), 50–58 (2004)

[93] Ernst, N.A., Yu, Y., Mylopoulos, J.: Visualizing Non-functional Requirements. In: Proceedings of the 1st International Workshop on Requirements Engineering Visualization, REV '06, pp. 2–. IEEE Computer Society, Washington, DC, USA (2006)

[94] Fabian, B., Gürses, S., Heisel, M., Santen, T., Schmidt, H.: A comparison of security requirements engineering methods. Requirements Engineering – Special Issue on Security Requirements Engineering **15**, 7–40 (2010)

[95] Farenhorst, R., Hoorn, J., Lago, P., van Vliet, H.: The lonesome architect. In: Software Architecture, 2009 European Conference on Software Architecture. WICSA/ECSA 2009. Joint Working IEEE/IFIP Conference on, pp. 61–70 (2009). DOI 10.1109/WICSA.2009.5290792

[96] Ford, C., Gileadi, I., Purba, S., Moerman, M.: Patterns for Performance and Operability. Auerbach Publications (2008)

[97] Forsell, M.: Improving Component Reuse in Software Development. Ph.D. thesis, Department of Computer Science and Information Systems, University of Jyväskylä (2002)

[98] Fowler, M.: Analysis Patterns: Reusable Object Models. Addison Wesley (1996)

[99] Frakes, W., Prieto-;Diaz, R., Fox, C.: Dare: Domain analysis and reuse environment. Annals of Software Engineering **5**(1), 125–141 (1998)

[100] France, R., Rumpe, B.: Model-driven development of complex software: A research roadmap. In: 2007 Future of Software Engineering, FOSE '07, pp. 37–54. IEEE Computer Society, Washington, DC, USA (2007)

[101] Gallagher, B.: Using the architecture tradeoff analysis method to evaluate a reference architecture: A case study. Tech. Rep. CMU/SEI-2000-TN-007, Software Engineering Institute, Carnegie Mellon University (2000)

[102] Galster, M., Eberlein, A., Moussavi, M.: Transition from requirements to architecture: A review and future perspective. In: Proceedings of the Seventh ACIS International Conference on Software Engineering, Artificial Intelligence, Networking, and Parallel/Distributed Computing (SNPD), pp. 9–16 (2006)

[103] Gamma, E., Helm, R., Johnson, R., Vlissides, J.: Design Patterns: Elements of Reusable Object-Oriented Software. Addison Wesley (1995)

[104] Garlan, D., Allen, R., Ockerbloom, J.: Architectural mismatch or why it's hard to build systems out of existing parts. In: Proceedings of the 17th International Conference on Software Engineering, ICSE '95, pp. 179–185. ACM, New York, NY, USA (1995)

[105] of Gas, O., Markets, E.: Smart Metering Implementation Programme, Response to Prospectus Consultation, Design Requirements. Tech. rep., Office of Gas and Electricity Markets (2011)

[106] of Gas, O., Markets, E.: Smart Metering Implementation Programme, Response to Prospectus Consultation, Overview Document. Tech. rep., Office of Gas and Electricity Markets (2011)

[107] Grunbacher, P., Egyed, A., Medvidovic, N.: Reconciling Software Requirements And Architectures With Intermediate Models. In: SOFTWARE AND SYSTEMS MODELING, pp. 202–211. Springer (2003)

[108] Hall, J.G., Rapanotti, L., Jackson, M.: Problem frame semantics for software development. Software and System Modeling 4(2), 189–198 (2005)

[109] Harrison, N.B., Avgeriou, P.: How Do Architecture Patterns and Tactics Interact? A Model and Annotation. Journal of Systems and Software 83(10), 1735–1758 (2010)

[110] Harrison, N.B., van Heesch, U., Sobernig, S., Sommerlad, P., Filipczyk, M., Fülleborn, A., Musil, A., Musil, J.: Software architecture patterns: Reflection and advances: [summary of the miniplop writers' workshop at ecsa'14]. ACM SIGSOFT Software Engineering Notes 40(1), 30–34 (2015)

[111] Hassenzahl, M., Wessler, R., Hamborg, K.C.: Exploring and understanding product qualities that users desire. In: Proceedings of the IHM/HCI Conference on Human-Computer Interaction, vol. 2 (2001)

[112] Hatebur, D.: Pattern- and component-based development of dependable systems. Ph.D. thesis, University of Duisburg-Essen (2012)

[113] Hatebur, D., Heisel, M.: A foundation for requirements analysis of dependable software. In: Proceedings of the International Conference on Computer

Safety, Reliability and Security (SAFECOMP), LNCS 5775, pp. 311–325. Springer (2009)

[114] Hatebur, D., Heisel, M.: A UML Profile for Requirements Analysis of Dependable Software. In: E. Schoitsch (ed.) Proceedings of the International Conference on Computer Safety, Reliability and Security (SAFECOMP), LNCS 6351, pp. 317–331. Springer (2010)

[115] Hatebur, D., Heisel, M.: Making Pattern- and Model-Based Software Development More Rigorous. In: J.S. Dong, H. Zhu (eds.) Proceedings of 12th International Conference on Formal Engineering Methods, LNCS 6447, pp. 253–269. Springer (2010)

[116] Hatebur, D., Heisel, M., Schmidt, H.: Security engineering using problem frames. In: Proceedings of the International Conference on Emerging Trends in Information and Communication Security (ETRICS), pp. 238–253. Springer Verlag (2006)

[117] Hatebur, D., Heisel, M., Schmidt, H.: A pattern system for security requirements engineering. In: Proceedings of the 7th International Conference on Availability, Reliability and Security (AReS), pp. 356–365. IEEE Computer Society, Los Alamitos, CA, USA (2007)

[118] Hatebur, D., Heisel, M., Schmidt, H.: Analysis and component-based realization of security requirements. In: Proceedings of the International Conference on Availability, Reliability and Security (AReS), pp. 195–203. IEEE Computer Society (2008)

[119] Hausmann, J.H., Heckel, R., Taentzer, G.: Detection of conflicting functional requirements in a use case-driven approach: a static analysis technique based on graph transformation. In: Proceedings of the 24th International Conference on Software Engineering (ICSE), pp. 105–115. ACM (2002)

[120] van Heesch, U., Avgeriou, P.: Naive architecting - understanding the reasoning process of students. In: M.A. Babar, I. Gorton (eds.) Software Architecture, LNCS 6285, pp. 24–37. Springer Berlin Heidelberg (2010)

[121] van Heesch, U., Avgeriou, P.: Mature architecting - a survey about the reasoning process of professional architects. In: Software Architecture (WICSA), 2011 9th Working IEEE/IFIP Conference on, pp. 260–269 (2011)

[122] van Heesch, U., Avgeriou, P., Tang, A.: Does decision documentation help junior designers rationalize their decisions? a comparative multiple-case study. J. Syst. Softw. **86**(6), 1545–1565 (2013)

[123] Heisel, M., Souquières, J.: A heuristic algorithm to detect feature interactions in requirements. In: Language Constructs for Describing Features, pp. 143–162. Springer (2000)

[124] Heyman, T., Yskout, K., Scandariato, R., Schmidt, H., Yu, Y.: The Security Twin Peaks. In: Proceedings of the International Symposium on Engineering Secure Software and Systems (ESSoS), LNCS 6542, pp. 167–180. Springer (2011)

[125] Hofmeister, C., Kruchten, P., Nord, R.L., Obbink, H., Ran, A., America, P.: A general model of software architecture design derived from five industrial approaches. Journal of Systems and Software 80(1), 106 – 126 (2007)

[126] Hofmeister, C., Nord, R., Soni, D.: Applied Software Architecture, 1st edn. Addison-Wesley Professional (2009)

[127] Hooks, I.F., Farry, K.A.: Customer-centered Products: Creating Successful Products Through Smart Requirements Management. AMACOM (2001)

[128] Hui, B., Liaskos, S., Mylopoulos, J.: Requirements Analysis for Customizable Software: A Goals-Skills-Preferences Framework. In: Proceedings of the 11th International Requirements Engineering Conference (RE), pp. 117–126 (2003)

[129] International Organization for Standardization (ISO), International Electrotechnical Commission (IEC): IEEE Recommended Practice for Architectural Description of Software-Intensive Systems (ISO/IEC 42010) (2007)

[130] International Organization for Standardization (ISO), International Electrotechnical Commission (IEC): ISO/IEC 25010. Systems and software engineering – Systems and software Quality Requirements and Evaluation (SQuaRE) – System and software quality models (2011)

[131] International Organization for Standardization (ISO), International Electrotechnical Commission (IEC), Institute of Electrical and Electronics Engineers(IEEE): Systems and software engineering - Architecture description (ISO/IEC/IEEE 42010) (2011)

[132] International Organization for Standardization (ISO) and International Electrotechnical Commission (IEC): Common Evaluation Methodology 3.1. ISO/IEC 15408 (2009)

[133] Jackson, M.: Problem Frames. Analyzing and structuring software development problems. Addison-Wesley (2001)

[134] Jansen, A., Bosch, J.: Software architecture as a set of architectural design decisions. In: Software Architecture, 2005. WICSA 2005. 5th Working IEEE/IFIP Conference on, pp. 109–120 (2005)

[135] Jansen, A., Bosch, J., Avgeriou, P.: Documenting after the fact: Recovering architectural design decisions. J. Syst. Softw. 81(4), 536–557 (2008)

[136] Jayaratna, N.: Understanding and Evaluating Methodologies: NIMSAD, a Systematic Framework. McGraw-Hill, Inc., New York, NY, USA (1994)

[137] Johansson, E., Wesslen, A., Bratthall, L., Host, M.: The importance of quality requirements in software platform development-a survey. In: Proceed-

ings of the 34th Annual Hawaii International Conference on System Sciences, pp. 10 pp.– (2001)

[138] Jones, L., Lattanze, A.: Using the architecture tradeoff analysis method to evaluate a wargame simulation system: A case study. Tech. Rep. CMU/SEI-2001-TN-022, Software Engineering Institute, Carnegie Mellon University (2001)

[139] Kang, K.C., Cohen, S.G., Hess, J.A., Novak, W.E., Peterson, A.S.: Feature-oriented domain analysis (foda) feasibility study. Tech. rep., Carnegie-Mellon University Software Engineering Institute (1990)

[140] Kang, K.C., Cohen, S.G., Hess, J.A., Novak, W.E., Peterson, A.S.: Feature-Oriented Domain Analysis (FODA) Feasibility Study. Tech. rep., Carnegie-Mellon University Software Engineering Institute (1990)

[141] Kang, K.C., Kim, S., Lee, J., Kim, K., Kim, G.J., Shin, E.: FORM: A Feature-Oriented Reuse Method with Domain-Specific Reference Architectures. Annals of Software Engineering 5, 143–168 (1998)

[142] Kazman, R.: Tool Support for Architecture Analysis and Design. In: Joint Proceedings of the Second International Software Architecture Workshop (ISAW-2) and International Workshop on Multiple Perspectives in Software Development (Viewpoints '96) on SIGSOFT '96 Workshops, ISAW '96, pp. 94–97. ACM, New York, NY, USA (1996)

[143] Kazman, R., Bass, L.: Categorizing business goals for software architectures. Tech. Rep. CMU/SEI-2005-TR-021, Software Engineering Institute, Carnegie Mellon University (2005)

[144] Kim, M., Park, S., Sugumaran, V., Yang, H.: Managing requirements conflicts in software product lines: A goal and scenario based approach. Data Knowl. Eng. 61, 417–432 (2007)

[145] Kitchenham, B.: Procedures for Performing Systematic Reviews. Tech. Rep. Keele University TR/SE-0401 and NICTA 0400011T.1, Keele University (UK) and National ICT Australia Ltd (2004)

[146] Kitchenham, B.: Procedures for performing systematic reviews. Tech. rep., Keele University and NICTA (2004)

[147] Kitchenham, B., Brereton, O.P., Budgen, D., Turner, M., Bailey, J., Linkman, S.: Systematic literature reviews in software engineering – A systematic literature review. Information and Software Technology 51(1), 7 – 15 (2009)

[148] Kitchenham, B., Brereton, P., Turner, M., Niazi, M., Linkman, S.G., Pretorius, R., Budgen, D.: Refining the systematic literature review process - two participant-observer case studies. Empirical Software Engineering 15(6), 618–653 (2010)

[149] Kitchenham, B., Charters, S., Budgen, D., Brereton, P., Turner, M., Linkman, S., Jørgensen, M., Mendes, E., Visaggio, G.: Guidelines for performing Systematic Literature Reviews in Software Engineering. Tech. rep., EBSE (2007)

[150] Konersmann, M., Alebrahim, A., Heisel, M., Goedicke, M., Kersten, B.: Deriving Quality-based Architecture Alternatives with Patterns. In: Software Engineering 2012: Fachtagung des GI-Fachbereichs Softwaretechnik, LNI 198, pp. 71–82. GI (2012)

[151] Konrad, S., Gall, M.: Requirements Engineering in the Development of Large-Scale Systems. In: Proceedings of the 16th IEEE International Requirements Engineering (RE), pp. 217–222 (2008)

[152] Koziolek, A.: Architecture-driven quality requirements prioritization. In: First International Workshop on the Twin Peaks of Requirements and Architecture (Twin Peaks), pp. 15–19 (2012)

[153] Koziolek, H.: Sustainability evaluation of software architectures: A systematic review. In: Proceedings of the Joint ACM SIGSOFT Conference – QoSA and ACM SIGSOFT Symposium – ISARCS on Quality of Software Architectures – QoSA and Architecting Critical Systems – ISARCS, pp. 3–12. ACM (2011)

[154] Krawczyk, H.: The order of encryption and authentication for protecting communications (or: how secure is ssl?). Cryptology ePrint Archive, Report 2001/045 (2001)

[155] Kreutzmann, H., Vollmer, S., Tekampe, N., Abromeit, A.: Protection profile for the gateway of a smart metering system. Tech. rep., BSI (2011)

[156] Kruchten, P.: The 4+1 View Model of architecture. IEEE Software 12(6), 42–50 (1995)

[157] Kruchten, P.: The Rational Unified Process: An Introduction. Addison-Wesley Professional (2003)

[158] van Lamsweerde, A.: Goal-oriented requirements engineering: a guided tour. In: Proceedings of the 5th IEEE International Symposium on Requirements Engineering (RE), pp. 249–262. IEEE Computer Society (2001)

[159] van Lamsweerde, A.: From system goals to software architecture. In: M. Bernardo, P. Inverardi (eds.) Formal Methods for Software Architectures, Lecture Notes in Computer Science, vol. 2804, pp. 25–43. Springer Berlin Heidelberg (2003)

[160] van Lamsweerde, A.: Reasoning about alternative requirements options. In: A. Borgida, V. Chaudhri, P. Giorgini, E. Yu (eds.) Conceptual Modeling: Foundations and Applications, vol. LNCS 5600, pp. 380–397. Springer (2009)

[161] van Lamsweerde, A.: Requirements Engineering: From System Goals to UML Models to Software Specifications. Wiley (2009)

[162] van Lamsweerde, A., Letier, E., Darimont, R.: Managing Conflicts in Goal-Driven Requirements Engineering. IEEE Trans. Softw. Eng. **24**(11), 908–926 (1998)

[163] Laney, R., Barroca, L., Jackson, M., Nuseibeh, B.: Composing requirements using problem frames. In: Proceedings of the 4th International Conference on Requirements Engineering (RE), pp. 122–131. Press (2004)

[164] Lee, K., Kang, K.C.: Usage Context as Key Driver for Feature Selection. In: Proceedings of the 14th International Conference on Software Product Lines: going beyond: going beyond (SPLC), pp. 32–46. Springer (2010)

[165] Lencastre, M., Botelho, J., Clericuzzi, P., Araújo, J.: A Meta-model for the Problem Frames Approach. In: Proceedings of the 4th Workshop in Software Modeling Engineering (WiSME) (2005)

[166] Li, Y., Kobro Runde, R., Stølen, K.: A meta-model approach to the fundamentals for a pattern language for context elicitation. In: Proceedings of the 20th Conference on Pattern Languages of Programs (PLOP) (2013)

[167] Lin, L., Nuseibeh, B., Ince, D., Jackson, M.: Using abuse frames to bound the scope of security problems. In: Proceedings of the 12th IEEE International Requirements Engineering Conference, pp. 354–355 (2004)

[168] Lin, L., Nuseibeh, B., Ince, D., Jackson, M., Moffett, J.: Introducing abuse frames for analysing security requirements. In: Requirements Engineering Conference, 2003. Proceedings. 11th IEEE International, pp. 371–372 (2003)

[169] Lindvall, M., Tvedt, R., Costa, P.: An Empirically-Based Process for Software Architecture Evaluation. Empirical Software Engineering **8**(1), 83–108 (2003)

[170] Luckham, D.C., Kenney, J.J., Augustin, L.M., Vera, J., Bryan, D., Mann, W.: Specification and Analysis of System Architecture Using Rapide. IEEE Trans. Softw. Eng. **21**(4), 336–355 (1995)

[171] Magee, J., Dulay, N., Eisenbach, S., Kramer, J.: Specifying distributed software architectures. In: W. Schäfer, P. Botella (eds.) Proceedings of the European Software Engineering Conference (ESEC), *Lecture Notes in Computer Science*, vol. 989, pp. 137–153. Springer Berlin Heidelberg (1995)

[172] Marew, T., Lee, J.S., Bae, D.H.: Tactics based approach for integrating non-functional requirements in object-oriented analysis and design. J. Syst. Softw. **82**(10), 1642–1656 (2009)

[173] Matinlassi, M.: Comparison of software product line architecture design methods: COPA, FAST, FORM, KobrA and QADA. In: Proceedings of the

26th International Conference on Software Engineering (ICSE), pp. 127–136 (2004)

[174] May, N.: A survey of software architecture viewpoint models. In: The Sixth Australasian Workshop on Software and System Architec- tures (AWSA), pp. 13–24 (2005)

[175] Mehta, N.R., Medvidovic, N.: Composing Architectural Styles from Architectural Primitives. In: Proceedings of the 9th European Software Engineering Conference Held Jointly with 11th ACM SIGSOFT International Symposium on Foundations of Software Engineering, ESEC/FSE-11, pp. 347–350. ACM, New York, NY, USA (2003)

[176] Mirakhorli, M., Carvalho, J., Cleland-Huang, J., Mader, P.: A domain-centric approach for recommending architectural tactics to satisfy quality concerns. In: Twin Peaks of Requirements and Architecture (TwinPeaks), 2013 3rd International Workshop on the, pp. 1–8 (2013)

[177] Mirakhorli, M., Cleland-Huang, J.: Traversing the twin peaks. IEEE Software **30**(2), 30–36 (2013)

[178] Modugno, F., Leveson, N., Reese, J., Partridge, K., Sandys, S.: Integrated safety analysis of requirements specifications. Requirements Engineering pp. 65–78 (1997)

[179] Montero, F., Navarro, E.: Atrium: Software architecture driven by requirements. In: Engineering of Complex Computer Systems, 2009 14th IEEE International Conference on, pp. 230–239 (2009)

[180] Navarro, E.: Architecture traced from requirements by applying a unified methodology. Ph.D. thesis, Computing Systems Department, University of Castilla-La Mancha (2007)

[181] Niknafs, A., Berry, D.M.: The impct of domain knowledge on the effectiveness of requirements idea generation during requirements elicitation. In: Proceedings of the 20th IEEE International Conference on Requirements Engineering, pp. 181–190 (2012)

[182] Nuseibeh, B.: Weaving Together Requirements and Architectures. IEEE Computer **34**(3), 115–117 (2001)

[183] Nuseibeh, B., Easterbrook, S.: Requirements Engineering: A Roadmap. In: Proceedings of the Conference on The Future of Software Engineering, ICSE, pp. 35–46. ACM, New York, NY, USA (2000)

[184] Nuseibeh, B., Easterbrook, S.: Requirements engineering: a roadmap. In: Proceedings of the 22nd International Conference on Software Engineering (ICSE) on The Future of Software Engineering, pp. 35–46. ACM (2000)

[185] Ovaska, E., Evesti, A., Henttonen, K., Palviainen, M., Aho, P.: Knowledge based quality-driven architecture design and evaluation. Inf. Softw. Technol. **52**(6), 577–601 (2010)

[186] Ozkaya, I., Bass, L., Nord, R., Sangwan, R.: Making practical use of quality attribute information. Software, IEEE **25**(2), 25–33 (2008)

[187] Pandey, R.K.: Architectural description languages (adls) vs uml: A review. ACM SIGSOFT Software Engineering Notes **35**(3), 1–5 (2010)

[188] Patidar, A., Suman, U.: A survey on software architecture evaluation methods. In: Proceedings of the 2nd International Conference on Computing for Sustainable Global Development (INDIACom), pp. 967–972 (2015)

[189] Peng, X., Lee, S., Zhao, W.: Feature-oriented nonfunctional requirement analysis for software product line. Journal of Computer Science and Technology **24**(2) (2009)

[190] Pérez, J., Ali, N., Carsí, J.A., Ramos, I.: Designing software architectures with an aspect-oriented architecture description language. In: I. Gorton, G. Heineman, I. Crnković, H.W. Schmidt, J.A. Stafford, C. Szyperski, K. Wallnau (eds.) Component-Based Software Engineering, LNCS 4063, pp. 123–138. Springer Berlin Heidelberg (2006)

[191] Perovich, D., Bastarrica, M., Rojas, C.: Model-driven approach to software architecture design. In: Sharing and Reusing Architectural Knowledge, 2009. SHARK '09. ICSE Workshop on, pp. 1–8 (2009)

[192] Perry, D.E., Wolf, A.L.: Foundations for the study of software architecture. SIGSOFT Software Engineering Notes **17**(4), 40–52 (1992)

[193] Pohl, K.: Requirement Engineering: Fundamentals, Principles, and Techniques. Springer (2010)

[194] Pohl, K., Böckle, G., Linden, F.J.v.d.: Software Product Line Engineering: Foundations, Principles and Techniques. Springer (2005)

[195] Pohl, K., Sikora, E.: Structuring the co-design of requirements and architecture. In: Proceedings of the 13th International Working Conference on Requirements Engineering: Foundation for Software Quality (REFSQ), pp. 48–62. Springer-Verlag, Berlin, Heidelberg (2007)

[196] Pomerol, J., Barba-Romero, S.: Multicriterion Decision in Management: Principles and Practice. Int. series in operations research & management science: ISOR. Kluwer (2000)

[197] Prieto-Díaz, R.: Domain analysis: an introduction. SIGSOFT Softw. Eng. Notes **15**(2), 47–54 (1990)

[198] Probst, G.J.B.: Practical Knowledge Management: A Model that Works. Prism (1998)

[199] Rashid, A., Moreira, A., Araújo, J.: Modularisation and composition of aspectual requirements. In: Proceedings of the 2nd International Conference on Aspect-oriented Software Development (AOSD), pp. 11–20. ACM, USA (2003)

[200] Remero, G., Tarruell, F., Mauri, G., Pajot, A., Alberdi, G., Arzberger, M., Denda, R., Giubbini, P., Rodríguez, C., Miranda, E., Galeote, I., Morgaz, M., Larumbe, I., Navarro, E., Lassche, R., Haas, J., Steen, A., Cornelissen, P., Radtke, G., Martáinez, C., Orcajada, A., Kneitinger, H., Wiedemann, T.: D1.1 Requ. of AMI. Tech. rep., OPEN meter proj. (2009)

[201] Remero, G., Tarruell, F., Mauri, G., Pajot, A., Alberdi, G., Arzberger, M., Denda, R., Rodríguez, C., Larumbe, I., Navarro, E., Lassche, R., Haas, J., Martáinez, C., Orcajada, A.: D1.2 Report on regulatory requirements. Tech. rep., OPEN meter project (2009)

[202] Robillard, P.N.: The Role of Knowledge in Software Development. Commun. ACM **42**, 87–92 (1999)

[203] Robinson, W.N., Pawlowski, S.D., Volkov, V.: Requirements interaction management. ACM Comput. Surv. **35**, 132–190 (2003)

[204] Rozanski, N., Woods, E.: Software Systems Architecture. Addison-Wesley (2005)

[205] Saaty, T.: The analytic hierarchy and analytic network processes for the measurement of intangible criteria and for decision-making. In: Multiple Criteria Decision Analysis: State of the Art Surveys, pp. 345–408. Springer (2005)

[206] Salifu, M., Nuseibeh, B., Rapanotti, L., Tun, T.T.: Using Problem Descriptions to Represent Variabilities For Context-Aware Applications. In: VaMoS'07, pp. 149–156 (2007)

[207] Sánchez, P., Magno, J., Fuentes, L., Moreira, A., Araújo, J.a.: Towards mdd transformations from ao requirements into ao architecture. In: Proceedings of the Third European Conference on Software Architecture, EWSA'06, pp. 159–174. Springer-Verlag, Berlin, Heidelberg (2006)

[208] Sangwan, R., Neill, C., Bass, M., Houda, Z.E.: Integrating a software architecture-centric method into object-oriented analysis and design. Journal of Systems and Software **81**(5), 727 – 746 (2008). Software Process and Product Measurement

[209] Schmidt, H., Hatebur, D., Heisel, M.: Software Engineering for Secure Systems: Academic and Industrial Perspectives, pp. 32–74. IGI Global (2011)

[210] Schmidt, H., Wentzlaff, I.: Preserving Software Quality Characteristics from Requirements Analysis to Architectural Design. In: Proceedings of the 3rd European Workshop on Software Architecture (EWSA), LNCS 4344, pp. 189–203. Springer (2006)

[211] Schumacher, M., Fernandez-Buglioni, E., Hybertson, D., Buschmann, F., Sommerlad, P.: Security patterns: integrating security and systems engineering. John Wiley & Sons (2005)

[212] Seater, R., Jackson, D., Gheyi, R.: Requirement progression in problem frames: deriving specifications from requirements. Requirements Engineering **12**(2), 77–102 (2007)

[213] Shaw, M., Clements, P.: The golden age of software architecture. Software, IEEE **23**(2), 31–39 (2006)

[214] Shaw, M., DeLine, R., Klein, D., Ross, T., Young, D., Zelesnik, G.: Abstractions for software architecture and tools to support them. Software Engineering, IEEE Transactions on **21**(4), 314–335 (1995)

[215] Shaw, M., Garlan, G.: Software Aechitecture: Perspectives on an emerging discipline. Prentice Hall (1996)

[216] Sikora, E.: Ein modellbasierter Ansatz zur verzahnten Entwicklung von Anforderungen und Architektur über mehrere Abstraktionsstufen hinweg. Ph.D. thesis, Institut für Informatik und Wirtschaftsinformatik (2009)

[217] Silva, F., Lucena, M., Lucena, L.: STREAM-AP: A process to systematize architectural patterns choice based on NFR. In: 3rd International Workshop on the Twin Peaks of Requirements and Architecture (TwinPeaks), pp. 27–34 (2013)

[218] Sindre, G., Opdahl, A.L.: Eliciting security requirements with misuse cases. Requir. Eng. **10**(1), 34–44 (2005)

[219] Smith, C., Williams, L.: Software performance engineering. In: L. Lavagno, G. Martin, B. Selic (eds.) UML for Real, pp. 343–365. Springer US (2004)

[220] Smith, C.U., Williams, L.G.: Performance solutions, a practical guide to creating responsive, scalable software. Addison-Wesley (2001)

[221] Smith, C.U., Williams, L.G.: Five steps to establish software performance engineering. In: Int. CMG Conference, pp. 507–516 (2006)

[222] Smolander, K., Hoikka, K., Isokallio, J., Kataikko, M., Mäkelä, T.: What is included in software architecture? a case study in three software organizations. In: Proceedings of the 9th Annual IEEE International Conference and Workshop on the Engineering of Computer-Based Systems, pp. 131–138 (2002)

[223] Sommerville, I., Sawyer, P.: Requirements Engineering: A Good Practice Guide, 1st edn. John Wiley & Sons, Inc. (1997)

[224] Sommerville, I., Sawyer, P., Viller, S.: Viewpoints for requirements elicitation: A practical approach. In: International Conference on RE: Putting Requirements Engineering to Practice, pp. 74–81. IEEE Computer Society (1998)

[225] Svahnberg, M., Wohlin, C.: Consensus Building when Comparing Software Architectures. In: M. Oivo, S. Komi-Sirviö (eds.) Product Focused Software Process Improvement, *Lecture Notes in Computer Science*, vol. 2559, pp. 436–452. Springer Berlin Heidelberg (2002)

[226] Svahnberg, M., Wohlin, C., Lundberg, L., Mattsson, M.: A method for understanding quality attributes in software architecture structures. In: Proceedings of the 14th International Conference on Software Engineering and Knowledge Engineering, SEKE '02, pp. 819–826. ACM, New York, NY, USA (2002)

[227] Svahnberg, M., Wohlin, C., Lundberg, L., Mattsson, M.: A Quality-Driven Decision Support Method for Identifying Software Architecture Candidates. International Journal of Software Engineering and Knowledge Management 13(5), 547–573 (2003)

[228] Svensson, R., Host, M., Regnell, B.: Managing quality requirements: A systematic review. In: Software Engineering and Advanced Applications (SEAA), 2010 36th EUROMICRO Conference on, pp. 261–268 (2010)

[229] Tang, A., Aleti, A., Burge, J., van Vliet, H.: What makes software design effective? Design Studies 31(6), 614 – 640 (2010). Special Issue Studying Professional Software Design

[230] Tang, A., Babar, M.A., Gorton, I., Han, J.: A survey of architecture design rationale. Journal of Systems and Software 79(12), 1792 – 1804 (2006)

[231] Tawhid, R., Petriu, D.: Integrating performance analysis in the model driven development of software product lines. In: Proceedings of the 11th International Conference on Model Driven Engineering Languages and Systems, MoDELS '08, pp. 490–504. Springer (2008)

[232] "UML Revision Task Force": UML Profile for Schedulability, Performance, and Time Specification (2005). Http://www.omg.org/spec/SPTP/1.1/PDF

[233] UML Revision Task Force: UML Profile for MARTE: Modeling and Analysis of Real-Time Embedded Systems (2009). Http://www.omg.org/spec/MARTE/1.0/PDF

[234] "UML Revision Task Force": Meta Object Facility (MOF) Query/View/-Transformation (2011). Http://www.omg.org/spec/QVT/1.1/PDF/

[235] "UML Revision Task Force": OMG Unified Modeling Language (UML), Superstructure (2011). Http://www.omg.org/spec/UML/2.4.1/Infrastructure/PDF/

[236] "UML Revision Task Force": Object Constraint Language Specification (2014). Http://www.omg.org/spec/OCL/2.0/PDF

[237] van der Ven, J., Jansen, A., Nijhuis, J., Bosch, J.: Design decisions: The bridge between rationale and architecture. In: A. Dutoit, R. McCall, I. Mistrík, B. Paech (eds.) Rationale Management in Software Engineering, pp. 329–348. Springer Berlin Heidelberg (2006)

[238] Vetterli, C., Brenner, W., Uebernickel, F., Petrie, C.: From Palaces to Yurts: Why Requirements Engineering Needs Design Thinking. IEEE Internet Computing pp. 91–94 (2013)

[239] Whalen, M., Gacek, A., Cofer, D., Murugesan, A., Heimdahl, M., Rayadurgam, S.: Your "What" Is My "How": Iteration and Hierarchy in System Design. IEEE Software **30**(2), 54–60 (2013)

[240] Wiegers, K.: Software Requirements, 2 edn. Microsoft Press (2003)

[241] Williams, L.G., Smith, C.U.: Information requirements for software performance engineering. In: Proceedings of the International Conference on Modeling Techniques and Tools for Computer Performance Evaluation, pp. 86–101. Springer (1995)

[242] Wohlin, C., Runeson, P., Höst, M., Ohlsson, M.C., Regnell, B., Wesslén, A.: Experimentation in Software Engineering: An Introduction. Kluwer Academic Publishers, Norwell, MA, USA (2000)

[243] Wohlin, C., Runeson, P., Höst, M., Ohlsson, M.C., Regnell, B., Wesslén, A.: Experimentation in Software Engineering. Springer (2012)

[244] Wojcik, R., Bachmann, F., Bass, L., Clements, P.C., Merson, P., Nord, R., Wood, W.G.: Attribute-Driven Design (ADD), Version 2.0. Tech. rep., Software Engineering Institute (2006)

[245] Woods, E., Rozanski, N.: The system context architectural viewpoint. In: Proceedings of the Joint Working IEEE/IFIP Conference on Software Architecture, European Conference on Software Architecture (WICSA/ECSA), pp. 333–336 (2009)

[246] Woodside, M., Petriu, D.C., Petriu, D.B., Shen, H., Israr, T., Merseguer, J.: Performance by unified model analysis (puma). In: Proceedings of the 5th International Workshop on Software and Performance, WOSP '05, pp. 1–12. ACM (2005)

[247] Yacoub, S.M., Ammar, H.H.: A methodology for architecture-level reliability risk analysis. IEEE Trans. Softw. Eng. **28**(6), 529–547 (2002)

[248] Yskout, K., Heyman, T., Scandariato, R., Joosen, W.: A system of security patterns. Report CW 469, K.U.Leuven, Department of Computer Science (2006)

[249] Yu, E.: Towards modelling and reasoning support for early-phase requirements engineering. In: Proceedings of the 3rd IEEE International Symposium on Requirements Engineering (RE), pp. 226–235 (1997)

[250] Yu, Y., do Prado Leite, J.C.S., Lapouchnian, A., Mylopoulos, J.: Configuring Features with Stakeholder Goals. In: Proceedings of the 2008 ACM Symposium on Applied Computing (SAC), pp. 645–649. ACM (2008)

[251] Yusop, N., Zowghi, D., Lowe, D.: The impact of non-functional requirements in web system projects. International Journal of Value Chain Management **2**(1), 18–32 (2008)

[252] Zave, P., Jackson, M.: Four dark corners of requirements engineering. ACM Trans. Softw. Eng. Methodol. **6**, 1–30 (1997)

[253] Zdun, U.: Systematic pattern selection using pattern language grammars and design space analysis. Softw. Pract. Exper. **37**(9), 983–1016 (2007)

[254] Zhang, H., Babar, M.A., Tell, P.: Identifying relevant studies in software engineering. Inf. Softw. Technol. **53**(6), 625–637 (2011)

[255] Ziadi, T., Hélouët, L., Jézéquel, J.M.: Towards a UML Profile for Software Product Lines. In: PFE'03, pp. 129–139. Springer (2003)

[256] Ziadi, T., Hélouët, L., Jézéquel, J.M.: Towards a UML Profile for Software Product Lines. In: F. Linden (ed.) Software Product-Family Engineering, *Lecture Notes in Computer Science*, vol. 3014, pp. 129–139. Springer (2004)

[257] Zuo, H., Mannion, M., Sellier, D., Foley, R.: An Extension of Problem Frame Notation for Software Product Lines. In: Proceedings of the 12th Asia-Pacific Software Engineering Conference (APSEC), pp. 499–505. IEEE Computer Society (2005)

Printed in the United States
By Bookmasters